BEST PLACES TO LIVE
for
AUTISM
COGNITIVE & PHYSICAL DISABILITIES

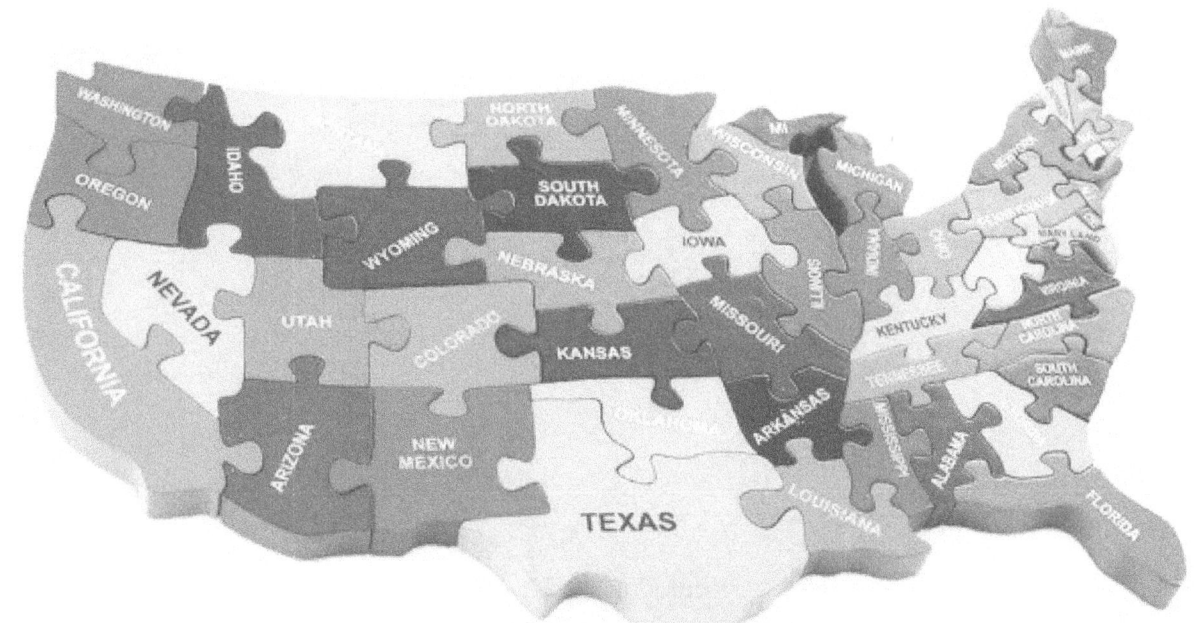

David H. Dudley

Best Places to Live for Autism, Cognitive and Physical Disabilities.

by David H. Dudley

Paperback ISBN: 978-0-9985377-6-4
ePUB ISBN: 978-0-9985377-7-1

Copyright 2017 David H. Dudley
Howard Publishing
All rights reserved.

No part of this document may be reproduced or transmitted in any form or by any means, electronic, mechanical, photocopying, recording, or otherwise, without prior written permission of your company name here.

Although the author has made every effort to ensure that the information in this book was correct at press time, the author and publisher do not assume and hereby disclaim any liability to any party for any loss, damage, or disruption caused by errors or omissions, whether such errors or omissions result from negligence, accident, or any other cause.

Cover Design by Tehsingul

Book Formatting by Stewart Stonger
http://design.nourishingdays.com/

Printed in the USA

Dedication

This book is dedicated to all the people striving to improve their life and/or the life of their loved ones. It takes courage to overcome the fear of change. Making improvements also takes commitment, persistence, hard work, and sacrifice to transition from the 'old' into the 'new'. I admire, respect, and salute you.

Epigraph

1. "A year from now you will wish you had started today." -Karen Lamb
2. "It doesn't matter where you are, you are nowhere compared to where you can go." -Bob Proctor
3. "Man cannot discover new oceans unless he has the courage to lose sight of the shore." -Andre Gide
4. "You miss 100 percent of the shots you never take." -Wayne Gretzky
5. Even if you stumble, you're still moving forward.
6. "Lay a firm foundation with the bricks that others throw at you." -David Brinkley
7. "In a chronically leaking boat, energy devoted to changing vessels is more productive than energy devoted to patching leaks." -Warren Buffett
8. "Don't say you don't have enough time. You have exactly the same number of hours per day that were given to Helen Keller, Pasteur, Michaelangelo, Mother Teresea, Leonardo da Vinci, Thomas Jefferson, and Albert Einstein." –Life's Little Instruction Book
9. "Someone was hurt before you, wronged before you, hungry before you, frightened before you, beaten before you, humiliated before you, raped before you… yet, someone survived… You can do anything you choose to do." –Maya Angelou
10. "Nobody can go back and start a new beginning, but anyone can start today and make a new ending." -Maria Robinson
11. "By changing nothing, nothing changes." -Tony Robbins
12. "Today is the first day of the rest of your life." -Anonymous
13. "All great changes are preceded by chaos." -Deepak Chopra
14. "You're braver than you believe, and stronger than you seem, and smarter than you think." –A.A. Milne
15. "You must do the thing you think you cannot do." -Eleanor Roosevelt
16. "Never, never, never, never give up." –Winston Churchill
17. "Courage doesn't always roar. Sometimes courage is the little voice at the end of the day that says I'll try again tomorrow." -Mary Anne Radmacher
18. "20 years from now you will be more disappointed by the things you didn't do than by the one's you did. So throw off the bowlines. Sail away from the safe harbor. Catch the trade winds in your sails. Explore. Dream. Discover." -Mark Twain
19. "One day your life will flash before your eyes. Make sure it's worth watching." –Unknown
20. "Getting over a painful experience is much like crossing monkey bars. You have to let go at some point in order to move forward." -C.S. Lewis
21. "Sometimes good things fall apart so better things can fall together." -Marilyn Monroe
22. "Whenever you find yourself on the side of the majority, it's time to pause and reflect." -Mark Twain
23. "If what you're doing is not your passion, you have nothing to lose."
24. "Use what talents you possess, the woods will be very silent if no birds sang there except those that sang best." -Henry van Dyke
25. "The best thing you can do is the right thing; the next best thing you can do is the wrong thing; the worst thing you can do is nothing." -Theodore Roosevelt
26. "Nothing diminishes anxiety faster than action." -Walter Anderson

27. "Live as if you were living for the second time and had acted as wrongly the first time as you are about to act now." -Viktor Frankl
28. "If you do what you've always done, you'll get what you've always gotten." -Tony Robbins
29. "Each person's task in life is to become an increasingly better person." -Leo Tolstoy
30. "All our dreams can come true – if we have the courage to pursue them." –Walt Disney
31. "Here is the test to find whether your mission on earth is finished. If you're alive, it isn't." -Richard Bach
32. "Your life does not get better by chance, it gets better by change." –Jim Rohn
33. "If today were the last day of my life, would I want to do what I am about to do today?" -Steve Jobs
34. "Fear, uncertainty and discomfort are your compasses toward growth."
35. The greatest mistake you can make in life is to be continually fearing you will make one.
36. "To create more positive results in your life, replace 'if only' with 'next time.'"
37. "As soon as anyone starts telling you to be "realistic," cross that person off your invitation list." –John Eliot
38. "I can accept failure, everyone fails at something. But I can't accept not trying." –Michael Jordan
39. "Believe you can and you're halfway there." – Theodore Roosevelt

Bottom line: You can improve your situation. You can transition, or proceed as close as is reasonably possible, into those areas of life that would give you the most fulfillment, Identify your preferences, define your goals, implore positive thinking, pray without ceasing, work hard, and make the necessary sacrifices to bring your dreams into fruition. Love others and be thankful along the way.

Moving to a place that is best for you and your family is possible and you can do it! My hope and desire is that this book will help you achieve your goals.

Table of Contents

DEDICATION 3

EPIGRAPH 5

TABLE OF CONTENTS 7

PREFACE 13

ACKNOWLEDGEMENTS 17

PART I - HOW TO FIND THE BEST PLACE & RELOCATING WITH EASE ... 19

Finding the Best Places to Live 20
Relocation Criteria (Dudley's Sample List) 22
'Avoidance' Sample List (Dudley's Personal Relocation Criteria) 23
S.M.A.R.T. Goals 24
Finding the Right Place Checklist For Individuals with Cognitive Disabilities . 27
Moving Checklist 29
Factors for Relocating a Business 36
Relocation (The Move) – Great Advice 37

PART II - CITIES & STATES RANKED ACCORDING TO YOUR WANTS & NEEDS 39

Unemployment rates for Metropolitan Areas (January 2016) 40
State Unemployment Rates (Dec. 2015) 41
U-6 Unemployment Rate Figures 43
Best Cities to Retire In... 44
By Affordability, Activities, Quality of Life, and Health Care 45
Most Favorable vs. Least Favorable... 49
Lowest/highest Adjusted Income Cities 49
Lowest/highest Cost Of In-Home Services 49
Highest/lowest % Of Employed People Aged 65 & Older 49
Most/fewest Recreation & Senior Centers Per Capita 49
Most/fewest Fishing Facilities Per Capita.. 49
Highest/lowest % Of The Population Aged 65 & Older 50
Best/Worst Mild Weather Ranking.. 50
Best and Worst States for Business 50

LEAST TAX-FRIENDLY STATES IN THE U.S. (2016)	61
BEST STATES TO MAKE A LIVING	62
VACCINE LAWS (STATE COMPARISONS)	63
FASTEST & SLOWEST GROWING MAJOR METROPOLITAN AREAS IN THE USA	64
THE 15 FASTEST GROWING CITIES IN AMERICA	64
FASTEST GROWING STATES IN AMERICA	65
BEST WEATHER U.S. CITIES	66
COMMUTE TIMES IN AMERICA	66
MOST FRIENDLY BIKE CITIES	67
MOST DANGEROUS CITIES IN AMERICA (2016)	68
HOME SCHOOL IN AMERICA: HOW STATES COMPARE	69
HOME SCHOOL STATE REGULATIONS	69
BEST LOCATIONS TO SEE THE NIGHT SKY	70
POPULATION STATISTICS (2010 CENSUS)	75
POPULATION CHANGE (2000 TO 2010)	75
NUCLEAR POWER PLANTS (LOCATIONS AND SAFETY)	76
MINIMUM PREFERRED DISTANCE FROM NUCLEAR POWER PLANTS	81
COAL AND OIL-FIRED POWER PLANT LOCATIONS & EMISSIONS (USA)	82
MAP OF FOSSIL FUEL POWER PLANT LOCATIONS AND EMISSIONS	84
SURVIVAL – BEST PLACES TO LIVE & CRITICAL PREPPER INFORMATION	84
ASTHMA - WORST CITIES TO LIVE	90
ALLERGIES - WORST CITIES	91
AIR QUALITY – BEST & WORST LOCATIONS	93
OZONE/PARTICULATE METROPOLITAN AREA STATISTICS	97
US AIR QUALITY MAP	106
THE HAPPIEST US STATES	106
THE HAPPIEST US CITIES	108
TOP 25 HAPPIEST RANKED CITIES	108
THE 25 LEAST HAPPIEST RANKED CITIES	109
PRIME FARM LAND & AGRICULTURE IN THE UNITED STATES	110
CONCENTRATION OF IMPORTANT ORGANIC MATTER FOUND IN THE SOIL.	110
NATURALLY OCCURRING SOIL MOISTURE IN THE UNITED STATES	110
DISTRIBUTION OF LAND USES IN THE CONTIGUOUS UNITED STATES	111
MAP OF VEGETABLE PRODUCTION IN THE CONTIGUOUS UNITED STATES	112
FOREIGN OWNED FARMLAND	112
AVERAGE DOLLAR VALUE OF AGRICULTURE PRODUCTS SOLD	114
	114
MAP OF FARMLAND RENTED OR LEASED IN UNITED STATES	114
MAP SHOWING THE AVERAGE PRICE PER ACRE IN THE USA (2009)	115
US HARDINESS ZONE MAP FOR PLANTS	115
OBESE ADULT POPULATION OF STATES	116

Section	Page
Earthquake Hazard Location Potential in the United States	117
Tornado Activity 1950-1995 Map	117
Hurricane Activity Map Showing Locations of Highest Probability	118
Hurricane Activity Locations	118
Lightning Density	119
State Shame (Worst Aspect of Each State)	119
Most Walkable Cities	120
10 Cities for Real Estate Bargains	123
Best Affordable Places to Live	123
10 Best Places to Raise a Family	124
Best & Worst State Capitals (2016)	124
By Affordability, Economic Well-being, Education, and Quality of Life	125
America's 50 Greenest Cities	126
Healthiest and Unhealthiest Cities in America	131
Safest Cities (2016 Rankings)	133
Safest States in America (2016)	135
Home & Community Safety Risk	136
Financial Safety Rank	136
Road Safety Rank	136
Workplace Safety Rank	136
Safety from Natural Disasters	136
US Crime/Safety Map	137
Most Favorable vs. Least Favorable	138
Assaults	138
Bullying	138
Employment Rate	138
Health Insurance	138
Automobile Fatalities	139
Law Enforcement	139
% of People with Rainy Day Funds	139
Property Losses from Climate Disasters	139
Fatal Occupational Injuries	139
Most/Fewest Law-Enforcement Employees per Capita	139
Fewest/Most Assaults per Capita	139
Lowest/Highest Bullying Incidents	139
Lowest/Highest Unemployment Rate	140
Lowest/Highest Share of Population Lacking Health Insurance	140
Highest/Lowest % of People with Rainy Day Funds	140
State Populations and Projections	140
Lowest/Highest Estimated Property Losses from Climate Disasters	140
Best Metropolitan Places to Live in the U.S. in 2017	142

PART III - BEST PLACES TO LIVE FOR PHYSICAL DISABILITIES (INCLUDING HELP FOR VETERANS & CARETAKERS) 143

- History: Attitudes Towards, and Treatment of, People with Disabilities 144
- Influence of Social Movements on Disability Rights 145
- Disability Defined 146
- Disability Resources: 152
- Disabilities (Classifications, Prevalence of each type of Disability, and State Comparisons) 153
- What is a disability? 154
- Employment Rate for Disabilities (State Comparisons) 155
- Earnings Average for Disabilities (State Comparisons) 156
- Disability Prevalence Rate 156
- Social Security Recipients by State 157
- Social Security Payments by State 158
- Veterans with a Service-Connected Disability 159
- Disability Prevalence Rate 159
- Health Insurance Coverage 160
- Type of Health Insurance by Disability Status 160
- Age Distribution of Disability 161
- Kinds of Disabilities and State Comparisons 161
- General Disability Statistics 166
- Working-Age People with a Disability / Employment 166
- Poverty 167
- Education 167
- Crime, Incarceration and Violence 167
- Obesity and Disabilities 168
- Binge Drinking Among the Disabled 168
- State Comparisons for Disability Services 169
- Four Key Aspects Of A High Functioning Medicaid Program 170
- State Comparisons for Disability Services (By Rank) 171
- State Comparisons for Disability Services (Alphabetical) 172
- The Best, The Worst And Facts About the Top Ranked States 174
- Facts About The Best Performing States 175
- The Proven Parenting And Programs To Help Kids With Intellectual And Developmental Disabilities Become Happy, Productive, Engaged Adults 176
- Key Family Characteristics for a Successful Transition within Two to Four Years 177
- Most Impactful Programs for a Successful Transition within Two to Four Years 178

HOW TO USE & HOW THE RANKINGS WERE DEVELOPED	181
MOST LIVABLE U.S. CITIES FOR WHEELCHAIR USERS	183
VETERAN'S WITH DISABILITIES (BEST PLACES)	184
ACCESS TO VA MEDICAL FACILITIES	184
ECONOMIC CONSIDERATIONS	185
PERCENTAGE OF VETERANS IN THE ADULT POPULATION	185
VETERAN UNEMPLOYMENT RATE IN 2013	185
MEDIAN INCOME FOR VETERANS	185
VETERANS WHO LIVE BELOW THE POVERTY LINE	185
AFFORDABLE HOUSING	186
PROXIMITY TO A MILITARY INSTALLATION	186
15 LOCATIONS TO CONSIDER	186
BEST PLACES TO LIVE FOR PEOPLE WITH DISABILITIES (OVERVIEW)	189
LOWEST COST OF LIVING CITIES	191
HIGHEST EMPLOYMENT RATE FOR PEOPLE WITH DISABILITIES	192
CONCLUSION	193
ADVOCACY	193
ADVOCACY RESOURCES	194
EMPLOYMENT FOR PERSONS WITH DISABILITIES AND THE BEST-AND WORST-STATES FOR WORKERS WITH DISABILITIES	197
EMPLOYMENT RESOURCES FOR PERSONS WITH DISABILITIES:	200
RANKING OF STATES ON EMPLOYMENT OF PEOPLE WITH DISABILITIES (PwDs)	201
INDEPENDENT LIVING	207
AMERICANS WITH DISABILITIES ACT (ADA) PAST, PRESENT, AND FUTURE	210
RESOURCES ON THE AMERICANS WITH DISABILITIES ACT	213
HOME MODIFICATION FOR PEOPLE WITH DISABILITIES	213
NEW ARCHITECTURE FOR DISABILITIES	214
HOME ADAPTABILITY CHECKLIST	216
ACCESSIBILITY CHECKLIST	217
DISABILITY LIVING CONDITIONS AND REMODELING RESOURCES	219
HELP FOR THE CAREGIVER	220
CAREGIVING SUPPORT AND ASSISTANCE	221
CAREGIVER STRESS AND BURNOUT	227
CAREGIVING TIPS SUMMARIZED	233
CAREGIVER RESOURCES	235
TOP 15 CHEAPEST STATES FOR LONG-TERM CARE COSTS	236

PART IV - BEST PLACES TO LIVE FOR AUTISM, INTELLECTUAL DEVELOPMENTAL DISABILITIES, AND MENTAL/COGNITIVE DISABILITIES 241

CHAPTER DEFINITIONS.. 242
"COGNITIVE DISABILITIES" VERSUS "INTELLECTUAL DISABILITY" 245
SERVICES AND FUNDING DATA FOR STATES AND STATE COMPARISONS 246
GROWTH OF FEDERAL, STATE, AND LOCAL SPENDING FOR IDD SERVICES IN THE UNITED STATES 247
SPENDING FOR IDD SERVICES PER CATEGORY IN THE UNITED STATES...................... 248
TOTAL IDD SERVICES AND SUPPORT SPENDING IN THE UNITED STATES 248
DISTRIBUTION OF SERVICES AVAILABLE THROUGH THE HCBS WAIVERS.................... 248
PUBLIC IDD SPENDING BY REVENUE SOURCE IN THE UNITED STATES 249
FEDERAL-STATE MEDICAID AS A PERCENTAGE OF TOTAL IDD SPENDING................... 250
IDD LIVING ARRANGEMENT TYPES (ESTIMATED NUMBERS) 250
ESTIMATED NUMBER OF INDIVIDUALS WITH IDD BY AGE GROUP LIVING WITH FAMILY CAREGIVERS 251
STATE IDD AGENCY SUPPORTED EMPLOYMENT PROGRAMS IN THE UNITED STATES........ 252
ESTIMATED NUMBER OF IDD CAREGIVING FAMILIES AND FAMILIES SUPPORTED BY IDD . 253
ESTIMATED NUMBER OF INDIVIDUALS WITH IDD BY AGE GROUP LIVING WITH FAMILY CAREGIVERS 253
ESTIMATED NUMBER OF PERSONS WITH IDD LIVING WITH A CAREGIVER WHO IS 60-YEARS OF AGE AND OLDER 254
ESTIMATED NUMBER OF IDD CAREGIVING FAMILIES COMPARED TO FAMILIES SUPPORTED BY STATE IDD AGENCY FEDERAL, STATE, AND LOCAL FUNDS. 255
CAREGIVERS AVERAGE HOURLY WAGES DISCOURSING PEOPLE FROM ENTERING THE PROFESSION... 256
FAMILY FINANCIAL SUPPORT IN EACH OF THE STATES FOR PARTICIPANTS WITH IDD 257
IDD FUNDING BUDGET OF EACH STATE.. 258
IDD FUNDING BUDGET IN UNITED STATES 307
WHAT IS APPLIED BEHAVIOR ANALYSIS (ABA)?... 308

APPENDIX 316

APPENDIX 1 - AQUAPONICS 317
APPENDIX 2 - AQUAPONIC DESIGN PLANS 321
APPENDIX 3 - AQUAPONICS FOR PROFIT... 323
APPENDIX 4 - AQUAPONICS PLANS AND INSTRUCTIONS 325
APPENDIX 5 - RELIABLE ALTERNATIVE NEWS SOURCES 327
APPENDIX 6 - RECOMMENDED RESOURCES... 328
APPENDIX 7 - ENCOURAGEMENT & KEYS TO SUCCESS 333

AUTISM COMMUNITY ADVICE...338
REQUEST FOR INPUT AND FEEDBACK 341

Preface

I would like to be able to tell you this book came into fruition through much enthusiasm and a strong interest in the topic. However, to make such a claim would be an egregious distortion of the truth.

To put it bluntly, this book was born out of a necessity to help our special needs daughter, and desperation to improve our family situation. Anyone who is a caretaker or has a family member with special needs knows the hardships, as well as the mental and emotional stress, that situation inflicts upon one's life. The strain is continuous and relentless. The burden is further exacerbated if living in an area that does not have adequate resources to help the special needs person or assist the caretaker.

Although I consider myself of sound mind, fairly intelligent (two college degrees, a professional engineer, and a business owner), maintain a positive attitude, and fully trust that God is in control, it has been - and remains to this day - a constant battle to not worry about our daughter who has severe autism, my wife, our son, our family's financial well-being, and our daughter's future.

Statistics show that stress-related health problems and life-altering undesired challenges for caretakers far outnumber those of non-caretakers. My wife and I have definitely experienced the difficulties and related consequences associated with caring for our daughter.

I strive to maintain a healthy lifestyle by exercising regularly, staying hydrated, avoiding substances harmful to my body, and trying my best to get adequate sleep. Admittedly, I have not perfected living this lifestyle; however, I feel I do fairly well. Nevertheless, the stress of taking care of, and being responsible for, someone with special needs, especially someone you love, takes its toll.

I have no doubt that I would have serious health problems if I were not striving to live a healthy lifestyle every day. I say this not to brag, but only to encourage you, if you are a caretaker or living with someone with special needs, to make healthy living a high priority and to not get discouraged. Your quality of life and the one you are caring for is dependent upon you being in good health and having a positive attitude. I would also presume your life has a positive impact on others as well, so be sure to take good care of yourself and try to laugh as much as sanely possible.

Although I do a lot to help care for our daughter and family, my wife is our daughter's primary caretaker and deserves the credit. Not to be disrespectful, but unless one lives this ordeal for months on end, year after year, they will not have an adequate understanding of how challenging such a situation can be. Your situation may be worse, and you have my sincere condolences. If your situation is not as difficult, I don't mean to belittle your hardships, you have my sympathy as well---life is challenging enough in itself. My point is only to say that it is impossible to understand how troubling our situation is unless you live it, as I am sure I could not fully understand your situation.

Now back to how this book came into fruition. Getting our daughter the best help possible has been our highest priority over the past couple of decades. Actually, it has been an imperative driving objective that has consumed us, but time marches on and other important matters that cannot and will not be ignored make their way into the reality of life. Such things as cost of living, employment opportunities, air quality, crime rate, economic circumstances, personal interests, proximity to relatives, educational opportunities, and professional goals are very important to one's well being, financial security, and level of happiness in life. The best situation for the entire family will also allow us to better help our daughter.

I have to admit that the weather in Sacramento is awesome and has spoiled to me to some degree. It is also great living close to so many attractions (theme parks, ocean, San Francisco, Sierra Nevada mountain range, Lake Tahoe, Yosemite National Park, giant redwoods, countless biking/ hiking/boating places, festivals, etc.). Our daughter has had a wonderful program for the past 13 years, and there are numerous resources in Sacramento for children and families with autism.

However, there are some big negatives as well. For instance, the California valley has some of the worst air quality in the country and is frequently detrimental to human health. The cost of living in California is ridiculous. The prices for groceries, fuel, utilities, real estate, food and supplies gobble up money faster than a hungry tiger can eat a gourmet steak. California is rated one of the worst states for entrepreneurs and small businesses, which is certainly in opposition to my goals. Land, for farming or a large yard for gardening, cost a fortune. The volume of traffic, high crime rate in many areas, the large percentage of illegal immigrants, gangs, abundance of vagrants, the concentration of people living here, and having so many early release prisoners in society requires one to be vigilant at all times in regards to safety precautions. I certainly do not mean to offend anyone by mentioning these groups, I only wish to emphasize that there are conditions and some people within these groups which make it prudent to avoid or at least be on high alert when near them. There are also other social considerations, such as conservative versus liberal views, democrat versus republican/independent/libertarian affiliation, religion and world views, etc. Before you pass judgment, please consider the fact that most of us would much rather prefer to live in communities where the people most closely align with our culture and views. Although most people applaud diversity studies show that people naturally gravitate towards other people who are similar. Much trepidation and disharmony occurs when we are at odds with our environment.

The frustration of trying to put a round peg into a square hole (our current living arrangement) has prompted us to search for a place to relocate that would be a better 'fit' for our entire family. Of course, meeting our daughter's needs remains a high priority but close behind is financial security, employment opportunities, living in a state that is friendly to small businesses, living in a healthy environment and safe community, and to have a good quality of life for our senior years.

Actually, we have a detailed list that describes our ideal location. We developed this list of items over time after running into roadblock after roadblock while living in Sacramento; and while considering our relocation needs. This list is shared in Part 1 as an example and guide to help you create your own list.

With our daughter transitioning into her adult years we began exploring new options for her and determined it would be a good time to relocate to a place better suited to the goals and needs of our entire family. When we first started researching our options several years ago we thought it would be an easy study: review the data, select the best option, and then make the move (simple as 1-2-3). To say that we were mistaken would be a gross understatement. We quickly learned that there was not one reliable resource that addressed all our needs; the information we obtained was sometimes suspect or conflicted with data from other sources. Other information we sought was often very difficult or next to impossible to find. There was not a single resource that came close to providing all the information we needed, so we had to go to many different sources.

That long and cumbersome journey is what has enabled and inspired me to create this resource. The information provided in this book is an accumulation of hundreds of hours of work and research. It was also developed at a considerable cost, as I hired four researchers to assist me in collecting, compiling, and processing enormous amounts of data for this book. There are many resources online and in print that have questionable or conflicting information, fail to examine the data comprehensively, or do not present the data in ways that can be easily understood. The data used for this book is only from RELIABLE sources. In other words, this book is a compilation of information obtained from many different trustworthy sources. Furthermore, the valuable information provided in this book is presented in a user-friendly format.

I trust you will find this one-stop resource for your relocation consideration is all you need to help you make an intelligent relocation decision that best fits your needs. You can be confident the information provided is thorough, accurate, and complete. Rest assured, this book is certainly a wise investment, as it will prevent you from having to sacrifice your limited and valuable time searching for answers. This investment will enable you to find the very best place for your preferences and needs.

At the time of this writing we are preparing to move to our selected location. We realize that no place is perfect, but I am confident our selected spot is the very best place for our family. I am not going to share it with you in this publication, as I do not want it to influence your decision, and because what works best for us may not be ideal for you.

Thank you for taking the time to check out this valuable resource. It is probably fair to say that we share a common connection in having a strong desire to live in the place that best meets our needs. Please feel free to give me your honest feedback and suggestions regarding this book. I truly welcome your input, as it will allow me to make improvements to future editions.

I would also like to hear your story, if you care to share it with me, about your situation and relocation preferences. And please do let me know how I can best pray for you. Thanks again. Now without any further delay, let's get started on your journey through this book to find the best place for you.

Please send comments, feedback, and suggestions to:
http://www.bestplacestoliveinamerica.info/contact-author/

Acknowledgements

This book would not be possible if not for the blessings from God. He alone is deserving of all praise and worship.

I must also thank my dear wife Connie and children Hannah and Nathan for their patience, sacrifices, and positive support during the creation of the book. This book would not have come into fruition without them on my team.

Much thanks and credit is due to all those who assisted me all the research, data collection, and formulating it into a user-friendly format. David Wolfe, Stewart Stonger, Robert Nash, Mitzi Cunningham, and Jennifer Groza were instrumental assistants in the preparation of this book.

To my parents, relatives, and in-laws, thank you for your love. Thank you also for being such a special part of my life.

Part I

How to Find the Best Place & Relocating with Ease

Finding the Best Places to Live

The reality of choosing a new place to live encompasses an incredibly large series of factors, all competing for your attention. In order to be successful in your search, you must determine what is most important to you and your family, do your homework, and then continue to be vigilant in your search until you find the right place to live. It can be intimidating and frustrating at times, but all that effort is worth it in the end once you are settled in best possible location.

Keep in mind that no place will be perfect. However, if you clearly define your goals, prioritize your needs, and prepare an organized list of things that are important to you, then you will be more confident and comfortable in your selection process. Following are some very important factors to consider when deciding where to live. Additional information on these topics is presented throughout this book. This book will also address many other topics and issues that are not presented in this overview, but certainly should not be overlooked.

Affordability — No matter what your income is, living comfortably and within your means should be your first concern. Affordability includes more than just housing expenses; the prices for consumable goods, like groceries, vary greatly from town to town. The price of gasoline, utility services including electric and water, and taxes, also varies.

> *One writer commented "When I moved from California to New Mexico, my expenses dropped like a rock overnight. My rent was cut in half, and I now spend a lot less money on groceries, gas, and utility bills. Because I'm a freelancer, my income stayed about the same, **so I felt like I had received a big raise!**"*

Employment Opportunities — Employment opportunities vary considerably from one location to another so spend time researching the <u>job markets</u> in different areas of the country. Start by analyzing quality employment opportunities within your industry, then determine where the highest concentration of jobs are located, and look at the opportunities in your industry.

Income levels for jobs will also vary considerably from state to state. Salary.com lets you compare pay rates for various careers across the country. Salaries are often based on where the job is located. Do your research before if employment is a 'must have' item on your relocation list.

Taxes — Did you know that some states have no <u>sales taxes</u>? In addition, some states don't collect individual <u>income taxes</u>. Some states provide property tax credits or homestead exemptions that can provide homeowners with some additional tax relief.

These are important factors to consider when choosing a place to live. The Tax Foundation measures the state-local tax burden, which calculates the percentage of income that taxpayers pay for state and local taxes. Consider local sales tax, income tax, and tax credits and exemptions when you're looking for the perfect place to live.

Real Estate Value — Since buying a home is the single largest investment you will probably ever make, this is an important factor in the relocation decision process. With real estate in a constant state of flux, it's important to research current home prices, the length of time homes are for sale, the resale values of homes, and probable long-term value estimates. In addition, carefully review local housing price trends. Websites like Zillow.com can help you gain a grasp of the local real estate market.

Proximity to Family and Friends —Do you spend the holidays with your family and friends? Do you have a large extended family? These are important factors to consider when choosing where to live.

If extended family and friends are important to you, choose a place either within driving distance or within a reasonable distance by plane. Otherwise, you'll constantly feel torn, and likely spend all of your vacation, time, money, and energy shuttling back and forth to visit friends and family.

Crime Rates and Statistics — No one wants to live in a high-crime area. By researching the crime rates and statistics for various areas, you can learn more about the safety of a town or neighborhood.

If you have already decided upon the city where you want to live, contact the local police stations to discuss the best areas. Most police stations have a person that will be happy to discuss any concerns you have about the area. You can also check out Crime Reports, which lets you review crime statistics for different neighborhoods. The Chamber of Commerce is another excellent resource.

Climate — Do long cold winters bother you? Then you probably shouldn't consider northern states. If you are not a fan of humidity it would probably be wise to avoid settling in the southeast United States. If you like to garden, the long summers are helpful.

The climate plays a large role in our lives as it impacts our hobbies, and behavior. Living in the climate in which you are most comfortable contributes to your mental health, so climates in your relocation options should be considered closely.

Education System — A good education is essential requirement for many families. Nonprofit websites like **GreatSchools** are a great source for parents looking for the ideal schools for their children. The quality of the public schools can also factor into your finances, since tuition for a private school can be extremely expensive.

Town or City Size — If you enjoy a friendly wave from everyone you pass while driving to the post office, then a smaller town is definitely for you. If you wish to remain relatively anonymous, a larger town or a big city is better suited to your personality.

Culture — If you crave constant cultural stimulation, you definitely want to choose a place that has a lot of cultural offerings. Larger cities have concerts, operas, sports teams, plays, museums, and musicals to offer. In smaller cities and towns cultural options are much more limited.

Many people need to be near their favorite team, or a vibrant music scene or the theater. If you have a favorite hobby or recreational activity, evaluate the options to make sure that you can continue to pursuing your interests. Finally, if you enjoy being around a specific religious or ethnic community with your same beliefs and interests, this should be a factor in where you choose to live.

> *One writer commented, "I commuted in Los Angeles for years and **you couldn't pay me enough money to do it again.**"*

Commute Time and Public Transportation Options — The explosive growth of the suburbs surrounding metropolitan areas have made commuting times in many areas unbearable. A recently released report from Sweden indicates that long-distance commuters actually have an increased risk of divorce. The length of time it takes to get to work can be a determining factor in the decision to move to a new locale.

If you have a family, commuting can drastically reduce the amount of time you spend at home. With gas prices rising and commute times becoming longer, utilizing public transportation options like light rail, train, or bus can be an inexpensive, time-saving way for you and your family to get around – and cut the cost of commuting to work. A good public transportation system is an essential item for those dependent upon such.

Food Options — If you're a foodie, and eating locally and sustainably is important to you, consider whether you can pursue this lifestyle in your new home. If trying new, diverse cuisines is one of your passions, a bigger metropolitan area is going to offer more choices than small-town America. For some, the ability to grow their own food year-round with a **home vegetable garden** is a determining factor for choosing where to live. 'Aquaponic Design Plans & Everything You Need to Know' by Dudley is the best resource for learning how to feed yourself and family year-round healthy organic food in any climate at a negligible cost.

Relocation Criteria
(Dudley's Sample List)

When we began our relocation search we listed the important items in our decision process. Following is a copy of our list. You will certainly want to develop your own list.

Must Have:

- Good for Hannah (our special needs daughter)
- Be a small business entrepreneur friendly state
- Warm /Temperate climate (no cold/north locations)

- Inexpensive Real Estate (farming is important to us)
- No Nuclear Facilities within 125 miles
- Classical Conversation home school program
- Air Quality Good
- Solid Church within 30 minutes
- Low Cost of Living

Must Have Resources:

- Funding Assistance for Hannah (our special needs daughter)
- Good School/Programs/Day-Care for Hannah

Negotiable:

- Low Unemployment
- Plentiful Employment Opportunities
- Within 35 miles of a large metropolitan area

Preferences:

- Low Allergies
- Good Soil
- Easy to recruit aids for Hannah (i.e. college/university. Metro demographics, etc.)
- Low cost for labor (aids for Hannah)

The above is a very simple list we put together. Your list can certainly be longer. Some things that are not on our list are cultural opportunities, food options, and public transportation. These items are not things that we placed a lot of value on in our decision process.

Also, since some items carry more weight than others it can be helpful to assign a number between 1 and 10 to each item, with "10" being very important and "1" being not so important. A numbered system will allow you to compare locations in terms of an overall total value score.

'Avoidance' Sample List
(Dudley's Personal Relocation Criteria)

After we narrowed our selection options and started looking at specific areas in our top three relocation choices, we examined them against another set of factors of items we wanted to avoid. Below is our 'avoidable' list, but you can certainly create your own list.

Dudley's Personal List of Items to Avoid

- Avoid being near an Airport
- Avoid being in direct Flight Paths of low and mid flying aircraft.
- Avoid being near or downwind of Waste Water Treatment Plants (WWTP)
- Avoid being near or downwind of Landfills

continued

- Avoid being near or downwind of mining and quarry operations.
- Cell Towers (1/4 mile+ distance)
- Avoid being near or downwind of Downwind of Industrial Businesses
- Avoid being near or downwind Nuclear Power Plants (a minimum of 125 miles away).
- Avoid being near or downwind of Coal & Gas Fired Power Plants
- Avoid being near or downwind of Livestock, Pig, and Poultry Operations
- Avoid living within the noise vicinity of a Hwy or Arterial Road

IMPORTANT NOTES:

1. Research climate data for the area being considered to identify the predominate wind directions.
2. Research what is upwind from any property you are considering as a home.
3. Air pollution is a major risk to our health and safety and is the contributing cause of nearly 100,000 premature deaths each year.
4. Experts recommend living at least 1 mile from highways (preferably at least 1.5 miles), and at least 600 to 1,000 feet from arterial roadways.

S.M.A.R.T. Goals

Before moving forward, it is important that you clearly define your goals and objectives. Only then can you create an effective plan that will produce the results you desire. Such is referred to as a strategic plan, and it should not be taken lightly. A strategic plan is your plan for success. It will define your mission, your present situation, where you want to be in three to five years, and help you get there efficiently. "If you fail to plan, you are planning to fail!" -- Benjamin Franklin

Clearly defining what you desire to get out of relocating, put together a realistic schedule, and define how to best execute the plan. Doing this most efficiency and effectively is achieved through a process called 'S.M.A.R.T.' goals. Writing out your S.M.A.R.T. goals creates a plan that promotes success in the least amount of time.

Defining your S.M.A.R.T. goals should be a process adopted early on in the relocation process, preferably before investing any money and much time. The S.M.A.R.T. goals should be an integral part of the decision and relocation process. The S.M.A.R.T. goal procedure also works well with all other endeavors in your life. In summary, the S.M.A.R.T. goals process is a clearly defined plan (in writing) that is consist of the following components:

S = Specific
M = Measurable
A = Achievable
R = Realistic
T = Time Bound

Specific - consider who, what, when where, why and how in developing the goal.

- What: What do I want to accomplish?
- Why: Specific reasons, purpose or benefits of accomplishing the goal.
- Who: Who is involved?
- Where: Identify a location.
- Which: Identify requirements and constraints.

Measurable - a numeric or descriptive measurement.

- How much?
- How many?
- How will I know when it is accomplished?
- You should be able to track and measure your progress along the way. Each measured success builds momentum and motivation by informing you of your current status as you make progress in the right direction.

Achievable - consider the resources needed and set a realistic goal.

- How: How can the goal be accomplished?

The goals that you set must also be attainable, which means that it <u>*can*</u> be achieved. Some things are just impossible to attain (world peace). However, most things can be achieved if you are strongly determined and put your heart and mind to it. History has proven this to be the case many times.

Big, long-term goals can be set if one is truly confident they can be achieved. However, one must also realize that success is achieved only by hard work, sacrifice, discipline and perseverance. Dream and plan for your long-term goal, but pursue many short-term goals along the way that are attainable at your current capability, skills and knowledge.

Relevant - make sure the goal is consistent with the mission

(Result-Based, Results-oriented, Resourced, Resonant, Realistic)

- Does this seem worthwhile?
- Is this the right time?
- Does this match other efforts and needs in my life?
- A realistic goal means **the goal is realistic when considering the other aspects and demands of your life**. It is inherently related to the *attainable* aspect of the goal.

If you are unable to carve extra time out of your schedule to pursue the goal, then it is not a realistic goal. Sometimes it is more important to first take control your current situation before taking on something else. So even if a goal is ultimately attainable, it may not necessarily be realistic. It is up to you to decide whether you can make it happen or not. And if not, what can you do different in your life to make it happen?

Time-bound - set a realistic deadline.

(Time-oriented, Time framed, Timed, Time-based, Time-boxed, Time-bound, Time-Specific, Timetabled, Time limited, Trackable, Tangible)

- When?
- What can I do 6 months from now?
- What can I do 6 weeks from now?
- What can I do today?
- **Without any timeframe, procrastination is likely; as there is no sense of urgency to take action to achieve the goal.** When setting the timeframe, you should not be overly ambitious and set unrealistic timeframes. You also do not want to set too long a timeframe as that will make you complacent and lose momentum. *What you want is to set a timeframe that gives you the right amount of positive pressure to push you.*
- Set an overall timeframe for achieving the goal, as well as other shorter timeframes for achieving the short- and medium-term milestones and targets of the goal.

Finishing Strong

Personally, I have found that doing at least one thing every day to achieve each of my long-term goals works well for me. Life is full. Furthermore, we are often bombarded with distractions and unplanned interruptions. However, keeping to a plan of doing at least one thing each day (no matter how small) will help in remain on track and moving forward to the ultimate goal. That one thing could be as simple as making a telephone call, looking something up on the internet, making a purchase, organizing a file, etc. It may be a small step, but it is one less step that has to be taken on the journey to achieving the goal.

> *Whatever your desire, use S.M.A.R.T. goal setting, and you will not go wrong. It is easy to remember and very effective at the same time.*
>
> *"Failing to plan is planning to fail"* -- Alan Lakein

Finding the Right Place Checklist
For Individuals with Cognitive Disabilities

Ideas on how to use the checklist

ASK, OBSERVE, ASK OTHERS

- ❖ First, try asking people who can read or understand words or sign to complete the checklist on their own or with help.
- ❖ Second, observe people who do not read or understand words or sign very well and act as their advocate (or choose someone else) in completing the checklist.
- ❖ Third, ask others who know the person well (like a friend or relative or service coordinator) to help complete the checklist.

The 'Place of My Own' Checklist

If you are thinking about finding a place of your own, here is a way to look at a house or apartment where you might want to live. It will help you decide what is good about the place and what could be better. The best way to use this checklist is as follows:

- Make sure' you get a chance to see the house or apartment and the immediate neighborhood.
- If you need assistance with the checklist, ask a friend, relative or your service coordinator or someone else you feel comfortable with.
- Write notes about what you find out about the place in the box provided.
- Think about all of these things before you decide if you want to live in the house or apartment.
- You may be looking at several different places – use this checklist to decide which house or apartment is best for you.

☐ The place is close to stores, banks, places to eat and other places I will need to go.

☐ The place is clean inside and outside.

☐ The place is in an area of my choice.

☐ The place is near and easy to get to the bus.

☐ The neighborhood feels safe and I'm comfortable when I leave the house or apartment.

☐ The rooms in the house or apartment are easy to get around in and you can move around in a wheelchair.

continued

- ☐ The place is in good repair.
- ☐ I can afford the deposit that I need to give the landlord.
- ☐ I have read over the rental agreement or had someone help me understand it.
- ☐ The stove is gas or electric and it works well.
- ☐ There is a refrigerator that works well.
- ☐ There is a dishwasher that works well.
- ☐ The heater/air conditioner works well.
- ☐ The neighbors are friendly and supportive.
- ☐ If I am living with roommates, we have talked about our own "house rules."
- ☐ I have my own bedroom or the place has enough privacy for me.
- ☐ The place has ramps and enough space to get through with a wheelchair.

Some "ideal" house elements to consider

House layout

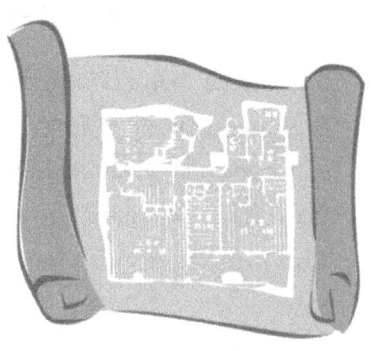

- ✓ One level or ranch style home
- ✓ Can be divided into separate areas with distinct spaces
- ✓ Large open spaces that make it easy to navigate
- ✓ Open/airy floor plan with spaces that flow into each other

House movement

- ✓ Wide hallways, doorways and doors
- ✓ Easy to open doors
- ✓ Doorways without saddles or sills that interfere with free movement
- ✓ Level floors that are easy to roll on
- ✓ Tough, durable surfaces that will not get damaged by a power chair

Bathroom

- ✓ Large and accessible.
- ✓ Roll in shower at least 5 feet by 5 feet.
- ✓ Hand held shower head.
- ✓ More than one shower.
- ✓ Bathtub with lift.
- ✓ Raised or side opening bathtub.
- ✓ Whirlpool or spa tub.

- ✓ Accessible toilet with raised seat, armrests and room for a rolling toilet chair, and a lift.
- ✓ Grab bars.
- ✓ Bathroom sink with adjustable heights.
- ✓ Lever/faucets with anti-scald controls.
- ✓ Space underneath sink for wheelchair.
- ✓ Pull lever soap dispenser.

Kitchen

- ✓ Large, open floor plan.
- ✓ Accessible features: lower sinks, counters and cabinets; sink and counter cut outs or knee openings; drawers and cabinets with accessible hardware.
- ✓ Ice/water dispenser in the refrigerator door.
- ✓ Higher or adjustable table.

Bedroom

- ✓ Accessible closets and other storage.
- ✓ Room by the bed for transferring safely from a wheelchair.

Getting in and out

- ✓ Ramps or on grade entries.
- ✓ Power lifts.
- ✓ Multiple wheelchair entries.
- ✓ Fire exits.

Garage

- ✓ Attached to the house.
- ✓ Large enough for conversion van and maneuverability.
- ✓ Equipped with a ramp.

Moving Checklist

Use this week-by-week checklist to plan your move to a new home.

When you make the decision to move, the clock starts clicking to your moving day.

But don't fret, this is a handy checklist of major accomplishments you should tackle before you move.

The tasks to accomplish further from moving day might seem trivial now, but staying on schedule will help you avoid last minute headaches. Time will be at a premium on the days right before your move, so be diligent in checking off these tasks.

60 Days Before You Move

This is the time to start strategically planning your move, step-by-step, to alleviate the stress of last-minute packing and planning.

Your Move

- Get quotes from at least three moving companies, and make sure they do in-home assessments so your quote is as accurate as possible. Talk to family and friends for recommendations, or get free moving quotes from websites like Relocation.com.
- Determine how many packing supplies you'll need, and designate a room where you can begin to store and organize them and other items that will assist you in your move.
- Research your new community and schools so you know as much as possible before you move.
- Got enough people to drive your cars to your new home? It not, you'll need a car mover.
- Get an appraisal on your expensive items so you can insure them for your move.
- If you are being transferred by work, understand your company's moving policy.
- Pare down -- use up, sell, recycle or donate anything you don't want to move. Make it a family project.
- Make a moving folder or booklet -- include an inventory of your household items with a video or photos.

Your Records

- Contact your insurance agent to transfer medical, property, fire and auto insurance policies, and while you have them on the phone -- be sure to ask about coverage while you're in transit.
- Create a designated folder for moving-related expenses where you can file all receipts. This will come in handy as many moving expenses are tax deductible. Obtain an IRS Change of Address form, Form 8822, by calling (800) 829-1040 or visiting the IRS website. You will be able to download and print form 8822 and most other IRS tax forms; e.g., Form 3903 to help deduct moving expenses.
- Notify old and new schools and arrange for the transfer of school records and begin the process of registering in new schools.
- Notify doctors and dentists of moves, and seek referrals and collect all medical, dental and school records to ensure you do not forget to obtain them at a later date; some require written permission for this. Keep these in a safe place.
- Belong to any membership associations? Be sure to transfer membership to your new hometown.

Your Family and Pets

- Make travel arrangements for you and your family. Whether it's renting a car, scheduling a flight or reserving a hotel room, book it at a time that will give you flexibility in case anything goes awry. Be sure to arrive well before your movers' scheduled arrival.
- If you're nearing a pet's regular exam, schedule it now, and start getting recommendations for veterinarians in your new town.

> **Quick Tips - 60 Days Before**
>
> - ❖ Contemplate holding a garage sale prior to your move; this will help you reduce the amount of stuff you need to move, and earn some extra cash on the side. Start planning one now, or think of charities that could take your stuff.
> - ❖ Unless you're buying packing materials new, keep an eye out of for used items that could be used for packing, like old towels and sheets that could be used as packing material.
> - ❖ Do you need storage? Start researching your storage options now.

30 Days Before You Move

Your Move

- By this point you should have already received estimates and hired a mover. Check with you mover to confirm all the details of the move are set. If you are packing on your own, make the proper arrangements and get the right supplies.
- Make the arrangements to connect and disconnect your cable, internet, electric and any other services you currently use and arranged for service at your new home. Dealing with this at an earlier date will prevent any date and time conflicts you may incur.
- If you need new blinds, curtains or furniture for your new home, buy them now and arrange it so they arrive at your new home when your things do.
- Start planning where things will go in your new home.
- Create an inventory of your stuff so that you can compare against the moving company's list to ensure you don't lose anything in the move. It's also a good aid in determining how much moving insurance you need.
- Are you taking appliances? If so, draw up a plan for how to handle them.
- Get a head start on your packing by packing things that you won't need before the move, like seasonal items such as summer sporting gear.
- Arrange childcare and pet care for the day of your move, or think about a "safe" room they can be during the move itself so they're out of the way.
- Make a packing plan -- assign everyone a task and involve the kids.
- Make an unpacking plan for the new home -- who does what and diagram where the furniture goes. The movers will not rearrange your furniture for you, so think this through.

Your Records

- Contact or visit your local Post Office to obtain a Change of Address form. You can also obtain this form online at the Postal Service website.

continued

- Give a change of address to the following: Banks, schools, friends and family, insurance company, doctors and specialists, cell phone company, credit card companies, and magazine and newspaper subscriptions.
- You may have to switch banks because your current bank doesn't have branches in your new town. Investigate the popular banks in the area you will be living in so that you can close and open new bank accounts as needed.
- Check the requirements for a new driver's license and complete auto registration at your new motor vehicle location.
- If you will be making an international move, make sure your passport is up to date and has not expired. Passports generally take three weeks to process.
- Let service providers -- landscapers, cleaning services -- know you're moving, and look for new ones in your new hometown.

Your Family and Pets

- If time permits, you may also want to take you and your family to your dentist and/or eye doctor to get your routine check ups done. It may take a while for you to find new family dentists and doctors in your new city that you are comfortable with so it can be a good idea to take care of these things while you still have access to professionals that you know.
- Encourage children to make an address book of friends.

Quick Tips - 30 Days Before

❖ Driving to your new house? Make sure your car's ready for the trip, and that you have all the proper maps -- make extra maps for the movers, just in case.

14 Days Before You Move

Your Move

- Begin cleaning any rooms in your house that have been emptied, such as closets, basements or attics, and check to make sure you did not leave anything unpacked.
- Moving plants? Check on their special moving needs.
- Make arrangements to clean your new home, and the home you're moving out of. Also, arrange for any services for your new home that will be easier to do before your things arrive: carpet-cleaning, wood floor cleaning, painting, etc.

Your Records

- Find pharmacies in your new town that you can transfer your family's prescriptions over to. Make sure you have enough required medication in case you don't locate a new pharmacist/doctor immediately.
- Organize important documents -- will, passport, deeds, financial statements -- to carry with you when move; make copies that you can pack with your household goods, but carry the originals with you.

Your Family and Pets

- Is your pet ready for the move? Make sure you have transportation arranged, and that you have someone who can watch the pet during the move. Also, make sure the pet is up to date on its shots.

Quick Tips - 14 Days Before

❖ Collect valuable items such as jewelry or heirlooms and keep them separate from the rest of your packed belongings so you don't risk losing them.

❖ Return any borrowed items, such as library books, and collect any clothing that you may have taken to be dry-cleaned.

One Week Before You Move

Your Move

- Pack any items you have not had a chance to pack yet. Your final week at home has the potential to be very stressful; don't push things off until the last minute.
- As you're packing, be sure you're labeling each box for where it goes in your new home -- if you don't do this now, you might very well forget what's in what box. Also, where applicable mark the boxes "Fragile," "Do not load," or "Load last."
- Call your mover and confirm your move date, and make any special arrangements for items like a piano.
- Arrange for payment for movers.
- Confirm closing/move-in dates with your real estate agent; confirm dates with your storage people.
- Discuss contingency plan for the movers running late. Where will you sleep?
- Disconnect and disassemble your computer and peripherals. Back up your computer files on a disk or flash memory drive. You should plan to take these files with you in the car or whatever mode of transportation you will be using to get to your new home. Exposure to extreme temperatures can damage your software and files.
- Dispose of paint, oil, and weed killers. Drain fuel out of mowers. Discard propane tanks from grills.

Your Records

- Make sure all scheduled deliveries (newspaper, milk, etc.) have been canceled or redirected to your new home.
- Open a new banking account. Don't close your old one until you move. If you bank online, be sure to update your address for statement delivery.
- Get together all keys, alarm codes and garage door openers and place them in a folder so that you can be prepared to hand them over to the new owner or real estate agent.

Your Family

- Start preparing your kids for the move. Talk about it, and engage them in the process -- maybe they can help color-code boxes to help the movers know where stuff goes.
- Empty all lockers at school, work or at your gym.
- Return any borrowed items from friends, the library or video store -- you don't want to fumble with this on your moving day.

Quick Tips - One Week Before

❖ Think about quick and easy meals you can prepare for your family to use up the remaining food in your refrigerator so that it does not go to waste, and also allow you to pack some kitchen items.

On Moving Day

Your Move

- Put together a moving day survival kit with items you will need for the trip and immediately when you arrive at your new home. These items include toilet paper, snacks, bottled water, dishes, toiletries, towels, a few days' worth of clothes. Be sure to plan for the contingency that your household items may arrive a day or even a few days late if you are doing a long distance move.
- Doublecheck any arrangements you might have made to transport your pet. Do you have proper travel gear?
- Write out a list for your movers of things they'll need: phone numbers; exact moving address and maps.
- Check the inventory list and sign it. Put your copy in your moving folder.
- Read the Bill of Lading carefully and sign it, if it is correct.
- Make sure you have the moving companies contact information with you in your moving folder.

- In your new home, tape names to doors to assist movers; map out the floor layout so movers know what's going where; finally, prepare your new home for moving to prevent any damage.
- If you don't have professional cleaners coming in, make sure you clean your home before leaving.
- Pack a moving day box of things you'll be moving yourself so you have access to them right away. Cell phone, light bulbs, tool kit, scissors, flashlight, trash bags, paper towels, toilet paper, aspirin and bed linens. Make sure you have extra packing material on hand for things that arise last minute.
- Pack pet food and pet litter.
- Be sure you have cash on hand for the move. Find out if you'll owe money after the move and find out what form of payment they accept.
- Double check to be sure you're on target for your utilities to be hooked up.
- Do the walkthrough with your real estate agent. Make sure everything's where it should be. Also ask for appliance manuals and such.

Quick Tips - Moving Day

- ❖ Empty, clean and defrost your refrigerator/freezer and use baking soda to rid it of any foul odors.
- ❖ Notify the police in your town if your home will be uninhabited for a long period of time.
- ❖ Before you move, mow your lawn one last time, especially if your home will not be unoccupied immediately after your departure.
- ❖ Make sure you know what to do with final trash.

One Week After You Move

- Get your kids involved in the unpacking process, and help them find activities in your new town.
- Did you get your moving deposits back yet?
- Make sure you have fire extinguishers and fire detectors in your new home.
- Do any quick repair work that needs to be done, if you didn't do it before moving in.
- Tackle some fun first projects to help make your house a home, like hanging pictures and other simple projects
- Explore the new town -- get acquainted, find out where everything is, etc.
- Replace the locks if you're uneasy about keeping the locks that came with the house.
- Check on licenses for pets.
- Update your address for all these: voter registration, drivers license, tax forms, new bank account, etc.
- Start thinking about the larger home-renovation projects you'd like to get started, and prioritize them.

Factors for Relocating a Business

Businesses grow. Products change. Economies flourish or flounder. Any combination of these or other factors can lead you to consider the possibility of relocating a business. As you consider the reasons to relocate your business, your primary concern has to be how the move is going to affect your bottom line. Don't make any move without first considering all the factors for relocation and determining what the move may do to your customer base.

Customer Base — Businesses that provide a service to their customers need to be near their source of income. As neighborhoods change, the customer base may dwindle. In that case, a business owner may want to relocate his business so he can attract a newer, larger group of clients. If the neighborhood is in an area that is deteriorating economically, the business owner may need to move his business to a locale where he can operate his business profitably.

Work Force — If you need a specially trained work force that works for reasonable wages, you want your business to be easily accessible to your source of labor in order to attract and retain qualified employees. Perhaps you may have had an ample supply of qualified workers when you started your business, but as the business grew you found it harder to find additional workers willing to work for the wages you wish to pay. If your employees must have special training, it may make more sense to relocate the business closer to educational facilities where the workers.

Facilities — It's not uncommon for a new business of any type to start in a small building. As business grows, the old facility is no longer large enough to serve the needs of the expanding business. It's only natural that the owner would list larger facilities in his business plan as one of his reasons to relocate. In some cases, the electrical, water, sewage and other utilities simply cannot handle the requirements of the business. In others, the building may be deteriorating to the point where repairs are no longer feasible. Rental costs may be increasing at a rapid rate, which makes it impractical to remain at the location.

Tax Considerations — Some cities offer tax breaks to attract new business to their community. These tax incentives may be in the form of property tax abatement, sales tax exceptions, income tax reductions or other tax breaks on infrastructure improvements. If your business meets their criteria, you may be able to relocate your business and save a considerable amount of money on taxes. While this is seldom the single reason for moving, it may provide the last push needed to make the decision to move.

Operating costs — The cost of labor (average salaries/hourly wages and benefits), utility costs and availability, environmental regulations, tax structure, transportation costs, raw materials, and real estate are all factors that impact operating costs. The locations under consideration can have vastly different expenses that impact operating costs.

New equipment or modernization of existing equipment — Any costs associated with new equipment or the modernization of existing equipment need to be evaluated in terms of the costs of relocation or expansion. In addition to the analysis of costs, technological advances and efficiencies are important considerations when evaluating the purchase of new equipment or modernization of existing equipment.

Proximity to key geographic markets — Reducing the distance of product to the key markets can affect speed, cost, and service. Being able to serve clients from a quality and cost standpoint is critical.

Clustering — Companies from similar industries and/or that are suppliers of one another tend to be located in close proximity to one another. This clustering effect creates a more collaborative environment, reduces transportation costs, and leverages an experienced work force.

Quality of life — An examination of the quality-of-life factors (parks, schools, neighborhoods, arts/cultural and sports amenities, recreational opportunities, etc.) can also be an important part of the process. This is more important when a company is considering the relocation of team members to the community where the project will be located.

Relocation (The Move) – Great Advice

Follow this advice for a successful move:

Stay organized. Much of moving related stress comes from managing all of the logistics, like leaving your current home, and finding a new one,. Try to be very organized. Keep to-do lists for both your departure and arrival locations so that you can stay on top of everything.

Know what's available to you. Many companies offer a variety of relocation services and most are flexible in what they provide. Make sure you take the time to learn what's available to you—and use it. For example, some companies will pay for things like house hunting trips, transportation of your cars, assistance in selling or buying your home, help figuring out how to rent out a property, and event organizers to settle you into your new home. They might also be able to help your spouse with job placement or employment leads in your new city.

If your employer doesn't typically offer relocation assistance, ask for it. If you learn that assistance isn't typically given, don't be afraid to negotiate.. Start by researching moving costs (truck rentals, quotes from professional movers, transportation expenses, temporary housing, storage, etc.) so that you can present your employer with a detailed estimate of how much your relocation is expected to cost you. Having this supporting information is crucial to the success of your request. Also ask about preferred providers when it comes to relocation companies and real estate agents. Reimbursement for your relocation may be contingent upon the usage of designated professionals with whom your employer has established relationships.

Take time to get to know your new environment before you move. If you have the luxury of taking some time to explore your new area before arriving, do so. Explore the neighborhoods in the area to make sure that you find the best suited one for your lifestyle.

If you're not able to visit the new city before you move, take the time talk to people that live there or used to live there, and "get as much perspective as you can on what you're walking into. You should also read the local news or any local blogs to understand the vibe and learn what's going in your new town, Terry adds.

Know the cost of living in the new city. There are significant differences in cost of living among US cities and states. Typically, these differences will be compensated for in your salary, but it's still important to check. Do the research and plan accordingly.

Don't make any long-term commitments. Renting at first is a great way to settle into a new city without making a commitment to a neighborhood you might end up not liking. A common mistake many people make when relocating for a job is to buy a home or commit to a long-term lease immediately, and later find that they don't like the neighborhood, or the job.

Part II

Cities & States Ranked According to YOUR Wants & Needs

Unemployment rates for Metropolitan Areas (January 2016)

Rank	Metropolitan Area	Rate
1	Salt Lake City, UT Metropolitan Statistical Area	2.8
2	Austin-Round Rock, TX Metropolitan Statistical Area	3.1
2	Denver-Aurora-Lakewood, CO Metropolitan Statistical Area	3.1
2	Minneapolis-St. Paul-Bloomington, MN-WI Metropolitan Statistical Area	3.1
5	Oklahoma City, OK Metropolitan Statistical Area	3.3
6	San Antonio-New Braunfels, TX Metropolitan Statistical Area	3.5
7	Dallas-Fort Worth-Arlington, TX Metropolitan Statistical Area	3.7
8	Kansas City, MO-KS Metropolitan Statistical Area	3.8
8	San Jose-Sunnyvale-Santa Clara, CA Metropolitan Statistical Area	3.8
8	Washington-Arlington-Alexandria, DC-VA-MD-WV Metropolitan Statistical Area	3.8
11	Cleveland-Elyria, OH Metropolitan Statistical Area	3.9
11	Columbus, OH Metropolitan Statistical Area	3.9
11	San Francisco-Oakland-Hayward, CA Metropolitan Statistical Area	3.9
14	Boston-Cambridge-Nashua, MA-NH Metropolitan NECTA	4.1
14	Indianapolis-Carmel-Anderson, IN Metropolitan Statistical Area	4.1
14	Philadelphia-Camden-Wilmington, PA-NJ-DE-MD Metropolitan Statistical Area	4.1
14	Richmond, VA Metropolitan Statistical Area	4.1
18	Nashville-Davidson--Murfreesboro--Franklin, TN Metropolitan Statistical Area	4.2
19	Cincinnati, OH-KY-IN Metropolitan Statistical Area	4.3
19	Orlando-Kissimmee-Sanford, FL Metropolitan Statistical Area	4.3
19	Pittsburgh, PA Metropolitan Statistical Area	4.3
19	St. Louis, MO-IL Metropolitan Statistical Area[1]	4.3
23	New York-Newark-Jersey City, NY-NJ-PA Metropolitan Statistical Area	4.4
23	Raleigh, NC Metropolitan Statistical Area	4.4

NOTES:
1. Current National Unemployment Rate is 4.8 percent
2. Only those Areas with one million or more people are included.
3. Data comes from the Bureau of Labor Statistics.

State Unemployment Rates (Dec. 2015)

Rank	State	Rate
	http://www.bls.gov/web/laus/laumstrk.htm	
1	NORTH DAKOTA	2.7
2	NEBRASKA	2.9
2	SOUTH DAKOTA	2.9
4	NEW HAMPSHIRE	3.1
5	HAWAII	3.2
6	IOWA	3.4
7	COLORADO	3.5
7	MINNESOTA	3.5
7	UTAH	3.5
10	VERMONT	3.6
11	IDAHO	3.9
11	KANSAS	3.9
13	MAINE	4.0
13	MONTANA	4.0
15	OKLAHOMA	4.1
16	VIRGINIA	4.2
17	WISCONSIN	4.3
17	WYOMING	4.3
19	INDIANA	4.4
19	MISSOURI	4.4
21	MASSACHUSETTS	4.7
21	OHIO	4.7
21	TEXAS	4.7
24	ARKANSAS	4.8
24	NEW YORK	4.8
24	PENNSYLVANIA	4.8
27	DELAWARE	5.0
27	FLORIDA	5.0
29	MARYLAND	5.1
29	MICHIGAN	5.1
29	NEW JERSEY	5.1
29	RHODE ISLAND	5.1
33	CONNECTICUT	5.2
34	KENTUCKY	5.3
35	OREGON	5.4
36	GEORGIA	5.5
36	SOUTH CAROLINA	5.5
36	WASHINGTON	5.5

continued

Rank	State	Rate
39	NORTH CAROLINA	5.6
39	TENNESSEE	5.6
41	ARIZONA	5.8
41	CALIFORNIA	5.8
43	ILLINOIS	5.9
44	LOUISIANA	6.1
45	ALABAMA	6.2
46	WEST VIRGINIA	6.3
47	MISSISSIPPI	6.4
47	NEVADA	6.4
49	ALASKA	6.5
50	DISTRICT OF COLUMBIA	6.6
51	NEW MEXICO	6.7

U-6 Unemployment Rate Figures

The U-6 rate is a more accurate way of looking at true unemployment. Currently if one works part-time, even a few hours a week he/she is considered employed. Also the unemployment rate does not include discouraged people who have stopped looking for work. The U-6 rate includes: unemployed and collecting benefits, discouraged workers, and part-time workers who desire full-time employment. Source: Bureau of Labor Statistics:

North Dakota	5.3
South Dakota	6.3
Nebraska	6.7
Iowa	7
Utah	7.5
Colorado	7.9
New Hampshire	8
Oklahoma	8
Kansas	8.2
Minnesota	8.2
Vermont	8.2
Wyoming	8.2
Wisconsin	8.3
Texas	8.4
Idaho	8.6
Indiana	9
Montana	9
Maryland	9.3
Missouri	9.3
Arkansas	9.5
Delaware	9.6
Hawaii	9.7
Massachusetts	9.7
Maine	9.8
Virginia	9.8
Ohio	10.1
Kentucky	10.3
United States	10.4
New Jersey	10.4
New York	10.6
Pennsylvania	10.7
Tennessee	10.7
Connecticut	10.9
District of Columbia	10.9
Illinois	10.9
Washington	11
Georgia	11.1
Louisiana	11.1
Alabama	11.2
North Carolina	11.3

Best Cities to Retire in

Fortune Magazine 2015

1. Phoenix, Arizona, including Mesa and Scottsdale
2. Arlington/Alexandria, VA
3. Prescott, Ariz.
4. Tucson, Ariz.
5. Des Moines, Iowa
6. Denver, including Aurora
7. Austin Texas, including Round Rock
8. Cape Coral, Fla., including Fort Myers
9. Colorado Springs
10. Franklin, Tenn.

Money Magazine 2015 (not ranked in order)

1. St. George, Utah
2. Richland, Washington
3. Vail, Arizona
4. Fayetteville, Arkansas
5. Mt. Juliet, Tennessee
6. Boise, Idaho
7. Sante Fe, New Mexico
8. Greenville, South Carolina
9. Dover, Delaware
10. Chattanooga, Tennessee
11. Northfield, Minnesota
12. Athens, Georgia
13. Asheville, North Carolina
14. Lexington, Kentucky
15. Bellingham, Washington
16. Prattville, Alabama
17. Tyler, Texas
18. Fishers, Indiana
19. Stillwater, Oklahoma
20. Clermont, Florida
21. Bluffton, South Carolina
22. Sarasota, Florida
23. Loveland, Colorado
24. Cape Coral, Florida
25. Traverse City, Michigan

Summary: Combining these lists, Florida and Arizona are tied with four cities and metropolitan areas while Tennessee has three. From a tax standpoint, this should not be a surprise. 11 of the 35 communities in this list come from states (Texas, Florida, Tennessee, and Washington) that collect no individual personal income taxes.

WalletHub compared the retirement-friendliness of the 150 largest U.S. cities across 24 key metrics. Data set ranges from the cost of living to the percentage of the elderly population to the availability of recreational activities. The results are provided on the next several pages.

By Affordability, Activities, Quality of Life, and Health Care

Overall Rank	City	'Affordability' Rank	'Activities' Rank	'Quality of Life' Rank	'Health Care' Rank
1	Tampa, FL	11	4	21	26
2	Scottsdale, AZ	50	5	2	33
3	Boise, ID	21	27	7	39
4	Cape Coral, FL	83	3	3	17
5	Orlando, FL	34	2	104	15
6	Sioux Falls, SD	69	8	47	3
7	Baton Rouge, LA	28	10	119	21
8	Port St. Lucie, FL	45	25	11	57
9	Overland Park, KS	103	62	9	1
10	Peoria, AZ	50	53	6	71
11	St. Petersburg, FL	11	71	56	74
12	Lincoln, NE	88	39	26	24
13	Springfield, MO	27	30	101	28
14	Amarillo, TX	10	91	44	100
15	Pembroke Pines, FL	62	52	10	72
16	Shreveport, LA	6	110	53	85
17	Salt Lake City, UT	49	1	129	16
18	Birmingham, AL	4	18	126	104
19	Augusta, GA	13	88	31	107
20	Colorado Springs, CO	91	26	39	29
21	Mesa, AZ	50	68	16	64
22	Tulsa, OK	23	69	54	75
23	Winston-Salem, NC	24	44	48	108
24	Omaha, NE	86	36	84	5
25	Nashville, TN	2	42	134	116
26	Lubbock, TX	17	109	72	34
27	Jackson, MS	15	22	105	78
28	Oklahoma City, OK	20	77	67	58
29	Tucson, AZ	76	35	45	47
30	Reno, NV	38	46	25	117
31	Raleigh, NC	33	50	102	36
32	Greensboro, NC	22	95	49	53
33	Tempe, AZ	50	41	64	37
34	Cincinnati, OH	38	7	118	92
T-35	Henderson, NV	73	56	1	144
T-35	Fort Wayne, IN	26	54	83	89
37	Knoxville, TN	3	32	130	141
38	Sacramento, CA	107	20	34	55
39	Denver, CO	115	13	107	4
40	Fort Lauderdale, FL	62	16	85	56

continued

Overall Rank	City	'Affordability' Rank	'Activities' Rank	'Quality of Life' Rank	'Health Care' Rank
41	Chattanooga, TN	8	19	122	133
42	Albuquerque, NM	48	49	58	87
T-43	El Paso, TX	19	106	27	129
T-43	Montgomery, AL	9	102	68	125
45	Gilbert, AZ	50	121	20	45
46	Mobile, AL	7	118	57	131
47	Miami, FL	62	11	123	61
48	Lexington, KY	29	74	52	114
49	Chandler, AZ	50	97	17	80
50	Jacksonville, FL	37	58	97	83
51	Toledo, OH	34	93	65	63
52	Chesapeake, VA	77	72	33	78
53	Irvine, CA	120	65	15	23
T-54	New Orleans, LA	38	43	98	103
T-54	Grand Rapids, MI	43	9	120	76
56	Glendale, CA	108	146	4	18
57	Richmond, VA	89	37	96	19
58	Norfolk, VA	77	40	88	50
59	San Diego, CA	123	33	42	32
60	Durham, NC	34	66	125	73
61	Las Vegas, NV	73	47	35	125
62	Laredo, TX	5	137	79	136
63	Phoenix, AZ	50	87	55	69
64	Newport News, VA	77	106	37	66
65	Wichita, KS	42	78	124	31
66	Glendale, AZ	50	82	78	59
67	Huntsville, AL	14	118	46	139
68	Madison, WI	141	14	63	7
69	Columbus, GA	16	112	91	118
70	Grand Prairie, TX	66	99	29	101
71	Huntington Beach, CA	108	135	8	26
72	Virginia Beach, VA	77	76	66	68
73	St. Louis, MO	61	34	149	13
74	Santa Rosa, CA	128	24	5	94
75	Long Beach, CA	108	81	40	30
76	Honolulu, HI	145	28	13	8
77	Louisville, KY	30	67	110	114
78	Pittsburgh, PA	92	23	99	88
79	Plano, TX	85	125	28	49
80	Kansas City, MO	95	59	111	35
81	Atlanta, GA	71	17	138	97
82	Memphis, TN	1	96	146	140

Part II - Cities & States Ranked According to YOUR Wants & Needs

Overall Rank	City	'Affordability' Rank	'Activities' Rank	'Quality of Life' Rank	'Health Care' Rank
83	Austin, TX	84	60	115	53
84	San Jose, CA	133	90	23	9
85	Tallahassee, FL	46	61	106	106
86	Hialeah, FL	62	103	30	119
87	Minneapolis, MN	134	15	127	2
88	Corpus Christi, TX	25	91	80	137
89	Charlotte, NC	31	111	109	84
90	Oceanside, CA	123	75	19	50
91	Garden Grove, CA	108	149	12	43
92	Columbus, OH	46	129	92	44
93	Vancouver, WA	129	55	32	42
94	Akron, OH	96	64	73	80
95	Los Angeles, CA	108	120	22	38
96	Des Moines, IA	94	84	112	20
97	Dallas, TX	44	104	121	60
98	San Francisco, CA	137	48	90	10
99	Fayetteville, NC	18	146	113	113
100	St. Paul, MN	135	45	114	6
101	Brownsville, TX	31	115	82	134
102	Irving, TX	66	114	93	66
103	Santa Clarita, CA	108	132	18	52
104	Garland, TX	66	128	51	96
105	Aurora, CO	115	98	89	11
106	Little Rock, AR	50	57	128	109
107	Oakland, CA	131	51	117	14
108	Riverside, CA	97	100	50	98
109	Fort Worth, TX	81	126	75	85
110	Portland, OR	130	21	95	102
111	Anaheim, CA	120	134	24	40
112	Arlington, TX	81	142	71	64
113	Indianapolis, IN	60	94	148	48
114	Spokane, WA	117	73	81	90
115	Santa Ana, CA	120	127	41	61
116	Seattle, WA	145	29	100	40
117	Fremont, CA	136	141	14	25
118	Stockton, CA	90	113	76	122
119	Milwaukee, WI	140	38	143	12
120	Fresno, CA	72	144	77	91
121	Moreno Valley, CA	97	79	70	124
122	San Antonio, TX	38	123	133	112
T-123	Bakersfield, CA	86	122	59	130
T-123	Oxnard, CA	106	116	38	127

continued

Overall Rank	City	'Affordability' Rank	'Activities' Rank	'Quality of Life' Rank	'Health Care' Rank
125	Anchorage, AK	119	89	132	22
126	Modesto, CA	93	143	62	110
127	Tacoma, WA	132	12	136	46
128	Rancho Cucamonga, CA	97	150	36	111
129	Houston, TX	59	123	147	80
130	Chula Vista, CA	123	139	43	76
131	Ontario, CA	97	133	74	121
132	North Las Vegas, NV	73	136	60	142
133	Cleveland, OH	104	63	145	94
134	Baltimore, MD	108	82	139	70
135	Rochester, NY	127	6	144	93
136	Fontana, CA	97	148	69	135
137	Buffalo, NY	105	70	141	127
138	Washington, DC	126	30	142	123
139	San Bernardino, CA	97	145	94	119
140	Philadelphia, PA	139	101	103	105
141	Detroit, MI	69	105	137	148
142	Worcester, MA	118	108	116	132
143	Boston, MA	149	86	131	99
144	Chicago, IL	143	80	140	143
145	Yonkers, NY	147	138	85	138
146	New York, NY	148	130	60	147
147	Aurora, IL	143	131	87	145
148	Providence, RI	150	85	135	146
149	Jersey City, NJ	141	140	108	149
150	Newark, NJ	138	117	150	150

Part II - Cities & States Ranked According to YOUR Wants & Needs

Most Favorable vs. Least Favorable

LOWEST/HIGHEST ADJUSTED INCOME CITIES			
Lowest Adjusted Cost of Living		**Highest Adjusted Cost of Living**	
1	Laredo, TX	146	San Jose, CA
2	Memphis, TN	147	Fremont, CA
3	Jackson, MS	148	New York, NY
4	Amarillo, TX	149	San Francisco, CA
5	Toledo, OH	150	Honolulu, HI

Best City vs. Worst City (2x Difference)

LOWEST/HIGHEST COST OF IN-HOME SERVICES			
Lowest Annual Cost of In-Home Services		**Highest Annual Cost of In-Home Services**	
1	Brownsville, TX	T-146	Seattle, WA
2	Shreveport, LA	T-146	Tacoma, WA
T-3	Montgomery, AL	T-146	San Francisco, CA
T-3	Fayetteville, NC	T-148	Oakland, CA
5	El Paso, TX	T-148	Fremont, CA

Best City vs. Worst City (2x Difference)

HIGHEST/LOWEST % OF EMPLOYED PEOPLE AGED 65 & OLDER			
Highest % Employed People Aged 65 & Older		**Lowest % Employed People Aged 65 & Older**	
1	Anchorage, AK	146	Brownsville, TX
2	Plano, TX	147	Cleveland, OH
3	Grand Prairie, TX	148	Hialeah, FL
4	Washington, DC	149	Detroit, MI
5	Lincoln, NE	150	Fontana, CA

Best City vs. Worst City (3x Difference)

MOST/FEWEST RECREATION & SENIOR CENTERS PER CAPITA			
Most Recreation & Senior Centers per Capita		**Fewest Recreation & Senior Centers per Capita**	
1	Baton Rouge, LA	92	Toledo, OH
2	Minneapolis, MN	93	New York, NY
3	Washington, DC	94	Boise, ID
4	Philadelphia, PA	94	Madison, WI
5	Norfolk, VA	96	Boston, MA

Most Opportunities vs. Fewest Opportunities

MOST/FEWEST FISHING FACILITIES PER CAPITA			
Most Fishing Facilities per Capita		**Fewest Fishing Facilities per Capita**	
1	Fort Lauderdale, FL	111	Memphis, TN
2	Tampa, FL	112	Phoenix, AZ
3	Miami, FL	113	Philadelphia, PA
4	Honolulu, HI	114	Fort Worth, TX
5	Cape Coral, FL	115	Columbus, OH

Most Opportunities vs. Fewest Opportunities

continued

Most Favorable vs. Least Favorable

HIGHEST/LOWEST % OF THE POPULATION AGED 65 & OLDER

#	Highest % of the Population Aged 65 & Older		#	Lowest % of the Population Aged 65 & Older
1	Scottsdale, AZ	Best City vs. Worst City (3x Difference)	T-146	Santa Ana, CA
2	Hialeah, FL		T-146	Aurora, IL
3	Cape Coral, FL		148	Gilbert, AZ
4	Honolulu, HI		149	Grand Prairie, TX
5	Henderson, NV		150	Fontana, CA

Best/Worst Mild Weather Ranking

#	Best Mild Weather-Ranking		#	Worst Mild Weather-Ranking
1	Glendale, CA	Best City vs. Worst City	146	Boston, MA
2	Riverside, CA		147	Indianapolis, IN
3	Bakersfield, CA		148	Providence, RI
4	Scottsdale, AZ		149	Rochester, NY
5	Henderson, NV		150	Buffalo, NY

Best and Worst States for Business

2015 rankings from *Public CEO* magazine. Public CEO annually polls CEO's from across the nation to determine what is important to a good business climate. They say that states that foster growth through progressive business development programs, low taxes and a quality living environment get top marks.

Top Five Cities: Texas, Florida, North Carolina, Tennessee, Georgia.

Bottom Five Cities: Massachusetts, New Jersey, Illinois, New York, California.

Summary: In terms of highest State-local tax burden as a percentage of income, three of the bottom cities (New York, New Jersey, California) make the list according to the most recent data offered up by the non-partisan Tax Foundation. Of Public CEO's top five cities, three (Tennessee, Texas, Florida) have no personal income tax.

2016 Tax Foundation Report on State Business Tax Climate.

The Tax Foundation report ranks states on corporate, individual income, sales, unemployment tax, and property tax rates. Not surprisingly, states at the top of this list have low or nonexistent tax rates. Wyoming, Nevada, South Dakota, and Texas have no corporate or individual income tax (though Nevada and Texas both impose gross receipts taxes); Alaska has no individual income or state-level sales tax; Florida has no individual income tax; and New Hampshire and Montana have no sales tax.

Part II - Cities & States Ranked According to YOUR Wants & Needs

	10 Best All-Around Tax States		10 Lowest Ranked, or Worst, All-Around Tax States
1	Wyoming	41	Maryland
2	South Dakota	42	Ohio
3	Alaska	43	Wisconsin
4	Florida	44	Connecticut
5	Nevada	45	Rhode Island
6	Montana	46	Vermont
7	New Hampshire	47	Minnesota
8	Indiana	48	California
9	Utah	49	New York
10	Texas	50	New Jersey

2016 State Business Tax Climate Index Ranks and Component Tax Ranks						
	Overall Rank	Corporate Tax Rank	Individual Income Tax Rank	Sales Rax Rank	Unemployment Insurance Tax Rank	Property Tax Rank
Alabama	29	25	22	41	26	17
Alaska	3	30	1	5	21	21
Arizona	24	22	19	49	9	6
Arkansas	38	42	29	43	43	27
California	48	35	50	40	13	13
Colorado	18	15	16	44	33	12
Connecticut	44	33	36	29	20	49
Delaware	14	50	33	1	4	15
Florida	4	17	1	17	3	20
Georgia	39	9	42	35	37	31
Hawaii	31	10	37	14	24	14
Idaho	19	24	23	20	45	4
Illinois	23	36	10	33	39	45
Indiana	8	20	11	11	14	5
Iowa	40	49	32	24	34	40
Kansas	22	40	18	32	10	19
Kentucky	28	29	30	9	46	23
Louisiana	37	38	27	50	5	28
Maine	34	45	26	10	41	41
Maryland	41	19	45	8	28	42
Massachusetts	25	39	13	18	47	46
Michigan	13	11	15	7	48	26
Minnesota	47	46	46	36	29	30
Mississippi	20	13	21	28	8	35

continued

	Overall Rank	Corporate Tax Rank	Individual Income Tax Rank	Sales Rax Rank	Unemployment Insurance Tax Rank	Property Tax Rank
Missouri	17	3	28	23	12	8
Montana	6	23	20	3	18	9
Nebraska	27	31	24	26	2	39
Nevada	5	4	1	39	42	7
New Hampshire	7	48	9	2	44	43
New Jersey	50	43	48	47	31	50
New Mexico	35	27	34	48	7	1
New York	49	12	49	42	32	47
North Carolina	15	7	14	31	11	32
North Dakota	26	14	35	22	16	3
Ohio	42	26	47	30	6	11
Oklahoma	33	8	40	38	1	18
Oregon	11	37	31	4	27	10
Pennsylvania	32	47	17	25	50	38
Rhode Island	45	34	38	27	49	44
South Carolina	36	16	41	19	35	25
South Dakota	2	1	1	34	40	22
Tennessee	16	18	8	46	25	37
Texas	10	41	6	37	15	34
Utah	9	5	12	16	19	2
Vermont	46	44	44	15	17	48
Virginia	30	6	39	6	38	29
Washington	12	28	6	45	23	24
West Virginia	21	21	25	21	22	16
Wisconsin	43	32	43	13	36	33
Wyoming	1	1	1	12	30	36
District of Columbia	42	36	34	40	27	39

Note: A rank of 1 is best, 50 is worst. Rankings do not average to the total. States without a tax rank equally as 1. DC's score and rank do not affect other states. The report shows tax systems as of July 1, 2015 (the beginning of Fiscal Year 2016).
Source: Tax Foundation.

State Business Tax Climate Index

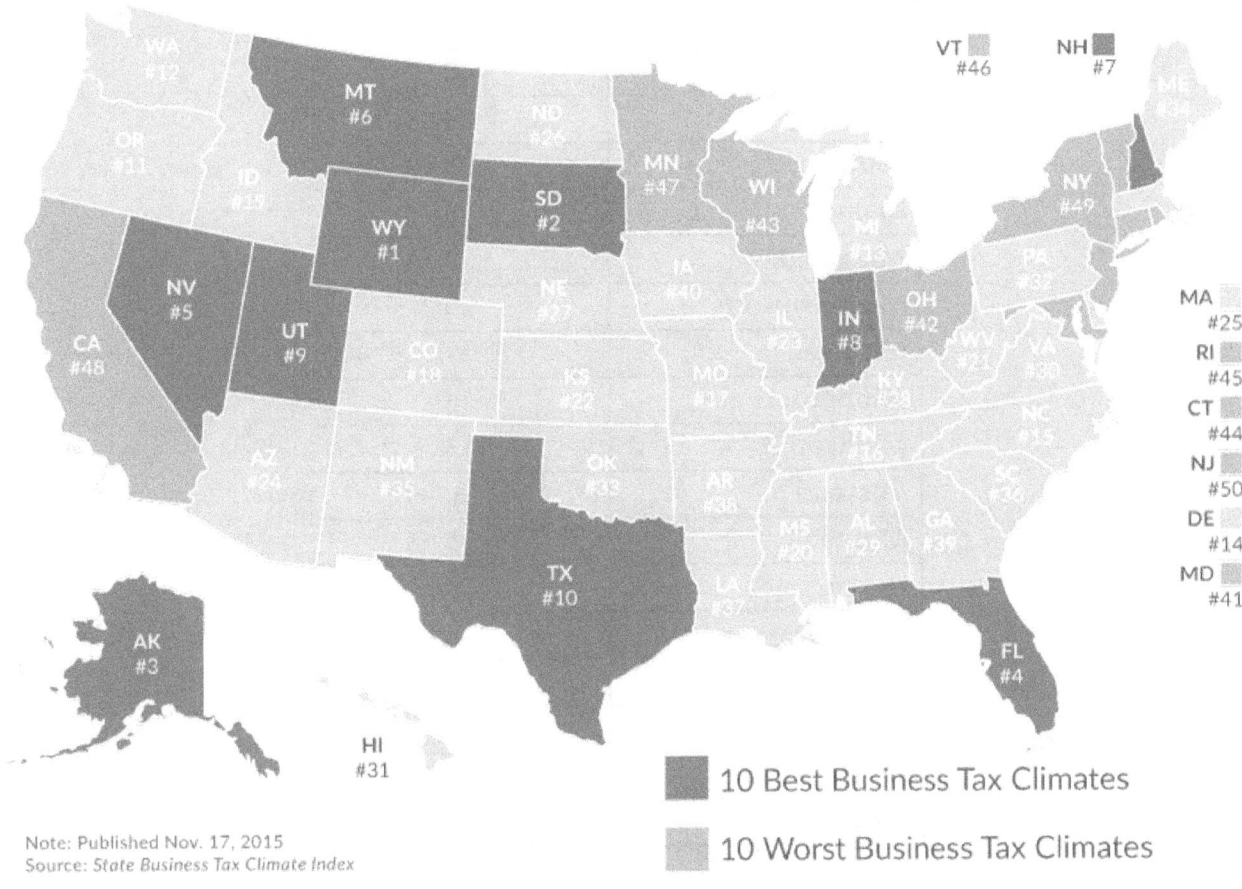

Corporate Tax Component of the State Business Tax Index

	Corporate Tax Rank
Alabama	25
Alaska	30
Arizona	22
Arkansas	42
California	35
Colorado	15
Connecticut	33
Delaware	50
Florida	17
Georgia	9
Hawaii	10

continued

	Corporate Tax Rank
Idaho	24
Illinois	36
Indiana	20
Iowa	49
Kansas	40
Kentucky	29
Louisiana	38
Maine	45
Maryland	19
Massachusetts	39
Michigan	11
Minnesota	46
Mississippi	13
Missouri	3
Montana	23
Nebraska	31
Nevada	4
New Hampshire	48
New Jersey	43
New Mexico	27
New York	12
North Carolina	7
North Dakota	14
Ohio	26
Oklahoma	8
Oregon	37
Pennsylvania	47
Rhode Island	34
South Carolina	16
South Dakota	1
Tennessee	18
Texas	41
Utah	5
Vermont	44
Virginia	6
Washington	28
West Virginia	21
Wisconsin	32

Wyoming	1
District of Columbia	36
Note: A rank of 1 is best, 50 is worst. Rankings do not average to the total. States without a tax rank equally as 1. DC's score and rank do not affect other states. The report shows tax systems as of July 1, 2015 (the beginning of Fiscal Year 2016). Source: Tax Foundation.	

Individual Income Tax Component of the State Business Tax Index

	Individual Income Tax Rank
Alabama	22
Alaska	1
Arizona	19
Arkansas	29
California	50
Colorado	16
Connecticut	36
Delaware	33
Florida	1
Georgia	42
Hawaii	37
Idaho	23
Illinois	10
Indiana	11
Iowa	32
Kansas	18
Kentucky	30
Louisiana	27
Maine	26
Maryland	45
Massachusetts	13
Michigan	15
Minnesota	46
Mississippi	21
Missouri	28
Montana	20
Nebraska	24
Nevada	1
New Hampshire	9
New Jersey	48
New Mexico	34
New York	49
North Carolina	14
North Dakota	35
Ohio	47
Oklahoma	40

	Individual Income Tax Rank
Oregon	31
Pennsylvania	17
Rhode Island	38
South Carolina	41
South Dakota	1
Tennessee	8
Texas	6
Utah	12
Vermont	44
Virginia	39
Washington	6
West Virginia	25
Wisconsin	43
Wyoming	1
District of Columbia	34

Note: A rank of 1 is best, 50 is worst. Rankings do not average to the total. States without a tax rank equally as 1. DC's score and rank do not affect other states. The report shows tax systems as of July 1, 2015 (the beginning of Fiscal Year 2016).
Source: Tax Foundation.

Sales Tax Component of the State Business Tax Index

	2016 Sales Rax Rank
Alabama	41
Alaska	5
Arizona	49
Arkansas	43
California	40
Colorado	44
Connecticut	29
Delaware	1
Florida	17
Georgia	35
Hawaii	14
Idaho	20
Illinois	33
Indiana	11
Iowa	24
Kansas	32
Kentucky	9
Louisiana	50
Maine	10
Maryland	8
Massachusetts	18
Michigan	7
Minnesota	36
Mississippi	28
Missouri	23
Montana	3
Nebraska	26
Nevada	39
New Hampshire	2
New Jersey	47
New Mexico	48
New York	42
North Carolina	31
North Dakota	22
Ohio	30
Oklahoma	38

	2016 Sales Rax Rank
Oregon	4
Pennsylvania	25
Rhode Island	27
South Carolina	19
South Dakota	34
Tennessee	46
Texas	37
Utah	16
Vermont	15
Virginia	6
Washington	45
West Virginia	21
Wisconsin	13
Wyoming	12
District of Columbia	40

Note: A rank of 1 is best, 50 is worst. Rankings do not average to the total. States without a tax rank equally as 1. DC's score and rank do not affect other states. The report shows tax systems as of July 1, 2015 (the beginning of Fiscal Year 2016).
Source: Tax Foundation.

Property Tax Component of the State Business Tax Index

	Property Tax Rank
Alabama	17
Alaska	21
Arizona	6
Arkansas	27
California	13
Colorado	12
Connecticut	49
Delaware	15
Florida	20
Georgia	31
Hawaii	14
Idaho	4
Illinois	45
Indiana	5
Iowa	40
Kansas	19
Kentucky	23
Louisiana	28
Maine	41
Maryland	42
Massachusetts	46
Michigan	26
Minnesota	30
Mississippi	35
Missouri	8
Montana	9
Nebraska	39
Nevada	7
New Hampshire	43
New Jersey	50
New Mexico	1
New York	47
North Carolina	32
North Dakota	3
Ohio	11
Oklahoma	18

	Property Tax Rank
Oregon	10
Pennsylvania	38
Rhode Island	44
South Carolina	25
South Dakota	22
Tennessee	37
Texas	34
Utah	2
Vermont	48
Virginia	29
Washington	24
West Virginia	16
Wisconsin	33
Wyoming	36
District of Columbia	39
Note: A rank of 1 is best, 50 is worst. Rankings do not average to the total. States without a tax rank equally as 1. DC's score and rank do not affect other states. The report shows tax systems as of July 1, 2015 (the beginning of Fiscal Year 2016). Source: Tax Foundation.	

Least Tax-Friendly States in the U.S. (2016)

Do you enjoying paying lots of taxes? Do you like giving a large percentage of your money to the government? If the answer to these questions is 'yes', then consider relocating to these states. The following states have the highest taxes in the US. California tops the list of all 50 states with the highest taxes. Coincidently, they are all Democratic Party states.

1. California

2. Connecticut

3. New Jersey

4. Hawaii

5. New York

6. Rhode Island

7. Vermont

8. Maine

9. Minnesota

10. Illinois

Best States to Make a Living

This annual study used five different criteria from federal government sources to put together the 2015 version of this list. Scores were then averaged and indexed to calculate the final figures. Criteria included:

- Average wages from the U.S. Bureau of Labor Statistics.
- State Tax Rates from the Tax Foundation
- Cost of Living, sourced from the Council for Community and Economic Research
- The unemployment rate from the U.S. Bureau of Labor Statistics
- Incidents of workplace illness, injuries and fatalities from the U.S. Bureau of Labor Statistics.

Of interest is the fact that the top three best states to make a living also have no state personal income tax.

1. Texas
2. Washington
3. Wyoming
4. Virginia
5. Illinois
6. Michigan
7. Colorado
8. Delaware
9. Ohio
10. Utah
11. Georgia
12. Minnesota
13. Tennessee
14. Arizona
15. Indiana
16. North Dakota
17. Kansas
18. Missouri
19. Oklahoma
20. Massachusetts
21. Nebraska
22. Alabama
23. Idaho
24. North Carolina
25. Maryland
26. Pennsylvania
27. Iowa
28. Kentucky
29. New Jersey
30. Wisconsin
31. Mississippi
32. Louisiana
33. Florida
34. New Hampshire
35. New Mexico
36. Arkansas
37. Nevada
38. Alaska
39. South Carolina
40. New York
41. Connecticut
42. Rhode Island
43. South Dakota
44. Montana
45. California
46. Vermont
47. West Virginia
48. Maine
49. Oregon
50. Hawaii

Part II - Cities & States Ranked According to YOUR Wants & Needs

Vaccine Laws (State Comparisons)

There are three types of exemptions to current vaccination laws: medical, philosophical, and religious. Only California, has expressly forbid people from applying for an exemption based on philosophical and religious grounds. While not outlawing it, Mississippi also does not allow for religious or philosophical vaccine exemptions. All states, including California and Mississippi, have a medical exemption. Only Oregon, Washington, Idaho, Utah, Arizona, Colorado, Texas, Oklahoma, North Dakota, Minnesota, Arkansas, Louisiana, Wisconsin, Minnesota, Ohio and Maine allow for philosophical objections to vaccines.

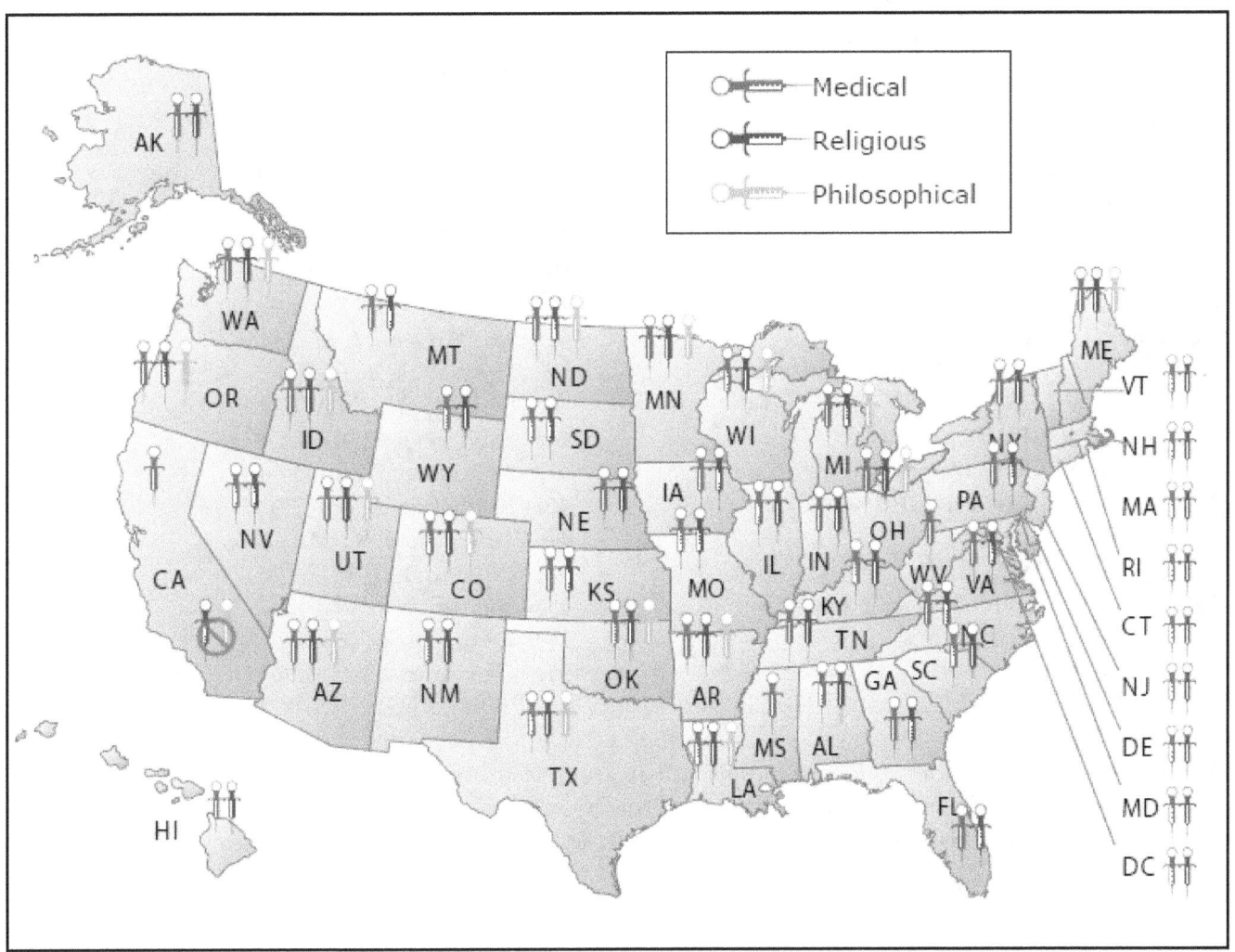

Fastest & Slowest Growing Major Metropolitan Areas in the USA

Data is from 2000-2012 and includes regions with one million people or more.

1. Raleigh, NC: 47.8%
2. Austin, TX: 44.9%
3. Las Vegas, NV: 43.6%
4. Orlando, FL: 34.2%
5. Charlotte, NC-SC: 32.8%
6. Riverside/San Bernardino, CA: 32.7%
7. Phoenix, AZ: 32.1%
8. Houston, TX: 31%
9. San Antonio, TX: 29.9
10. Dallas-Fort Worth: 27.9%
11. Atlanta, GA: 27%
12. Nashville, TN: 24.5%
13. Jacksonville, FL: 22.3%
14. Sacramento, CA: 21.5%
15. Denver, CO: 20.6%
16. Washington DC-VA-MD-WV: 20.5%
17. Salt Lake City: 19.2%
18. Portland, OR-WA: 18.3%
19. Tampa-St. Petersburg, FL: 18.2%
20. Oklahoma City, OK: 18.1%
21. Seattle, WA: 16.4%
22. Richmond, VA: 16.4%
23. Indianapolis, IN: 15.9%
24. Columbus, OH: 15.6%
25. Miami, FL: 14.7%
26. San Diego, CA: 12.5%
27. Minneapolis- St. Paul, MN-WI: 12.4%
28. Kansas City, MO-KS: 12.1%
29. Louisville, KY-IN: 11.3%
30. Memphis, TN-MS-AR: 10.3%
31. San Jose, CA: 8.9%
32. Birmingham, AL: 7.9%
33. San Francisco-Oakland, CA: 7.7%
34. Baltimore, MD: 7.6%
35. Grand Rapids, MI: 7.6%
36. Virginia Beach-Norfolk, VA-NC: 7.3
37. Cincinnati, OH-KY-IN: 6.4%
38. Philadelphia, PA-NJ-DE-MD: 5.7%
39. Hartford, CT: 5.5%
40. Boston, MA-NH: 5.4%
41. Los Angeles, CA: 5.3%
42. New York, NY-NJ-PA: 4.5%
43. Chicago, IL-IN-WI: 4.4%
44. Saint Louis, MO-IL: 4.4%
45. Milwaukee, WI: 4.3%
46. Rochester, NY: 1.5%
47. Providence, RI-MA: .9%
48. Pittsburgh, PA: -2.8%
49. Buffalo, NY: -3%
50. Detroit, MI: -3.7%
51. Cleveland, OH: -3.9%
52. New Orleans, LA -8.2%

Note: Seven of the bottom 25 lowest/no-growth areas come from states with the top five highest income tax. Conversely six of the top ten fastest growing regions, and 11 of the top 25 come from states with no income tax. Of the 25 fastest growing regions, only four come from states with the highest income tax.

The 15 Fastest Growing Cities in America

By Forbes, 2015

The census data focuses on cities with the largest population increase percentages between July 1, 2014 and July 1, 2015, but only cities with more than 50,000 people were included. According to the numbers, Texas is the most popular state for new residents, claiming four out of the ten spots on the list. The city of Georgetown, Texas, had the largest increase, followed by New Braunfels, which is about 75 miles away.

The cities in the top 15 are not large metropolitan cities like New York, Houston, or Atlanta. The US Census reports that those cities did have larger numerical increases during the same time frame, and they are still the most populous cities in America, but smaller cities (like Frisco, Texas; Milpitas, California; and Ankeny, Iowa) are attracting people more quickly. Check out the list below, as well as an interactive map we created as a visual guide to show where the action is.

1. Georgetown, TX
2. New Braunfels, TX
3. Ankeny, IA
4. Frisco, TX
5. South Jordan, UT
6. Dublin, CA
7. Pearland, TX
8. Milpitas, CA
9. Broomfield, CO
10. Mount Pleasant, SC
11. Pflugerville, TX
12. Fort Myers, FL
13. Murfreesboro, TN
14. Goodyear, AZ
15. Buckeye, AZ

Fastest Growing States in America

by percentage population growth 2010-2014

1. North Dakota: 9.9%
2. District of Columbia: 9.5%
3. Texas: 7.2%
4. Colorado: 6.5%
5. Utah: 6.5%
6. Florida: 5.8%
7. Arizona: 5.3%
8. Nevada: 5.1%
9. Washington: 5%
10. South Dakota: 4.8%
11. South Carolina, 4.5%
12. Hawaii: 4.4%
13. Idaho: 4.3%
14. North Carolina: 4.3%
15. California: 4.2%
16. Delaware: 4.2%
17. Georgia: 4.2%
18. Virginia: 4.1%
19. Alaska: 3.7%
20. Oregon: 3.6%
21. Wyoming: 3.6%
22. Maryland: 3.5%
23. Montana: 3.5%
24. Oklahoma: 3.4%
25. **United States (cumulative): 3.3%**
26. Tennessee: 3.2%
27. Massachusetts: 3%
28. Nebraska: 3%
29. Minnesota: 2.9%
30. Louisiana: 2.6%
31. Iowa: 2.0%
32. New York: 1.9%
33. Kansas: 1.8%
34. Arkansas: 1.7%
35. Indiana: 1.7%
36. Kentucky: 1.7%
37. New Jersey: 1.7%
38. Alabama: 1.5%
39. New Mexico: 1.3%
40. Missouri: 1.2%
41. Wisconsin: 1.2%
42. Mississippi: .9%
43. New Hampshire: .8%
44. Pennsylvania: .7%
45. Connecticut: .6%
46. Ohio: .5%
47. Illinois: .4%
48. Michigan: .3%
49. Rhode Island: .2%
50. Maine: .1%
51. Vermont: .1%
52. West Virginia: -.1%

Best Weather U.S. Cities

Business Insider Publication: Pleasant weather is defined as a mean average temperature between 55 and 75 degrees, nothing colder than 45 or warmer than 85. Essentially, any rain or snow in a day meant it was not "pleasant.

The top five most pleasant places using the last 23 years of weather data under the above parameters are:

- Los Angeles — 183 days/year
- San Diego— 182 days/year
- Oxnard — 166 days/year
- Simi Valley — 156 days/year
- San Francisco — 153 days/year

Commute Times in America

Average Travel time to work (in minutes) from the 30 largest U.S. Cities in 2013. The average U.S. Commute time is 25.8 minutes

1. Oklahoma City, OK: 20.7 minutes
2. Columbus, OH: 21.4 minutes
3. Louisville, KY: 21.4 minutes
4. Memphis, TN: 21.6 minutes
5. El Paso, TX: 22.1 minutes
6. Indianapolis, IN: 22.6 minutes
7. Nashville, TN: 23.3 minutes
8. San Diego, CA: 23.3 minutes
9. San Antonio, TX: 23.4 minutes
10. Austin, TX 23.5 minutes
11. Charlotte, NC: 24.1 minutes
12. Jacksonville, FL: 24.3 minutes
13. Phoenix, AZ: 24.7 minutes
14. Denver, CO: 24.8 minutes
15. Las Vegas, NV: 24.9 minutes
16. Portland, OR: 25.3 minutes
17. Dallas, TX: 25.8 minutes
18. **USA Average: 25.8**
19. Seattle, WA: 26.2 minutes
20. Houston, TX: 26.3 minutes
21. Fort Worth, TX: 26.5 minutes
22. Detroit, MI: 26.8 minutes
23. San Jose, CA: 27.3 minutes
24. Boston, MA: 29.5 minutes
25. Los Angeles, CA: 29.9 minutes
26. Washington, DC: 29.9 minutes
27. Baltimore, MD: 30.5 minutes
28. San Francisco, CA 31.5 minutes
29. Philadelphia, PA: 32 minutes
30. Chicago, IL: 33.7 minutes
31. New York, NY: 39.7 minutes

Most Friendly Bike Cities

Forbes Magazine: Cities on this list were given a score from 1-100 based on four equally weighted factors: miles of bike lanes, hills road connectivity, and percent of commuters traveling by bicycle.

1) Minneapolis
2) San Francisco
3) Portland
4) Denver
5) Boston
6) Chicago
7) Washington D.C.
8) Sacramento
9) Tucson, AZ
10) Philadelphia, PA
11) Long Beach
12) New York
13) Seattle
14) Oakland
15) Aurora, CO

However, just because a city/metro region is bike friendly, it still doesn't mean a lot of people bike to work. Only seven of the 51 largest metro areas post a one percent average for bicycling, Following is a list of the most commute biked cities

1. Portland-Vancouver-Hillsboro, OR-WA: 2.3%
2. San Francisco-Oakland-Fremont, CA: 1.9%
3. San Jose-Sunnyvale-Santa Clara, CA: 1.9%
4. Sacramento–Arden–Arcade–Roseville, CA: 1.8%
5. Austin-Round Rock-San Marcos, TX: 1.0%
6. New Orleans-Metairie-Kenner, LA: 1.0%
7. Phoenix-Mesa-Glendale, AZ: 1.0%
8. Seattle-Tacoma-Bellevue, WA: 0.9%
9. Denver-Aurora-Broomfield, CO: 0.9%
10. Los Angeles-Long Beach-Santa Ana, CA: 0.9%

Most Dangerous Cities in America (2016)

Cities listed here have populations over 25,000 and are ranked based on violent crime per 1,000 residents. Violent crime includes murder, rape, armed robbery and aggravated assault as reported to the FBI.

1. East Saint Louis, IL
2. Camden, NJ
3. Detroit, MI
4. Alexandria, LA
5. Wilmington, DE
6. Memphis, TN
7. Flint, MI
8. Saginaw, MI
9. Oakland, CA
10. Saint Louis, MO
11. Ardmore, OK
12. Birmingham, AL
13. Chester, PA
14. Newburgh, NY
15. Milwaukee, WI
16. West Memphis, AR
17. Myrtle Beach, SC
18. Little Rock, AR
19. Baltimore, MD
20. Stockton, CA
21. Atlantic City, NJ
22. East Point GA
23. Cleveland, OH
24. Homestead, FL
25. Harvey, IL
26. Atlanta, GA
27. Elkhart, IN
28. Daytona Beach, FL
29. Indianapolis, IN
30. Pine Bluff, AR
31. Rockford, IL
32. New Bedford, MA
33. Charleston, WV
34. Kansas City, MO
35. Washington DC
36. Buffalo, NY
37. Weslaco, TX
38. Niagara Falls, NY
39. Kalamazoo, MI
40. Riviera Beach, FL
41. Springfield, MO
42. San Bernardino, CA
43. Fall River, MA
44. Compton, CA
45. Nashville, TN
46. Chelsea, MA
47. Lake Worth, FL
48. Harrisburg, PA
49. Trenton, NJ
50. Lansing, MI
51. Newark, NJ
52. Lawrence, MA
53. Hartford, CT
54. Fort Myers, FL
55. Jackson, TN
56. Springfield, MA
57. Danville, IL
58. Fort Pierce, FL
59. Springfield, IL
60. New Haven, CT
61. Albany, GA
62. Brockton, MA
63. Miami, FL
64. Bridgeton, NJ
65. Philadelphia, PA
66. Canton, OH
67. Minneapolis, MN,
68. Houston, TX
69. Gadsden, AL
70. New Orleans, LA
71. Chattanooga, TN
72. Miami Beach, FL
73. Worcester, MA
74. Spartanburg, SC
75. Holyoke, MA
76. Jackson, MS
77. Anderson, SC
78. Rocky Mount, NC
79. Jackson, MI
80. Odessa, TX
81. Waterloo, IA
82. Tallahassee, FL
83. Poughkeepsie, NY
84. Battle Creek, MI
85. Salisbury, MD
86. North Miami, FL
87. Gary, IN
88. Baton Rouge, LA
89. Albuquerque, NM
90. Batch Springs, TX
91. Lawton, OK
92. Lima, OH
93. Goldsboro, NC
94. Reading, PA
95. Panama City, FL
96. Bridgeport, CT
97. Orlando, FL
98. Cincinnati, OH
99. Elizabeth, NJ
100. Beaumont, TX

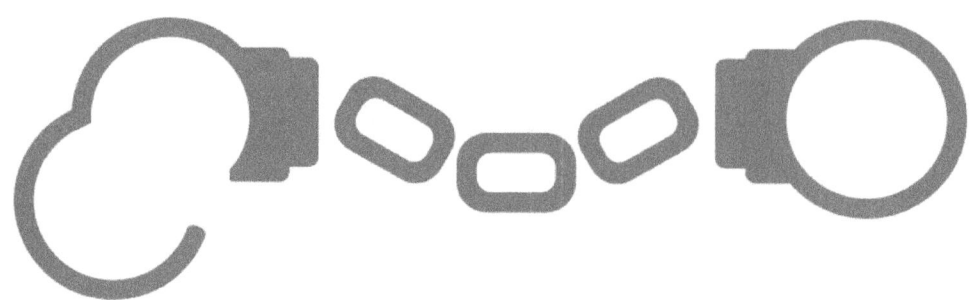

Home School in America: How States Compare

According to the Homeschool Legal Defense Association (HSLDA) while all states currently allow homeschooling, some are more restrictive than others.

- **States requiring no notice before engaging in homeschooling:** Alaska, Connecticut, Idaho, Illinois, Indiana, Michigan, Missouri, New Jersey, Oklahoma and Texas.
- **States with low regulation (parental notification only) include:** Alabama, Arizona, California, Delaware, Kansas, Kentucky, Mississippi, Montana, Nebraska, Nevada, New Mexico, Utah, Washington D.C., Wisconsin and Wyoming.
- **States with moderate regulation (parental notification, plus test scores and/or professional student progress evaluations) include:** Arkansas, Colorado, Florida, Georgia, Hawaii, Iowa, Louisiana, Maine, Maryland, Minnesota, New Hampshire, North Carolina, North Dakota, Ohio, Oregon, South Carolina, South Dakota, Tennessee, Virginia, Washington and West Virginia.
- **States with high regulation (all the above, plus other requirements — e.g. curriculum approval by the state, teacher qualification of parents or home visits by state officials) include:** Massachusetts, New York, Pennsylvania, Rhode Island and Vermont.

Home School State Regulations

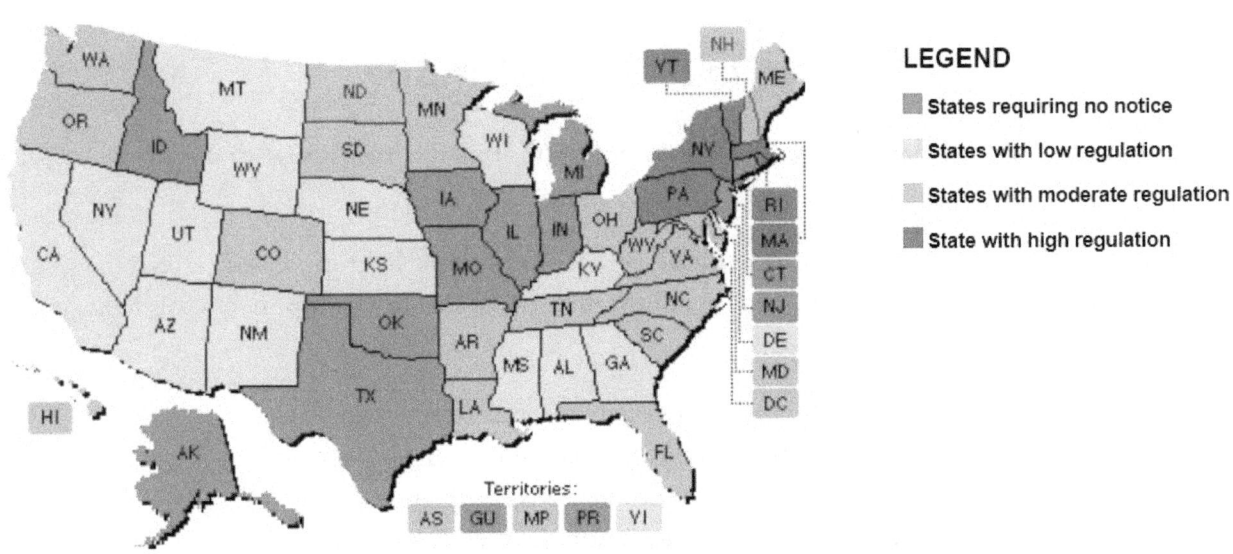

Best Locations to See the Night Sky

Less than 100 years ago, everyone could look up and see a spectacular starry night sky. Now, millions of children across the globe will never experience the Milky Way where they live. The increased and widespread use of artificial light at night is not only impairing our view of the universe, it is adversely affecting our environment, our safety, our energy consumption and our health.

What is Light Pollution?

Most of us are familiar with air, water, and land pollution, but did you know that light can also be a pollutant?

The inappropriate or excessive use of artificial light – known as light pollution – can have serious environmental consequences for humans, wildlife, and our climate. Components of light pollution include:

- **Glare** – excessive brightness that causes visual discomfort
- **Skyglow** – brightening of the night sky over inhabited areas
- **Light trespass** – light falling where it is not intended or needed
- **Clutter** – bright, confusing and excessive groupings of light sources

Light pollution is a side effect of industrial civilization. Its sources include building exterior and interior lighting, advertising, commercial properties, offices, factories, streetlights, and illuminated sporting venues.

The fact is that much outdoor lighting used at night is inefficient, overly bright, poorly targeted, improperly shielded, and, in many cases, completely unnecessary. This light, and the electricity used to create it, is being wasted by spilling it into the sky, rather than focusing it on to the actual objects and areas that people want illuminated.

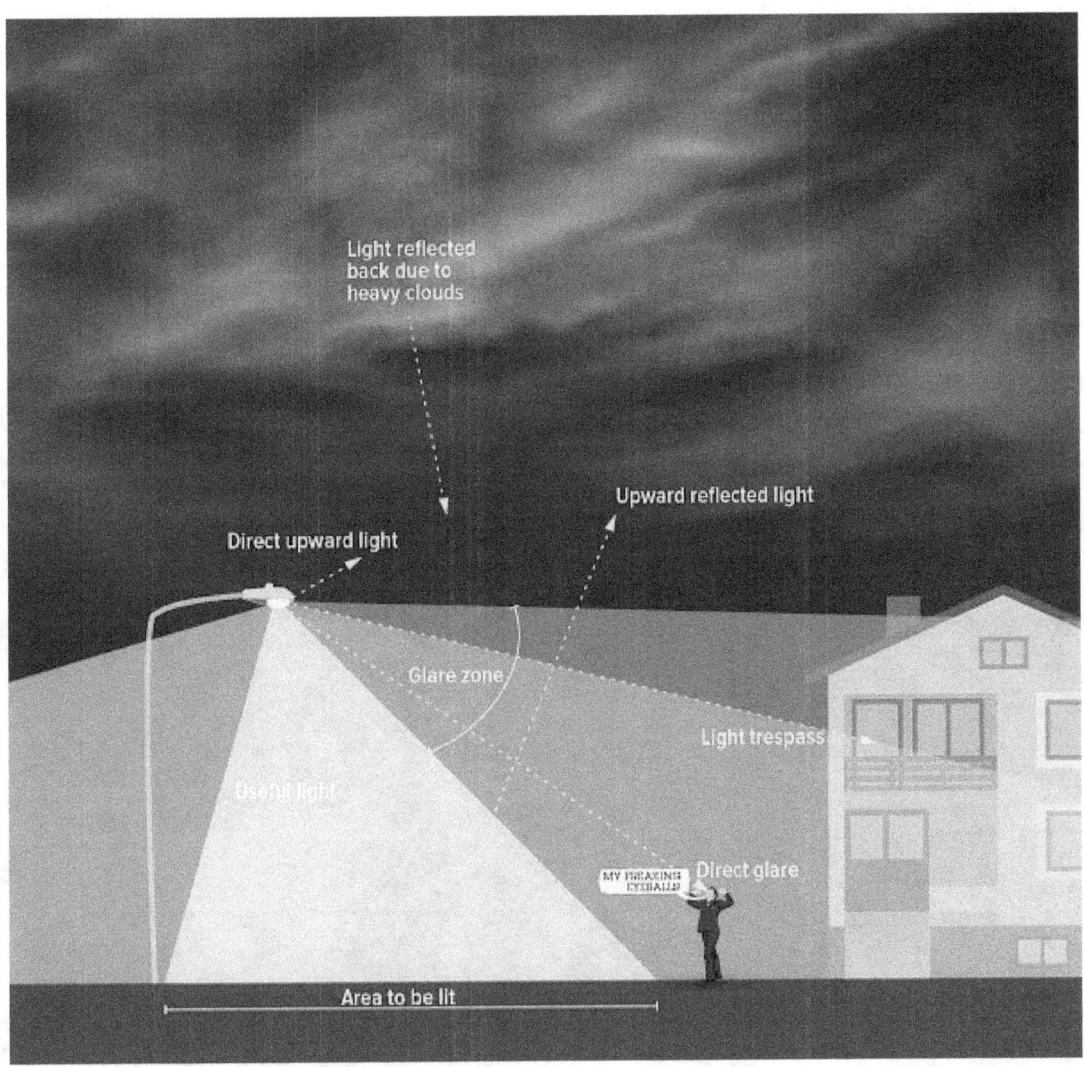

The Natural Night Sky Inspires

Until recently, for all of human history, our ancestors experienced a sky brimming with stars – a night sky that inspired science, religion, philosophy, art and literature, including some of Shakespeare's most famous sonnets.

The natural night sky is our common and universal heritage, yet is rapidly becoming unknown to the newest generations.

"For my part I know nothing with any certainty, but the sight of the stars makes me dream." — Vincent van Gogh

Van Gogh painted his famous "Starry Night" in Saint Rémy, France, in 1889. Now, the Milky Way can no longer be seen from there. If he were alive today, would he still be inspired to paint "Starry Night"?

Experiencing the night sky provides perspective, inspiration, and leads us to reflect on our humanity and place in the universe. The history of scientific discovery and even human curiosity itself is indebted to the natural night sky.

How Bad is Light Pollution?

With much of the Earth's population living under light-polluted skies, over lighting is an international concern. If you live in an urban or suburban area all you have to do to see this type of pollution is go outside at night and look up at the sky.

ABOVE: Before and during the 2003 Northeast blackout, a massive power outage that affected 55 million people.

If you want to find out how bad light pollution is where you live use the "NASA Blue Marble Navigator" online for a bird's eye view of the lights in your town or check out the Globe at Night interactive light pollution map data created with 8 years of data collected by citizen scientists: http://www.globeatnight.org/map/?2013

ABOVE: The Brooklyn Bridge, New York City – Shown without artificial lighting.

Lighting, Crime and Safety (The Myth is Busted)

There is no clear scientific evidence that increased outdoor lighting deters crimes. It may make us feel safer, but has not been shown to make us safer.

A 2015 study published in the Journal of Epidemiology and Community Health found that streetlights don't prevent accidents or crime, but do cost a lot of money. The researchers looked at data on road traffic collisions and crime in 62 local authorities in England and Wales and found that lighting had no effect, whether authorities had turned them off completely, dimmed them, turned them off at certain hours, or substituted low-power LED lamps.

According to the study, "When risks are carefully considered, local authorities can safely reduce street lighting saving both costs and energy ... without necessarily impacting negatively upon road traffic collisions and crime."

According to a 2011 study of London street lighting and crime, there is no good evidence that increased lighting reduces total crime." A 1997 National Institute of Justice study concluded, "We can have very little confidence that improved lighting prevents crime."

The truth is bad outdoor lighting can decrease safety by making victims and property easier to see. A Chicago Alley Lighting Project showed a correlation between brightly lit alleyways and increased crime.

Brighter Does Not Mean Safer:

According to a 2012 report of the American Medical Association, "Glare from nighttime lighting can create hazards ranging from discomfort to frank visual disability."

Outdoor lighting is intended to enhance safety and security at night, but too much lighting can actually have the opposite effect. Visibility should always be the goal. Glare from bright, unshielded lights actually decreases safety because it shines into our eyes and constricts our pupils. This cannot only be blinding, it also makes it more difficult for our eyes to adjust to low-light conditions.

Glare from bright, unshielded lights actually decreases safety. In fact, most property crime occurs in the light of the day. And some crimes like vandalism and graffiti actually thrive on night lighting.

What are the best places in the US for stargazing?

The short version: Arizona, New Mexico, and the Big Island of Hawaii.

The long version: an ideal stargazing site depends on clear and dark skies. Clear skies are a function of cloud cover, atmospheric transparency and seeing (for example, aerosols and other air pollution, humidity, turbulence, altitude, etc.). Dark skies are a function of light pollution: in general, the further away you are from a populated area, the better off you are, because even small towns can cast a light dome that drowns out fainter objects. But it's better to deal with a small town's light dome than a big city's light dome.

Dry, high-altitude locations far away from major cities are considered the best locations. It's why there are observatories on Mauna Kea and in northern Chile (the Atacama Desert is the driest place in the world), and why, in the continental U.S., the southwest is so attractive to amateur astronomers. Many regions in the eastern U.S. are most challenged with stargazing opportunities.

Population Statistics (2010 Census)

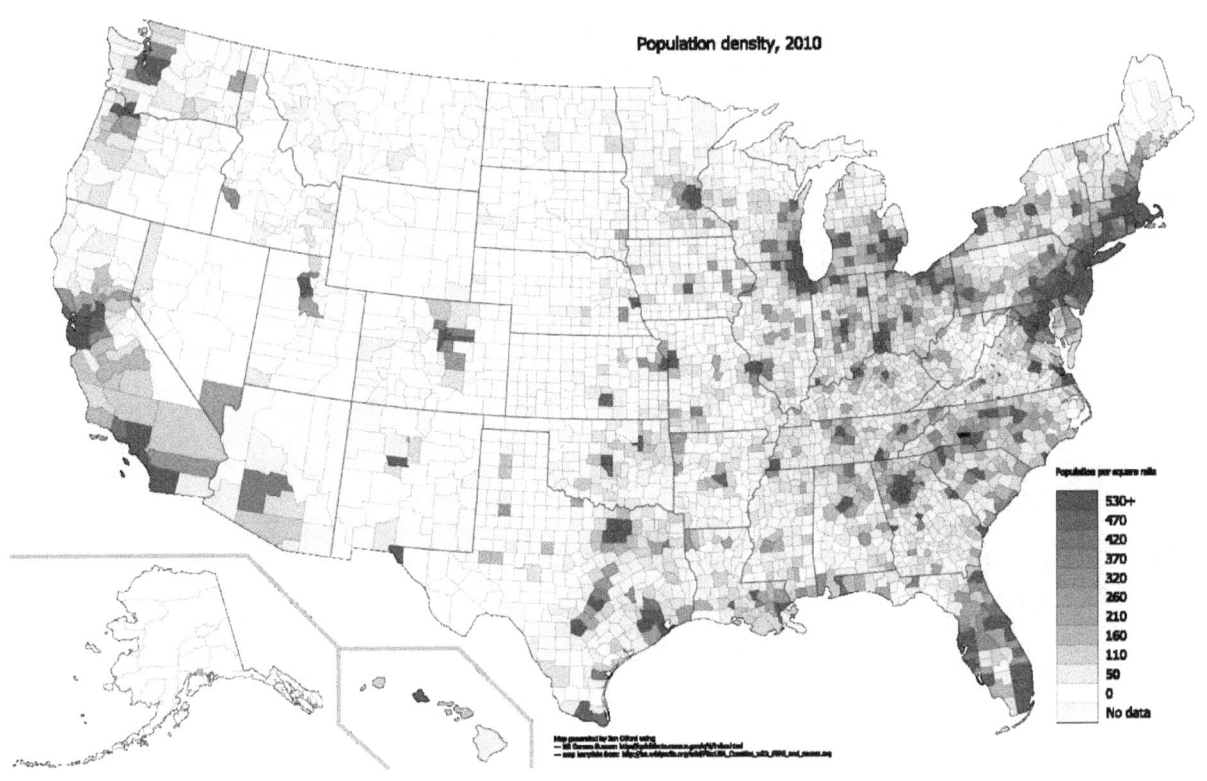

Population Change (2000 to 2010)

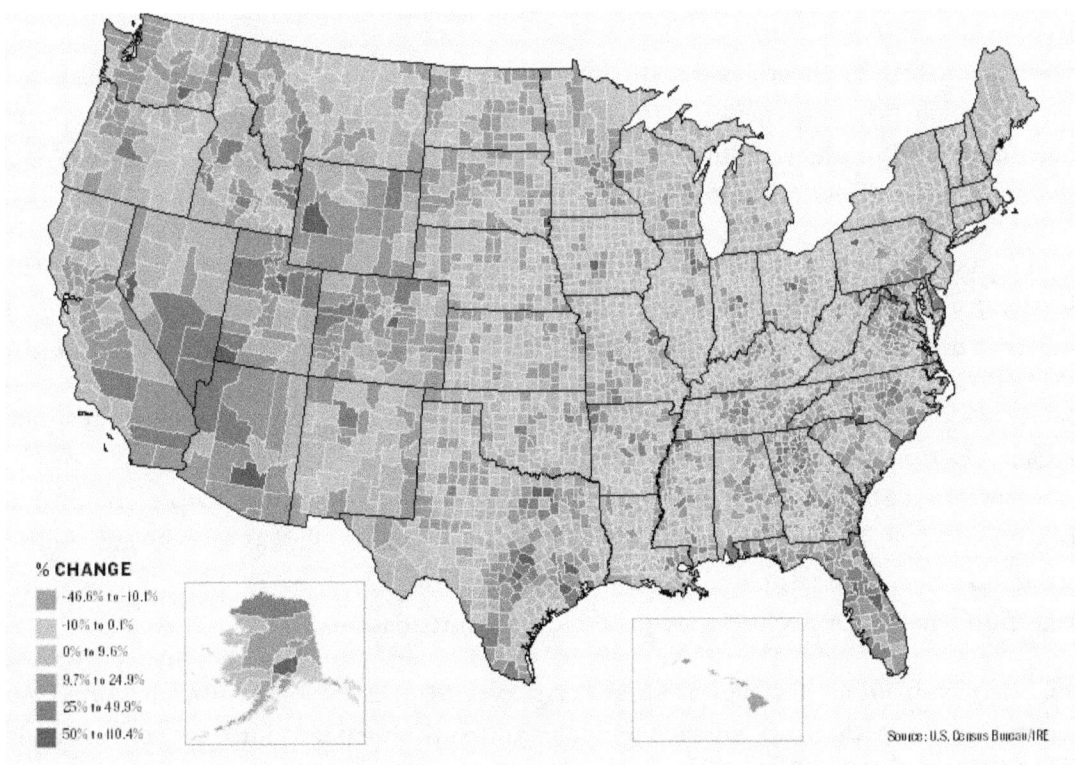

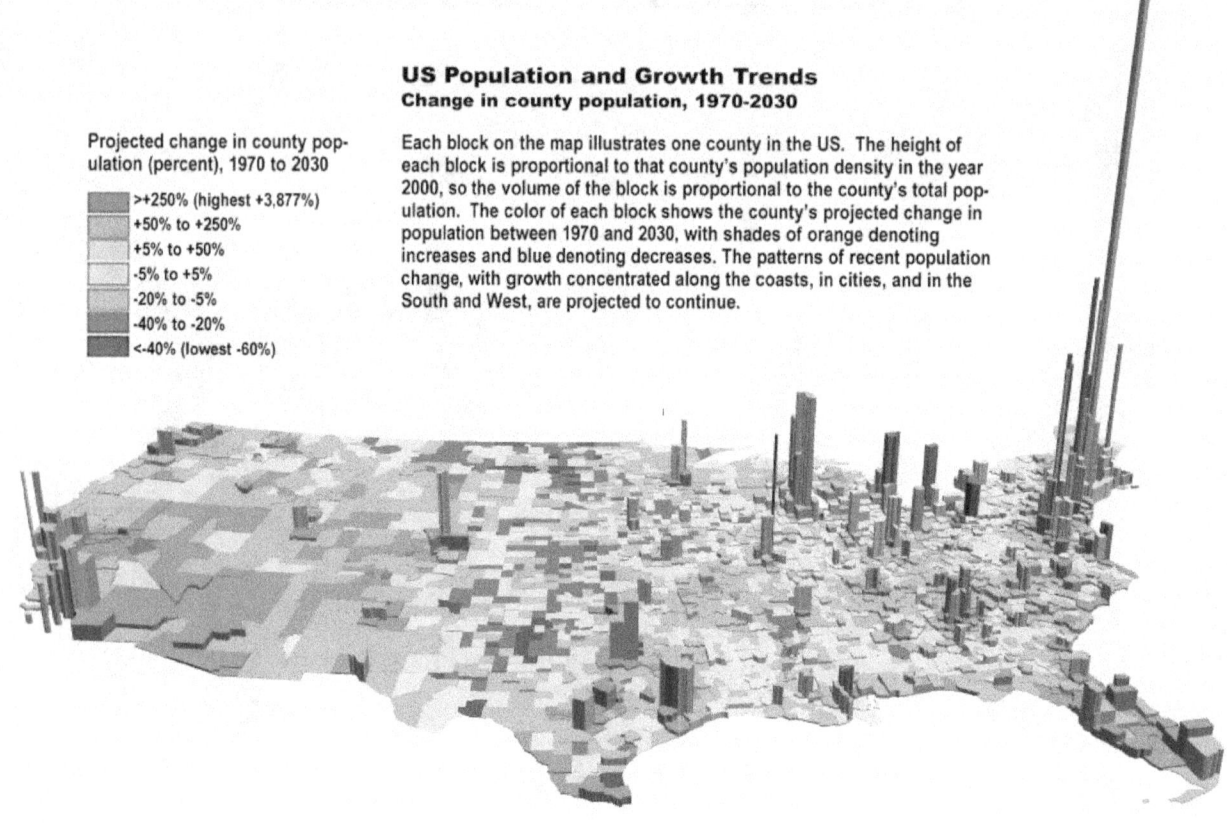

Nuclear Power Plants (Locations and Safety)

Nuclear power plants use the heat generated from nuclear fission in a contained environment to convert water to steam, which powers generators to produce electricity. Nuclear power plants operate in most states in the country and produce about 20 percent of the nation's power. Nearly 3 million Americans live within 10 miles of an operating nuclear power plant.

Although the construction and operation of these facilities are closely monitored and regulated by the Nuclear Regulatory Commission (NRC), accidents are possible. An accident could result in dangerous levels of radiation that could affect the health and safety of the public living near the nuclear power plant.

Local and state governments, federal agencies, and the electric utilities have emergency response plans in the event of a nuclear power plant incident. The plans define two "emergency planning zones." One zone covers an area within a 10-mile radius of the plant, where it is possible that people could be harmed by direct radiation exposure. The second zone covers a broader area, usually up to a 50-mile radius from the plant, where radioactive materials could contaminate water supplies, food crops and livestock. However, one must question whether or not these are prudent recommendations.

The potential danger from an accident at a nuclear power plant is exposure to radiation. This exposure could come from the release of radioactive material from the plant into the environment, usually characterized by a plume (cloud-like formation) of radioactive gases and particles. The major hazards to people in the vicinity of the plume are radiation exposure to the body from the cloud and particles deposited on the ground, inhalation of radioactive materials and ingestion of radioactive materials.

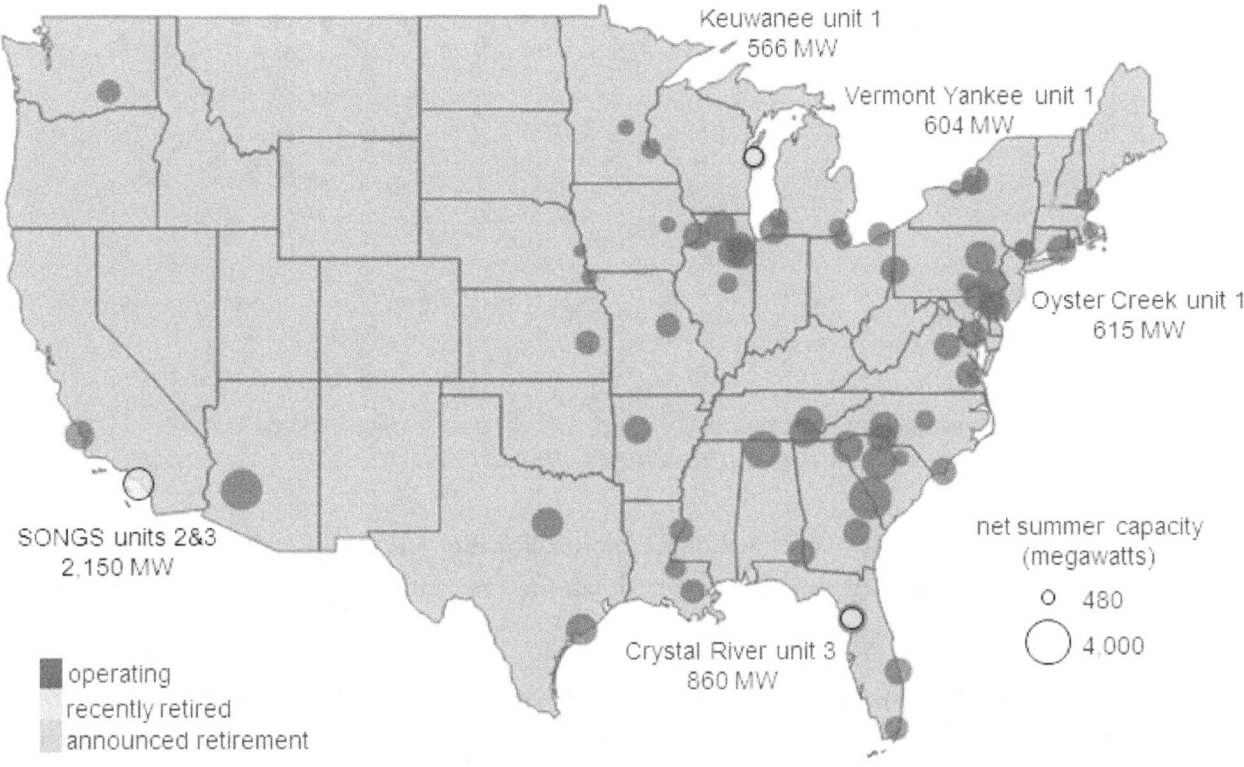

Radioactive materials are composed of atoms that are unstable. An unstable atom gives off its excess energy until it becomes stable. The energy emitted is radiation. Each of us is exposed to radiation daily from natural sources, including the Sun and the Earth. Small traces of radiation are present in food and water. Radiation also is released from man-made sources such as X-ray machines, television sets and microwave ovens. Radiation has a cumulative effect. The longer a person is exposed to radiation, the greater the effect. A high exposure to radiation can cause serious illness or death.

The following map shows where all the nations' nuclear power plants are located in relation to potential seismic hazards

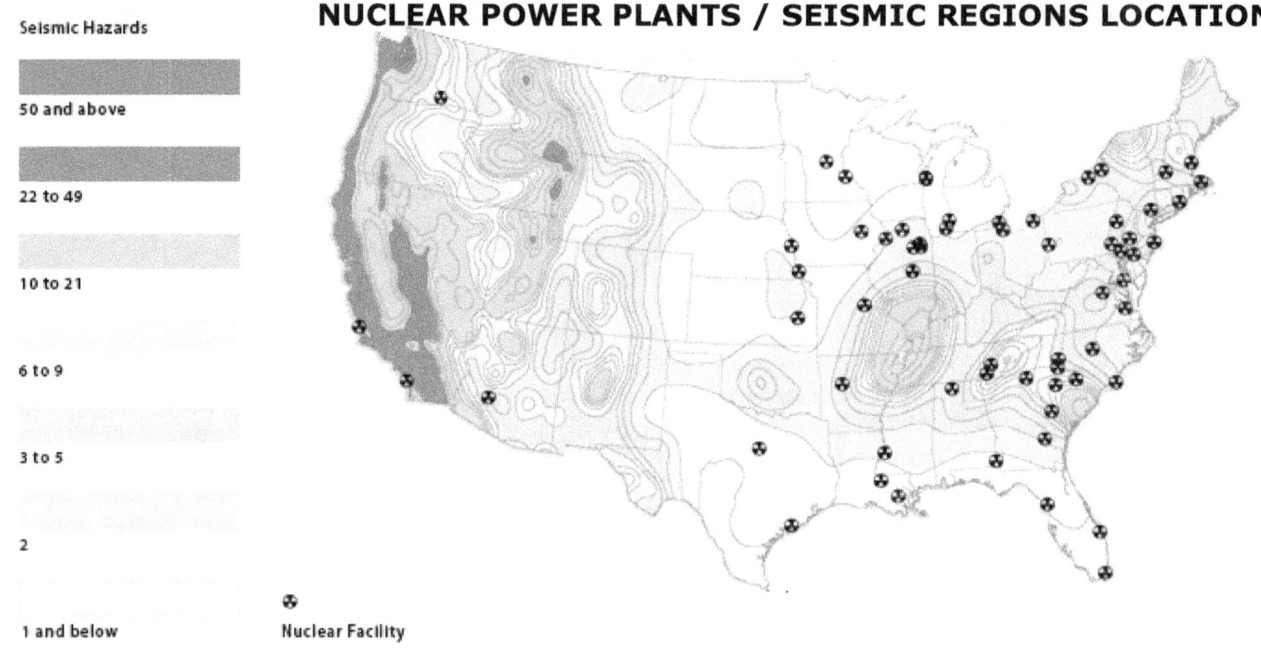

The problem at Fukushima was that the earthquake, and following tsunami, resulted in a complete lack of electrical power; which then led to a meltdown situation. The underlying issue was power sufficient enough to run the powerful cooling pumps.

Taking a simple look at the risks that may exist around any nuclear power plant, the worst-case-scenario is always going to be one where the 'issue' leads to complete power failure. Without electricity, any one of these nuclear reactors will melt down, just like Fukushima, Chernobyl, or worse.

A nuclear power plant being what it is, we would like to think that there is the utmost highest regard and oversight for safety built in to the design, construction, and operation of each one. However, from what we have seen happen in Japan and the USSR, we now know that a nuclear disaster is a very real possibility.

It has been well over a century since the last major solar storm hit the earth, but sooner or later, it will happen again. It's only a question of when, and many scientists believe that the recurrence of such an event is overdue.

In fact, scientists claim that the likelihood of a coronal mass ejection on the scale of the 1859 Carrington Event - the most devastating solar storm on record - is around one percent annually, which means that it should have already happened, statistically speaking.

As previously reported by Natural News, the Carrington Event fried telegraph networks in several countries and lit up the sky with auroral displays so bright they could be seen even near the equator.

When a solar storm of this magnitude hits the earth again, the consequences will be far more disastrous given our complete dependence on electronic devices, electronic systems and the power grid - all of which will almost certainly be wiped out. This will include items such as cell phones, toasters, automobile ignition systems, and the electrical power that we take for granted and rely on more heavily than most of us would care to imagine.

It could take years or even a decade before the power grid and some sense of normalcy can be restored. In the meantime, there is a strong likelihood that millions of people -- particularly those living in urban areas -- will perish within a short time after the event.

Without power to the cities, social order will quickly collapse and mayhem will ensue. The worst part would be the potential of nuclear power plant meltdowns.

For years experts have been warning that the U.S. electrical infrastructure is vulnerable to both manmade and natural threats. Either from an electromagnetic pulse (EMP) weapon fired at the U.S. by an enemy. all the technology that supports our advanced society - from our electrical, banking, water and communications systems, among others - are currently at risk of being totally, and irreparably, destroyed. Again, one cannot help but think of the dangers that may result if the power supply to our nuclear power plants becomes significantly disrupted.

The New Madrid Seismic Zone is a major seismic zone and a prolific source of intraplate earthquakes in the southern and midwestern United States, stretching to the southwest from New Madrid, Missouri.

The New Madrid fault system was responsible for the 1811–12 New Madrid earthquakes and may have the potential to produce large earthquakes in the future. Since 1812, frequent smaller earthquakes have been recorded in the area.

Earthquakes that occur in the New Madrid Seismic Zone potentially threaten parts of seven American states: Illinois, Indiana, Missouri, Arkansas, Kentucky, Tennessee and Mississippi.

There are 15 nuclear power plants in the New Madrid fault zone. The USGS predicts that a major quake would create horrific scenes like something out of a science fiction movie, potentially cutting the Eastern part of the country off from the West in terms of vehicular traffic and road commerce.

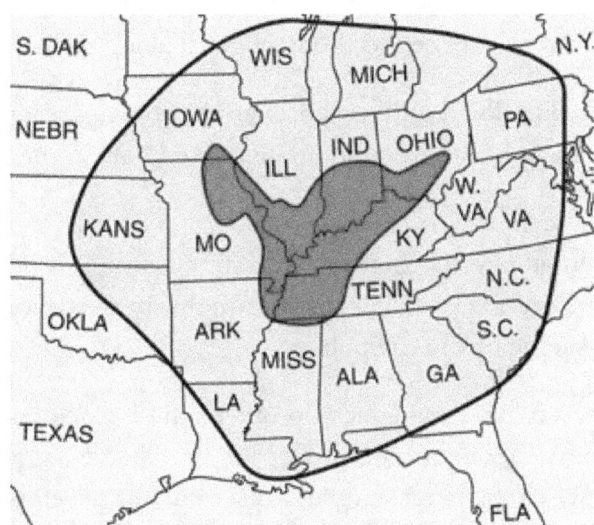

Earthquakes have rocked the powerful San Andreas fault that splits California far more often than previously thought, according to UC Irvine and Arizona State University researchers who have charted temblors there stretching back 700 years.

The findings, to be published in the Sept. 1 issue of *Geology*, conclude that large ruptures have occurred on the Carrizo Plain portion of the fault – about 100 miles northwest of Los Angeles – as often as every 45 to 144 years. But the last big quake was in 1857, more than 150 years ago.

Diablo Canyon is designed to handle 20 foot tsunami waves. However, a massive earthquake of 9+ could produce a tsunami in the region as never experienced within the last couple of centuries. Worst yet, is the nucler fallout that may occur from the earthquake itself.

A senior federal nuclear expert is urging regulators to shut down California's last operating nuclear plant until they can determine whether the facility's twin reactors can withstand powerful shaking from any one of several nearby earthquake faults.

Michael Peck, who for five years was Diablo Canyon's lead on-site inspector, says in a 42-page, confidential report, uncovered by the Associate Press in 2014, that the Nuclear Regulatory Commission is not applying the safety rules it set out for the plant's operation.

What's striking about Peck's analysis is that it comes from within the NRC itself, and gives a rare look at a dispute within the agency. At issue are whether the plant's mechanical guts could survive a big jolt, and what yardsticks should be used to measure the ability of the equipment to withstand the potentially strong vibrations that could result.

According to Peck's filing, PG&E research in 2011 determined that any of three nearby faults - the Shoreline, Los Osos and San Luis Bay - is capable of producing significantly more ground motion during an earthquake than was accounted for in the design of important plant equipment. In the case of San Luis Bay, it is as much as 75 percent more.

Those findings involve estimates of what's called peak ground acceleration, a measurement of how hard the earth could shake in a given location. The analysis says PG&E failed to demonstrate that the equipment would remain operable if exposed to the stronger shaking, violating its operating license.

The agency should shut the facility down until it is proven that piping, reactor cooling and other systems can meet higher stress levels, or approve exemptions that would allow the plant to continue to operate, according to Peck's analysis.

The revelation of this confidential internal analysis and safety warning is not only alarming in regards to the Diablo Canyon Nuclear Power Plant, but makes one very suspicious of what NRC and other government agencies may be keeping from the public.

Another concern is an unforeseen 'physical' attack on one of these reactors (internal sabotage or external (domestic or foreign terrorist). Also, one must consider the possibilities of a cyber 'virus' attack along the lines of the Stuxnet computer virus that attacked the Iranian nuclear development facilities?

It is difficult to impossible to answer the question, "How far away is a safe distance from a nuclear reactor?", much depends on the wind and severity of the nuclear power plant accident so following is a 100 mile radius zones (200 mile diameter) around each nuclear plant to provide some visual perspective.

Minimum Preferred Distance from Nuclear Power Plants

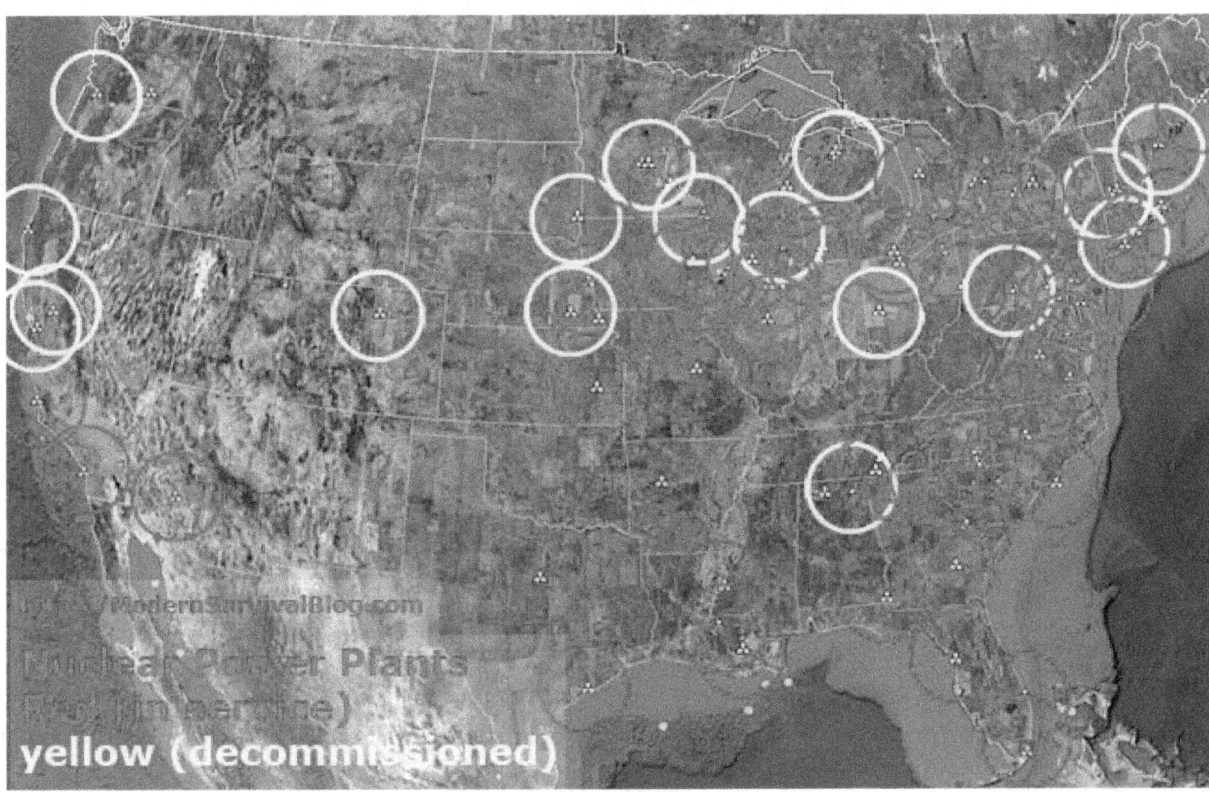

Nuclear industry hides from public huge radiation spikes at power plant reactors

Wednesday, September 03, 2014 by: Ethan A. Huff, staff writer, Natural News

A nuclear insider has unleashed a bombshell about how radiation is actually released from nuclear power plant reactors -- and what he has to say might shock you. During a recent interview with *Nuclear Hotseat* host Libbe HaLevy, radiation biologist Dr. Ian Fairlie spoke about massive radiation spikes that occur when plant reactors are refueled, a common occurrence that the industry has long withheld from the public.

From time to time, nuclear power plants require fresh infusions of fuel in order to keep operating. During this process, nuclear reactors are depressurized and their valves opened up, resulting in a release of gas containing some radioactive elements. The radioactive concentration of this release is said to be minimal, and plant operators are required to report it to regulators annually.

When these reports are made, however, plant operators typically average out the total radioactive release across a 365-day period, which makes it appear small. In truth, the bulk of the release occurs in a very short period of time, often in just one afternoon, which means workers and those living downwind are sustaining high amounts of radioactive exposure.

"Up until 2012, we didn't really know what happened with emissions from nuclear reactors," explained the independent nuclear consultant during the segment. "The only data that we had was annual data.... We didn't really know the time pattern -- now we do."

Up to 75 percent of total radioactive release at nuclear power plants occurs in just one instance

According to Dr. Fairlie, it is a common misconception that small bursts of radiation are released from nuclear power plants throughout the year, representing a minimal overall threat. Up to three-quarters, or 75 percent, of what is recorded annually as radiation releases occurs in just one large spike, typically during the refueling of reactors.

"Instead of having even, little bits of emissions throughout the 365 days, you have one big, massive spike which happens over a day-and-a-half period," said Dr. Fairlie. "That's important... because it results in doses which are at least 20 times higher, maybe even as much as 100 times higher."

This is significant because current regulatory guidelines do not require plant operators to disclose when and how often such releases occur, which creates an illusion of safety. If people knew that nuclear plants operated in this manner, they would likely avoid being near them on the few days when large radiation releases occur.

"These spikes have been hidden from us ever since the beginning of the nuclear power program," explained Dr. Fairlie. "Nobody knew about them apart from people who work in the nuclear industry and they keep really quiet about it."

Though the data from which Dr. Fairlie came to these conclusions was compiled in Germany, he says similar radioactive releases are likely occurring at U.S. reactors as well. He is now urging Americans to contact the Nuclear Regulatory Commission and demand that such information be disclosed in the interest of public health.

Coal and Oil-Fired Power Plant Locations & Emissions (USA)

Coal is the largest energy source for generating electricity at U.S. power plants. There are approximately 450 coal-fired facilities in the United States.

Coal-fired power plants are among the country's greatest sources of pollution. They are the biggest industrial emitters of mercury and arsenic into the air. They emit 84 of the 187 hazardous air pollutants identified by the Environmental Protection Agency (EPA) as posing a threat to human health and the environment.

Coal-fired power plants also emit cadmium, chromium, dioxins, formaldehyde, furans, lead, nickel, and polycyclic aromatic hydrocarbons. They emit volatile organic compounds, including benzene, toluene, and xylene. Emissions include acid gases such as hydrogen chloride and hydrogen fluoride. Small amounts of radioactive materials such as radium, thorium, and uranium are also emitted.

Burning coal in power plants emits sulfur dioxide and nitrogen oxides. Sulfur dioxide and nitrogen oxides react with precipitation in the atmosphere to form acid rain. Burning coal also produces particulate matter.

Coal-fired and oil-fired power plants are also called fossil-fueled power plants. Oil-fired power plants generate only 1 percent of the country's electricity.

About 60 percent of sulfur dioxide emissions, 50 percent of mercury emissions, and 13 percent of nitrogen oxide emissions come from fossil-fueled power plants. Coal- and oil-fired power plants also account for about 60 percent of arsenic emissions, 30 percent of nickel emissions, and 20 percent of chromium emissions.

Coal-fired power plants account for 81 percent of the electric power industry's greenhouse gas emissions, which contribute to global warming and climate change. The most significant greenhouse gas emitted by coal-fired power plants is carbon dioxide. They also emit smaller amounts of methane and nitrous oxide.

The hazardous air emissions from coal-fired power plants cause serious human health impacts. Arsenic, benzene, cadmium, chromium compounds, TCDD dioxin, formaldehyde, and nickel compounds are listed as carcinogens in the 'Thirteenth Report on Carcinogens' published by the National Toxicology Program. Furan and lead are listed as "reasonably anticipated to be human carcinogens" in the Thirteenth Report on Carcinogens.

Hazardous air pollutants emitted by coal-fired power plants can cause a wide range of health effects, including heart and lung diseases, such as asthma. Exposure to these pollutants can damage the brain, eyes, skin, and breathing passages. It can affect the kidneys, lungs, and nervous and respiratory systems. Exposure can also affect learning, memory, and behavior.

Mercury pollutes lakes, streams, and rivers, and accumulates in fish. Nearly all fish and shellfish contain mercury. People who eat large amounts of fish from mercury-contaminated lakes and rivers, including Native Americans, are at the greatest risk of exposure to mercury.

The EPA and Food and Drug Administration issue fish advisories to recommend that people limit or avoid eating certain kinds or amounts of fish. Exposure to mercury is a particular concern for women who may become pregnant, pregnant women, nursing mothers, and young children. Fish advisories have been issued in every state.

People who live near coal-fired power plants have the greatest health risks from power plant pollution. Many pollutants such as metals and dioxins may attach to fine particles and travel hundreds or even thousands of miles.

Map of Fossil Fuel Power Plant Locations and Emissions

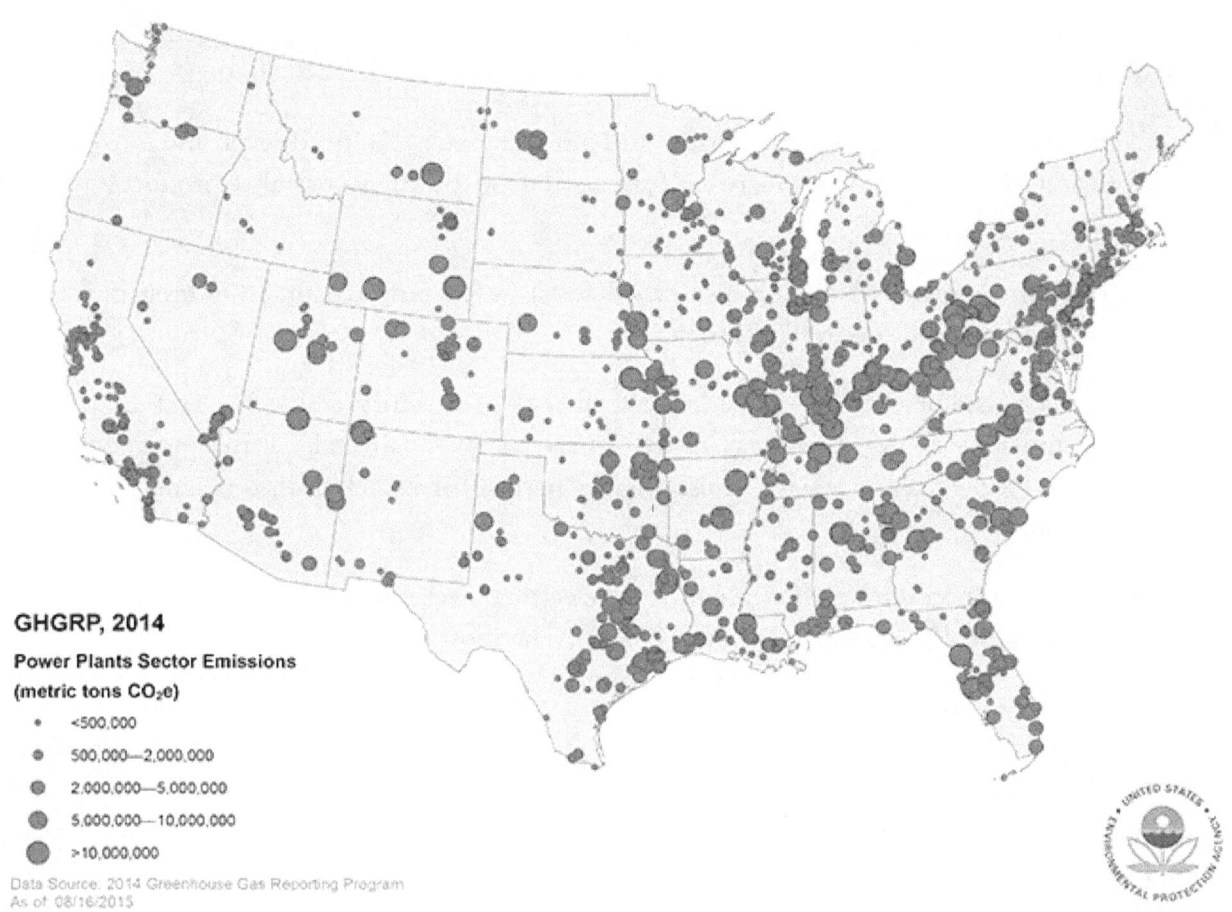

Survival – Best Places to Live & Critical Prepper Information

Most of us have not suffered through unmitigated poverty, hopelessness, or relentless fear. We do not know what crisis really is. However, there are many threats to our way of life, and we need to prepare for the reality of disaster. The key is to come up with a plan and work towards accomplishing that plan.

Bug Out Bags

The first step in a plan is knowing what to take with you, when you need to leave your home in times of emergency. A Bug Out Bag is just that – a bag with the essentials for survival, when you need to bug out. While recommended contents of a bug out bag vary, and each individual should come up with his/her own personalized list, there are some essentials that should be in every bug out bag:

Drinking Water	Water Bottle	Water Filters/Purification Systems
Water Purification Tablets	Protein/Energy Bars	MREs
Spork	Can Opener	Metal Cooking Pot

Metal Cup	Pot Scrubber	Portable Stove
Stove Fuel	Lightweight Long Sleeve Shirt	Convertible (Zip-Off) Pants
Underwear	Wool Hiking Socks	Medium Weight Fleece
Hat with Flex Brim	Gloves	Rain Poncho
Tarp	Tent	Sleeping Bag
Ground Pad	Wool Blanket	Ignition Source
Tinder	Waterproof Storage	First Aid Kit
Insect Repellant	Hand Sanitizer	All-Purpose Camp Soap
Travel Toilet Paper	Travel Size Toothbrush & Toothpaste	Personal Hygiene Necessities
Survival Knife	LED Headlamp	Mini LED Keychain
Lantern	Candles	Batteries
Cell Phone	Crank Power Charger	Emergency Radio with Hand Crank
$500 in Small Bills	Local Area Map	Compass
Small Note Pad and Pencil	Pepper Spray	Handgun
Rifle	Ammunition	Parachute Cord
Duct Tape	Sunglasses	Latex Tubing
Fishing Kit	Garbage Bags	Ziploc Bags

Safe Place

Independence, self-sustainability, true community, and redundancy in systems are all in a day's work for the prepper. However, the one thing that weighs upon our minds above all else is home - the home where we will take refuge during times of crisis. Some call it a retreat, a bunker, a hideout, or a bugout place. Whatever he calls it, every prepper has to have that place set aside that gives him the utmost advantage while facing calamities such as terrorist attacks, nuclear fallout, civil unrest, economic disasters, natural disasters – whatever the case may be.

There are seven key factors that must be addressed in choosing a location for your haven in times of distress: accessibility, water, food, sustainable energy, climate, defensibility/vulnerability, and population density.

Accessibility

First and foremost, you have to be able to get to your bug out location. Depending on the disaster you are encountering, you may not have the time or means to go very far. Therefore, it may be wise to choose a location close to where you live. In addition, you do not want to be dependent on major roadways to get to your location. If people panic and clog the highways, you may be cut off from your retreat.

The ideal location for your hideout is a combination of rugged terrain and varied topography that is just accessible enough. It should not be easy to wander into; people should have to spend a lot of time and energy to reach it. A refuge in times of disaster should be off the beaten path and reachable by a single dirt road with other escape routes in case unwanted visitors find your location.

Water

You must have water. The human body can only go without water for 72 hours. It is generally recommended that a person consume at least one liter of water per day. If you are able to stock your hideout before disaster strikes, store as much bottled water as possible.

However, your survival location should have at least one source of water, preferably more, in case you need to stay for an extended period of time. Digging a well is always an alternative, but having your shelter near a stream, river, or lake is even better. Rainwater collection is another viable option.

Food

Your survival retreat should not only have storage areas for stocking up on non-perishables, but should also allow you to grow food for the future. Bountiful hunting and fishing should be available close by.

A traditional garden will help supply you with food. Another option to traditional gardening is raised bed gardening which requires less water than typical gardens and often produces more food. In harsher climates, a greenhouse can be built with makeshift materials, at little cost, and will allow you to produce food year round. A root cellar will allow you to store potatoes, beets, carrots, onions and the like for your winter meals, or a cool, underground storage space will keep them fresh for much of the winter.

You should also familiarize yourself with any fruit, berries, and nuts growing naturally in the area. In addition, learn the routes game such as deer, elk, bear, etc. take through or by your property and know which water sources are the best places to fish.

Goats, chickens, and rabbits are much easier to squeeze into a smaller parcel than cattle or horses and will draw less attention to your retreat. However, a cow and a bull have the ability could keep your family healthy and fed for a long time. The trade-off is up to the individual prepper. The bottom line is, the number of animals you plan to raise determines the amount of open field you will need to clear on your property to provide the grasses and feeding area they will require. Not every survival situation will allow for raising your own meat, eggs, milk, and fiber from livestock.

Sustainable Energy

Your cabin should be equipped with at least one fireplace or wood stove for cooking and heat. Having plenty of firewood cut, seasoned, and stacked will make your life much easier. Make sure your location has plenty of hardwood trees to harvest for the future. For long-term survival situations you may want to prepare some alternative forms of energy to pump water, heat your cabin, cook food, etc. A few options include solar panels on the roof, if there is good southern exposure to the sun; a wind turbine to pump water and provide energy; or using a stream to provide hydro power.

Climate

Climate is an important consideration when choosing your survival location. Is it prone to extremely cold/hot temperatures, flooding, or excessive snowfall? These factors need to be considered in regards to their effect on your ability to reach your bugout place, maintain access to water, and produce food.

Defensibility/Vulnerability

Make sure your surroundings work for you. Is the retreat actually protecting you or not? How easy would it be for others to overtake your bug out location? Is it easily seen from a road? Are there trees around it to provide cover if you need to defend it? Look for natural land features that will prevent invasion. Folds in the land topography offer greater cover and concealment. Mountainous terrain, cliffs, steep hills, rocky outcrops, etc. will discourage most intruders, and having high ground for a look out spot will help you see intruders before they see you. An underground bunker will also increase security and camouflage of your survival domicile.

Population Density

Isolation is not necessarily the goal when calamities hit. You should have a network of like-minded people in the general area of your retreat if possible. Ideally, choosing a retreat location, especially for a homestead in which you will be living on a day to day basis, should be done with multiple families involved. The more preppers involved, the larger the perimeter of warning and defense, and the safer everyone will be. It is not enough to have a friend or two on the other side of town, or to have a couple neighbors who are open to preparing for disasters. A return to a true community foundation is the surest way to secure your retreat.

However, you certainly do not want to be in close proximity to highly populated areas, either. If the entire nation is experiencing a disaster of any sort, you do not want thousands of close neighbors to deal with. In addition major cities and popular hubs of activities are more likely to be targets of man-made catastrophes.

It is a good idea to have your hideout within 10 to 20 miles of a village or small town where you can go (by foot, if necessary) for additional supplies, news and other contact with the outside world should the emergency stretch into months or longer.

Additional Ideas to Consider

- ✓ Consider developing your survival retreat close to national forest areas or unclaimed and unpurchased acreage. This could give you the potential use of thousands of acres, while guaranteeing that no unpleasant or unaware neighbors will move in too close. Abundant resources such as timber, wild game, possible minerals, caching sites, and secondary retreat locations will be at your disposal.
- ✓ Ensure your survival location is provisioned with enough food to keep your family safe for at least three months, preferably a year; provisioned with tools necessary for long-term self-sufficiency, should it become necessary; and stocked with enough weapons and ammunition to defend it from small groups of marauding invaders, should it come to that.
- ✓ Choose a survival retreat in an area of low seismic and volcanic activity, located away from the coast, out of reach of flood waters, and with access to an underground tornado shelter.
- ✓ Consider having a secondary retreat location. Back-up retreat locations should be chosen in remote areas near your primary retreat, and very few, if any, people should be told about this place. This is a last ditch survival spot, not ideal for long-term living arrangements. Little if any infrastructure will be built here, and all shelter materials should be heavily concealed. Caching sites should be set up well in advance and placed on at least two separate routes to the same location. Hidden approaches to the area should be scouted ahead of time, and a viable water source should be present nearby.
- ✓ It may be best for you to secure the home you live in now and make it your survival retreat due to financial and/or family obligations.

Conclusion

In research for this chapter we reviewed many reputable sources. The vast majority offered great survival tips and recommendations. Most were consist with one another on those points. However, the one variable that was not consistent among our studies of survival resources was that of 'location'. Most all resources made recommendations on the best places, regions, states, or cities to be for attaining the highest probability of survival during a catastrophic event. Unfortunately, not only were there inconsistencies between our resources, many of the recommendations on the best places to be for survival was in direct conflict with information being offered from another viable source.

The fact is, the perfect survival location is a rare thing. Depending on the hardships you will face and the area you live in, you may just have to make do with what you can find. Even the best laid plans can be derailed by circumstances beyond your control. Your survival retreat could be destroyed by wildfires, crushed by landslides, or looted by vandals before you can reach it. Don't depend entirely on a remote retreat as your only survival plan. Have alternative locations where you can go in emergencies, and be sure you keep survival gear at home *and* in your survival bunker. Learn as many survival techniques as possible, from identifying wild edibles and medicinal herbs, to defense and hunting skills. Knowledge will be with you wherever you go. Having a survival property could very well be a lifesaver in desperate times, but don't let it lull you into a false sense of security.

There are all kinds of excuses for not doing what needs to be done, but everyone needs a strategy for an emergency or survival situation. No one is immune to catastrophic events.

Asthma - Worst Cities to Live

A list of the 100 worst cities in America, starting with the worst cities for asthma (Source: *Asthma and Allergy Foundation*):

1. Scranton, Pa.
2. Richmond, Va.
3. Philadelphia
4. Atlanta
5. Milwaukee
6. Cleveland
7. Greensboro, N.C.
8. Youngstown, Ohio
9. St. Louis
10. Detroit
11. Knoxville, Tenn.
12. Cincinnati
13. Toledo, Ohio
14. Canton, Ohio
15. Baton Rouge, La.
16. Pittsburgh
17. Little Rock, Ark.
18. Phoenix-Mesa, Ariz.
19. Memphis, Tenn.
20. Baltimore
21. Lancaster, Pa.
22. Chicago
23. Charlotte, N.C.
24. Houston
25. Harrisburg, Pa.
26. McAllen, Texas
27. Washington
28. Hartford, Conn.
29. Birmingham, Ala.
30. Kalamazoo, Mich.
31. Grand Rapids, Mich.
32. Indianapolis
33. Fresno, Calif.
34. Dayton, Ohio
35. Louisville, Ky.
36. Allentown, Pa.
37. Salt Lake City
38. San Diego
39. San Antonio
40. Bakersfield, Calif.
41. Columbia, S.C.
42. Las Vegas
43. Chattanooga, Tenn.
44. Lansing, Mich.
45. Stockton, Calif.
46. Mobile, Ala.
47. Omaha, Neb.
48. Augusta, Ga.
49. Los Angeles
50. Dallas-Fort Worth
51. Johnson City, Tenn.
52. Fort Wayne, Ind.
53. Raleigh-Durham, N.C.
54. Seattle
55. Denver
56. Kansas City, Mo.
57. Oklahoma City
58. New York
59. Norfolk, Va.
60. Springfield, Mass.
61. Modesto, Calif.
62. New Orleans
63. Spokane, Wash.
64. Tulsa, Okla.
65. Columbus, Ohio
66. Buffalo, N.Y.
67. Nashville, Tenn.
68. Greenville, S.C.
69. Sacramento, Calif.
70. Boston
71. Boise City, Idaho
72. Charleston, S.C.
73. Portland, Ore.
74. Colorado Springs, Colo.
75. Rochester, N.Y.
76. El Paso, Texas
77. Des Moines, Iowa
78. Lexington, Ky.
79. Albuquerque, N.M.
80. Sarasota, Fla.
81. Wichita, Kan.
82. Syracuse, N.Y.
83. Providence, R.I.
84. Austin, Texas
85. Fort Myers, Fla.
86. Tucson, Ariz.
87. Jackson, Miss.
88. Madison, Wis.
89. Miami
90. Pensacola, Fla.
91. San Francisco
92. Orlando, Fla.
93. Lakeland, Fla.
94. Melbourne, Fla.
95. Daytona Beach, Fla.
96. Jacksonville, Fla.
97. West Palm Beach, Fla.
98. Albany, N.Y.
99. Minneapolis
100. Tampa, Fla.

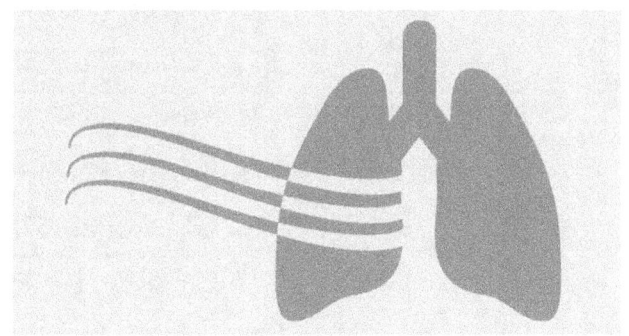

Allergies - Worst Cities

The major cities of the U.S. have been ranked according to how challenging they are to live in for people with allergies. The list is provided below with Witchita, Kansas being ranked as the worst city. The rankings come from the Asthma and Allergy Foundation of America.

1. Wichita, Kan. (100.00)
2. Jackson, Miss. (96.44)
3. Knoxville, Tenn. (94.32)
4. Louisville, Ky. (89.12)
5. Memphis, Tenn. (88.72)
6. McAllen, Texas (88.37)
7. Baton Rouge, La. (87.87)
8. Dayton, Ohio (86.91)
9. Chattanooga, Tenn. (85.76)
10. Oklahoma City (85.65)
11. New Orleans (84.54)
12. Madison, Wisc. (83.67)
13. Omaha, Neb. (82.64)
14. Little Rock, Ark. (80.02)
15. Tulsa, Okla. (77.50)
16. Buffalo, N.Y. (77.10)
17. Grand Rapids, Mich. (76.88)
18. Dallas (76.63)
19. Detroit (76.27)
20. Toledo, Ohio (75.59)
21. Birmingham, Ala. (74.54)
22. Des Moines, Iowa (73.86)
23. San Antonio (73.53)
24. Nashville, Tenn. (72.37)
25. Syracuse, N.Y. (72.35)
26. Charleston, S.C. (70.96)
27. Augusta, Ga. (70.71)
28. Providence, R.I. (70.15)
29. St. Louis (70.08)
30. Greenville, S.C. (69.63)
31. Youngstown, Ohio (69.47)
32. Houston (68.95)
33. Columbia, S.C. (68.12)
34. Virginia Beach, Va. (67.82)
35. Rochester, N.Y. (67.67)
36. Akron, Ohio (67.33)
37. Minneapolis (66.99)
38. Kansas City, Mo. (66.80)
39. Portland, Maine (66.32)
40. Columbus, Ohio (65.52)
41. Cleveland (65.06)
42. Philadelphia (64.98)

continued

43. Milwaukee (64.86)
44. Charlotte, N.C. (64.73)
45. Austin, Texas (64.45)
46. Pittsburgh (64.37)
47. Riverside, Calif. (63.48)
48. Albany, N.Y. (62.40)
49. Greensboro, N.C. (61.99)
50. Indianapolis (61.80)
51. Scranton, Pa. (60.04)
52. El Paso, Texas (59.84)
53. Hartford, Conn. (59.21)
54. Poughkeepsie, N.Y. (59.09)
55. Cincinnati (58.73)
56. New York (58.71)
57. Richmond, Va. (58.27)
58. Chicago (58.25)
59. Jacksonville, Fla. (58.18)
60. Allentown, Pa. (58.16)
61. Springfield, Mass. (58.00)
62. New Haven, Conn. (57.64)
63. Lakeland, Fla. (56.79)
64. Fresno, Calif. (56.40)
65. Cape Coral, Fla. (56.38)
66. Bridgeport, Conn. (56.32)
67. Miami (55.55)
68. Harrisburg, Pa. (55.48)
69. Worcester, Mass. (55.25)
70. Las Vegas (55.22)
71. Tampa, Fla. (54.22)
72. Phoenix (54.06)
73. Tucson, Ariz. (53.96)
74. Atlanta (53.67)
75. Boston (52.88)
76. Los Angeles (52.28)
77. Lancaster, Pa. (51.92)
78. Bakersfield, Calif. (51.89)
79. Orlando, Fla. (51.33)
80. Ogden, Utah (50.57)
81. Baltimore (48.62)
82. Albuquerque, N.M. (48.62)
83. Washington, D.C. (48.06)
84. Seattle (47.05)
85. Raleigh, N.C. (47.00)
86. Sarasota, Fla. (46.55)
87. Modesto, Calif. (46.28)
88. San Francisco (45.74)
89. Palm Bay, Fla. (45.64)
90. Oxnard, Calif. (45.26)
91. San Diego (44.36)
92. Salt Lake City (43.16)
93. Boise, Idaho (43.11)
94. Denver (42.97)
95. San Jose, Calif. (42.78)
96. Daytona Beach, Fla. (41.60)
97. Colorado Springs, Colo. (40.86)
98. Stockton, Calif. (40.08)
99. Sacramento, Calif. (37.95)
100. Portland, Ore. (37.87)

BELOW MAP: Elevated ozone levels and increased ragweed pollen combine to make life miserable for those that are affected by hay fever who live in the dark areas.

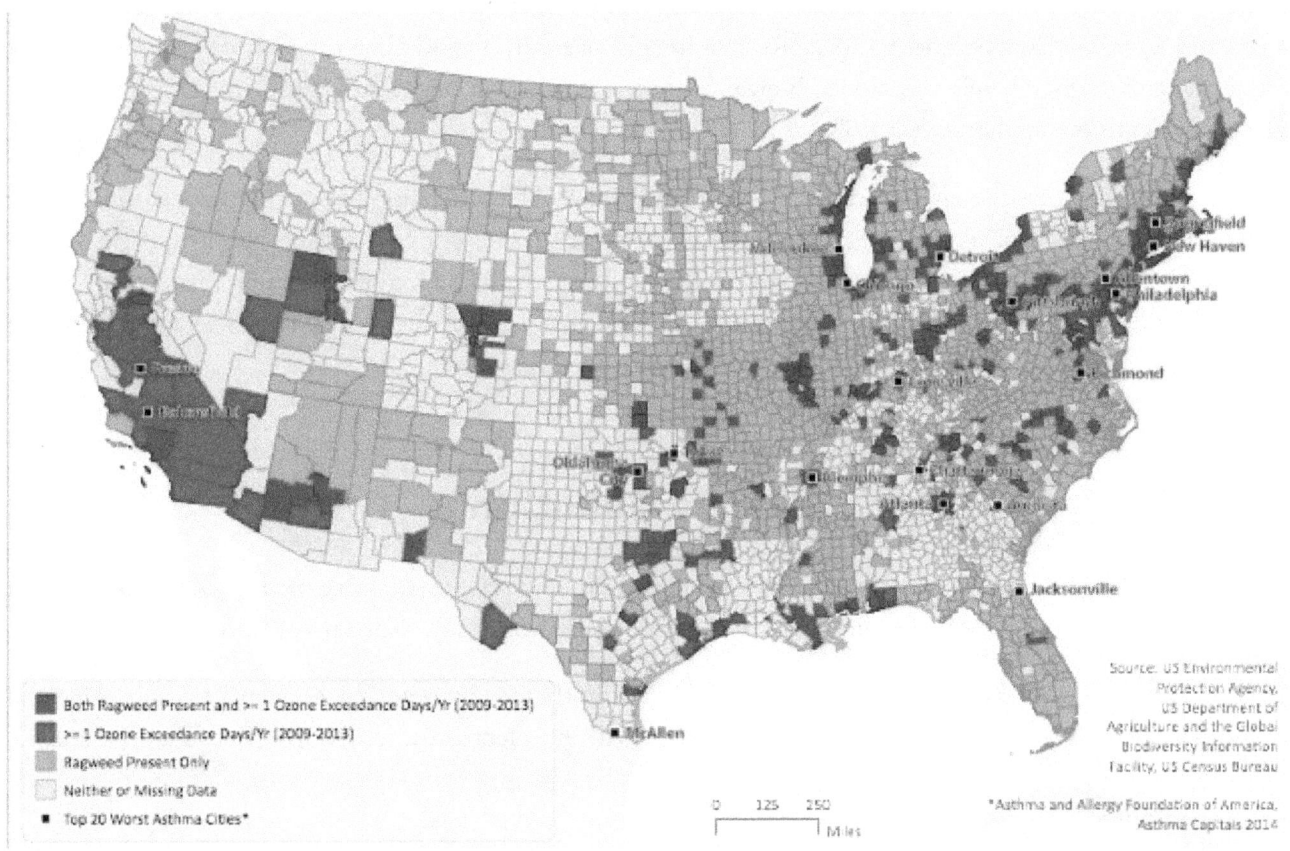

Air Quality – Best & Worst Locations

The American Lung Association *State of the Air 2015* report looks at levels of ozone and particle pollution found in official monitoring sites across the United States. The report uses the most current quality-assured nationwide data available for these analyses.

Two types of air pollution dominate in the U.S.: ozone and particle pollution. These two pollutants threaten the health and the lives of millions of Americans.

Ozone

It may be hard to imagine that pollution could be invisible, but ozone is. The most widespread pollutant in the U.S. is also one of the most dangerous. Scientists have studied the effects of ozone on health for decades. Hundreds of research studies have confirmed that ozone harms people at levels currently found in the United States. In the last few years, we've learned that it can also be deadly.

Ozone (O3) is a gas molecule composed of three oxygen atoms. Often called "smog," ozone is harmful to breathe. Ozone aggressively attacks lung tissue by reacting chemically with it. Breathing ozone can shorten your life. Strong evidence exists of the deadly impact of ozone in large studies conducted in cities across the U.S., in Europe and in Asia. Researchers repeatedly found that the risk of premature death increased with higher levels of ozone. Newer research has confirmed that ozone increased the risk of premature death even when other pollutants.

Even low levels of ozone may be deadly. A large study of 48 U.S. cities looked at the association between ozone and all-cause mortality during the summer months. Ozone concentrations by city in the summer months ranged from 16 percent to 80 percent lower than the U.S. Environmental Protection Agency (EPA) currently considers safe. Researchers found that ozone at those lower levels was associated with deaths from cardiovascular disease, strokes, and respiratory causes.

Particle Pollution

Particle pollution refers to a mix of very tiny solid and liquid particles that are in the air we breathe. But nothing about particle pollution is simple. And it is so dangerous it can shorten your life.

Particles themselves are different sizes. Some are one-tenth the diameter of a strand of hair. Many are even tinier; some are so small they can only be seen with an electron microscope. Because of their size, you can't see the individual particles. You can only see the haze that forms when millions of particles blur the spread of sunlight.

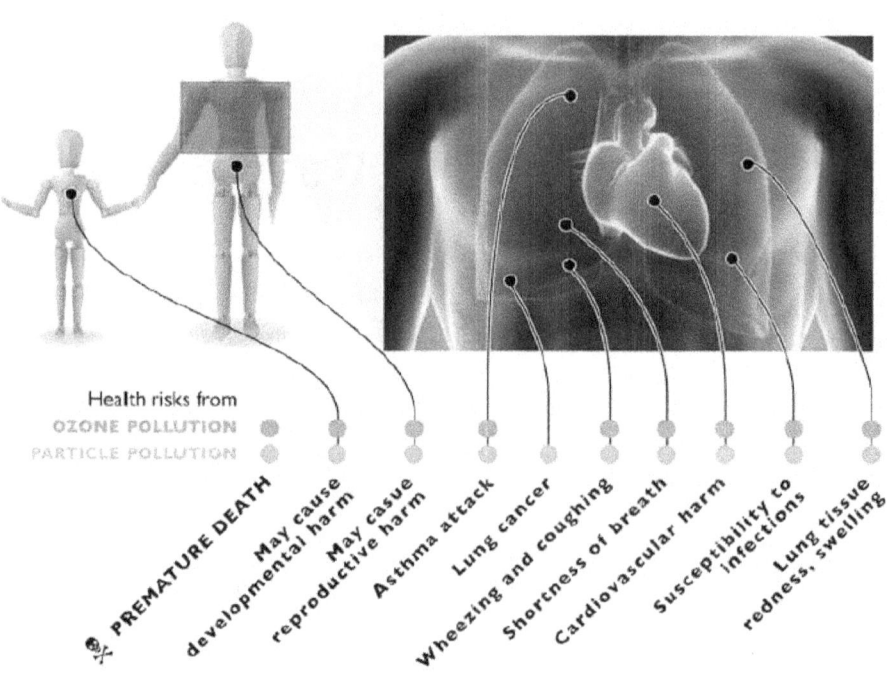

The differences in size make a big difference in how they affect us. Our natural defenses help us to cough or sneeze larger particles out of our bodies. But those defenses don't keep out smaller particles, those that are smaller than 10 microns (or micrometers) in diameter, or about one-seventh the diameter of a single human hair. These particles get trapped in the lungs, while the smallest are so minute that they can pass through the lungs into the bloodstream, just like the essential oxygen molecules we need to survive.

94

Researchers categorize particles according to size, grouping them as coarse, fine and ultrafine. Coarse particles fall between 2.5 microns and 10 microns in diameter and are called $PM_{10-2.5}$. Fine particles are 2.5 microns in diameter or smaller and are called $PM_{2.5}$. Ultrafine particles are smaller than 0.1 micron in diameter and are small enough to pass through the lung tissue into the blood stream, circulating like the oxygen molecules themselves. No matter what the size, particles can harm your health.

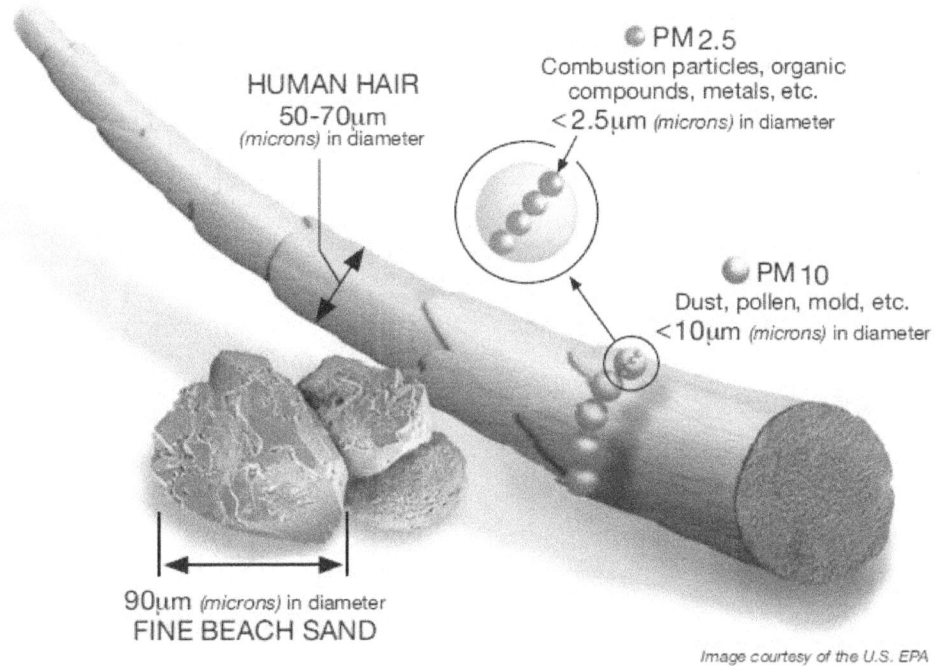

Image courtesy of the U.S. EPA

Because particles are formed in so many different ways, they can be composed of many different compounds. Although we often think of particles as solids, not all are. Some are completely liquid; some are solids suspended in liquids. As the EPA puts it, particles are really "a mixture of mixtures."

The mixtures differ between the eastern and western United States and in different times of the year. For example, the Midwest, Southeast and Northeast states have more sulfate particles than the West on average, largely due to the high levels of sulfur dioxide emitted by large, coal-fired power plants. By contrast, nitrate particles from motor vehicle exhaust form a larger proportion of the unhealthful mix in the winter in the Northeast, Southern California, the Northwest, and North Central US. However, anyone who lives where particle pollution levels are high is at risk.

EPA Concludes Fine Particle Pollution Poses Serious Health Threats

- Causes early death (both short-term and long-term exposure)
- Causes cardiovascular harm (e.g. heart attacks, strokes, heart disease, congestive heart failure)
- Likely to cause respiratory harm (e.g. worsened asthma, worsened COPD, inflammation)
- May cause cancer
- May cause reproductive and developmental harm

—U.S. Environmental Protection Agency, Integrated Science Assessment for Particulate Matter, December 2009. EPA 600/R-08/139F.

Ozone/Particulate Metropolitan Area Statistics

The next several tables were acquired from the American Lung Association *State of the Air 2015* report. Note on following tables: Ranked using highest weighted average of data.

The 25 Most Polluted Cities for Short-term Particle Pollution (24-hour $PM_{2.5}$)

2015 Rank	Metropolitan Statistical Areas
1	Fresno-Madera, CA
2	Bakersfield, CA
3	Visalia-Porterville-Hanford, CA
4	Modesto-Merced, CA
5	Los Angeles-Long Beach, CA
6	San Jose-San Francisco-Oakland, CA
7	Salt Lake City-Provo-Orem, UT
8	Logan, UT-ID
9	Fairbanks, AK
10	Pittsburgh-New Castle-Weirton, PA-OH-WV
11	Missoula, MT
12	Phoenix-Mesa-Scottsdale, AZ
13	Yakima, WA
14	Sacramento-Roseville, CA
15	New York-Newark, NY-NJ-CT-PA
15	Reno-Carson City-Fernley, NV
17	El Paso-Las Cruces, TX-NM
18	Seattle-Tacoma, WA
19	Harrisburg-York-Lebanon, PA
20	Eugene, OR
20	Lancaster, PA
22	Philadelphia-Reading-Camden, PA-NJ-DE-MD
23	Boise City-Mountain Home-Ontario, ID-OR
23	Indianapolis-Carmel-Muncie, IN
25	Medford-Grants Pass, OR

The 25 Most Polluted Cities for Year-Round Particle Pollution (Annual PM$_{2.5}$)

2015 Rank	Metropolitan Statistical Areas
1	Fresno-Madera, CA
2	Bakersfield, CA
3	Visalia-Porterville-Hanford, CA
4	Modesto-Merced, CA
5	Los Angeles-Long Beach, CA
6	El Centro, CA
7	San Jose-San Francisco-Oakland, CA
8	Cincinnati-Wilmington-Maysville, OH-KY-IN
9	Pittsburgh-New Castle-Weirton, PA-OH-WV
10	Cleveland-Akron-Canton, OH
11	Philadelphia-Reading-Camden, PA-NJ-DE-MD
12	Harrisburg-York-Lebanon, PA
12	Johnstown-Somerset, PA
14	New York-Newark, NY-NJ-CT-PA
15	Louisville/Jefferson County --Elizabethtown--
15	Madison, KY-IN
16	Lancaster, PA
17	Altoona, PA
17	Birmingham-Hoover-Talladega, AL
17	Indianapolis-Carmel-Muncie, IN
20	Houston-The Woodlands, TX
20	Macon-Warner Robins, GA
22	Little Rock-North Little Rock, AR
23	El Paso-Las Cruces, TX-NM
23	Erie-Meadville, PA
23	Shreveport-Bossier City, LA
23	Wheeling, WV-OH

The 25 Most Ozone Polluted Cities

2015 Rank	Metropolitan Statistical Areas
1	Los Angeles-Long Beach, CA
2	Visalia-Porterville-Hanford, CA
3	Bakersfield, CA
4	Fresno-Madera, CA
5	Sacramento-Roseville, CA
6	Houston-The Woodlands, TX
7	Dallas-Fort Worth, TX-OK
8	Modesto-Merced, CA
9	Las Vegas-Henderson, NV-AZ
10	Phoenix-Mesa-Scottsdale, AZ
11	New York-Newark, NY-NJ-CT-PA
12	Tulsa-Muskogee-Bartlesville, OK
13	Denver-Aurora, CO
14	El Centro, CA
15	Oklahoma City-Shawnee, OK
16	Fort Collins, CO
16	St. Louis-St. Charles-Farmington, MO-IL
18	Grand Rapids-Wyoming-Muskegon, MI
19	Chicago-Naperville, IL-IN-WI
20	Sheboygan, WI
21	Pittsburgh-New Castle-Weirton, PA-OH-WV
22	Washington-Baltimore-Arlington, DC-MD-VA-WV-PA
23	Cincinnati-Wilmington-Maysville, OH-KY-IN
24	Kansas City-Overland Park-Kansas City, MO-KS
25	Memphis-Forrest City, TN-MS-AR
25	South Bend-Elkhart-Mishawaka, IN-MI

The 25 Most Polluted Counties for Short-term Particle Pollution (24-hour PM$_{2.5}$)

2015 Rank	County
1	Fresno
2	Kern
3	Kings
4	Stanislaus
5	Riverside
6	Lemhi
7	Madera
8	Los Angeles
9	Ravalli
10	San Joaquin
11	Salt Lake
12	Cache
13	Merced
14	Franklin
15	Utah
16	Fairbanks North
16	Star borough
17	Shoshone
18	Weber
19	Tulare
20	Allegheny
21	Inyo
22	Lake
23	Silver Bow
24	Missoula
25	Maricopa

The 25 Most Polluted Counties for Year-Round Particle Pollution (Annual PM$_{2.5}$)

2015 Rank	County
1	Madera
2	Kern
3	Kings
4	Tulare
5	Fresno
6	Stanislaus
7	Riverside
8	Imperial
9	San Joaquin
10	Butler
11	Allegheny
12	Merced
13	Los Angeles
14	Plumas
14	Shoshone
16	San Bernardino
17	Cuyahoga
18	Delaware
19	Hamilton
19	Cambria
19	Lebanon
22	Northampton
23	Stark
23	Clark
25	Lancaster
25	Lemhi

The 25 Most Ozone Polluted Counties (2014 – most recent data)

2014 Rank	County
1	San Bernardino
2	Riverside
3	Tulare
4	Los Angeles
5	Kern
6	Fresno
7	Uintah
8	Madera
9	Sacramento
10	Harris
11	Kings
12	Tarrant
13	Stanislaus
14	Denton
15	Duchesne
16	Clark
17	Maricopa
18	El Dorado
19	Fairfield
20	Tulsa
21	Jefferson
22	Dallas
23	Imperial
24	Oklahoma
25	Collin

The Top 25 Cleanest U.S. Cities for Year-Round Particle Pollution

Rank[2]	Design Value[3]	Metropolitan Statistical Area	Population
1	4.2	Prescott, AZ	215,133
2	4.7	Farmington, NM	126,503
3	4.8	Casper, WY	80,973
3	4.8	Cheyenne, WY	95,809
5	5.3	Flagstaff, AZ	136,539
6	6.1	Duluth, MN-WI	279,887
6	6.1	Kahului-Wailuku-Lahaina, HI	160,292
6	6.1	Palm Bay-Melbourne-Titusville, FL	550,823
6	6.1	Salinas, CA	428,826
10	6.2	Anchorage, AK	396,142
10	6.2	Bismarck, ND	123,751
10	6.2	Rapid City-Spearfish, SD	166,341
13	6.5	Cape Coral-Fort Meyers-Naples, FL	1,000,757
13	6.5	Elmira-Corning, NY	187,156
15	6.6	North Port-Sarasota, FL	931,788
16	6.7	Albuquerque-Santa Fe-Las Vegas, NM	1,163,966
16	6.7	Sierra Vista-Douglas, AZ	129,473
18	6.9	Burlington-South Burlington, VT	214,796
19	7.0	Fargo-Wahpeton, ND-MN	246,386
19	7.0	Homosassa Springs, FL	139,271
19	7.0	Lakeland-Winter Haven, FL	623,009
19	7.0	Orlando-Deltona-Daytona Beach, FL	2,975,658
23	7.1	Bangor, ME	153,364
23	7.1	Miami-Fort Lauderdale-Port St. Lucie, FL	6,447,610
23	7.1	Tampa-St. Petersburg-Clearwater, FL	2,870,569
23	7.1	Urban Honolulu, HI	983,429

Notes:
1. This list represents cities with the lowest levels of annual PM2.5 air pollution.
2. Cities are ranked by using the highest design value for any county within that metropolitan area.
3. The Design Value is calculated concentration of a pollutant based on the form of the Annual PM2.5 National Ambient Air Quality Standard, and is used by EPA to determine whether the air quality in a county meets the current (2012) standard. (U.S. EPA).

The Cleanest U.S. Cities for Ozone Air Pollution[1]

Metropolitan Statistical Area	Population	Metropolitan Statistical Area	Population
Bellingham, WA	206,353	Medford-Grants Pass, OR	291,851
Bend-Redmond-Prineville, OR	186,769	Missoula, MT	111,807
Bismarck, ND	123,751	Monroe-Ruston-Bastrop, LA	253,035
Blacksburg-Christiansburg-Radford, VA	180,351	Montgomery, AL	373,510
Brownsville-Harlingen-Raymondville, TX	439,197	New Bern-Morehead City, NC	196,091
Brunswick, GA	113,807	Panama City, FL	190,816
Burlington-South Burlington, VT	214,796	Rapid City-Spearfish, SD	166,341
Cape Coral-Fort Myers-Naples, FL	1,000,757	Rochester-Austin, MN	251,180
Charleston-North Charleston, SC	712,220	Rockford-Freeport-Rochelle, IL	443,748
Cheyenne, WY	95,809	Rome-Summerville, GA	120,959
Crestview-Fort Walton Beach-Destin, FL	253,618	Salinas, CA	428,826
Des Moines-Ames-West Des Moines, IA	755,200	Savannah-Hinesville-Statesboro, GA	518,020
Dothan-Enterprise-Ozark, AL	248,513	Sebring, FL	97,616
Eau Claire-Menomonie, WI	208,692	Sioux City-Vermillion, IA-SD-NE	182,649
Elmira-Corning, NY	187,156	Sioux Falls, SD	243,513
Eugene, OR	356,212	Spokane-Spokane Valley-	
Fairbanks, AK	100,436	Coeur d-Alene, WA-ID	679,989
Fargo-Wahpeton, ND-MN	246,386	Steamboat Springs-Craig, CO	36,616
Gadsden, AL	103,931	Tallahassee-Bainbridge, FL-GA	400,614
Gainesville-Lake City, FL	337,925	Tuscaloosa, AL	235,628
Harrisonburg-Staunton-Waynesboro, VA	248,661	Urban Honolulu, HI	983,429
Idaho Falls-Rexburg-Blackfoot, ID	232,740	Utica-Rome, NY	297,766
Ithaca-Cortland, NY	152,593	Waterloo-Cedar Falls, IA	169,484
La Crosse-Onalaska, WI-MN	135,512	Wausau-Stevens Point-	
Lincoln-Beatrice, NE	335,989	Wisconsin Rapids, WI	308,439
Logan, UT-ID	129,763	Williamsport-Lock Have, PA	156,708
McAllen-Edinburg, TX	877,959		

Note:
1. This list represents cities with no monitored ozone air pollution in unhealthful ranges using the Air Quality Index based on 2008 NAAQS.

The Top 25 Cleanest Counties for Year-Round Particle Pollution

2014 Rank[2]	County	State	Design Value[3]
1	Lake	CA	3.8
2	Custer	SD	3.9
3	Yavapai	AZ	4.2
3	Jackson	SD	4.3
3	Essex	NY	4.3
5	Billings	ND	4.4
7	Park	WY	4.6
8	Hancock	ME	4.7
8	San Juan	NM	4.7
10	Laramie	WY	4.8
10	Natrona	WY	4.8
12	Albany	WY	4.9
12	Santa Fe	NM	4.9
14	Ashland	WI	5.1
14	Forest	WI	5.1
16	Coconino	AZ	5.3
16	Teton	WY	5.3
18	Vilas	WI	5.4
19	San Benito	CA	5.5
19	Litchfield	CT	5.5
21	Anchorage Municipality	AK	5.6
22	Sweetwater	WY	5.7
22	Palm Beach	FL	5.7
24	Pima	AZ	5.8
25	Mercer	ND	5.9
25	Missaukee	MI	5.9

Notes:
1. This list represents counties with the lowest levels of monitored long term PM2.5 air pollution.
2. Counties are ranked by Design Value
3. The Design Value is calculated concentration of a pollutant based on the form of the Annual PM2.5 National Ambient Air Quality Standard and is used by EPA to determine whether the air quality in a county meets the current (2012) standard. (U.S. EPA).

US Air Quality Map

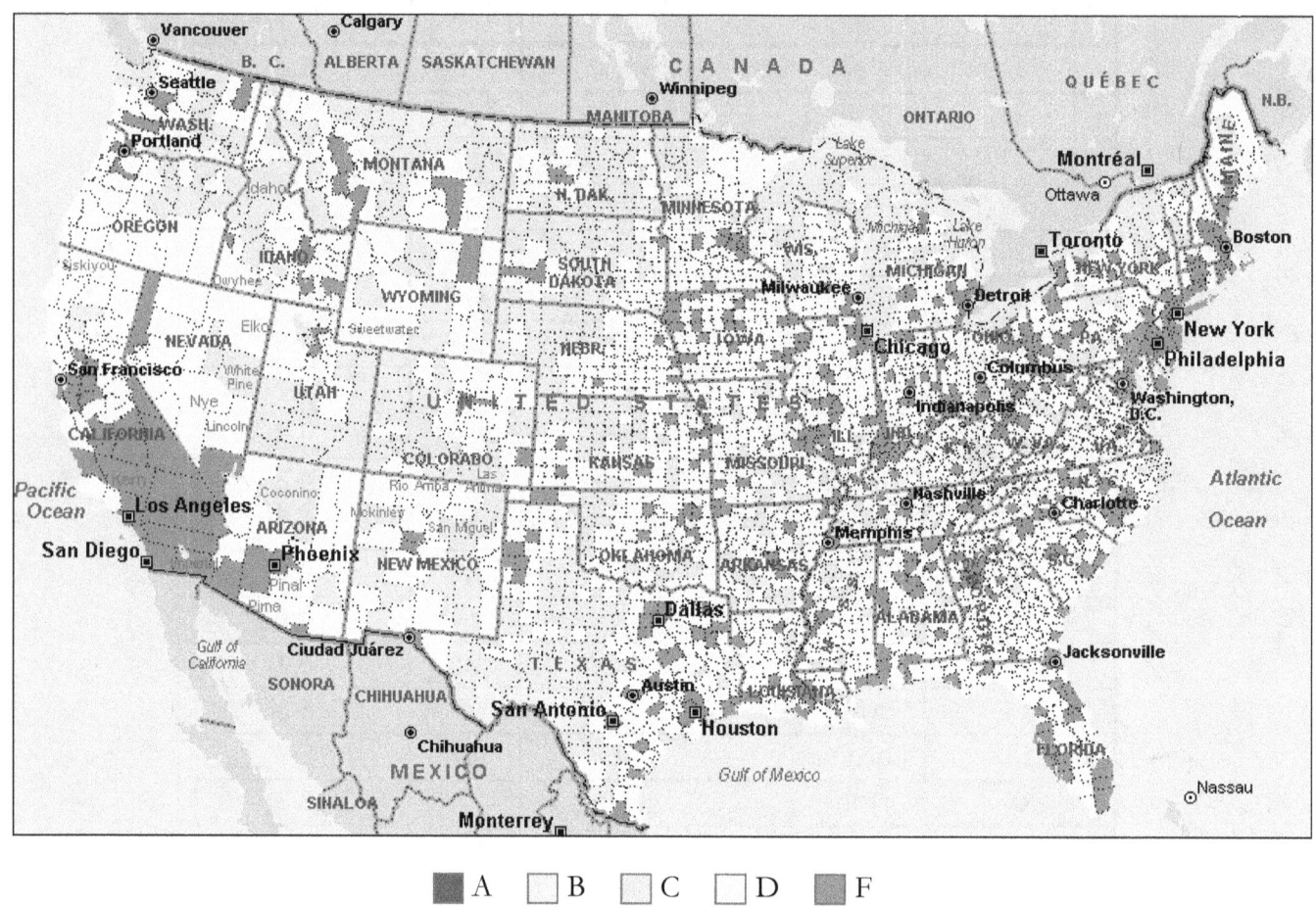

A = Best/Cleanest in the US; F = Worst/Dirtiest in the US.

The Happiest US States

by Jeanna Bryner, Live Science Managing Editor, February 27, 2012

For the third year in a row, the Aloha State gets kudos as the happiest U.S. state, with Hawaii residents scoring highest in the Gallup-Healthways Well-Being Index.

But you don't have to jet to an island for a smile, as North Dakota and Minnesota came in second and third, respectively. West Virginia's residents showed the lowest well-being scores.

Following a trend that has been consistent over the past four years, Western and Midwestern states fared well on the happiness index, accounting for nine of the slots on the top 10 happiest states' list, with Southern states sliding into half of the bottom 10 states.

The 2011 telephone survey was carried out between Jan. 2 and Dec. 29, 2011 and included a random sample of 353,492 adults, ages 18 and older, living in all 50 U.S. states and the District of Columbia. To understand state well-being, Gallup relied on six measures: life evaluation (self-evaluation about your present life situation and anticipated one in five years); emotional health; work environment (such as job satisfaction); physical health; healthy behavior; and basic access (access to health care, a doctor, a safe place to exercise and walk, and community satisfaction).

The entire list with all states listed in order of happiest (#1) to least happiest (#50):

1. Hawaii: 70.2
2. North Dakota: 70.0
3. Minnesota: 69.2
4. Utah: 69.0
5. Alaska: 69.0
6. Colorado: 68.4
7. Kansas: 68.4
8. Nebraska: 68.3
9. New Hampshire: 68.2
10. Montana: 68.0
11. South Dakota: 67.8
12. Vermont: 67.7
13. Maryland: 67.6
14. Virginia: 67.4
15. Iowa: 67.4
16. Massachusetts: 67.4
17. California: 67.3
18. Washington: 67.3
19. Connecticut: 67.2
20. Oregon: 67.1
21. Wyoming: 66.9
22. Wisconsin: 66.9
23. Idaho: 66.9
24. New Mexico: 66.8
25. Maine: 66.7
26. Arizona: 66.6
27. Texas: 66.4
28. Georgia: 66.3
29. New Jersey: 66.2
30. North Carolina: 66.1
31. Pennsylvania: 66.0
32. Illinois: 65.9
33. South Carolina: 65.7
34. New York: 65.7
35. Rhode Island: 65.6
36. Louisiana: 65.5
37. Michigan: 65.3
38. Oklahoma: 65.1
39. Indiana: 65.1
40. Nevada: 65.0
41. Tennessee: 65.0
42. Florida: 64.9
43. Missouri: 64.8
44. Arkansas: 64.7
45. Alabama: 64.6
46. Ohio: 64.5
47. Delaware: 64.2
48. Mississippi: 63.4
49. Kentucky: 63.3
50. West Virginia: 62.3

The Happiest US Cities

by Live Science (http://www.livescience.com) March 26, 2013

A survey called the Gallup-Healthways Well-Being Index reveals which metropolitan regions in the United States are happiest by measuring factors of well-being such as residents' health, job satisfaction, and access to basic necessities.

The results of the 2012 Gallup-Healthways poll, released today (March 26), were consistent with a state-level poll, which found the happiest U.S. states tended to be nestled in the Western and Midwestern parts of the country; the lowest well-being scores clustered in Southern states.

The poll was conducted through telephone interviews of more than 350,000 adults in 189 metropolitan areas, from Jan 2 until Dec. 29, 2012. To measure well-being, Gallup calculated an average of six measures: life evaluation (self-evaluation about present and future life situation); emotional health; work environment (such as job satisfaction); physical health; healthy behavior (such as frequent exercise and less smoking); and basic access (access to health care, a doctor, a safe place to exercise and walk, and community satisfaction). The same measures are used for state well-being.

Top 25 Happiest Ranked Cities

1. Lincoln, Neb.: 72.8
2. Boulder, Colo.: 72.7
3. Burlington-South Burlington, Vt.: 72.4
4. Provo-Orem, Utah: 71.7
5. Fort Collins-Loveland, Colo.: 71.6
6. Barnstable Town, Mass.: 71.5
7. Honolulu, Hawaii: 71.5
8. Ann Arbor, Mich.: 71.4
9. Washington-Arlington-Alexandria, (D.C.-Va.-Md.-W.V.): 71.3
10. San Luis Obispo-Paso Robles, Calif.: 71.2
11. Charlottesville, Va.: 71.1
12. San Francisco-Oakland-Fremont, Calif.: 71.0
13. San Jose-Sunnyvale-Santa Clara, Calif.: 70.8
14. Denver-Aurora, Colo.: 70.4
15. Madison, Wis.: 70.4
16. Minneapolis-St. Paul-Bloomington, Minn.-Wis.: 70.3
17. Bellingham, Wash.: 70.2
18. Raleigh-Cary, N.C.: 70.0
19. Bremerton-Silverdale, Wash.: 70.0
20. Naples-Marco Island, Fla.: 69.9
21. Des Moines-West De Moines, Iowa: 69.9
22. Portland-South Portland-Biddeford, Maine: 69.8
23. Lancaster, Penn.: 69.6
24. Cedar Rapids, Iowa: 69.6
25. Salt Lake City, Utah: 69.5

The 25 Least Happiest Ranked Cities

1. Charleston, W.Va.: 60.8
2. Huntington-Ashland, W.Va.-Ky.-Ohio: 61.2
3. Mobile, Ala.: 62.4
4. Beaumont-Port Arthur, Texas: 62.5
5. Hickory-Lenoir-Morganton, N.C.: 62.7
6. Fort Smith, Ark.-Okla.: 62.9
7. Bakersfield, Calif.: 63.1
8. Rockford, Ill.: 63.1
9. Spartanburg, S.C.: 63.4
10. Utica-Rome, N.Y.: 63.4
11. Binghamton, N.Y.: 63.5
12. Corpus Christi, Texas: 63.5
13. Chattanooga, Tenn.-Ga.: 63.5
14. McAllen-Edinburgh-Mission, Texas: 63.7
15. Redding, Calif.: 63.7
16. Yakima, Wash.: 63.8
17. Topeka, Kan.: 63.8
18. Pensacola-Ferry Pass-Brent, Fla.: 64.0
19. Dayton, Ohio: 64.0
20. Shreveport-Bossier City, La.: 64.2
21. Hagerstown-Martinsburg, Md.-W.Va.: 64.3
22. Scranton-Wilkes-Barre, Penn.: 64.4
23. Stockton, Calif.: 64.5
24. Youngstown-Warren-Boardman, Ohio-Penn.: 64.5
25. Palm Bay-Melbourne-Titusville, Fla.: 64.6

Prime Farm Land & Agriculture in the United States

Concentration of important organic matter found in the soil.

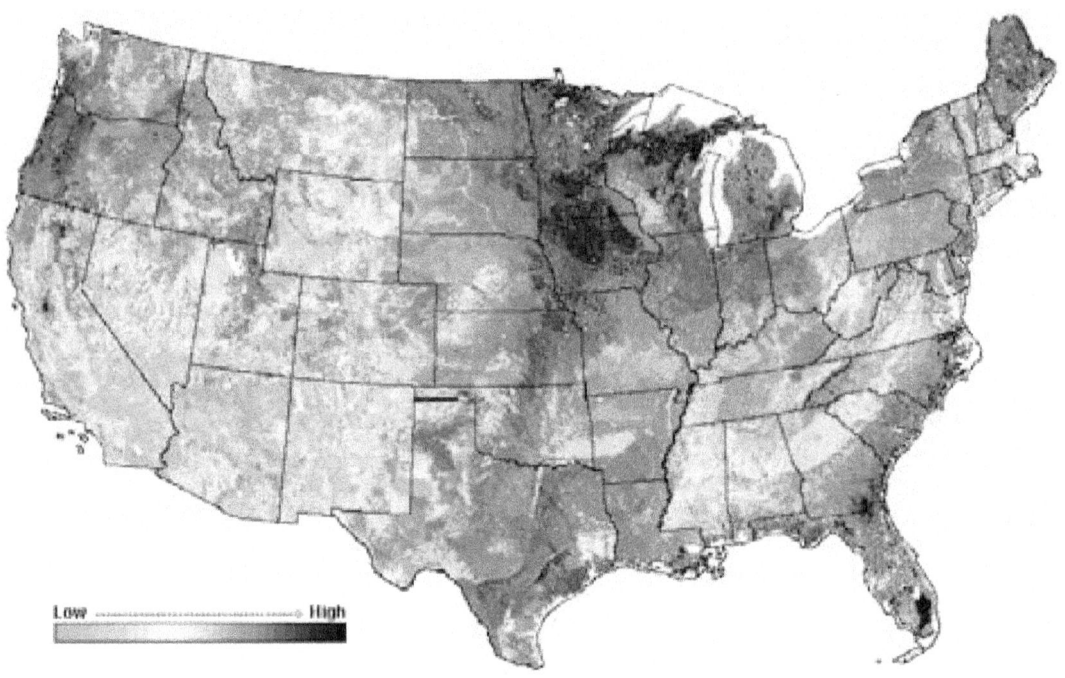

Naturally occurring soil moisture in the United States

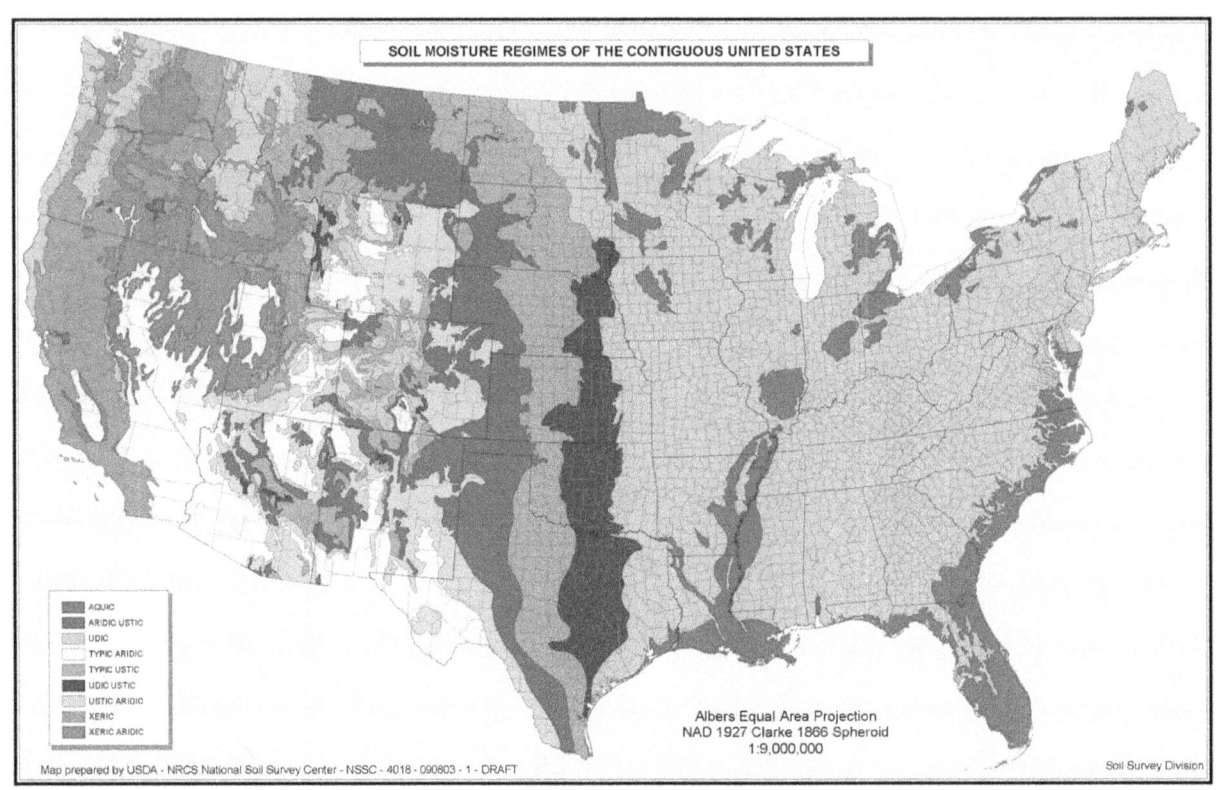

UN/FAO Soils Map of the U.S.
Soils Ranked by FCC Limiting Factors

ABOVE: A soils map of the United States created from the United Nations Food and Agriculture Organization digital soils map of the world. Soils are classified by their number of agronomic limiting factors. Soils with a high number of limiting factors are problematic and require remediation for agricultural production. The best soils for agriculture have no or few limiting factors.

Distribution of Land Uses in the Contiguous United States

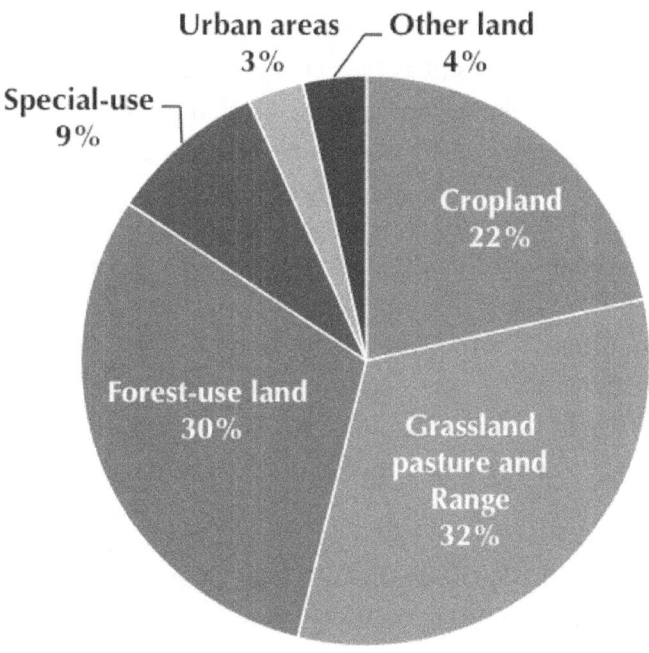

Map of Vegetable Production in the Contiguous United States

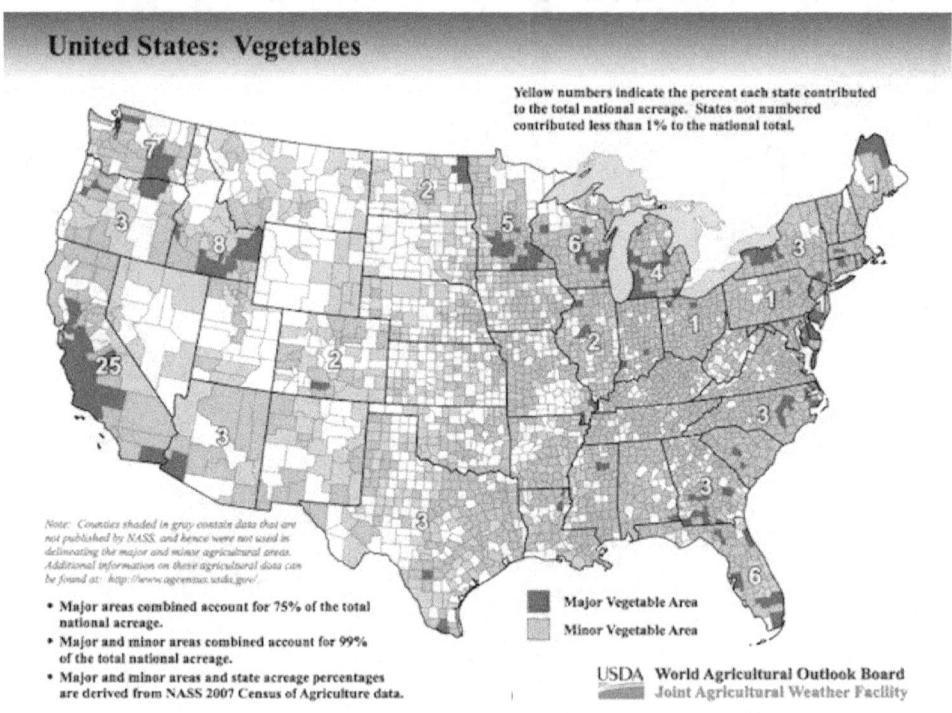

Foreign Owned Farmland

Another disturbing practice, occurring at an exponential rate over the last decade, is the purchase of real estate by foreign countries and companies. A slew of foreigners — primarily Chinese state corporations and Gulf sheiks— are buying up farmland throughout the world at an accelerated pace to acquire as much precious soil, farmland, and water as possible. This phenomenon is known as "land grabbing," This practice displaces family farms and drives up food costs. Large companies and foreign countries are rapidly obtaining the ability to control food supply and distribution. The economic outlook of forthcoming higher food prices in the near future is alarming.

Data shows that this troubling trend, of foreign governments with trillion dollar budgets and large foreign corporate companies with million dollar budgets, purchasing enormous amounts of precious limited farmland. Although this has been occurring since the 70's it has been increasing at an exponential rate over the past decade. For instance, in 2011 foreign ownership of agricultural land increased by 1,490,781 acres in the United States alone. Unfortunately, most American's are ill-informed about this issue, and so many other critical matters, due to mainstream media's continued failure to truly and accurate inform the public on important issues.

The USDA released a report in 2013 (most recent report as of this writing) detailing foreign holdings of U.S. agricultural land as of December 2011. "Foreign persons" are defined as individuals who are not citizens of the U.S., foreign businesses and governments that have their principal place of business in a foreign country and U.S. entities in which there is a significant foreign interest. The report showed that foreign investors held an interest in 25.7 million acres of U.S. agricultural land (forest land and farmland) as of December 31, 2011. This is an increase of approximately 1.5 million acres from December 31, 2010.

The report also stated that foreign persons have reported acreage holdings in all 50 States and Puerto Rico. Forest land accounted for 54 percent of all foreign held agricultural acreage, cropland for 19 percent, and pasture and other agricultural land for 27 percent. Together, 9,511,437 acres or 36 percent of foreign-held acres are owned by individuals or entities from these countries. Foreign entities are also buying up critical farmland and water source acreage in enormous quantities in Mexico, Central America, South America, Caribbean, Asia, and Africa. Again, the pace and amount of land being grabbed is astonishing and truly disturbing.

As of 2013 "water grabbing" by corporations amounted to 454 billion cubic meters per year globally. Cooperate and foreign investors from seven countries – the United States, United Arab Emirates, India, United Kingdom, Egypt, China and Israel – accounted for 60 percent of the water acquired under these deals.

Between 2000 and 2012 nearly two-thirds of the land being purchased was in Eastern Africa and Southeast Asia. During this period over 205 million acres of land were been purchased by foreigners and large corporations. About 62 percent of these deals were in Africa, totaling about 138 million acres. In September 2010 the World Bank, showed that over 460,000 square kilometers (180,000 sq mi) or 46,000,000 hectares (110,000,000 acres) in large-scale farmland acquisitions or negotiations were announced between October 2008 and August 2009 alone. More than one economist has stated that China is buying Africa to feed its rapidly growing population.

These large land grabs push out small farmers and destabilizes the local economy. In Sudan, for instance, the local population is becoming increasingly dependent on food aid and international food subsidies because the land grabbers are pushing out small farmers, and the produce being harvested is shipped to markets in other parts of the world. Evidence also shows that these large land grabs lead to lost natural ecosystems, as a result of farming at such a large commercial scale. Another problem resulting from these land grabs is the large-scale displacement of local peoples without adequate compensation, in either land or money. These displacements often result in resettlement in marginal lands, loss of livelihoods especially in the case of pastoralists, and the erosion of social networks. Lastly, the reduction of available land drives up land prices and is going to make it all the more difficult for the average person to afford real estate.

Some examples for foreign corporate land purchases include the company Cargill purchased 775,000 acres of Brazil's valuable soybean farmland. Nile Trading and Development purchase of 1,482,632 acres of east Africa's rich farmland. BHP Billiton, a large mining company, purchase of 877,000 acres in Indonesia. Ted Turner of AOL and CNN fame, purchase of 111,000 acres in Argentina. The South Korean corporation Daewoo purchase of 1.3 million hectares, half of all Madagascar's agricultural land, to produce corn and palm oil. This is just a small fraction of some of the land grab transactions.

Average Dollar Value of Agriculture Products Sold

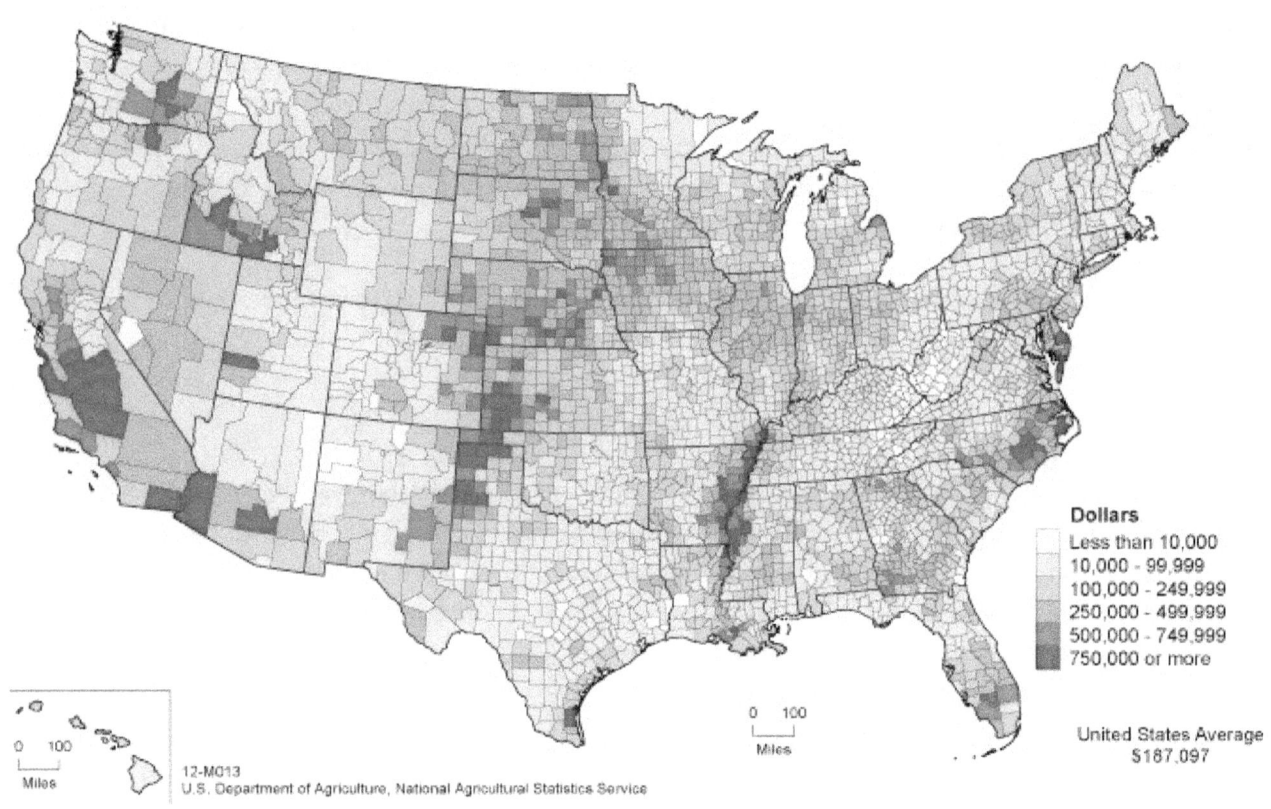

Map of Farmland Rented or Leased in United States

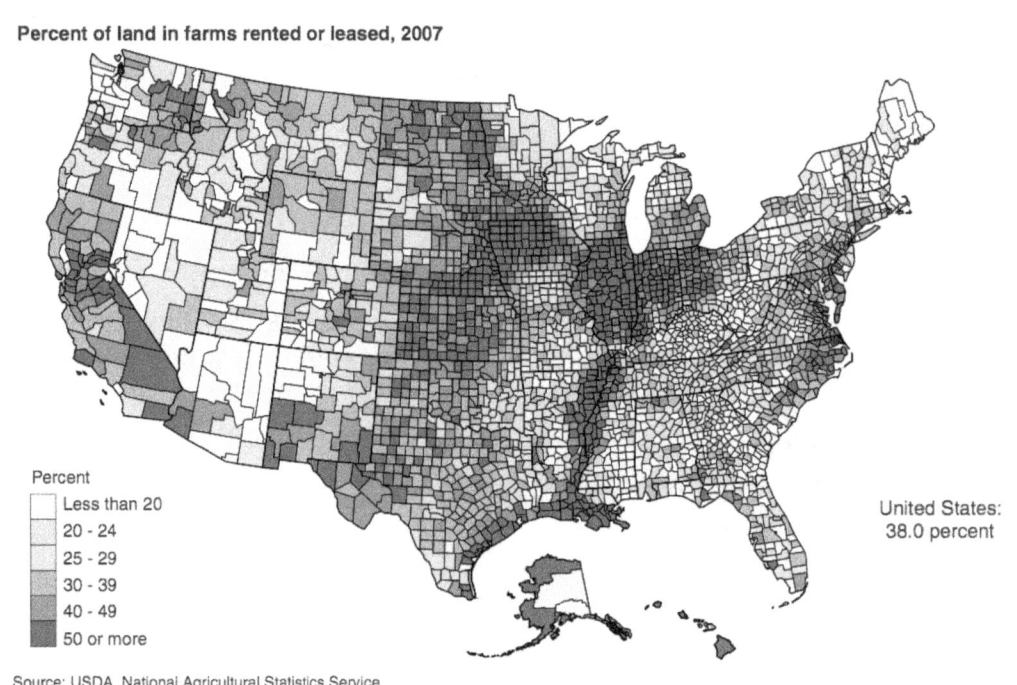

Map showing the average price per acre in the USA (2009)

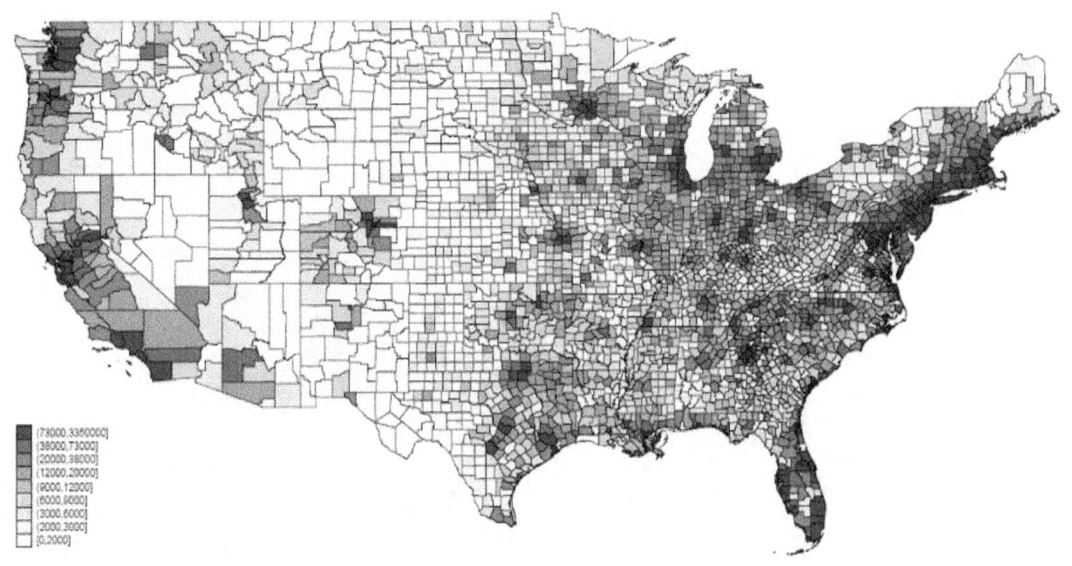

US Hardiness Zone Map for Plants

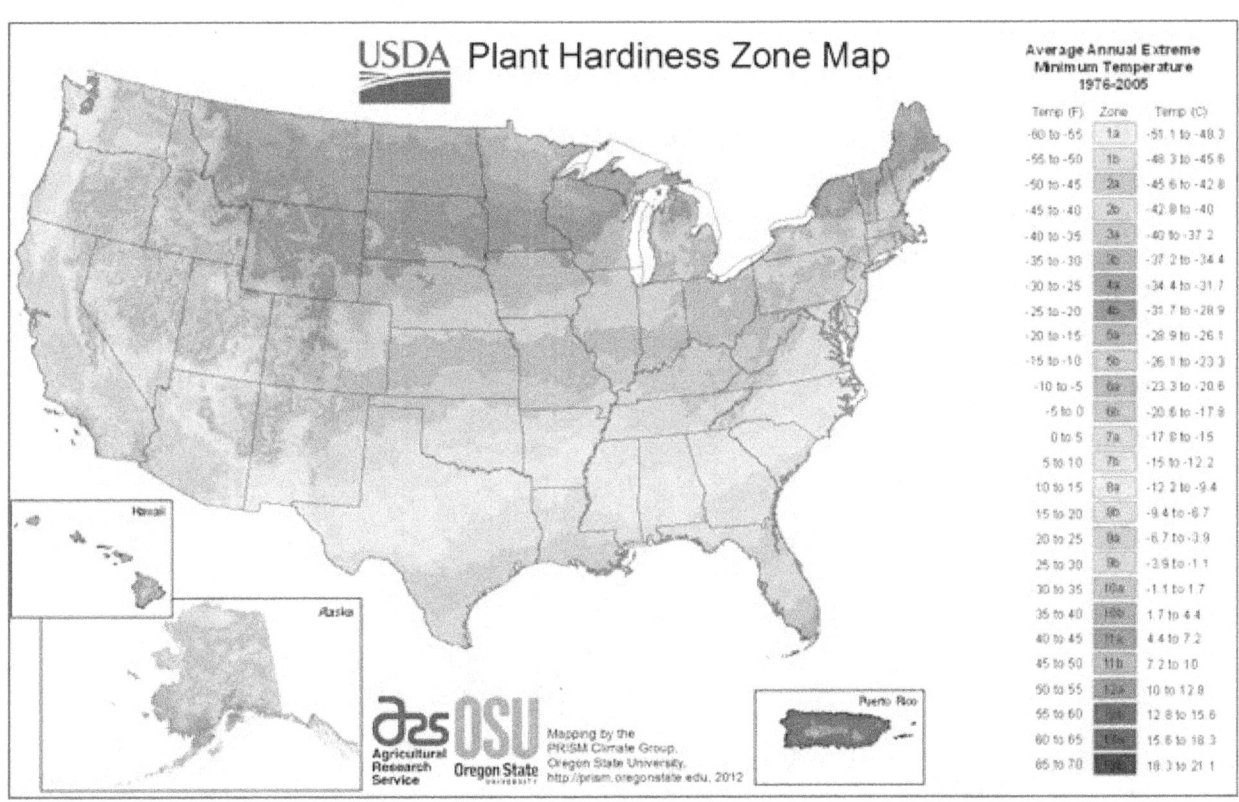

Precipitation Map of the United States (Annual Average)

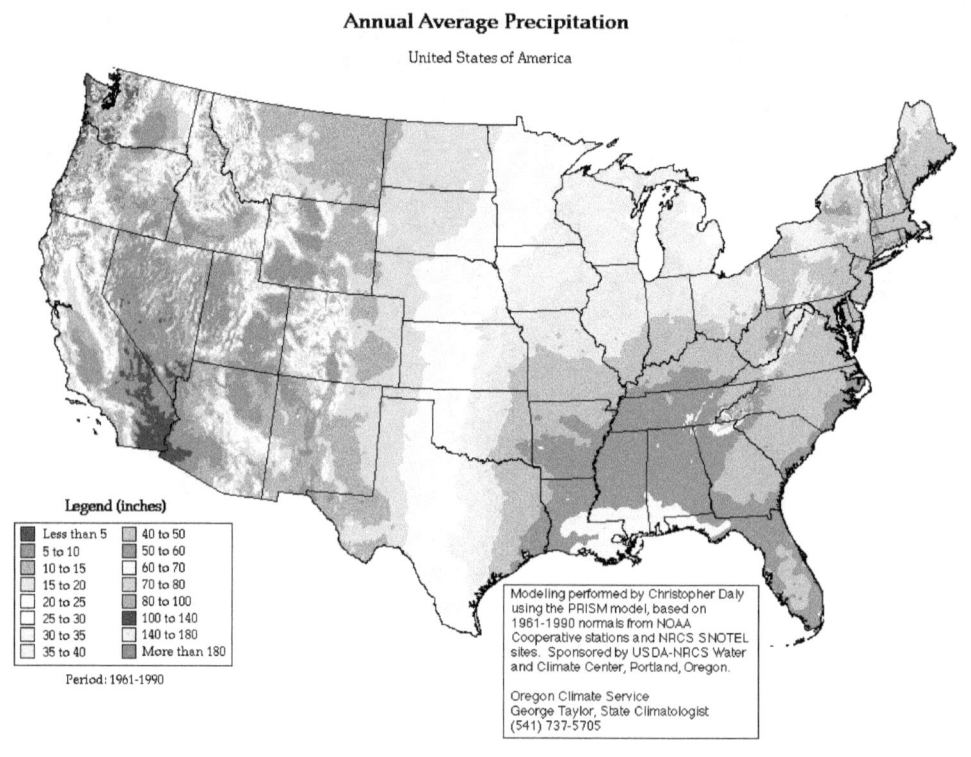

Obese Adult Population of States

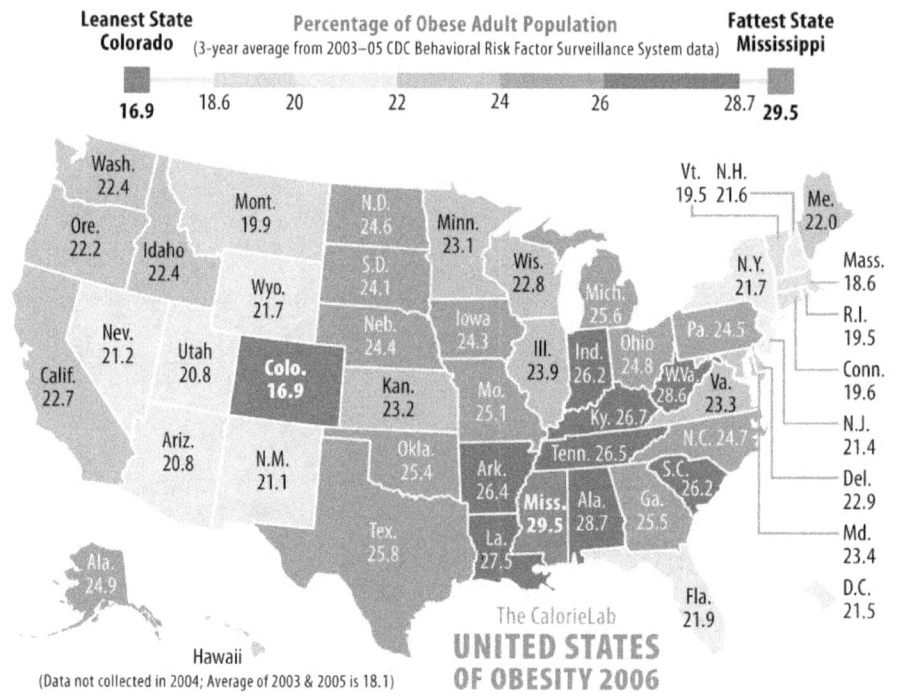

Earthquake Hazard Location Potential in the United States

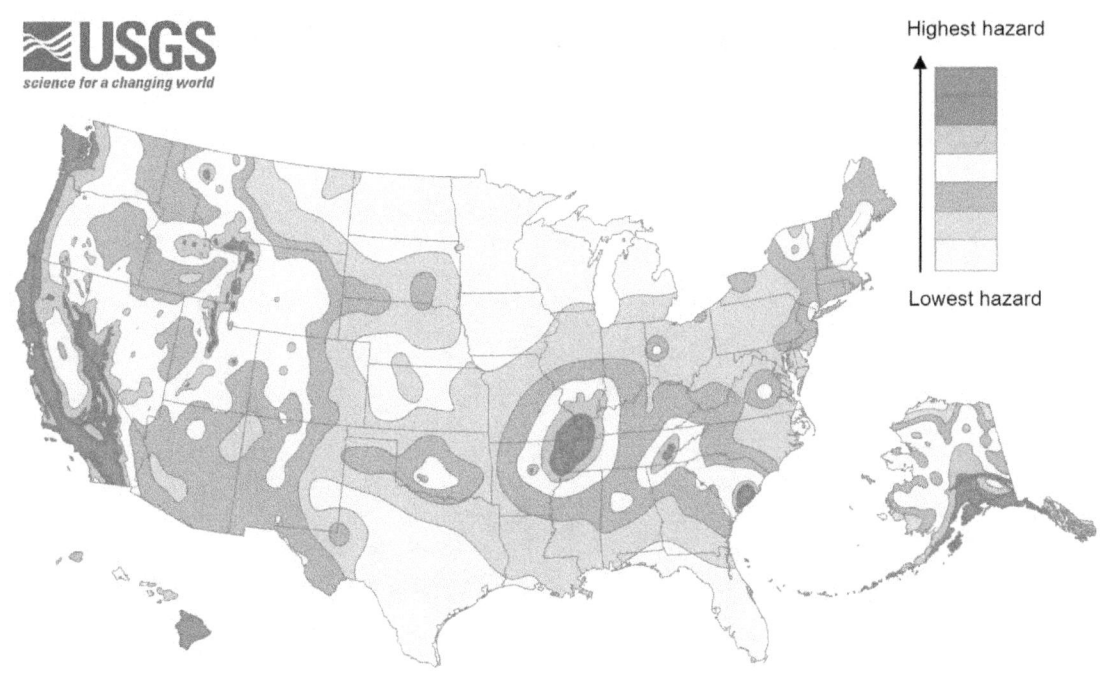

Tornado Activity 1950-1995 Map.

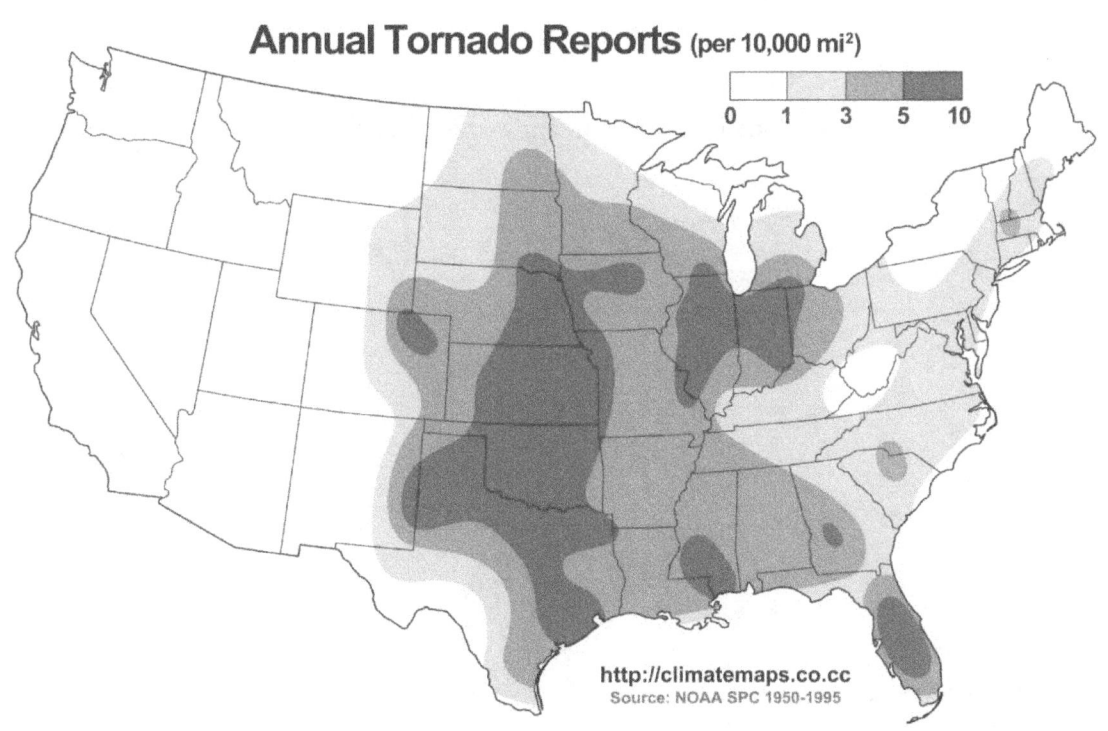

Hurricane Activity Map Showing Locations of Highest Probability

Hurricane Activity Locations

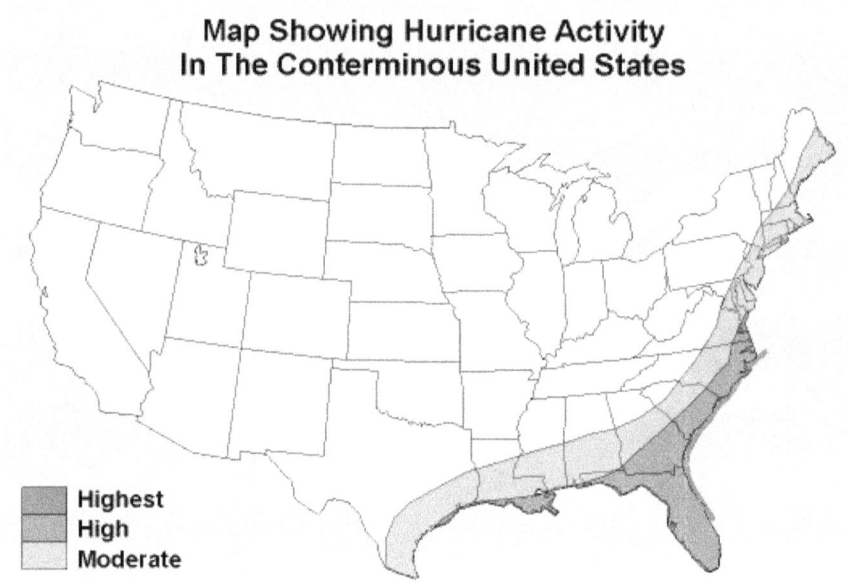

Combined Highest Probability of Hurricane, Tornado, and Earthquake Hazards Map

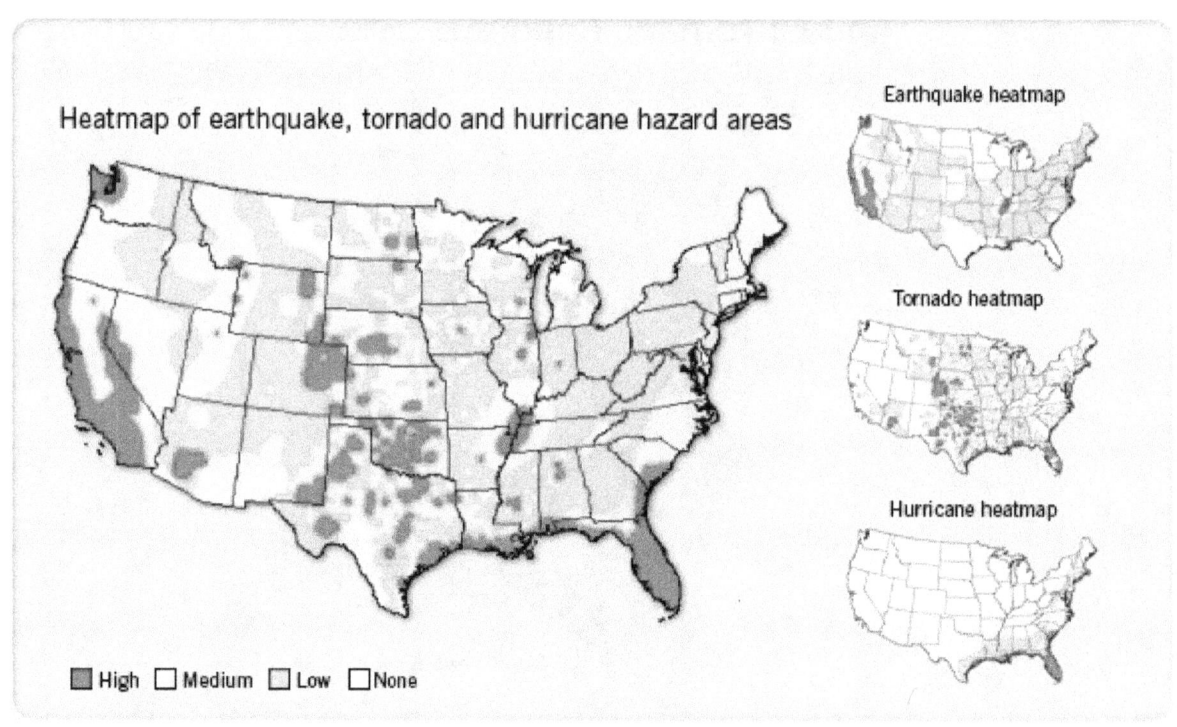

Lightning Density

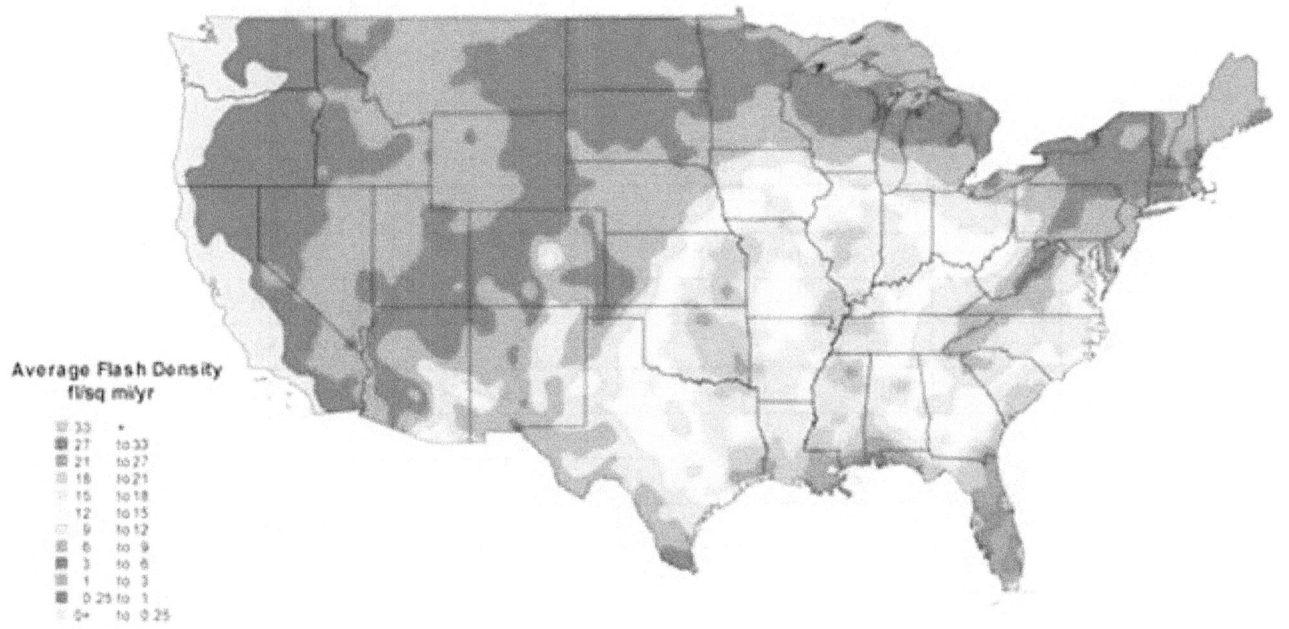

State Shame (Worst Aspect of Each State)

Most Walkable Cities

The following cities with a population of 200,000 or greater were ranked by 'WalkScore' in 2016 as being the most walk-friendly cities in the United States. Walk Score is available for any address in the United States, Canada, and Australia. Walk Score also ranked the largest 3,000 cities and over 10,000 neighborhoods so you can find a walkable home or apartment. https://www.walkscore.com/cities-and-neighborhoods/ The best ranked walking city is New York, ranked as #1.

Rank	City	State	Population
1	New York	NY	8,175,133
2	Los Angeles	CA	3,792,621
3	Chicago	IL	2,695,598
4	Houston	TX	2,099,451
5	Philadelphia	PA	1,526,006
6	Phoenix	AZ	1,445,632
7	San Antonio	TX	1,327,407
8	San Diego	CA	1,307,402
9	Dallas	TX	1,197,816
10	San Jose	CA	945,942
11	Jacksonville	FL	821,784
12	Indianapolis	IN	820,445
13	San Francisco	CA	805,235
14	Austin	TX	790,390
15	Columbus	OH	787,033
16	Fort Worth	TX	741,206
17	Charlotte	NC	731,424
18	Detroit	MI	713,777
19	El Paso	TX	649,121
20	Memphis	TN	646,889
21	Baltimore	MD	620,961
22	Boston	MA	617,594
23	Seattle	WA	608,660
24	Washington D.C.	DC	601,723
25	Nashville-Davidson	TN	601,222
26	Denver	CO	600,158
27	Louisville-Jefferson	KY	597,337
28	Milwaukee	WI	594,833
29	Portland	OR	583,776
30	Las Vegas	NV	583,756
31	Oklahoma City	OK	579,999
32	Albuquerque	NM	545,852

33	Tucson	AZ	520,116
34	Fresno	CA	494,665
35	Sacramento	CA	466,488
36	Long Beach	CA	462,257
37	Kansas City	MO	459,787
38	Mesa	AZ	439,041
39	Virginia Beach	VA	437,994
40	Atlanta	GA	420,003
41	Colorado Springs	CO	416,427
42	Omaha	NE	408,958
43	Raleigh	NC	403,892
44	Miami	FL	399,457
45	Cleveland	OH	396,815
46	Tulsa	OK	391,906
47	Oakland	CA	390,724
48	Minneapolis	MN	382,578
49	Wichita	KS	382,368
50	Arlington	TX	365,438
51	Bakersfield	CA	347,483
52	New Orleans	LA	343,829
53	Honolulu	HI	337,256
54	Anaheim	CA	336,265
55	Tampa	FL	335,709
56	Aurora	CO	325,078
57	Santa Ana	CA	324,528
58	St. Louis	MO	319,294
59	Pittsburgh	PA	305,704
60	Corpus Christi	TX	305,215
61	Riverside	CA	303,871
62	Cincinnati	OH	296,943
63	Lexington-Fayette	KY	295,803
64	Anchorage	AK	291,826
65	Stockton	CA	291,707
66	Toledo	OH	287,208
67	St. Paul	MN	285,068
68	Newark	NJ	277,140
69	Greensboro	NC	269,666
70	Buffalo	NY	261,310
71	Plano	TX	259,841
72	Lincoln	NE	258,379
73	Henderson	NV	257,729

continued

74	Fort Wayne	IN	253,691
75	Jersey City	NJ	247,597
76	St. Petersburg	FL	244,769
77	Chula Vista	CA	243,916
78	Norfolk	VA	242,803
79	Orlando	FL	238,300
80	Chandler	AZ	236,123
81	Laredo	TX	236,091
82	Madison	WI	233,209
83	Winston-Salem	NC	229,617
84	Lubbock	TX	229,573
85	Baton Rouge	LA	229,493
86	Durham	NC	228,330
87	Garland	TX	226,876
88	Glendale	AZ	226,721
89	Reno	NV	225,221
90	Hialeah	FL	224,669
91	Paradise	NV	223,167
92	Chesapeake	VA	222,209
93	Scottsdale	AZ	217,385
94	North Las Vegas	NV	216,961
95	Irving	TX	216,290
96	Fremont	CA	214,089
97	Irvine	CA	212,375
98	Birmingham	AL	212,237
99	Rochester	NY	210,565
100	San Bernardino	CA	209,924
101	Spokane	WA	208,916
102	Gilbert	AZ	208,453
103	Arlington	VA	207,627
104	Montgomery	AL	205,764
105	Boise City	ID	205,671
106	Richmond	VA	204,214
107	Des Moines	IA	203,433
108	Fayetteville	NC	200,564

10 Cities for Real Estate Bargains

By US News Money Report based upon Moody's Economy.com research

Homes in the following locations are undervalued when compared with their longer-term averages. As a result, some very good bargains on real estate can be achieved.

1. Memphis
2. Salinas, California
3. Medford, Oregon
4. Washington D.C.
5. Mobile, Ala.
6. Las Cruces, N.M.
7. Fayetteville, N.C
8. Phoenix
9. Fort Worth/Arlington, Texas
10. Cincinnati

Best Affordable Places to Live

Livability explores what makes small-to-medium sized cities great places to live. Their research examines community amenities, education, sustainability, transportation, housing and the economy. LIVABILITY.COM

What follows isn't merely a list of the cheapest places to live in America. Instead, these 10 cities are less expensive than most but still great places to live by all usual metrics (year 2015).

To find these cities, Livability looked at cost of living across a number of categories such health care, food, housing, and transportation using data from C2ER and the U.S. Department of Housing and Urban Development. They also examined the tax climate in the state. Then they assigned a value score. Sure, there are some cheaper places to live. But these are cities where most people can afford to live and would still want to live.

Rank	City	State
1	RoundRock	TX
2	Dayton	OH
3	Lawton	OK
4	Lansing	MI
5	Appleton	WI
6	Fort Wayne	IN
7	Rochester	MN
8	Nampa	ID
9	Topeka	KS
10	Cedar Rapids	IA

10 Best Places to Raise a Family

Many of the key reasons Americans move revolve around doing what's best for their families. The communities we choose to live in as we raise children are arguably the most important, as they tend to be some of the places we live the longest. Thus, in 2016 Livability created this 10 Best Cities for Families list to offer some great examples of metros that truly stand out as great places to raise your kids.

Liveability looked at the quality of the schools, the crime rate, and measures of the quality of healthcare and economy. They gave points to communities that are walkable, diverse, have lots of parks and active children's sections in their libraries. They favored communities with shorter commute times (so working parents can be home more and on the road less) and larger populations of other kids to play with. You can check out more information on each of these 10 cities – and thousands more – on Livability.com.

Rank	City	State
1	Rockville	MD
2	Chandler	AZ
3	Newton	MA
4	Holland	MI
5	Chula Vista	CA
6	Oak Park	IL
7	St. George	UT
8	Hollywood	AL
9	Bowling Green	OH
10	Palo Alto	CA

Best & Worst State Capitals (2016)

WalletHub's analysts compared the 50 state capitals to identify which among them combines the best of everything an ideal city has to offer: affordability, a strong economy, high education standards and overall excellent quality of life. Our data set of 35 key metrics ranges from cost of living to K–12 school-system quality to number of attractions. For more information and other rankings check out: www.WalletHub.com

By Affordability, Economic Well-being, Education, and Quality of Life

Overall Rank	City	State Capital Index	'Affordability' Rank	'Economic Well-Being' Rank	'Education & Health' Rank	'Quality of Life' Rank
1	Austin, TX	65.43	11	2	5	18
2	Lincoln, NE	65.34	4	8	3	20
3	Bismarck, ND	64.73	10	1	6	42
4	Madison, WI	63.78	26	12	1	8
5	Raleigh, NC	62.42	3	5	19	23
6	Boise, ID	61.07	9	24	11	14
7	Montpelier, VT	60.18	25	15	4	19
8	Pierre, SD	59.84	14	32	2	44
9	Helena, MT	59.52	19	7	30	15
10	Columbus, OH	59.38	12	14	10	22
11	Des Moines, IA	58.70	8	19	14	27
12	Olympia, WA	58.23	24	36	17	1
13	Denver, CO	57.91	38	3	31	6
14	Salt Lake City, UT	57.77	28	30	16	4
15	Nashville, TN	57.46	21	4	25	28
16	Atlanta, GA	57.18	31	33	13	5
17	Cheyenne, WY	56.07	2	10	40	37
18	Jefferson City, MO	55.41	6	22	35	34
19	Annapolis, MD	55.26	34	18	27	10
20	Topeka, KS	55.22	13	25	23	41
21	Oklahoma City, OK	55.19	5	6	43	47
22	Juneau and, AK	53.90	27	17	20	46
23	St. Paul, MN	53.83	36	21	9	25
24	Springfield, IL	53.39	1	31	42	38
25	Concord, NH	52.93	41	11	8	45
26	Columbia, SC	52.81	29	42	34	7
27	Phoenix, AZ	52.50	22	27	33	32
28	Tallahassee, FL	51.61	37	46	12	17
29	Charleston, WV	50.98	7	13	49	48
30	Lansing, MI	50.73	18	40	32	39
31	Augusta, ME	50.70	39	23	28	29
32	Santa Fe, NM	50.64	35	38	41	2
33	Richmond, VA	50.56	33	26	46	12
34	Indianapolis, IN	49.86	17	34	37	43
35	Albany, NY	49.66	46	43	15	11
36	Salem, OR	49.57	40	28	29	30
37	Frankfort, KY	49.53	15	29	47	35
38	Sacramento, CA	49.21	44	41	26	13
39	Little Rock, AR	48.72	16	20	44	50
40	Harrisburg, PA	48.65	42	39	36	9
41	Boston, MA	47.54	48	16	7	16
42	Baton Rouge, LA	46.83	30	35	45	36

continued

43	Dover, DE	46.81	32	44	39	26
44	Honolulu, HI	46.35	50	9	18	3
45	Trenton, NJ	45.60	43	50	22	33
46	Providence, RI	44.54	47	37	24	21
47	Jackson, MS	43.08	23	48	48	49
48	Montgomery, AL	42.85	20	49	50	40
49	Carson City, NV	42.03	45	47	38	24
50	Hartford, CT	39.47	49	45	21	31

America's 50 Greenest Cities

Popular Science used raw data from the U.S. Census Bureau and the National Geographic Society's Green Guide, which collected survey data and government statistics for American cities of over 100,000 people in more than 30 categories, including air quality, electricity use and transportation habits. They then compiled these statistics into four broad categories, each scored out of either 5 or 10 possible points. The sum of these four scores determines a city's place in the rankings. The categories are:

- **Electricity (E; 10 points):** Cities score points for drawing their energy from renewable sources such as wind, solar, biomass and hydroelectric power, as well as for offering incentives for residents to invest in their own power sources, like roof-mounted solar panels.
- **Transportation (T; 10 points):** High scores go to cities whose commuters take public transportation or carpool. Air quality also plays a role.
- **Green living (G; 5 points):** Cities earn points for the number of buildings certified by the U.S. Green Building Council, as well as for devoting area to green space, such as public parks and nature preserves.
- **Recycling and green perspective (R; 5 points):** This measures how comprehensive a city's recycling program is (if the city collects old electronics, for example) and how important its citizens consider environmental issues.

NOTE: Just because a city is ranked high as being a 'green' city doesn't necessarily mean that it is a healthy city. For instance, several of the top 50 green cities have very poor air quality.

1. Portland, Ore. 23.1

Electricity: 7.1 Transportation: 6.4 Green Living: 4.8 Recycling/Perspective: 4.8

America's top green city has it all: Half its power comes from renewable sources, a quarter of the workforce commutes by bike, carpool or public transportation, and it has 35 buildings certified by the U.S. Green Building Council.

2. San Francisco, Calif. 23.0

Electricity: 6.8 Transportation: 8.8 Green Living: 3.5 Recycling/Perspective: 3.9

3. Boston, Mass. 22.7

Electricity: 5.7 Transportation: 8.7 Green Living: 3.4 Recycling/Perspective: 4.9

CASE STUDY: Grass Power

Boston has preliminary plans for a plant that would turn 50,000 tons of fall color into power and fertilizer. The facility would first separate yard clippings into grass and leaves. Anaerobic bacteria feeding on the grass would make enough methane to power at least 1.5 megawatts' worth of generators, while heat and agitation would hasten the breakdown of leaves and twigs into compost.

4. Oakland, Calif. 22.5

Electricity: 7.0 Transportation: 7.5 Green Living: 3.1 Recycling/Perspective: 4.9

5. Eugene, Ore. 22.4

Electricity: 10.0 Transportation: 4.7 Green Living: 2.9 Recycling/Perspective: 4.8

CATEGORY LEADER: Electricity

Much of the wet Pacific Northwest draws its energy from hydroelectric dams. But Eugene draws an additional 9 percent of its municipal electricity from wind farms. It also buys back excess power from residents who install solar panel

6. Cambridge, Mass. 22.2

Electricity: 6.1 Transportation: 7.5 Green Living: 3.9 Recycling/Perspective: 4.7

7. Berkeley, Calif. 22.2

Electricity: 6.2 Transportation: 8.4 Green Living: 2.9 Recycling/Perspective: 4.7

8. Seattle, Wash. 22.1

Electricity: 6.2 Transportation: 7.3 Green Living: 4.7 Recycling/Perspective: 3.9

9. Chicago, Ill. 21.3

Electricity: 5.4 Transportation: 7.3 Green Living: 5.0 Recycling/Perspective: 3.6

CATEGORY LEADER: Green Space

In addition to the 12,000 acres Chicago has devoted to public parks and waterfront space, the U.S. Green Building Council has awarded four city projects with a "Platinum" rating, its highest award.

10. Austin, Tex. 21.0

Electricity: 6.9 Transportation: 5.9 Green Living: 3.3 Recycling/Perspective: 4.9

11. Minneapolis, Minn. 20.3

Electricity: 7.8 Transportation: 7.4 Green Living: 2.8 Recycling/Perspective: 2.3

CASE STUDY: Citizen Enviro-Grants

If you've got a world-saving idea, the City of Lakes will give you, your church or your community group the money to get it done. Twenty $1,000 mini-grants and five $10,000 awards were distributed last year to programs ranging from household power-consumption monitors to "block club talks" about global warming. A similar initiative has sprung up in Seattle.

12. St. Paul, Minn. 20.2

Electricity: 8.0 Transportation: 4.0 Green Living: 3.5 Recycling/Perspective: 4.7

13. Sunnyvale, Calif. 19.9

Electricity: 7.3 Transportation: 6.8 Green Living: 2.2 Recycling/Perspective: 3.6

14. Honolulu, Hawaii 19.9

Electricity: 6.0 Transportation: 7.8 Green Living: 2.6 Recycling/Perspective: 3.5

15. Fort Worth, Tex. 19.7

Electricity: 8.3 Transportation: 4.6 Green Living: 2.4 Recycling/Perspective: 4.4

16. Albuquerque, N.M. 19.1

Electricity: 7.6 Transportation: 5.5 Green Living: 2.4 Recycling/Perspective: 3.6

17. Syracuse, N.Y. 18.9

Electricity: 7.0 Transportation: 4.9 Green Living: 2.6 Recycling/Perspective: 4.4

18. Huntsville, Ala. 18.4

Electricity: 6.2 Transportation: 4.1 Green Living: 3.6 Recycling/Perspective: 4.5

19. Denver, Colo. 18.2

Electricity: 5.9 Transportation: 5.2 Green Living: 3.0 Recycling/Perspective: 4.1

CASE STUDY: Green Concrete

Fly ash, a by-product of coal-burning power plants, usually ends up in landfills. Researchers at the University of Colorado Denver found a way to reuse this industrial by-product. They add it at concentrations of about 20 percent to a new green concrete mix. The addition of fly ash also reduces the amount of sulfur- and carbon-spewing concrete production needed to finish a job. The mayor has signed an executive order requiring the use of green concrete in new city projects, and a $550-million infrastructure bond makes demand for the mix likely to grow.

20. New York, N.Y. 18.2

Electricity: 2.8 Transportation: 10.0 Green Living: 3.4 Recycling/Perspective: 2.0

CATEGORY LEADER: Transportation

More than 54 percent of New Yorkers take public transportation to work, beating the next-best metropolis, Washington, D.C., by 17 percent.

21. Irvine, Calif. 18.1

Electricity: 4.2 Transportation: 6.8 Green Living: 2.9 Recycling/Perspective: 4.2

22. Milwaukee, Wis. 17.3

Electricity: 5.0 Transportation: 4.9 Green Living: 3.1 Recycling/Perspective: 4.3

23. Santa Rosa, Calif. 17.2

Electricity: 7.0 Transportation: 3.4 Green Living: 2.4 Recycling/Perspective: 4.4

24. Ann Arbor, Mich. 17.2

Electricity: 4.6 Transportation: 4.8 Green Living: 2.9 Recycling/Perspective: 4.9

25. Lexington, Ky. 16.8

Electricity: 5.9 Transportation: 3.6 Green Living: 2.3 Recycling/Perspective: 5.0

CATEGORY LEADER: Recycling and green perspective

Lexingtonians recycle everything from surplus electronics to scrap metal, and they listed the environment as their third most important concern (behind only employment and public safety)—the highest ranking in the study.

26. Tulsa, Okla. 16.7

Electricity: 5.0 Transportation: 3.9 Green Living: 3.4 Recycling/Perspective: 4.4

27. Rochester, N.Y. 16.1

Electricity: 4.5 Transportation: 4.4 Green Living: 3.1 Recycling/Perspective: 4.1

28. Riverside, Calif. 16.0

Electricity: 7.5 Transportation: 3.1 Green Living: 2.1 Recycling/Perspective: 3.3

29. Springfield, Ill. 15.7

Electricity: 5.3 Transportation: 3.0 Green Living: 3.2 Recycling/Perspective: 4.2

30. Alexandria, Va. 15.7

Electricity: 2.7 Transportation: 6.3 Green Living: 3.1 Recycling/Perspective: 3.6

31. St. Louis, Mo. 15.0

Electricity: 2.7 Transportation: 5.0 Green Living: 3.7 Recycling/Perspective: 3.6

32. Anchorage, Alaska 14.4

Electricity: 2.7 Transportation: 4.7 Green Living: 2.1 Recycling/Perspective: 4.9

CASE STUDY: Power-Saving Streetlights

Since Anchorage spends a good part of the year buried under highly reflective snow, it doesn't make sense to keep the street lamps at full bore when moonlight can do the job. The fix? Install citywide dimmers. On top of that, the city is planning to upgrade its 16,000 streetlamps to either LED or induction bulbs, depending on the results of computer simulations designed to find the type of light that helps humans see best and disturbs wildlife the least. The swap should be complete by year's end, and the initial $5-million investment is expected to save up to $3 million in energy costs annually.

33. Athens-Clarke, Ga. 14.1

Electricity: 2.4 Transportation: 4.7 Green Living: 3.2 Recycling/Perspective: 3.8

34. Amarillo, Tex. 14.0

Electricity: 5.2 Transportation: 2.9 Green Living: 2.3 Recycling/Perspective: 3.6

35. Kansas City, Mo. 13.8

Electricity: 2.7 Transportation: 3.7 Green Living: 2.7 Recycling/Perspective: 4.7

36. Salt Lake City, Utah 13.5

Electricity: 3.6 Transportation: 4.1 Green Living: 2.3 Recycling/Perspective: 3.5

37. Pasadena, Calif. 13.2

Electricity: 5.8 Transportation: 3.1 Green Living: 1.8 Recycling/Perspective: 2.5

38. Norwalk, Calif. 13.0

Electricity: 3.5 Transportation: 3.1 Green Living: 2.5 Recycling/Perspective: 3.9

39. Laredo, Tex. 12.9

Electricity: 4.4 Transportation: 2.5 Green Living: 1.7 Recycling/Perspective: 4.3

40. Joliet, Ill. 12.0

Electricity: 1.3 Transportation: 4.3 Green Living: 2.6 Recycling/Perspective: 3.8

41. Newport News, Va. 11.9

Electricity: 2.7 Transportation: 2.7 Green Living: 2.7 Recycling/Perspective: 3.8

42. Louisville, Ky. 11.9

Electricity: 1.3 Transportation: 4.0 Green Living: 2.5 Recycling/Perspective: 4.1

43. Concord, Calif. 11.9

Electricity: 3.0 Transportation: 3.2 Green Living: 2.2 Recycling/Perspective: 3.5

44. Fremont, Calif. 11.3

Electricity: 3.0 Transportation: 3.0 Green Living: 1.5 Recycling/Perspective: 3.8

45. Elizabeth, N.J. 10.5

Electricity: 2.6 Transportation: 2.8 Green Living: 1.8 Recycling/Perspective: 3.3

46. Livonia, Mich. 10.2

Electricity: 2.7 Transportation: 2.1 Green Living: 1.8 Recycling/Perspective: 3.6

47. San Bernardino, Calif. 10.2

Electricity: 2.8 Transportation: 2.3 Green Living: 1.6 Recycling/Perspective: 3.5

48. Thousand Oaks, Calif. 10.2

Electricity: 2.9 Transportation: 2.9 Green Living: 1.6 Recycling/Perspective: 2.8

49. Stockton, Calif. 10.1

Electricity: 2.8 Transportation: 2.5 Green Living: 1.0 Recycling/Perspective: 3.8

50. Greensboro, N.C. 10.0

Healthiest and Unhealthiest Cities in America

To create the study, Bert Sperling of Sperling's BestPlaces culled data on 50 U.S. cities from both public and private sources and tested each city against 50 select measures in five major categories: Physical Activity, Health Status, Nutrition, Lifestyle Pursuits, and Mental Wellness. According to the Sperling "report card," in the nationwide battle for healthiest cities, West easily trumps East.

NOTE: Scores indicate percentile rankings within each category (100 is highest, 1 is lowest).

Rank	City	State	Points	Mental	Lifestyle	Activity	Health	Diet
1	San Jose	CA	1,272	55	93	87	100	93
2	Washington	DC-MD-VA-WV	1,207	100	89	85	83	95
3	San Francisco	CA	1,141	30	97	97	91	85
4	Seattle-Bellevue-Everett	WA	1,121	48	100	100	71	73
5	Salt Lake City-Ogden	UT	1,067	83	75	89	63	77
6	Oakland	CA	1,065	59	79	77	93	71
7	Sacramento	CA	1,059	32	77	81	85	91
8	Orange County	CA	1,025	95	95	75	18	57
9	Denver	CO	1,017	71	73	93	20	83
10	Austin-San Marcos	TX	999	73	69	95	2	79
11	Boston	MA-NH-ME	992	65	46	83	67	55
12	San Diego	CA	978	69	71	67	51	67
13	Minneapolis-St. Paul	MN-WI	976	93	91	91	6	40
14	Bergen-Passaic	NJ	973	91	6	61	89	51
15	Nassau-Suffolk	NY	968	79	24	73	69	48
16	Portland-Vancouver	OR-WA	958	18	83	79	44	59
17	Raleigh-Durham-Chapel Hill	NC	954	97	44	24	24	89
18	Nashville	TN	940	85	42	12	40	97
19	Baltimore	MD	933	24	26	71	48	65
20	Riverside-San Bernardino	CA	927	6	40	57	97	42
21	Phoenix-Mesa	AZ	924	38	48	63	55	61
22	Pittsburgh	PA	918	89	2	69	73	26
23	Los Angeles-Long Beach	CA	910	8	85	34	81	75
24	Philadelphia	PA-NJ	888	61	30	65	77	32
25	Newark	NJ	883	63	4	48	87	44
26	Atlanta	GA	872	67	63	59	1	69
27	Milwaukee-Waukesha	WI	834	42	67	53	42	28
28	Fort Lauderdale	FL	829	34	36	4	57	87
29	Chicago	IL	827	81	87	20	4	53
30	Kansas City	MO-KS	824	77	51	30	46	30
31	Greensboro-Winston-Salem-High Point	NC	813	46	8	6	59	81
32	Charlotte-Gastonia-Rock Hill	NC-SC	813	53	12	14	30	63
33	Miami	FL	810	20	16	2	26	100
34	St. Louis	MO-IL	807	57	81	40	32	18
35	Dallas	TX	798	75	28	44	12	34
36	Houston	TX	796	36	20	36	34	38
37	Fort Worth-Arlington	TX	788	40	32	38	61	22
38	Providence-Fall River-Warwick	RI-MA	781	14	18	46	75	14
39	Norfolk-Virginia Beach-Newport News	VA-NC	778	87	38	42	28	4
40	Tampa-St. Petersburg-Clearwater	FL	776	10	10	22	79	36
41	Indianapolis	IN	774	28	53	51	36	10
42	Las Vegas	NV-AZ	745	44	55	28	16	16
43	New York	NY	725	12	59	8	38	46
44	Detroit	MI	719	1	22	26	95	2
45	Columbus	OH	702	51	57	55	8	1
46	Orlando	FL	700	4	65	16	10	20
47	Cleveland-Lorain-Elyria	OH	683	16	34	18	65	6
48	Cincinnati	OH-KY-IN	681	2	61	32	22	8
49	San Antonio	TX	674	22	14	10	53	12
50	New Orleans	LA	582	26	1	1	14	24

Safest Cities (2016 Rankings)

The 2016 Safest Cities ranking (generated by Neighborhood Scout, www.Neighborhoodscout.com) reveals the 100 safest cities in America with 25,000 or more people, based on the total number of crimes per 1,000 residents. Crimes include burglary, larceny-theft, motor vehicle theft, homicide, rape, armed robbery, and aggravated assault. Data used for this research are 1) the number of crimes reported to the FBI to have occurred in each city, and 2) the population of each city.

Rank	City
100	North Andover, MA
99	Highland Park, IL
98	Foster City, CA
97	Leander, TX
96	Cibolo, TX
95	Lakeville, MN
94	Wylie, TX
93	Cary, NC
92	Upper Arlington, OH
91	Shoreview, MN
90	Hoffman Estates, IL
89	Royal Oak, MI
88	San Clemente, CA
87	Elmhurst, IL
86	Apex, NC
85	Sayreville, NJ
84	Mount Prospect, IL
83	Los Altos, CA
82	Yorba Linda, CA
81	Walnut, CA
80	Ossining, NY
79	Lincoln, CA
78	Spring Hill, TN
77	Dublin, OH
76	Madison, MS
75	Milton, GA
74	Northbrook, IL
73	Melrose, MA
72	Fair Lawn, NJ
71	West Linn, OR
70	The Colony, TX
69	Carol Stream, IL
68	Newton, MA
67	Poway, CA
66	Arlington Heights, IL

continued

65	Milton, MA
64	Cliffside Park, NJ
63	South Kingstown, RI
62	Arlington, MA
61	Billerica, MA
60	Syracuse, UT
59	Palatine, IL
58	Saratoga, CA
57	Shelton, CT
56	Hanover Park, IL
55	Lake Forest, CA
54	Flower Mound, TX
53	Fishers, IN
52	Mission Viejo, CA
51	Holly Springs, NC
50	Laguna Niguel, CA
49	Carmel, IN
48	Bethel Park, PA
47	Westfield, NJ
46	Brunswick, OH
45	Little Elm, TX
44	Friendswood, TX
43	Keller, TX
42	Brentwood, TN
41	Moorpark, CA
40	Long Beach, NY
39	Glastonbury, CT
38	Mundelein, IL
37	Glenview, IL
36	Marshfield, MA
35	Huntley, IL
34	Rexburg, ID
33	Cheshire, CT
32	Plainfield, IL
31	Independence, KY
30	Johns Creek, GA
29	Greenwich, CT
28	Wellesley, MA
27	Sammamish, WA
26	Andover, MA
25	Belmont, MA
24	Merrimack, NH
23	Fort Lee, NJ
22	Bella Vista, AR

21	Wheaton, IL
20	North Ridgeville, OH
19	Ridgewood, NJ
18	Buffalo Grove, IL
17	Ballwin, MO
16	Lexington, MA
15	Pleasant Grove, UT
14	Florence, AZ
13	Parkland, FL
12	Needham, MA
11	Weston, FL
10	Aliso Viejo, CA
9	Zionsville, IN
8	Bartlett, IL
7	Shrewsbury, MA
6	Lake in the Hills, IL
5	Bergenfield, NJ
4	Franklin, MA
3	Rancho Santa Margarita, CA
2	Winona, MN
1	Ridgefield, CT

Safest States in America (2016)

WalletHub (www.wallethub.com) compared the 50 states and the District of Columbia across five key dimensions: 1) Home & Community Safety, 2) Financial Safety, 3) Road Safety, 4) Workplace Safety, and 5) Safety from Natural Disasters.

They identified 25 relevant metrics, Each metric was given a value between 0 and 100, wherein 100 represents the highest level of safety and 0 the lowest. Finally, they calculated the overall score for each state using the weighted average across all metrics and ranked the states accordingly.

Data used to create these rankings were collected from the U.S. Census Bureau, Bureau of Labor Statistics, Federal Bureau of Investigation, Parents for Megan's Law, U.S. Fire Administration, National Highway Traffic Safety Administration, National Centers for Environmental Information, Centers for Disease Control and Prevention, Verisk Analytics, stopbullying.gov, Kaiser Family Foundation, FINRA Investor Education Foundation, TransUnion and CoreLogic.

Best Places to Live in America

Overall Rank	State	Total Score	Home & Community Safety Risk	Financial Safety Rank	Road Safety Rank	Workplace Safety Rank	Safety from Natural Disasters
51	Mississippi	34.00	36	49	50	49	43
50	Oklahoma	35.29	34	32	32	48	51
49	Alaska	36.12	49	29	48	46	3
48	New Mexico	36.94	47	51	51	44	12
47	Tennessee	37.98	43	33	35	28	47
46	South Carolina	39.98	48	48	44	26	29
45	Louisiana	40.01	40	46	39	43	34
44	Arkansas	41.27	51	38	25	32	33
43	Nevada	41.33	42	50	43	25	14
42	Missouri	41.70	41	21	22	20	49
41	Kansas	42.02	28	12	29	30	50
40	Alabama	42.48	37	40	27	11	48
39	Texas	42.99	38	30	36	17	45
38	Florida	43.51	46	43	42	9	17
37	South Dakota	44.11	29	5	46	50	28
36	Wyoming	44.73	17	13	49	47	25
35	Colorado	45.69	31	11	34	22	42
34	Kentucky	46.56	13	42	38	37	40
33	Oregon	46.84	35	45	20	31	24
32	Georgia	47.00	33	44	21	14	37
31	Delaware	47.35	45	34	30	13	13
30	District of Columbia	47.40	50	47	7	4	8
29	Arizona	47.53	39	14	45	6	23
28	Montana	48.15	30	20	40	34	21
27	Hawaii	48.20	24	24	37	45	1
26	Nebraska	48.60	26	3	24	38	44
25	Michigan	48.66	44	17	19	29	10
24	Idaho	49.26	18	25	26	42	22
23	North Carolina	49.90	14	41	41	5	38
22	Indiana	50.37	22	37	16	27	35
21	Washington	51.25	27	31	18	24	20
20	North Dakota	51.30	16	1	47	51	7
19	California	51.38	23	35	33	40	11
18	Maryland	52.15	25	26	23	10	26
17	Illinois	52.29	20	22	2	33	39
16	West Virginia	52.58	15	39	28	39	15
15	New Jersey	53.40	2	28	17	21	46
14	Pennsylvania	53.53	9	15	31	36	27
13	Ohio	54.03	19	23	12	8	31

12	New York	54.15	5	19	10	35	41
11	Wisconsin	55.54	21	8	14	18	19
10	Iowa	55.68	6	6	11	41	36
9	Utah	55.79	32	9	13	19	5
8	Virginia	56.58	12	16	8	2	32
7	Minnesota	60.54	11	2	3	3	30
6	Connecticut	60.70	3	18	6	15	18
5	Maine	61.22	8	27	15	12	2
4	Rhode Island	61.30	4	36	4	1	16
3	New Hampshire	62.57	10	4	9	7	6
2	Massachusetts	63.86	7	7	1	23	9
1	Vermont	66.78	1	10	5	16	4

US Crime/Safety Map

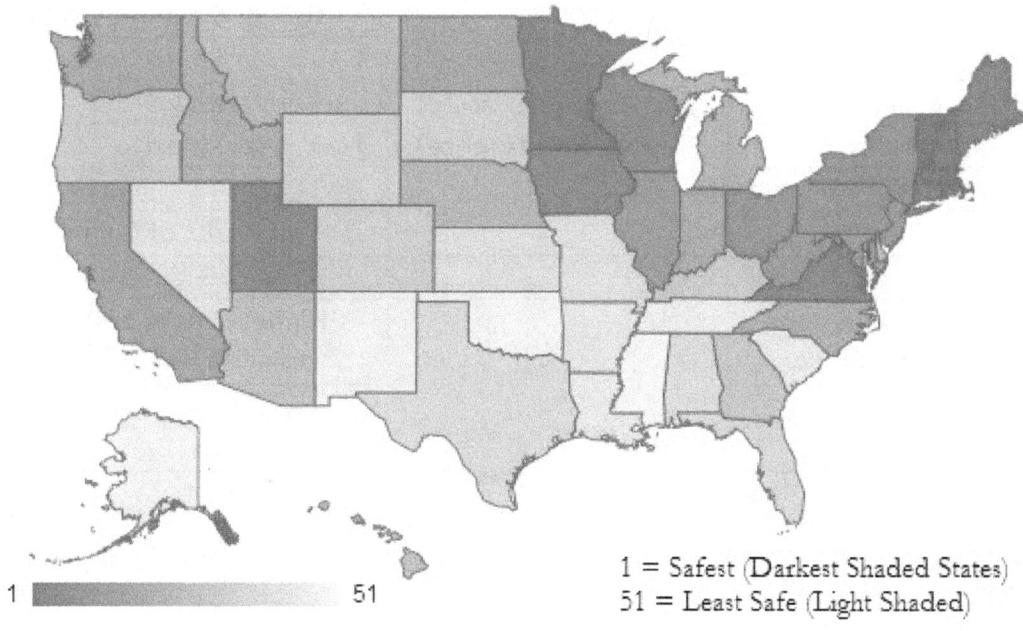

1 = Safest (Darkest Shaded States)
51 = Least Safe (Light Shaded)

Most Favorable vs. Least Favorable

	Assaults			
Fewest Assaults per Capita			**Most Assaults per Capita**	
1	Maine	Best States vs. Worst States (10x Difference)	47	Nevada
2	Vermont		48	New Mexico
3	Kentucky		49	Alaska
4	New Hampshire		50	Tennessee
5	Virginia		51	District of Columbia
	Bullying			
Lowest Bullying Incident Rate			**Highest Bullying Incident Rate**	
1	District of Columbia	Lowest States vs. Highest States	38	Michigan
2	Florida		39	Idaho
3	Massachusetts		40	Montana
4	Mississippi		41	Missouri
5	New Mexico		42	Maine
	Employment Rate			
Lowest Unemployment Rate			**Highest Unemployment Rate**	
T-1	Nebraska	Best States vs. Worst States (3x Difference)	T-46	Alaska
T-1	North Dakota		T-46	Mississippi
3	South Dakota		T-49	New Mexico
4	New Hampshire		T-49	West Virginia
5	Utah		51	District of Columbia
	Health Insurance			
Lowest Share of Population Lacking Health Insurance			**Highest Share of Population Lacking Health Insurance**	
1	Massachusetts	Best States vs. Worst States (6x Difference)	47	Georgia
2	District of Columbia		48	Alaska
T-3	Hawaii		49	Florida
T-3	Vermont		50	Nevada
5	Minnesota		51	Texas

Automobile Fatalities

	Fewest Fatalities per 100 Million Vehicle Mile of Travel	Best States vs. Worst States (3x Difference)		Most Fatalities per 100 Million Vehicle Mile of Travel
1	Massachusetts		47	Louisiana
2	Vermont		48	Mississippi
3	Minnesota		49	Montana
4	District of Columbia		50	Wyoming
5	Rhode Island		51	South Carolina

Law Enforcement

	Most Law-Enforcement Employees per Capita	Best States vs. Worst States (4x Difference)		Fewest Law-Enforcement Employees per Capita
1	District of Columbia		46	Vermont
2	Illinois		47	Utah
3	Louisiana		48	Michigan
4	New Jersey		49	Maine
5	New York		50	Washington

% of People with Rainy Day Funds

	Highest % of People with Rainy Day Funds	Best States vs. Worst States (2x Difference)		Lowest % of People with Rainy Day Funds
1	Arizona		48	Kentucky
2	New York		49	Indiana
3	Massachusetts		T-49	Mississippi
4	North Dakota		T-49	New Mexico
5	California			

Property Losses from Climate Disasters

	Lowest Estimated Property Losses from Climate Disasters	Lowest States vs. Highest States		Highest Estimated Property Losses from Climate Disasters
1	California		41	Alabama
2	Florida		42	Missouri
T-3	Utah		43	New Jersey
T-3	North Dakota		T-44	Kansas
5	Maine		T-44	Oklahoma

Fatal Occupational Injuries

	Fewest Fatal Occupational Injuries per Total Employees	Best States vs. Worst States		Most Fatal Occupational Injuries per Total Employees
1	Massachusetts		47	Mississippi
2	California		48	South Dakota
T-3	Connecticut		49	Alaska
T-3	New Jersey		T-50	North Dakota
T-3	Rhode Island		T-50	Wyoming

State Populations and Projections

State	2000 Census Population	2000 Rank	2030 Projections Population	2030 Rank	Change: 2000 to 2030 Number	Change: 2000 to 2030 Percent	Change: 2000 to 2030 Rank in percent change
United States	**281,421,906**	(x)	**363,584,435**	(x)	**82,162,529**	**29.2**	(x)
California	33,871,648	1	46,444,861	1	2,283,845	114.3	1
Texas	20,851,820	2	33,317,744	2	5,581,765	108.8	2
New York	18,976,457	3	28,685,769	3	12,703,391	79.5	3
Florida	15,982,378	4	19,477,429	4	12,465,924	59.8	4
Illinois	12,419,293	5	13,432,892	5	1,252,198	56.1	5
Pennsylvania	12,281,054	6	12,768,184	6	675,671	52.2	6
Ohio	11,353,140	7	12,227,739	7	4,178,426	51.9	7
Michigan	9,938,444	8	12,017,838	8	3,831,385	46.8	8
New Jersey	8,414,350	9	11,550,528	9	2,730,680	46.3	9
Georgia	8,186,453	10	10,712,397	10	1,412,519	41.3	10
North Carolina	8,049,313	11	10,694,172	11	2,746,504	38.8	11
Virginia	7,078,515	12	9,825,019	12	240,742	38.4	12
Massachusetts	6,349,097	13	9,802,440	13	12,573,213	37.1	13
Indiana	6,080,485	14	8,624,801	14	1,491,096	34.7	14
Washington	5,894,121	15	7,380,634	15	410,685	33.2	15
Tennessee	5,689,283	16	7,022,251	16	1,725,765	32.6	16
Missouri	5,595,211	17	7,012,009	17	1,691,351	29.7	17
Wisconsin	5,363,675	18	6,810,108	18	229,058	29.2	18
Maryland	5,296,486	19	6,430,173	19	1,136,557	28.3	19
Arizona	5,130,632	20	6,306,130	20	1,386,651	28.2	20
Minnesota	4,919,479	21	6,150,764	21	566,808	21.2	21
Louisiana	4,468,976	22	5,792,357	22	254,509	21	22
Alabama	4,447,100	23	5,148,569	23	103,040	16.9	23
Colorado	4,301,261	24	4,874,243	24	1,388,090	16.5	24
Kentucky	4,041,769	25	4,833,918	25	142,703	15.8	25
South Carolina	4,012,012	26	4,802,633	26	280,662	15.4	26
Oklahoma	3,450,654	27	4,554,998	27	834,962	14.9	27
Oregon	3,421,399	28	4,282,102	28	787,089	14.7	28
Connecticut	3,405,565	29	3,913,251	29	462,597	13.4	29
Iowa	2,926,324	30	3,688,630	30	513,229	12.7	30
Mississippi	2,844,658	31	3,485,367	31	729,623	12	31
Kansas	2,688,418	32	3,240,208	32	136,174	10.7	32
Arkansas	2,673,400	33	3,092,410	33	662,912	10.4	33
Utah	2,233,169	34	2,955,172	34	104,622	10	34
Nevada	1,998,257	35	2,940,084	35	427,143	9.6	35
New Mexico	1,819,046	36	2,099,708	36	251,666	9.4	36
West Virginia	1,808,344	37	1,969,624	37	247,752	8.7	37
Nebraska	1,711,263	38	1,820,247	38	283,065	8.3	38
Idaho	1,293,953	39	1,719,959	39	1,013,599	8.2	39

Part II - Cities & States Ranked According to YOUR Wants & Needs

State	2000 Census Population	2000 Rank	2030 Projections Population	2030 Rank	Change: 2000 to 2030 Number	Change: 2000 to 2030 Percent	Change: 2000 to 2030 Rank in percent change
Maine	1,274,923	40	1,646,471	40	755,728	7.6	40
New Hampshire	1,235,786	41	1,466,046	41	333,657	7.5	41
Hawaii	1,211,537	42	1,411,097	42	108,984	6.4	42
Rhode Island	1,048,319	43	1,152,941	43	45,618	6	43
Montana	902,195	44	1,044,898	44	29,197	5.9	44
Delaware	783,600	45	1,012,658	45	487,130	4	45
South Dakota	754,844	46	867,674	46	500,972	2.6	46
North Dakota	642,200	47	800,462	47	197,388	1.7	47
Alaska	626,932	48	711,867	48	28,848	1	48
Vermont	608,827	49	606,566	49	-88,385	-4.9	49
District of Columbia	572,059	50	522,979	50	-35,634	-5.5	50
Wyoming	493,782	51	433,414	51	-138,645	-24.2	51

U.S. Census Bureau, Population Division, Interim State Population Projections, 2005. Internet Release Date: April 21, 2005

Best Metropolitan Places to Live in the U.S. in 2017

Article by U.S. News & World Report, 2017

According to a 2017 *U.S. News & World Report* study, the following metro areas offer the best combination of jobs, desirability, cost of living, quality of life and more. The 2017 *U.S. News & World Report* study assessed statistics for the nation's 100 largest metro areas, including the job market, cost of living, crime rates, educational quality, availability of top-notch health care, and more. Each category was weighted based in a survey of 2,000 people across the country.

1. Austin, TX
2. Denver, CO
3. San Jose, CA
4. Washington, DC
5. Fayetteville, AR
6. Seattle, WA
7. Raleigh & Durham, NC
8. Boston, MA
9. Des Moines, IA
10. Salt Lake City, UT
11. Colorado Springs, CO
12. Boise, ID
13. Nashville, TN
14. Charlotte, NC
15. Dallas-Fort Worth, TX
16. San Francisco, CA
17. Minneapolis-St. Paul, MN
18. Madison, WI
19. Gran Rapids, MI
20. Houston, TX
21. Sarasota, FL
22. San Diego, CA
23. San Antonio, TX
24. Richmond, VA
25. Omaha, NE
26. Portland, ME
27. Charleston, SC
28. Syracuse, NY
29. Grenville, SC
30. Albany, NY
31. Hartford, CT
32. Portland, OR
33. Buffalo, NY
34. Harrisburg, PA
35. Tampa, FL
36. Oklahoma City, OK
37. Winston-Salem, NC
38. Little Rock, AR
39. Rochester, NY
40. Orlando, FL
41. Lancaster, PA
42. Chattanooga, TN
43. Louisville, KY
44. Phoenix, AZ
45. Jacksonville, FL
46. Honolulu, HI
47. Milwaukee, WI
48. Kansas City, MO
49. Melbourne, FL
50. Atlanta, GA
51. Greensboro, NC
52. Santa Rosa, CA
53. Cincinnati, OH
54. Worchester, MA
55. Indianapolis, IN
56. Columbia, SC
57. Columbus, OH
58. Pittsburgh, PA
59. Tulsa, OK
60. Spokane, WA
61. Knoxville, TN
62. Tucson, AZ
63. Baton Rouge, LA
64. Lakeland, FL
65. St. Louis, MO
66. Sacramento, CA
67. Springfield, MA
68. Wichita, KS
69. Virginia Beach, VA
70. Fort Meyers, FL
71. Toledo, OH
72. Augusta, GA
73. Baltimore, MD
74. Albuquerque, NM
75. Dayton, OH
76. El Paso, TX
77. Philadelphia, PA
78. Las Vegas, NV
79. Allentown, PA
80. New York City, NY
81. New Haven, CT
82. Daytona Beach, FL
83. Chicago, IL
84. Cleveland, OH
85. Providence, RI
86. Scranton PA
87. Youngstown, OH
88. Los Angeles, CA
89. Detroit, MI
90. Birmingham, Al
91. Jackson, MS
92. Miami, FL
93. Memphis, TN
94. McAllen, TX
95. New Orleans, LA
96. Fresno, CA
97. Bakersfield, CA
98. Stockton, CA
99. Modesto, CA
100. San Juan, PR

Part III

Best Places to Live For Physical Disabilities (Including Help for Veterans & Caretakers)

History: Attitudes Towards, and Treatment of, People with Disabilities

A. **Nomadic Tribes** People with disabilities were considered useless because they could not contribute to food gathering or to the wealth of the tribe. Nomads often left people with disabilities to die whenever the tribe moved to a new location. Many tribal cultures believed that disability implied possession by evil spirits.

B. The **Greeks** sought rational explanations for disability, with insufficient medical science. They reached such conclusions as: epilepsy is a disturbance of the mind; people who are deaf cannot learn without verbal communication.

C. **Early Christianity**, building on Judaic concepts of charity, brought a gentler approach, focusing on sympathy and pity toward people with disabilities. Sympathy and pity, however, led to condescension and paternalism, resulting in a general loss of autonomy. Some believed that enough prayer and ritual could eliminate the disability.

D. During **the Middle Ages**, as the attraction to supernaturalism increased, Christians became fearful of people with disabilities. People with disabilities were ridiculed, such as the court jester who was actually someone with a humped back. Ridicule often turned to persecution and "impurity" turned into a vision of disability as a manifestation of evil.

E. **The Renaissance** brought new strides in medical science and treatment for people with disabilities. During this time, the "charity model" and "medical model" began to determine the attitude toward disability. Education was available to people with disabilities for the first time in recorded Western history. An enlightened approach to social norms and dreams for a better future seemed to encourage active participation of people with disabilities in their communities. The "charity model" is based upon a benevolent society which provides services based upon an assumption of "what is best" for those served. The charity model led to the promotion of institutionalization during the Renaissance, as a method of doing 'what is best" for those with disabilities. From the Renaissance through World War II, society believed that people with disabilities might be educated, but in "special" segregated programs or schools, often far from populated areas.

F. In the early years, the **American colonies** would not admit people with disabilities because they believed such individuals would require financial support. Colonists enacted settlement laws whose restrictions included people with disabilities.

G. But by 1880, after the development of almshouses for people who were poor or in need of basic support, most states and territories had programs for people with specific types of disabilities. Most of these programs were large institutions where people who were blind, deaf, mentally retarded, or otherwise physically disabled were sent for treatment, education or to spend their entire lives.

H. The movement west, otherwise known as the **American Frontier Movement**, inspired a peculiarly American belief that social ills could be eradicated by local initiatives. The concept of "rugged individualism" was born in the American Frontier and maintains a powerful hold over political debate today. In fact, the desire for "independent living" carries with it the seed of the "rugged individualist" ideals. Some community-based services began to emerge, but people with disabilities were usually segregated from society as a whole. Rural areas were the only places where people with disabilities tended to live with their families in integrated settings.

I. The **Eugenics** movement got its start in the United States in the early decades of the century. The movement quickly took hold in Europe and, in some cases, was closely tied, theoretically, to calls for euthanasia of "defectives."

J. **Rehabilitation services** on a broad scale were introduced as a federal program following World War I. The emphasis in these first rehabilitation programs was on the veteran with a disability who was returning home to the United States. The need for training or re-training created the first federally funded program for people with disabilities - a program now known as the federal-state vocational rehabilitation system.

K. Institutionalization--separation from the community at large--and the growing Eugenics movement paved the way to the ultimate abuse of people with disabilities in 1930's **Hitler's Germany**. People with disabilities, most notably those with mental retardation and mental illness, became the first guinea pigs for the Third Reich's medical experiments and mass execution. Before Hitler's SS began mass extermination of Jews, Gypsies, Gays, and Lesbians, it perfected its skills and knowledge on people with disabilities. The experiments and euthanasia were in the hands of doctors and nurses, many of whom were later transferred to duty in the concentration camps.

L. During the 1940s, the **blind community** argued for separate services for people who were blind, based upon the belief that people who were blind needed education not rehabilitation. Advocates argued that rehabilitation is based upon a "medical model" in which the person who is blind needs to be treated and cured, rather than educated to live with blindness. The debate over what approach to use resulted in a "split" within the vocational rehabilitation program, allowing state vocational rehabilitation agencies and agencies serving the blind to become separate entities within a state.

M. Other major services for people with disabilities were not seriously considered by federal policy makers until the social change movements of the 1960s. Although the Social Security system provided benefits to those who had earned sufficient income over a long enough time period and had become disabled (i.e., unable to work), there was no attempt to broaden the base of services for people with disabilities beyond the vocational rehabilitation approach. For the first time in U.S. history, consumers, advocates, and service professionals began an intensive examination of the human service delivery system to decide what was missing. Community-based programs for people with disabilities began growing all over the nation in an attempt to fill the gaps left by these missing services. New concepts, new technology, and new attitudes were beginning to make a difference in the lives of people with disabilities.

Influence of Social Movements on Disability Rights

A. Influenced by the **civil rights** movement led by African-Americans during the 1960s, people with disabilities pointed out that - just like other minorities - they were being denied access to basic services and opportunities such as employment, housing, transportation, education and the like. Like Rosa Parks, people with disabilities want and need to be able to ride the bus. The only difference is that Rosa Parks as an African-American woman was not permitted to sit in the front of the bus while people with disabilities just want to get on the bus.

B. **Consumerism**, a movement led by well-known national figures such as Ralph Nader, contributed another element to the growing disability rights and independent living movement. People with disabilities were, for the first time, stressing their role as consumers first, and "patients" last. In other words, individuals with disabilities wanted the right to decide for themselves what services and products they wished to purchase (even if a third arty was paying for the service or product). As "clients" or "patients," people with disabilities were rarely given any autonomy or power over the services and products they would use.

C. **Self-help** is nothing new in the United States, but organized self-help programs are relatively new. The original non-professional, self-help program that is best known in the U.S. is Alcoholics Anonymous, which provides peer-to-peer support. Having a severe disability may not be exactly the same as having a problem with alcohol, but a strong parallel remains. Leaders of the disability rights and independent living movement believe that only persons with disabilities know best how to serve others who have the same or similar disabilities. The concept of "peer" counseling and peer groups are the most common methods of self-help.

D. **De-medicalization** and de-institutionalization share certain common characteristics. De-medicalization for people with disabilities means removing the involvement of medical professionals from the daily lives of individuals with disabilities. People with disabilities are not "sick." They are disabled and not dependent upon medical professionals for every day needs. The perfect example of a "de-medicalized" service for persons with severe mobility disabilities is that of "personal assistance." Personal assistance is a consumer-directed service whereby the person with the disability recruits, hires, trains, manages and fires his or her own personal assistants. When consumers with disabilities are allowed to buy the services they need for daily survival from whomever they choose, they have "de-medicalized" the service. Unfortunately, the vast majority of services provided to people with disabilities are still rooted in the "medical model," regardless of the individual's needs and desires.

E. **De-institutionalization**, which began in response to large facilities for those who are mentally ill or mentally retarded, follows the principles of de-medicalization. Medical personnel staff most institutions, even if residents are not ill. Since many such individuals are only disabled by some permanent type of condition, placement in institutions is inappropriate and far more costly than providing those same residents with the support services they need to live in their chosen communities. The disability rights and independent living movement is working towards the development of those other non-medical and community-based services which would assist institutionalized persons to move back to their home towns or areas. The disability rights and independent living movements are a compilation of all five social movements as they pertain to and are defined by people who have disabilities.

Disability Defined

The Definition of Disability Perspective of the Disability Community The questions of the definition of "person with a disability" and how persons with disabilities perceive themselves are knotty and complex. It is no accident that these questions are emerging at the same time that the status of persons with disabilities in society is changing dramatically. The Americans with Disabilities Act (ADA) is the cause of some of these changes, as well as the result of the corresponding shift in public policy.

Questions of status and identity are at the heart of disability policy. One of the central goals of the disability rights movement, which can claim primary political responsibility for the ADA, is to move American society to a new and more positive understanding of what it means to have a disability.

Disability policy scholars describe four different historical and social models of disability: A moral model of disability which regards disability as the result of sin; A medical model of disability which regards disability as a defect or sickness which must be cured through medical intervention; A rehabilitation model, an offshoot of the medical model, which regards the disability as a deficiency that must be fixed by a rehabilitation professional or other helping professional; and the disability model, under which "the problem is defined as a dominating attitude by professionals and others, inadequate support services when compared with society generally, as well as attitudinal, architectural, sensory, cognitive, and economic barriers, and the strong tendency for people to generalize about all persons with disabilities overlooking the large variations within the disability community."

THE MORAL MODEL is historically the oldest and is less prevalent today. However, there are many cultures that associate disability with sin and shame, and disability is often associated with feelings of guilt, even if such feelings are not overtly based in religious doctrine. For the individual with a disability, this model is particularly burdensome. This model has been associated with shame on the entire family with a member with a disability. Families have hidden away the disabled family member, keeping them out of school and excluded from any chance at having a meaningful role in society. Even in less extreme circumstances, this model has resulted in general social ostracism and self-hatred.

THE MEDICAL MODEL came about as "modern" medicine began to develop in the 19th Century, along with the enhanced role of the physician in society. Since many disabilities have medical origins, people with disabilities were expected to benefit from coming under the direction of the medical profession. Under this model, the problems that are associated with disability are deemed to reside within the individual. In other words, if the individual is "cured" then these problems will not exist. Society has no underlying responsibility to make a "place" for persons with disabilities, since they live in an outsider role waiting to be cured. The individual with a disability is in the sick role under the medical model. When people are sick, they are excused from the normal obligations of society: going to school, getting a job, taking on family responsibilities, etc. They are also expected to come under the authority of the medical profession in order to get better. Thus, until recently, most disability policy issues have been regarded as health issues, and physicians have been regarded as the primary authorities in this policy area. One can see the influence of the medical model in disability public policy today, most notably in the Social Security system, in which disability is defined as the inability to work. This is consistent with the role of the person with a disability as sick. It is also the source of enormous problems for persons with disabilities who want to work but who would risk losing all related public benefits, such as health care coverage or access to Personal Assistance Services (for in-home chores and personal functioning), since a person loses one's disability status by going to work.

THE REHABILITATION MODEL is similar to the medical model; it regards the person with a disability as in need of services from a rehabilitation professional who can provide training, therapy, counseling or other services to make up for the deficiency caused by the disability. Historically, it gained acceptance after World War II when many disabled veterans needed to be re-introduced into society. The current Vocational Rehabilitation system is designed according to this model. Persons with disabilities have been very critical of both the medical model and the rehabilitation model. While medical intervention can be required by the individual at times, it is naive and simplistic to regard the medical system as the appropriate locus for disability related policy matters. Many disabilities and chronic medical conditions will never be cured. Persons with disabilities are quite capable of participating in society, and the practices of confinement and institutionalization that accompany the sick role are simply not acceptable.

THE DISABILITY MODEL has taken hold as the disability rights and independent living movements have gained strength. This model regards disability as a normal aspect of life, not as a deviance and rejects the notion that persons with disabilities are in some inherent way "defective". As Professor David Pfeiffer has put it, "...paralyzed limbs may not particularly limit a person's mobility as much as attitudinal and physical barriers. The question centers on 'normality'. What, it is asked, is the normal way to be mobile over a distance of a mile? Is it to walk, drive one's own car, take a taxicab, ride a bicycle, use a wheelchair, roller skate, or use a skate board, or some other means? What is the normal way to earn a living?" Most people will experience some form of disability, either permanent or temporary, over the course of their lives. Given this reality, if disability were more commonly recognized and expected in the way that we design our environments or our systems, it would not seem so abnormal.

The disability model recognizes social discrimination as the most significant problem experienced by persons with disabilities and as the cause of many of the problems that are regarded as intrinsic to the disability under the other models. The cultural habit of regarding the condition of the person, not the built environment or the social organization of activities, as the source of the problem, runs deep. For example, it took me several years of struggling with the heavy door to my building, sometimes having to wait until a person stronger came along, to realize that the door was an accessibility problem, not only for me, but for others as well. And I did not notice, until one of my students pointed it out, that the lack of signs that could be read from a distance at my university forced people with mobility impairments to expend a lot of energy unnecessarily, searching for rooms and offices. Although I have encountered this difficulty myself on days when walking was exhausting to me, I interpreted it, automatically, as a problem arising from my illness (as I did with the door), rather than as a problem arising from the built environment having been created for too narrow a range of people and situations.

The United Nations uses a definition of disability that is different from the ADA: ***Impairment***: Any loss or abnormality of psychological, or anatomical structure or function. ***Disability***: Any restriction or lack (resulting from an impairment) of ability to perform an activity in the manner or within the range considered normal for a human being.

Handicap: A disadvantage for a given individual, resulting from an impairment or disability, that limits or prevents the fulfillment of a role that is normal, depending on age, sex, social and cultural factors, for that individual. Handicap is therefore a function of the relationship between disabled persons and their environment. It occurs when they encounter cultural, physical or social barriers which prevent their access to the various systems of society that are available to other citizens. Thus, handicap is the loss or limitation of opportunities to take part in the life of the community on an equal level with others.

This definition reflects the idea that to a large extent, disability is a social construct. Most people believe they know what is and is not a disability. If you imagine "the disabled" at one end of a spectrum and people who are extremely physically and mentally capable at the other, the distinction appears to be clear. However, there is a tremendous amount of middle ground in this construct, and it's in the middle that the scheme falls apart. What distinguishes a socially "invisible" impairment - such as the need for corrective eyeglasses - from a less acceptable one - such as the need for a corrective hearing aid, or the need for a walker? Functionally, there may be little difference. Socially, some impairments create great disadvantage or social stigma for the individual, while others do not. Some are considered disabilities and some are not.

The following examples further illustrate the difficulty of defining disability without consideration of social factors: * A person who has a cochlear implant; * A person who has a digestive disorder that requires following a very restrictive diet and following a strict regime of taking medications, and could result in serious illness if such regime is not adhered to; * A person with serious carpal tunnel syndrome; * A person who is very short. It is likely that different people could have different responses to the question of whether any of the above-listed characteristics would result in "disability", and some might say , "It depends".

This illustrates the differences in the terms "disability" and "handicap", as used by the U.N. Any of the above traits could become a "handicap" if the individual were considered disabled and also received disparate treatment as a result. Another example of the social construction of disability is when society discriminates against an individual who may have an "impairment" (in the sense of the U.N. definition) without a corresponding functional limitation. "The power of culture alone to construct a disability is revealed when we consider bodily differences - deviations from a society's conception of a 'normal' or acceptable body - that, although they cause little or no functional or physical difficulty for the person who has them, constitute major social disabilities. An important example is facial scarring, which is a disability of appearance only, a disability constructed totally by stigma and cultural meanings. Stigma, stereotypes, and cultural meanings are also the primary components of other disabilities, such as mild epilepsy and not having a 'normal' or acceptable body size."

The definition of disability in the ADA reflects a recognition of the social construction of disability, especially by including coverage for persons who are perceived by others as having a disability. The U.S. Equal Employment Opportunity Commission's ADA Title I Technical Assistance Manual provides the following explanations of how this prong of the definition is to be interpreted:

1. The individual may have an impairment which is not substantially limiting, but is treated by the employer as having such an impairment. For example: An employee has controlled high blood pressure which does not substantially limit his work activities. If an employer reassigns the individual to a less strenuous job because of unsubstantiated fear that the person would suffer a heart attack if he continues in the present job, the employer has "regarded" this person as disabled.

2. The individual has am impairment that is substantially limiting because of attitudes of others toward the condition. For example: An experienced assistant manager of a convenience store who has a prominent facial scar was passed over for promotion to store manager. The owner believed that customers and vendors would not want to look at this person. The employer discriminated against her on the basis of disability, because he perceived and treated her as a person with a substantial limitation.

3. The individual may have no impairment at all, but is regarded by an employer as having a substantially limiting impairment. For example: An employer discharged an employee based on a rumor that the individual had HIV disease. This person did not have any impairment, but was treated as though she had a substantially limiting impairment. This part of the definition protects people who are "perceived" as

having disabilities from employment decisions based on stereotypes, rumors, or misconceptions about disability. It applies to decisions based on unsubstantiated concerns about productivity, safety, insurance, liability, attendance, costs of accommodation, accessibility, workers' compensation costs or acceptance by co-workers and customers. Accordingly, if an employer makes an adverse employment decision based on unsubstantiated beliefs or fears that a person's perceived disability will cause problems in areas such as those listed above, and cannot show a legitimate, nondiscriminatory reason for the action, that action would be discriminatory under this part of the definition.

The definitions within a statute are related to the purpose of the statute. This is especially relevant in the field of disability policy, as one can find many different statutes, all with different definitions of this term. The purpose of the ADA is to prevent discrimination and to provide a remedy for people who have experienced it. This is consistent with the disability model of understanding disability, which places great importance on <u>discrimination as a major cause of disadvantage</u>. In order to provide an appropriate remedy to the full range of individuals who experience discrimination based on disability, it is necessary to explicitly recognize that there are people who would not consider themselves "disabled", nor would they be considered so by most others, but who receive the same disparate treatment as "the disabled". The courts have had a difficult time interpreting this complex definition. There are numerous cases in which judges have treated the ADA definition as though the purpose of the law is to provide a social benefit, rather than protect an individual from discrimination. In some cases, the courts have placed an individual with a disability in a Catch-22 situation: if the individual has held a job, then this is proof that the individual is not disabled and therefore cannot use the ADA to seek a remedy for employment discrimination.

The notion that the ADA should only be used to protect persons who are somehow "truly" disabled reflects an unsophisticated or naive understanding of the nature of disability. Given the significance of social and cultural influences in determining who is regarded as disabled, it makes little sense to refuse to take these same influences into account. Another important issue related to the topic of the definition of disability has to do with disability identity. There are many persons who unarguably fit within the first prong of the ADA definition who do not consider themselves disabled. "...there are many reasons for not identifying yourself as disabled, even when other people consider you disabled. First, disability carries a stigma that many people want to avoid, if at all possible. For newly disabled people, and for children with disabilities who have been shielded from knowledge of how most non-disabled people regard people with disabilities, it takes time to absorb the idea that they are members of a stigmatized group. Newly disabled adults may still have the stereotypes of disability that are common among non-disabled people. They may be in the habit of thinking of disability as total, believing that people who are disabled are disabled in all respects. ...They may fear, with good reason, that if they identify themselves as disabled others will see them as wholly disabled and fail to recognize their remaining abilities, or perhaps worse, see their every ability and achievement as 'extraordinary' or 'courageous'."

The reason that so many people reject the label "disabled" is that they seek to avoid the harsh social reality that is still so strong today. Having a disability, even though the ADA has been in place for almost a decade, still carries with it a great deal of stigmatization and stereotyping. It is ironic that those who could benefit from the law choose not to do so because they wish to avoid the very social forces that this law seeks to redress and eradicate. People who may fall under the coverage of the ADA because of the presence of a genetic marker are certainly not likely to think of themselves as disabled. While there may be discomfort at the thought of coming under this label, it is worthwhile to recognize that no one with a disability, visible or otherwise, wants to experience the stigma and discrimination that is still all too common for those who society considers disabled. There are many others who do not consider themselves to be disabled but who do experience discrimination.

The ADA provides a legal remedy when this occurs. Since the ADA definition recognizes the social construction of disability, whether it can apply to a person is a function of the social treatment that the individual receives. In other words, the question of whether a person with a genetic marker is covered by the definition does not arise in the abstract. If the individual has experienced discrimination based on the individual's physical or mental characteristics, then that individual may take advantage of the ADA to redress that discrimination. The question of whether a group of people fits within society's concept of who might be disabled, or who is treated in the same negative way, is not an option that the group has the chance to select. No group of people would willfully opt to be treated disparately.

From a policy point of view, there are two possible options that could be pursued to avoid coming under the coverage of the ADA: (1) an amendment to the ADA to explicitly state that persons with genetic markers are excluded from coverage under the definition; and/or (2) separate legislation to redress discrimination based on genetic characteristics. The first option would operate like the proverbial phrase, cutting off one's nose to spite one's face. The possibility of genetic discrimination is quite real, and it would be a poor bargain to lose one's civil rights in exchange for avoiding disability based stigma. It could also cause significant problems with legal interpretation of the ADA definition; the risk is that courts could use any exclusion to deny ADA coverage to others.

The second option is also politically and legally fraught with risk. Politically, people with genetic markers are a much smaller group than the very large confederation of disability organizations and individuals who came together to work towards passage of the ADA. Thus, the chances of gaining the strong legal protections that are now available in the ADA are not very high. It could also be expected that well-financed corporate interests would oppose such legislation. Enactment of any new legislation would be a tough, uphill battle that would probably result in a compromised version of the original proposal. In addition, the existence of two overlapping pieces of legislation could result in unfavorable judicial interpretation.

For those within the disability movement who have no problem being identified as disabled, there are advantages to coming under the coverage of the ADA, and indeed to being part of a community that is actively working to eradicate the discrimination and stigma that are our legacy. After decades of disparate treatment with no meaningful legal protection or remedy, it is quite satisfying to fight discrimination and to stand together to reject the stigma and stereotypes that are the basis of disability-based discrimination. Most disability activists welcome the inclusion of persons with invisible disabilities, as well as those who have faced discrimination even though they have no real impairment. This is because we understand that freedom from injustice is not an entitlement to be doled out in small doses. The nature of disability discrimination is that it often has very little to do with the individual's capabilities and true characteristics. The stigma and stereotypes are the cause of the discrimination, much more than the disability itself. It could be argued that the disability per se is not the cause at all, that the social reaction to disability is the cause.

In seeking to avoid the stigma associated with disability, there is a choice of strategies. Social and legal activism that challenge the assumptions behind the disability discrimination address the issues head on. The goal is to eradicate the stigma. The decision to disassociate from those who have historically been stigmatized tends to perpetuate the stereotypes and discrimination. The disability rights movement is working towards a society in which physical and mental differences among people are accepted as normal and expected, not abnormal or unusual. We have plenty of methods and tools at our disposal to accommodate human differences should we choose to. Ironically, the growth of technology in our lives provides us with both the ability to detect more human differences than ever before, as well as the ability to make those differences less meaningful in practical terms. How we react to human differences is a social and a policy choice. We prefer to advocate for a social structure that focuses on including all people in the social fabric, rather than drawing an artificial line that separates "disabled people" from others.

Disability Resources:

504 Sit-In 20th Anniversary
http://dredf.org/504/history.html

Section 504 of the Rehabilitation Act of 1973 prohibited programs receiving federal funds from discriminating against qualified individuals with disabilities. This site provides information and photos about the history of the law.

Beyond Affliction: The Disability History Project
http://www.npr.org/programs/disability/ba_shows.dir/index_sh.html

"History Project is a four hour documentary radio series about the shared experience of people with disabilities and their families since the beginning of the 19th century. This Web site includes excerpts from the Shows as well as many of the primary source documents - extended interviews, images, and texts- from which the on-air programs were developed." A winner from National Public Radio.

Disability History Museum
http://www.disabilitymuseum.org/dhm/index.html

The mission of this new cybermuseum "is to promote understanding about the historical experience of people with disabilities by recovering, chronicling, and interpreting their stories." There are supposed to be three main components: the museum, the library, and education. As of this writing (11/30/01), only the library was "open" - but it was well worth the visit! It currently includes two collections: a well organized, documented, full-text collection of historical documents, and a collection of visual stills (photographs, paintings, postcards, lithographs, etc.)

Disability Social History Project
http://www.disabilityhistory.org/dshp.html

Presented as "an opportunity for disabled people to reclaim our history and determine how we want to define ourselves and our struggles," this fascinating site includes an overview of disability in history, time lines, famous people, bibliographies and links. Whether you're interested in famous personalities in the history of disability or want to learn more about 19th century "freak shows," you're sure to find something here.

The Museum of DisAbility History
http://museumofdisability.org/

"Dedicated to the collection, preservation and display of artifacts pertaining to the history of people with disabilities," this museum in Buffalo, New York, and on the World Wide Web, offers a variety of online educational exhibits and activities.When we last visited in November 2001, there were exhibits of "The Birth of Newborn Screening" and "Idiocy in America: The Path to the Institution 1850-1920." The site also includes information about some of the museum's collections and services.

The History of the ADA: A Movement Perspective
http://www.empowermentzone.com/ada_hist.txt

From The Empowerment Zone, a history of the Americans with Disabilities Act by Arlene Mayerson.

Smithsonian National Museum of American History, Virtual Exhibitions - The Disability Rights Movement
http://americanhistory.si.edu/disabilityrights/welcome.html

We heard lots of good things about this exhibit in the "real" (physical) Smithsonian, and now you can see them online. The website is based on the accessible kiosks developed for the "real" facility. It is easy to navigate and features text, photos and ephemera of the disability rights movement.

Disabilities
(Classifications, Prevalence of each type of Disability, and State Comparisons)

According to a recent report by the United States Census Bureau nearly 20 percent of the United States population has a disability. That amounts to 56.7 million people classified as having some sort of disability.

Eight percent of children under the age of 15 have a disability. The report also indicated that the disabled person aged 15 to 64 were three times more likely to experience poverty as opposed to individuals with no disability. The point of this chapter is to define what disability is and recognize that disability will almost certainly impact either us or a close loved one at some point in our lives. It is not a curse or something to shy away from, in fact, if it is confronted and handled directly, disability can become a beautiful encouragement to those challenged with such and others. However, before that can occur, it is important to gain knowledge and know the facts. Just what is disability? What are the major types? Which states have the greatest number of disabled people? What is the growth rate and state distribution of people with disabilities? This chapter will answer those questions, and allow us to better examine which states are best for people with disabilities.

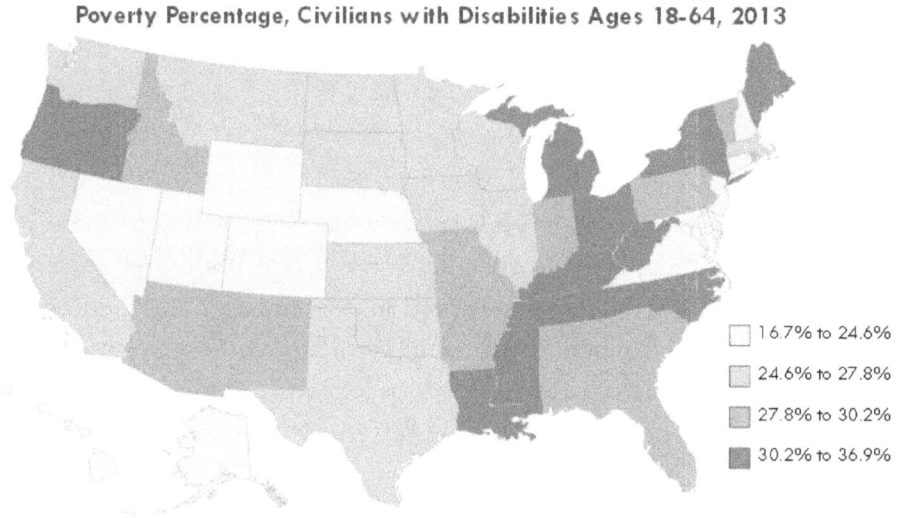

Poverty Percentage, Civilians with Disabilities Ages 18-64, 2013

- 16.7% to 24.6%
- 24.6% to 27.8%
- 27.8% to 30.2%
- 30.2% to 36.9%

What is a disability?

The Social Security Administration (SSA) has a definition of disability that it employs prior to qualifying one as being 'disabled' and subsequently sending out disability benefits to beneficiaries. SSA states that a person must not be able to engage in any Substantial Gainful Activity (SGA) because of a medically-determinable physical or mental impairment that either results in death or has/will last for a continuous period of at least 12 months. SGA can be considered either full or part-time work. It includes work performed for pay or profit, work that could be performed for pay or profit, and work intended for profit, whether profit is realized or not.

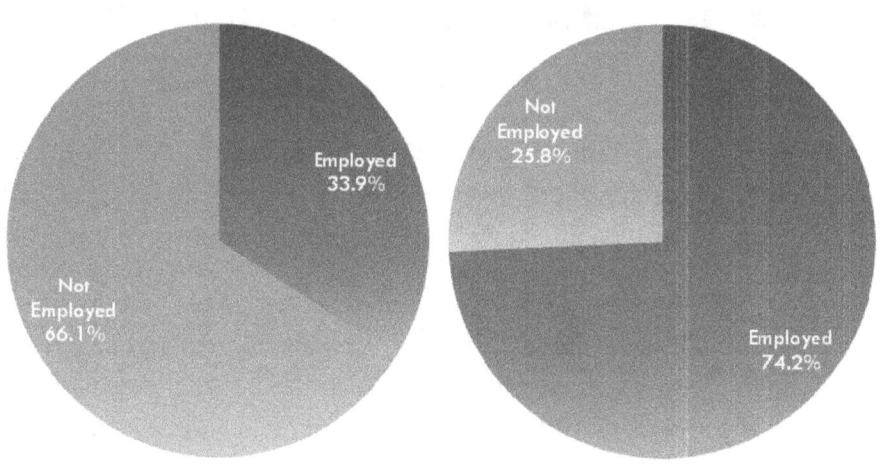

Employment Percentages of People with and without Disabilities, 2013

Employment Rate
(ages 21-64)

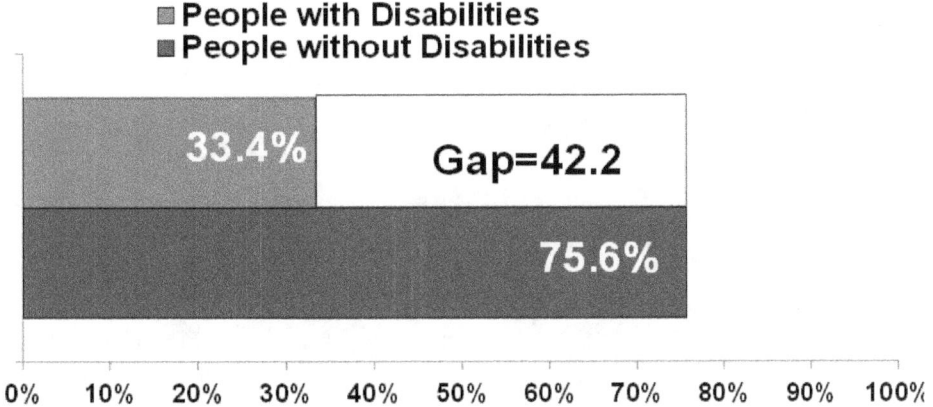

Employment Rate for Disabilities (State Comparisons)

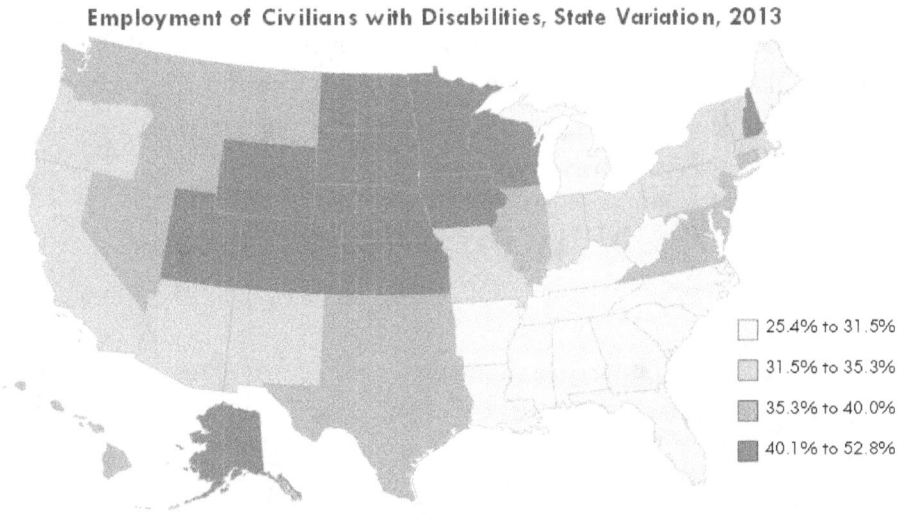

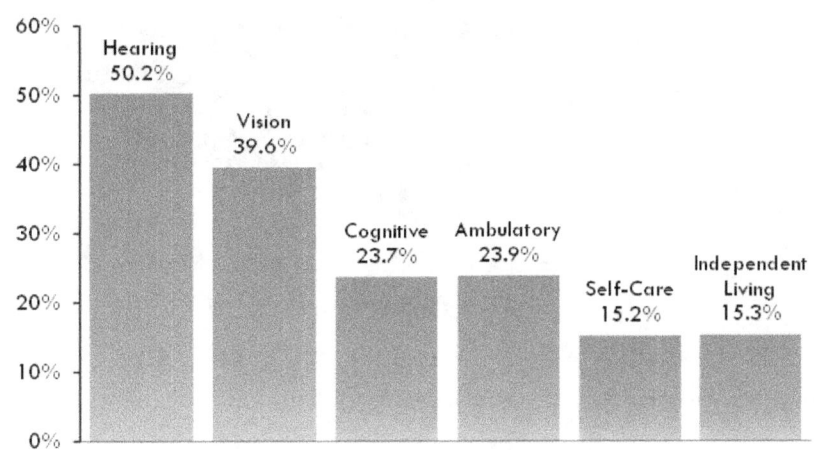

Earnings Average for Disabilities (State Comparisons)

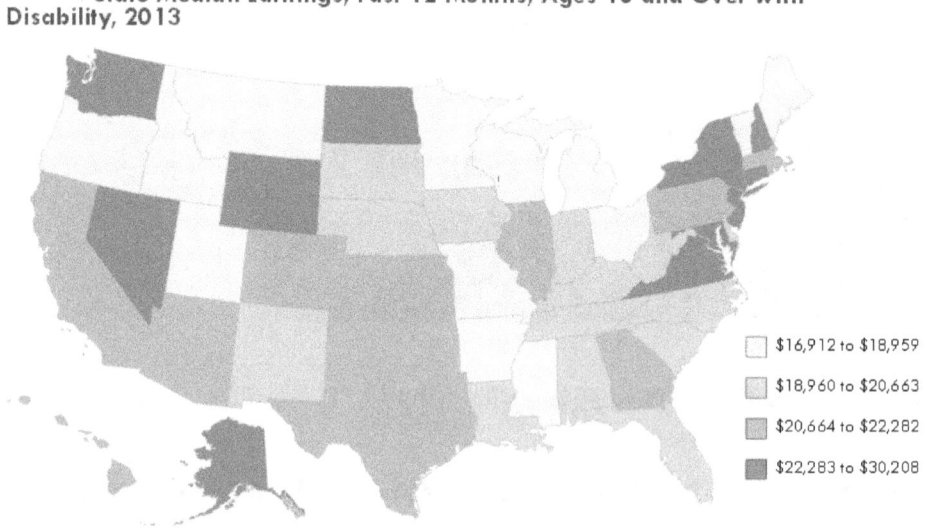

Based on this definition of disability, 10.2 million people received some sort of financial support from the Social Security Administration in 2014. Surprisingly, the states with the largest populations did not have the highest rates of disability beneficiaries. The states with the highest rates (over seven percent) were: Alabama, Arkansas, Kentucky, Maine, Mississippi, and West Virginia.

Disability Prevalence Rate

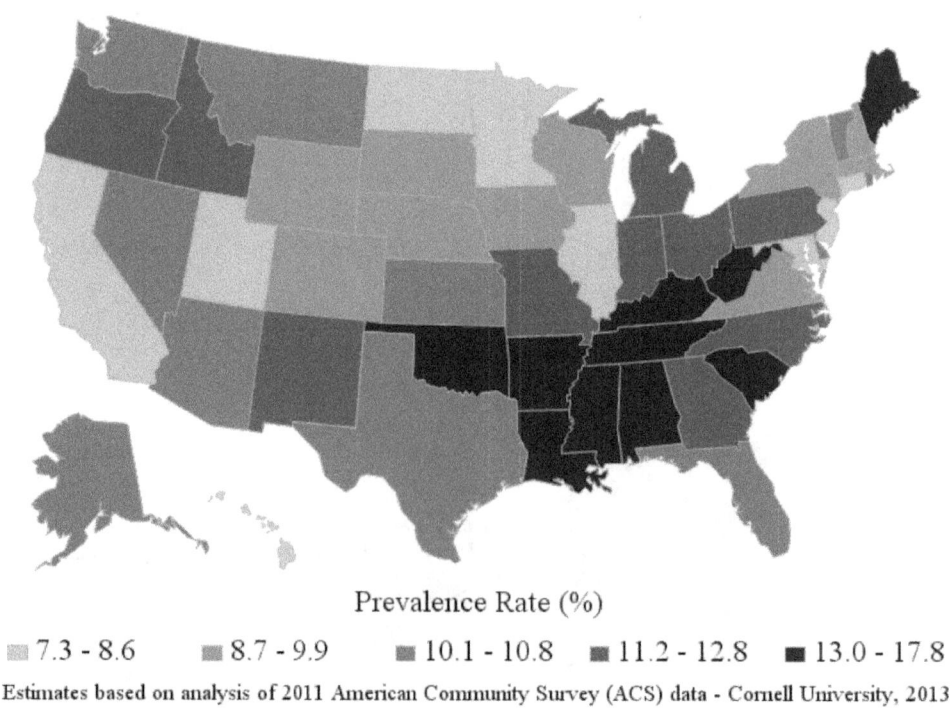

Social Security Recipients by State

Social Security
Number of recipients by state or other area, eligibility category, age, and receipt of OASDI benefits, December 2014

State or area	Total	Category		Age			SSI recipients also receiving OASDI
		Aged	Blind and disabled	Under 18	18–64	65 or older	
All areas	8,335,457	1,151,881	7,183,576	1,299,743	4,912,937	2,122,777	2,748,976
Alabama	174,524	9,574	164,950	27,624	118,618	28,282	62,796
Alaska	12,399	1,777	10,622	1,258	8,040	3,101	4,280
Arizona	119,510	15,780	103,730	20,978	69,564	28,968	38,363
Arkansas	111,482	5,560	105,922	28,863	67,733	14,886	37,974
California	1,304,400	360,514	943,886	118,869	619,855	565,676	498,979
Colorado	72,872	9,071	63,801	9,991	46,688	16,193	23,772
Connecticut	63,259	6,681	56,578	8,938	39,679	14,642	19,719
Delaware	16,687	1,229	15,458	3,601	10,428	2,658	4,963
District of Columbia	26,782	1,979	24,803	4,079	18,040	4,663	6,519
Florida	561,125	127,975	433,150	107,287	268,648	185,190	179,468
Georgia	256,314	24,346	231,968	46,318	158,291	51,705	83,754
Hawaii	25,235	5,819	19,416	1,660	14,797	8,778	8,808
Idaho	30,493	1,807	28,686	5,576	20,834	4,083	10,246
Illinois	275,671	30,306	245,365	41,073	171,403	63,195	75,560
Indiana	127,957	5,448	122,509	24,593	89,423	13,941	38,961
Iowa	51,227	3,149	48,078	8,300	35,824	7,103	18,548
Kansas	48,920	2,953	45,967	9,516	32,481	6,923	16,478
Kentucky	188,401	9,607	178,794	27,941	128,445	32,015	64,025
Louisiana	181,279	12,377	168,902	36,143	113,096	32,040	58,832
Maine	37,591	1,787	35,804	4,262	27,937	5,392	15,330
Maryland	118,184	15,020	103,164	18,741	73,404	26,039	32,111
Massachusetts	188,726	22,213	166,513	23,980	116,812	47,934	57,302
Michigan	277,309	18,158	259,151	41,883	191,686	43,740	85,175
Minnesota	94,207	10,611	83,596	13,714	59,844	20,649	28,074
Mississippi	125,595	8,790	116,805	23,372	78,828	23,395	45,633
Missouri	142,768	7,241	135,527	23,610	99,671	19,487	48,609
Montana	18,248	1,287	16,961	2,427	12,762	3,059	6,831
Nebraska	27,719	2,169	25,550	4,105	19,190	4,424	9,972
Nevada	50,919	12,162	38,757	9,807	28,093	13,019	15,590
New Hampshire	19,671	899	18,772	2,516	15,034	2,121	6,695
New Jersey	181,606	35,697	145,909	25,894	98,369	57,343	57,868
New Mexico	64,059	8,496	55,563	9,262	37,578	17,219	24,647
New York	653,601	118,456	535,145	88,442	340,372	224,787	199,079
North Carolina	235,300	18,590	216,710	43,410	148,316	43,574	81,935
North Dakota	8,224	700	7,524	1,025	5,599	1,600	3,182
Ohio	313,259	15,226	298,033	50,469	219,044	43,746	89,746
Oklahoma	96,975	6,127	90,848	17,322	65,073	14,580	32,051
Oregon	85,136	9,099	76,037	10,735	57,067	17,334	27,882
Pennsylvania	374,111	24,297	349,814	72,103	236,902	65,106	105,709
Rhode Island	33,280	3,232	30,048	4,646	21,539	7,095	11,208
South Carolina	118,354	8,296	110,058	20,459	76,209	21,686	40,971
South Dakota	14,905	1,434	13,471	2,614	9,252	3,039	5,228
Tennessee	183,890	11,856	172,034	24,959	126,835	32,096	64,133
Texas	666,301	105,048	561,253	146,148	345,640	174,513	225,103
Utah	31,212	2,747	28,465	5,385	20,661	5,166	9,256
Vermont	15,783	1,000	14,783	1,627	11,602	2,554	6,786
Virginia	155,501	18,228	137,273	23,905	97,541	34,055	51,399
Washington	151,262	17,120	134,142	18,310	98,797	34,155	42,424
West Virginia	77,715	2,565	75,150	8,066	57,771	11,878	25,237
Wisconsin	117,679	6,904	110,775	22,627	78,180	16,872	39,012
Wyoming	6,786	330	6,456	1,002	4,908	876	2,544
Outlying area							
Northern Mariana Islands	1,044	144	900	308	534	202	209

SOURCES: Social Security Administration, Master Beneficiary Record and Supplemental Security Record, 100 percent data; and U.S. Postal Service geographic data.

CONTACT: (410) 965-0090 or statistics@ssa.gov.

File available from:
U.S. Social Security Administration • Office of Retirement and Disability Policy • Office of Research, Evaluation, and Statistics
SSI Recipients by State and County, 2014
http://www.socialsecurity.gov/policy/docs/statcomps/ssi_sc/2014/

Social Security Payments by State

Social Security
Amount of payments, by state or other area, eligibility category, and age, December 2014
(in thousands of dollars)

State or area	Total	Category		Age		
		Aged	Blind and disabled	Under 18	18–64	65 or older
All areas	4,686,160	484,298	4,201,862	862,438	2,916,177	907,545
Alabama	93,376	2,376	91,000	18,109	66,558	8,708
Alaska	6,366	600	5,766	730	4,503	1,133
Arizona	66,366	6,067	60,300	13,945	40,947	11,475
Arkansas	60,491	1,248	59,243	19,155	37,198	4,137
California	817,219	185,057	632,162	86,290	430,394	300,536
Colorado	39,932	3,661	36,271	6,379	27,120	6,433
Connecticut	35,702	2,691	33,011	6,092	23,506	6,104
Delaware	9,350	453	8,897	2,289	6,059	1,001
District of Columbia	16,333	762	15,571	2,749	11,633	1,951
Florida	305,132	55,137	249,994	70,293	155,628	79,211
Georgia	142,070	7,581	134,489	30,941	93,850	17,279
Hawaii	14,655	2,549	12,106	1,049	9,538	4,068
Idaho	16,345	549	15,796	3,526	11,464	1,356
Illinois	156,021	12,749	143,272	27,655	100,936	27,430
Indiana	72,464	1,776	70,687	16,236	51,401	4,826
Iowa	27,155	960	26,195	5,321	19,482	2,352
Kansas	26,608	996	25,612	6,182	17,990	2,436
Kentucky	100,954	2,597	98,357	18,478	71,913	10,562
Louisiana	98,441	3,303	95,138	23,950	64,158	10,334
Maine	19,692	474	19,218	2,671	15,343	1,678
Maryland	69,192	6,313	62,879	12,313	45,979	10,900
Massachusetts	102,391	9,408	92,983	15,394	66,220	20,777
Michigan	160,054	7,567	152,487	27,923	113,827	18,304
Minnesota	53,139	4,912	48,227	8,909	34,400	9,831
Mississippi	66,681	1,961	64,720	15,346	44,490	6,845
Missouri	78,271	2,316	75,955	15,617	56,060	6,593
Montana	9,558	366	9,192	1,611	6,973	973
Nebraska	14,810	754	14,056	2,569	10,697	1,545
Nevada	28,853	4,975	23,878	6,564	16,970	5,319
New Hampshire	10,344	336	10,008	1,533	8,046	764
New Jersey	100,791	15,011	85,780	17,219	59,300	24,271
New Mexico	33,842	2,587	31,255	6,164	21,765	5,913
New York	360,332	49,273	311,059	59,400	201,339	99,593
North Carolina	127,056	5,066	121,990	28,066	85,407	13,583
North Dakota	4,034	254	3,780	605	2,865	565
Ohio	179,732	5,715	174,017	33,823	128,691	17,217
Oklahoma	53,100	1,718	51,382	11,260	37,227	4,613
Oregon	48,366	3,457	44,909	7,085	34,571	6,710
Pennsylvania	214,328	9,442	204,886	47,413	139,463	27,452
Rhode Island	17,962	1,181	16,780	3,035	12,148	2,779
South Carolina	64,278	2,174	62,104	13,347	44,062	6,869
South Dakota	7,697	478	7,219	1,648	4,996	1,053
Tennessee	100,557	3,258	97,300	16,275	73,821	10,461
Texas	345,934	34,609	311,325	94,115	192,710	59,109
Utah	17,255	1,135	16,120	3,355	11,797	2,103
Vermont	8,535	333	8,202	1,125	6,530	880
Virginia	85,387	7,066	78,322	15,824	56,500	13,064
Washington	87,344	7,950	79,394	11,890	59,679	15,775
West Virginia	42,701	672	42,029	5,355	33,273	4,073
Wisconsin	64,810	2,280	62,530	14,772	43,788	6,250
Wyoming	3,509	81	3,428	622	2,631	256
Outlying area						
Northern Mariana Islands	645	65	581	221	329	95

SOURCES: Social Security Administration, Supplemental Security Record, 100 percent data; and U.S. Postal Service geographic data.
CONTACT: (410) 965-0090 or statistics@ssa.gov.

File available from:
U.S. Social Security Administration • Office of Retirement and Disability Policy • Office of Research, Evaluation, and Statistics
SSI Recipients by State and County, 2014
http://www.socialsecurity.gov/policy/docs/statcomps/ssi_sc/2014/

Part III - Best Places to Live For Physical Disabilities

Veterans with a Service-Connected Disability

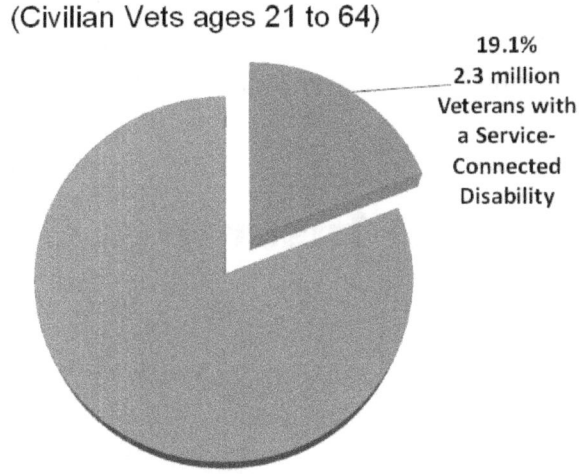

Resource for information of the above: Social Security Annual Statistical Report on the Social Security Disability Insurance Program, 2014
https://www.ssa.gov/policy/docs/statcomps/di_asr/2014/di_asr14.pdf

Disability Prevalence Rate

Disability is a broad term that varies based on the federal for state agency defining it. For instance, the Centers for Disease Control (CDC) issued a report that coincided with the 25th anniversary of the enactment of the Americans with Disabilities Act, a law prohibiting discrimination against a person because of a disability—in the workplace, in matters of transportation, and in community life in general. A disability is defined by the CDC as "anything that impedes vision, cognition, mobility, self-care or independent living."

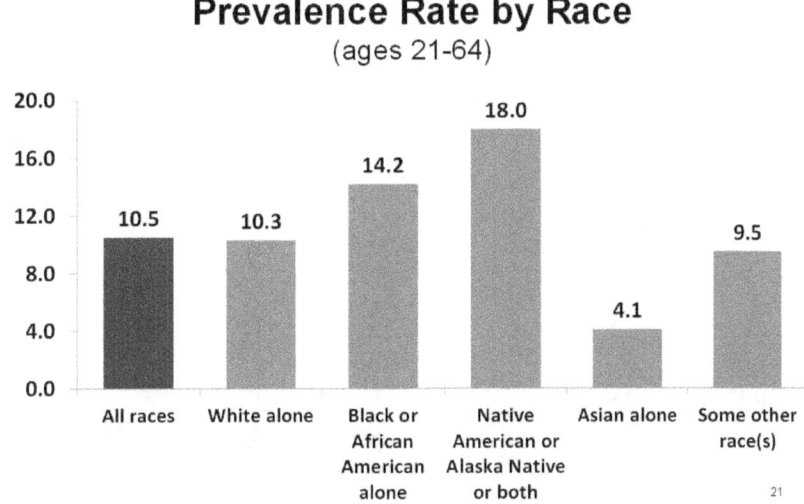

The Social Security Administration defines disability a bit more specifically and also includes the use of sub-categories. Two major categories, Musculo- skeletal system and connective tissue, as well as mental

159

disabilities, which make up over half of those currently receiving benefits. Mental illness is broken into nine separate diagnostic categories including autism, schizophrenia/paranoia/psychotic disorders, anxiety, substance addiction, etc. "Musculo- skeletal system and connective tissue" could include joint or back pain, spinal issues, or hereditary, infectious or degenerative processes. What this intends to show is that defining disability is complex and can include many different categories.

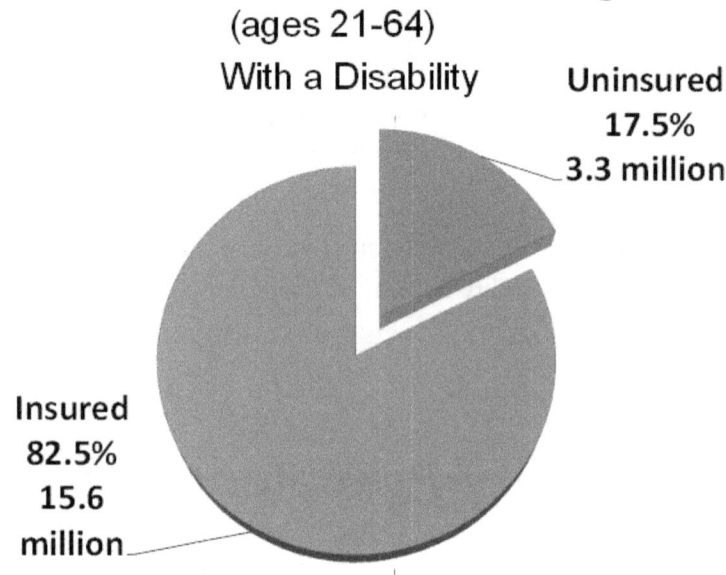

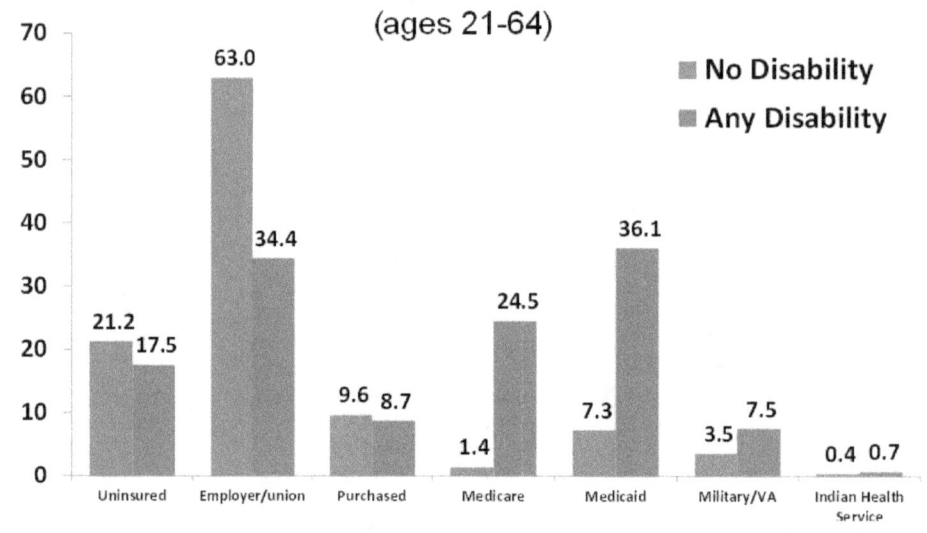

Age Distribution of Disability

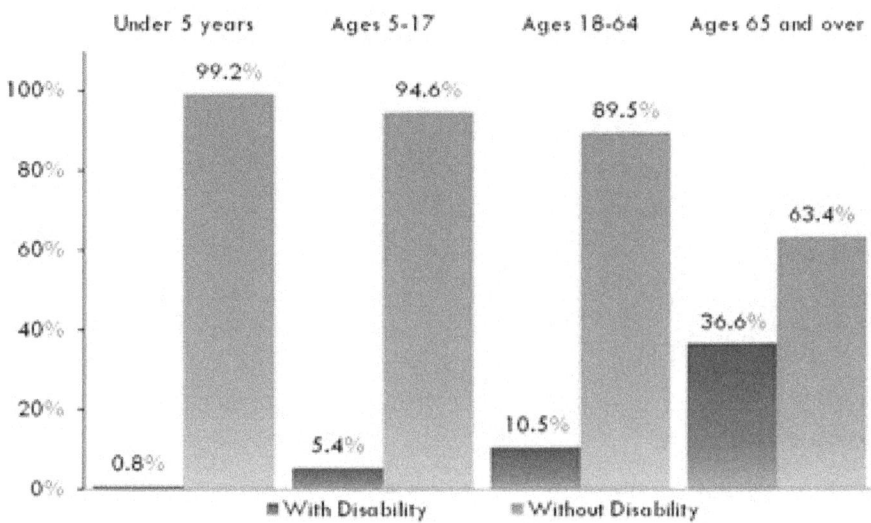

Kinds of Disabilities and State Comparisons

The Social Security Administration breaks these kinds of disabilities down into two broad categories: Part 'A' and Part 'B'

Part A of the Listing of Impairments contains medical criteria that apply to the evaluation of impairments in adults age 18 and over. They are as follows:

- Musculoskeletal System
- 2.00 Special Senses and Speech
    - Respiratory System
    - Cardiovascular System
- 5.00 Digestive System
- 6.00 Genitourinary Disorders
- 7.00 Hematological Disorders
    - Skin Disorders
- 9.00 Endocrine Disorders
    - Congenital Disorders that Affect Multiple Body Systems
- 11.00 Neurological
- 12.00 Mental Disorders
- 13.00 Cancer (malignant neoplastic diseases)
- 14.00 Immune System Disorders

Listing of Impairments - Childhood Listings (Part B)

The following sections provide medical criteria for the evaluation of impairments of children under age 18 (where criteria in Part A - Adult listings do not give appropriate consideration to the particular disease process in childhood).

- 100.00 Low Birth Weight and Failure to Thrive
- 101.00 Musculoskeletal System
- 102.00 Special Senses and Speech
- 103.00 Respiratory System
- 104.00 Cardiovascular System
- 105.00 Digestive System
- 106.00 Genitourinary Disorders
- 107.00 Hematological Disorders
- 108.00 Skin Disorders
- 109.00 Endocrine Disorders
- 110.00 Congenital Disorders that Affect Multiple Body Systems
- 111.00 Neurological
- 112.00 Mental Disorders
- 113.00 Cancer (malignant neoplastic diseases)
- 114.00 Immune System Disorders

What follows is a list of these major disability types, a short description, and the current percentage of the 10.2 million people disability benefit recipients that the disability impacts.

Congenital anomalies. This primarily includes Down Syndrome and other chromosomal disorders, and makes up .4% of those receiving benefits.

Endocrine, nutritional, and metabolic diseases: This can include hormonal imbalances, thyroid disorders, hypoglycemia, and diabetes. This makes up 2.7% of those receiving benefits.

Mental Disorders: At over 35% of recipients, this is easily the largest category in this list. This includes autism (.5%) intellectual disability (defined as needing to be dependent upon others for basic personal needs or an I.Q. score of less than 59, 8.3%) Mood disorders (including oddity of thought or seclusiveness, 13.8%) or schizophrenic/psychotic disorders (5%)

Diseases of the Blood, Circulatory, and Digestive system: About 11% of recipients, this could include Crohn's disease, disorders that impact the heart and circulatory system, and Hepatitis C.

Musculoskeletal system and connective tissue: The biggest single category of disability at 28%, with nearly three million people impacted. This is perhaps due to workplace injuries, as workers are one of the biggest recipients of disability benefits from SSA. This could include bone and joint deformity requiring reconstructive surgery, burns, amputations, fractures of hips or legs, broken arms, or any limitation that might prevent moving at a brisk pace or the inability to engage in fine motor skills including reaching, grasping, pulling, etc. as well as preparing a meal and feeding one's self. Other examples in this category could include osteoarthritis, spina bifida, a from-birth spinal defect, and spine curvature.

Nervous system and sense organs: This category, affecting 9.4% of recipients includes all from birth neurological disorders such as cerebral palsy, hereditary diseases like muscular dystrophy, degenerative diseases like multiple sclerosis, head/brain trauma, Parkinson's disease and epilepsy and other seizure disorders. Of these, one of the most common disabilities is cerebral palsy, a neurological condition that stems from a lack of oxygen to the brain due to premature birth. It is estimated roughly 10,000 children each year are diagnosed with cerebral palsy.

Respiratory system: At 2.6 percent, this category includes asthma, hereditary disorders like cystic fibrosis which can lead to respiratory infection, or Chronic pulmonary insufficiency, where the body cannot take in enough oxygen to remain healthy.

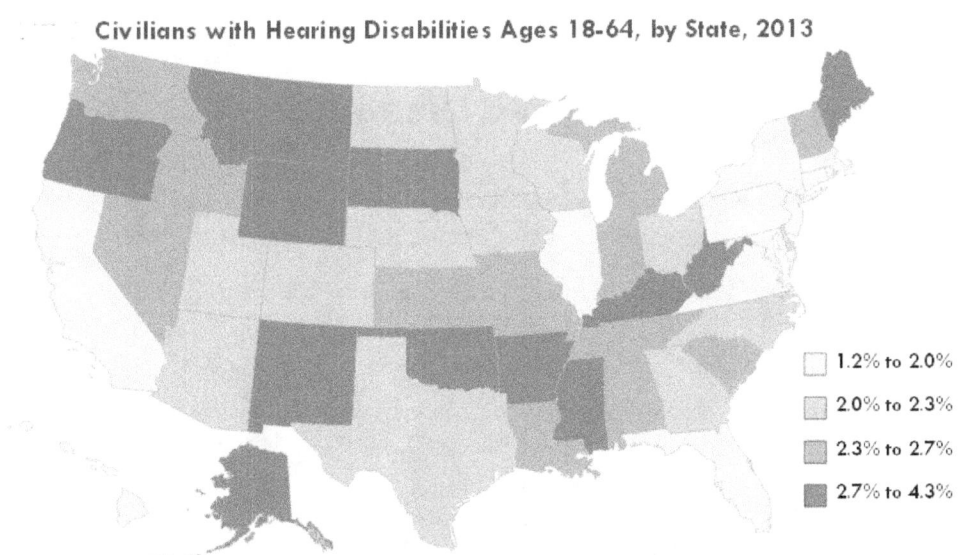

Vision Disabilities

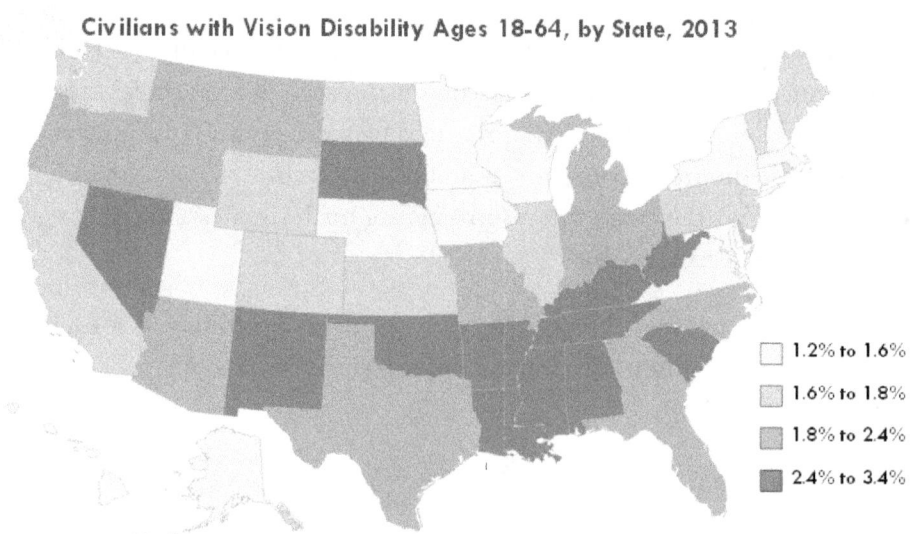

Cognitive Disability

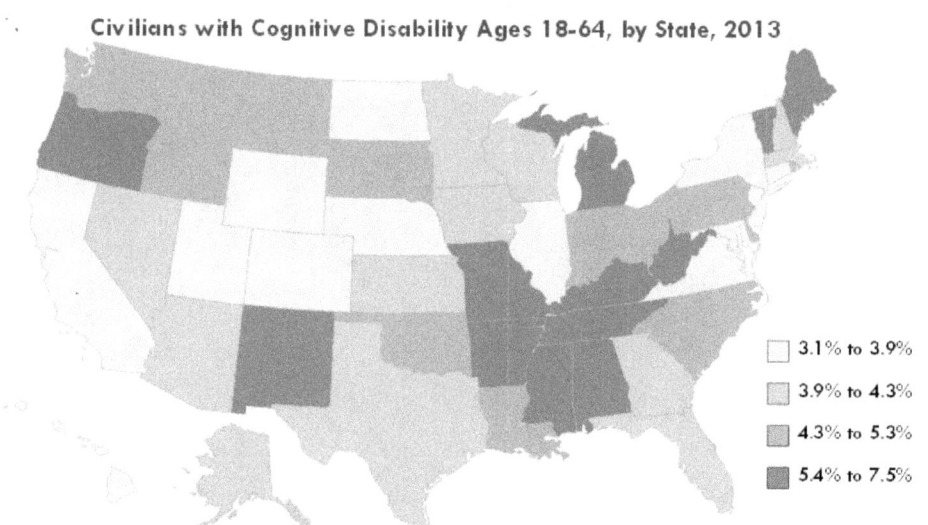

Ambulatory Disability

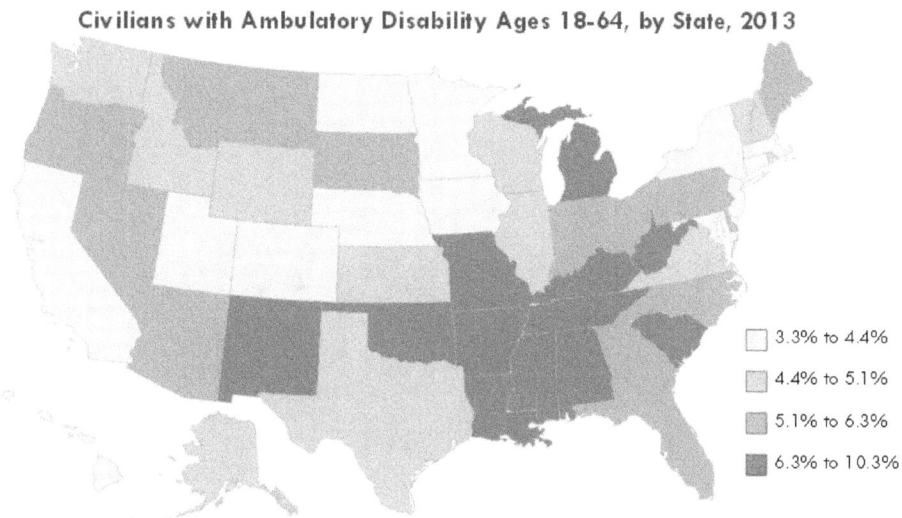

Self-Care Disability

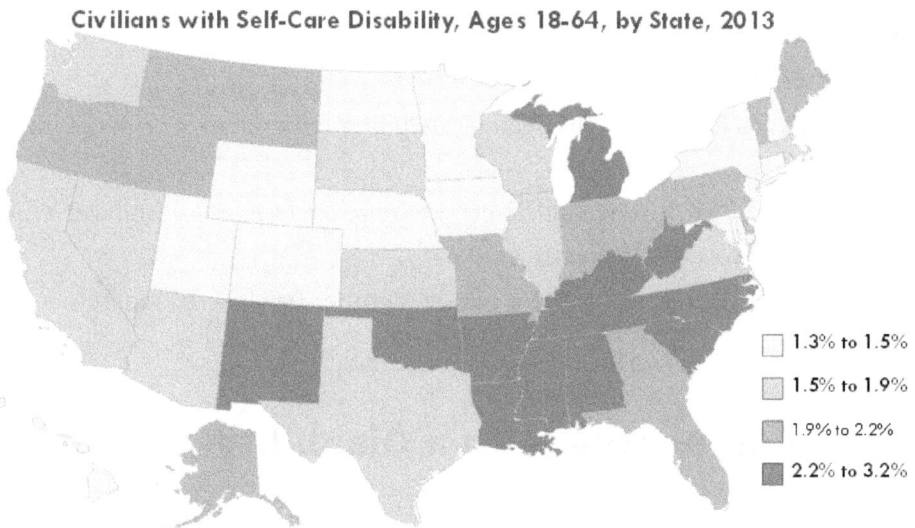

Independent Living Disability

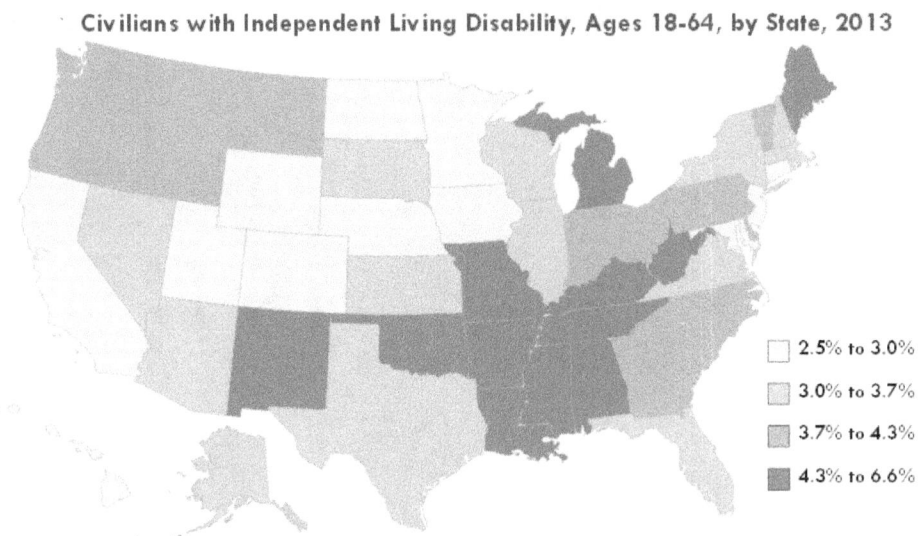

General Disability Statistics

- One-in-five Americans have a disability.
- 56.7 million Americans have a disability.
- 8.1 million Americans have difficulty seeing, including 2.0 million who were blind or unable to see at all.
- 7.6 million Americans experience difficulty hearing, including 1.1 million whose difficulty was severe. About 5.6 million used a hearing aid.
- 51 percent of Americans report having a family member or close friend with a disability.

Working-Age People with a Disability / Employment

- 21 million working-age people with disabilities.
- 34 percent of working age people with disabilities are employed.
- 40.2 percent of people with visual impairment are employed.
- 24 percent of people with ambulatory or cognitive difficulties are employed.
- 57.1 percent gap in labor force participation rates between those with and without disabilities.
- The gap in labor force participation between people with and without disabilities in 1981 was 45.2 percent. In 2013 it had grown to 57.1 percent – a roughly 12 percent increase.
- 1.3 million young Americans ages 16-20 with disabilities.
- 300,000 young people with disabilities age into what should be the workforce each year.

Poverty

- 28.5 percent of people with disabilities live in poverty.
- More people with disabilities live in poverty (28.5 percent) than any other minority. 26.2 percent of African Americans live in poverty while 23.6 percent of Hispanic Americans do. 15.3 percent of women live in poverty and just 10.1 perent of white people live in poverty. Obviously, there is an even higher poverty rate for people who fall into multiple categories, such as an African American woman with a disability.
- Working-age adults (ages 21 to 64) with disabilities had median monthly earnings of $1,961 compared with $2,724 for those with no disability.
- 11 million working-age Americans with disabilities live on government benefits.

Education

- Seven percent of people with disabilities will earn a college degree.
- 53 percent of college graduates with disabilities are employed.

Crime, Incarceration and Violence

- People with disabilities are twice as likely to be victims of crime than people without disabilities. People with disabilities between the ages of 12-15 and 35-49 were three times more likely to be victims of violent crimes.
- 32 percent of federal prisoners report having at least one disability.
- 40 percent of jail inmates report having at least one disability.
- At least half of the estimated 375 to 500 people shot and killed by police each year in this country have mental health problems.

NOTE: Statistics above provided by the organization, 'RespectAbility'. RespectAbility is on the front lines in the battle to reduce stigmas, failed government policies, and other obstacles that deny people with disabilities the opportunity to achieve the American Dream. They are highly recommended. More about RespectAbility can be found on their website at: http://respectabilityusa.com

Obesity and Disabilities

In 2013, 40.1% of adults with disabilities were obese. For people without disabilities, the obesity percentage was 24.9%.

State obesity percentages for people with disabilities ranged from 28.9% to 46.6%. State obesity percentages for people without disabilities ranged from 19.3% to 31.7%. Since 2009, the obesity percentage increased for both people with disabilities (from 36.9% in 2009 to 40.1% in 2013) and people without disabilities (from 23.5% in 2009 to 25.0% in 2013). In 2013, the gap between the percentages of obesity for people with and without disabilities increased from 13.4% in 2009 to 15.1%, the largest difference in this period.

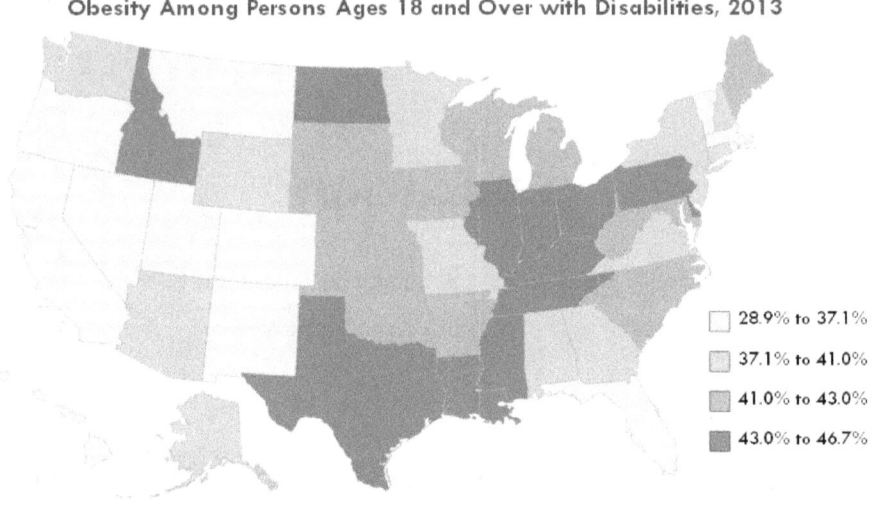

Obesity Among Persons Ages 18 and Over with Disabilities, 2013

Binge Drinking Among the Disabled

The 2013 state percentages for binge drinking among people with disabilities, ages 18 and over ranged from 5.6% in Tennessee to 15.8% in Massachusetts. In the years 2009 through 2013, the binge drinking percentage for people with disabilities varied from a high of 13.2% in 2009 to a low of 10.2% in 2010.

For people without disabilities the percentages were higher, varying from 16.0% in 2009 to 20.4% in 2011. The binge drinking gap measures the degree to which people with disabilities have less binge drinking; the gap was 6.5% in 2013, lower in 2009 (2.8%) and 2010 (5.9%), and higher in 2011 (7.8%) and 2012 (6.7%).

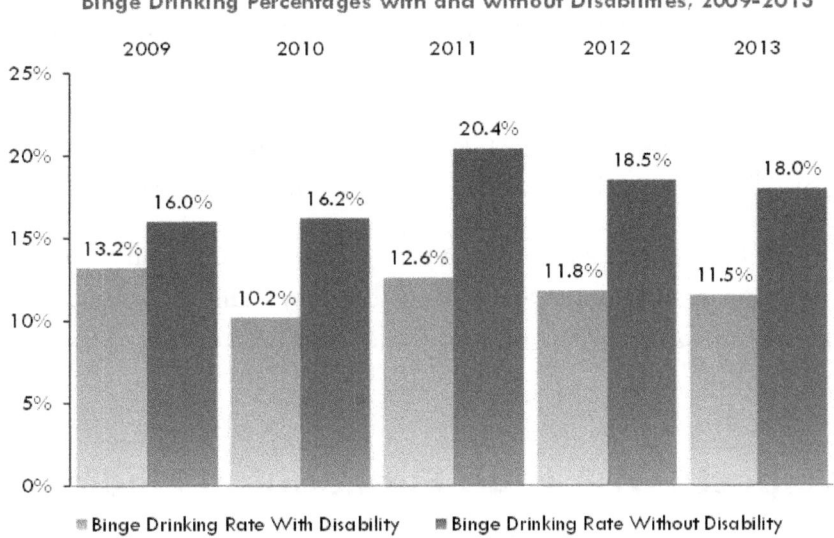

Binge Drinking Percentages with and without Disabilities, 2009-2013

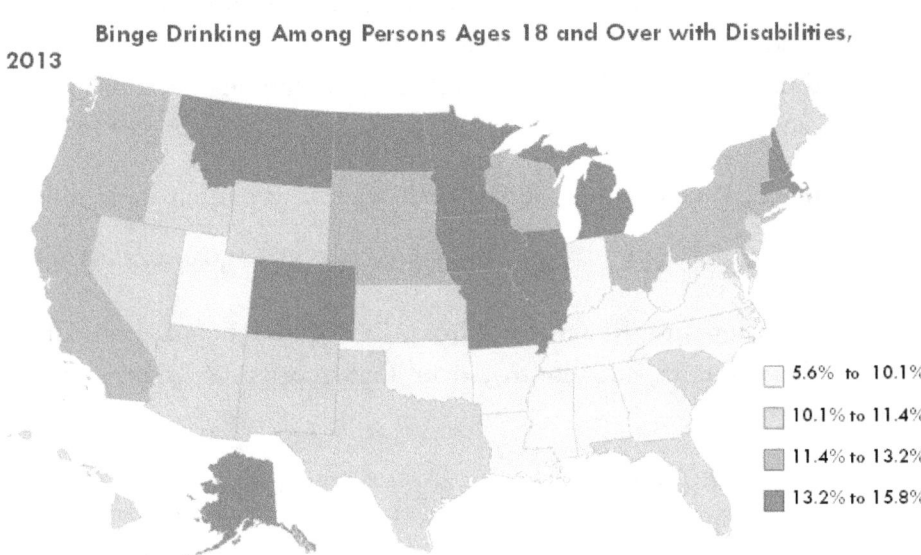

Binge Drinking Among Persons Ages 18 and Over with Disabilities, 2013

State Comparisons for Disability Services

Every year since 2006, United Cerebral Palsy (UCP) produces he *Case for Inclusion*, an annual ranking of how well State Medicaid programs serve Americans with intellectual and developmental disabilities (ID/DD) and their families. Individuals with ID/DD, including the young and the aging, want and deserve the same opportunities and quality of life as all Americans.

Medicaid impacts so many—children and adults with disabilities, the elderly and families living in poverty. It is the critical safety net that provides financial and health care security and community support to Americans, including those with ID/DD, so their desired opportunities, quality of life and community participation can be fully realized.

It is both a duty and a necessity of a civil society such as ours to aid and empower these individuals, who are often the most vulnerable among us, to succeed. We are all stronger together.

Yet some States do much better than others in demonstrating the needed political will and sound policies necessary to achieve this ideal. *The Case for Inclusion* ranks all 50 States and the District of Columbia (DC)—not on their spending – but on their **outcomes** for Americans with ID/DD.

The Case for Inclusion is a tool that gives us glimpses at how well each individual State is performing overall; how each State matches up against other States regarding key data measures; and, most importantly, the policies and practices of top performing States that may be considered as best practices.

Four Key Aspects Of A High Functioning Medicaid Program

The University of Minnesota's Research and Training Center on Community Living identifies the four key aspects of a high functioning and effective Medicaid program, which have also been articulated in a number of legislative, administrative and judicial statements describing national policy.1 *The Case for Inclusion's* five major outcome areas align, as indicated, with the following four-part holistic approach:

1. **Promoting Independence:** People with disabilities will live in and participate in their communities.

2. **Promoting Productivity:** People with disabilities will have satisfying lives and valued social roles.

3. **Keeping Families Together and Reaching Those in Needs:** People with disabilities will have sufficient access to needed support, and control over that support so that assistance they receive contributes to lifestyles they desire.

4. **Tracking Health, Safety, and Quality of Life:** People will be safe and healthy in the environments in which they live.

The rankings in this report are a snapshot in time. Most data is from 2013, which is the most recent data available from credible, national sources. All data is sourced directly from the States to the federal government and in response to public surveys.

State Comparisons for Disability Services (By Rank)

States	2015 Rankings	States	2015 Rankings
Arizona	1	Washington	26
Maryland	2	Florida	27
Missouri	3	New Jersey	28
New York	4	Michigan	29
Hawaii	5	West Virginia	30
Colorado	6	Nevada	31
Minnesota	7	Tennessee	32
Dist. of Columbia	8	Wisconsin	33
South Carolina	9	North Carolina	34
Ohio	10	Delaware	35
Georgia	11	New Mexico	36
Maine	12	Nebraska	37
Alabama	13	South Dakota	38
Massachusetts	14	Rhode Island	39
Utah	15	Alaska	40
California	16	Virginia	41
Connecticut	17	North Dakota	42
Oregon	18	Oklahoma	43
Kentucky	19	Iowa	44
Kansas	20	Wyoming	45
Vermont	21	Idaho	46
Pennsylvania	22	Illinois	47
Indiana	23	Montana	48
Louisiana	24	Arkansas	49
New Hampshire	25	Texas	50
		Mississippi	51

State Comparisons for Disability Services (Alphabetical)

States	2015 Rankings	States	2015 Rankings
Alabama	13	Montana	48
Alaska	40	Nebraska	37
Arizona	1	Nevada	31
Arkansas	49	New Hampshire	25
California	16	New Jersey	28
Colorado	6	New Mexico	36
Connecticut	17	New York	4
Delaware	35	North Carolina	34
Dist. of Columbia	8	North Dakota	42
Florida	27	Ohio	10
Georgia	11	Oklahoma	43
Hawaii	5	Oregon	18
Idaho	46	Pennsylvania	22
Illinois	47	Rhode Island	39
Indiana	23	South Carolina	9
Iowa	44	South Dakota	38
Kansas	20	Tennessee	32
Kentucky	19	Texas	50
Louisiana	24	Utah	15
Maine	12	Vermont	21
Maryland	2	Virginia	41
Massachusetts	14	Washington	26
Michigan	29	West Virginia	30
Minnesota	7	Wisconsin	33
Mississippi	51	Wyoming	45
Missouri	3		

Sub-Ranking By Major Category

Although the overall ranking presents a comprehensive view of each State and the District of Columbia, it is more important to consider the top-performing States in each of the five major categories, in addition to how improvement in any category would have the biggest impact on better State performance and subsequent ranking. For example, Arizona ranks #1 overall, but ranks low (sub-ranking #41) for promoting productivity. Arizona could potentially learn from Washington State (sub-ranking #1) how it might improve in this area.

Part III - Best Places to Live For Physical Disabilities

	Promoting Independence		Tracking, Health Safety & Quality of Life		Keeping Families Together		Promoting Productivity		Reaching Those in Need		Overall	
	50% of total		14% of total		8% of total		12% of total		16% of total		100%	
	Score	Rank	Score	Rank	Score	Rank	Score	Rank	Score	Rank	Score	Rank
Alabama	43.5	12	12.1	1	1.5	44	5.4	46	10.5	38	73	13
Alaska	43.2	14	0	32	1.6	42	6.6	20	10.4	40	61.8	40
Arizona	47.3	2	11.3	21	7.1	1	5.8	41	14.3	5	85.8	1
Arkansas	25	50	12	2	1.2	48	5.9	40	11.3	28	55.5	49
California	45.1	7	0	32	4.5	7	7.6	7	14.9	2	72.2	16
Connecticut	38.3	34	11.9	4	3.3	20	8.2	5	9.8	44	72	17
Delaware	41.5	26	0	32	4.2	13	5.3	47	13.5	8	64.4	35
Dist. of Columbia	42.6	18	11.7	9	2.3	33	4.6	48	13.3	10	74.5	8
Florida	30.9	28	11.6	12	3	26	3.3	50	10.2	41	69	27
Georgia	44.3	11	11.6	11	1.5	46	7.1	11	9	46	73.5	11
Hawaii	46.8	4	10.5	29	3.4	17	2.8	51	13.3	9	76.8	5
Idaho	38.5	36	0	32	1.1	51	6.1	34	13.1	12	58.7	46
Illinois	27.8	49	11.5	13	1.7	41	5.8	43	9.7	45	56.5	47
Indiana	37.9	38	11.6	10	2.6	32	6.7	18	11.2	30	70	23
Iowa	37.1	41	0	32	1.6	43	6.6	22	14.4	6	59.5	44
Kansas	39.2	30	11.1	24	2	37	6.5	25	12.5	19	71.3	20
Kentucky	41.2	27	10.8	28	1.2	47	6.3	29	12.2	22	71.7	19
Louisiana	35.4	42	11	25	6.4	3	6.2	30	10.7	35	69.8	24
Maine	42.4	19	10.8	27	1.5	35	5.9	37	12.8	17	73.4	12
Maryland	44.8	8	11.3	22	1.2	49	8.3	3	12.4	21	78	2
Massachusetts	42.4	20	11.5	16	1.7	40	6.5	23	10.7	34	72.8	14
Michigan	44.7	10	0	32	4	14	7	14	13.2	11	68.8	29
Minnesota	41.8	23	11.5	15	3.3	21	6.9	16	11.2	29	74.6	7
Mississippi	8.4	51	2.6	30	2.1	35	5.6	45	10.5	37	29.2	51
Missouri	42.2	21	11.4	19	4.5	8	7	12	12.8	17	77.8	3
Montana	35.1	44	0	32	3.4	18	6	36	11.4	26	55.9	48
Nebraska	41.7	24	0	32	1.9	38	7	13	12.5	20	63.1	37
Nevada	45.6	6	0	32	3	25	6.7	19	10.1	42	65.4	31
New Hampshire	47	3	0	32	2.7	28	7.2	10	12.8	15	69.7	25
New Jersey	35.4	43	11.9	5	2.6	31	6.2	31	12.9	14	69	28
New Mexico	43.2	15	2.4	31	4.5	9	6.2	32	7.5	47	63.8	36
New York	39.2	32	11.4	20	4.3	12	6.4	26	15.5	1	76.8	4
North Carolina	30.3	48	11.8	6	4.4	11	6.5	24	11.8	23	64.9	34
North Dakota	37.3	40	0	32	2.2	34	6.6	21	14.3	4	60.4	42
Ohio	39.2	31	11.4	17	5.9	4	6.1	33	11.2	31	73.8	10
Oklahoma	34.6	45	11.4	18	2	36	5.9	38	5.6	49	59.5	43

continued

	Promoting Independence		Tracking, Health Safety & Quality of Life		Keeping Families Together		Promoting Productivity		Reaching Those in Need		Overall	
	Score	Rank	Score	Rank	Score	Rank	Score	Rank	Score	Rank	Score	Rank
Oregon	45.8	5	0	32	4.4	10	7.7	6	14	7	72	18
Pennsylvania	39.2	33	11.8	7	3.2	22	6.4	28	10	43	70.6	22
Rhode Island	43.4	13	0	32	2.7	29	5.7	44	10.6	36	62.4	39
South Carolina	38.3	37	11.7	8	6.4	2	6.9	15	10.9	32	74.3	9
South Dakota	37.8	39	0	32	3.1	24	7.6	8	14.5	3	63	38
Tennessee	42.7	171	12	3	1.7	39	4	49	4.7	50	65.1	32
Texas	31.6	47	0	32	3.3	19	5.8	42	0.8	51	41.5	50
Utah	40.2	29	10.9	26	3.7	16	6.4	27	11.6	25	72.8	15
Vermont	47.3	1	0	32	3.8	15	8.6	2	10.9	33	70.6	21
Virginia	33.9	46	11.2	23	2.7	30	5.9	39	7.3	48	61	41
Washington	41.8	22	0	32	4.6	6	10.1	1	13	13	69.5	26
West Virginia	41.7	25	0	32	3.1	23	8.3	4	12.6	18	65.7	30
Wisconsin	42.8	16	0	32	4.7	5	6.1	35	11.3	27	64.9	33
Wyoming	38.8	35	0	32	2.9	27	6.8	17	10.4	39	58.9	45

The Best, The Worst And Facts About the Top Ranked States

The Best Performing States

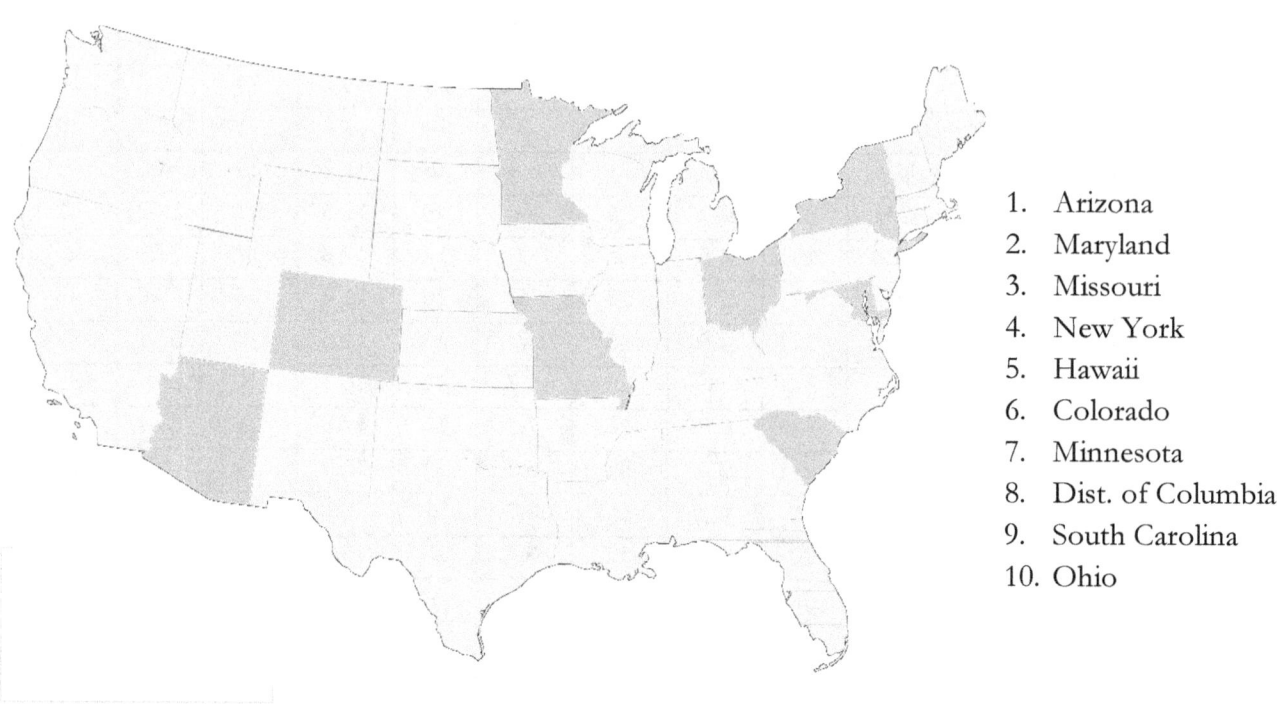

1. Arizona
2. Maryland
3. Missouri
4. New York
5. Hawaii
6. Colorado
7. Minnesota
8. Dist. of Columbia
9. South Carolina
10. Ohio

The Worst Performing States

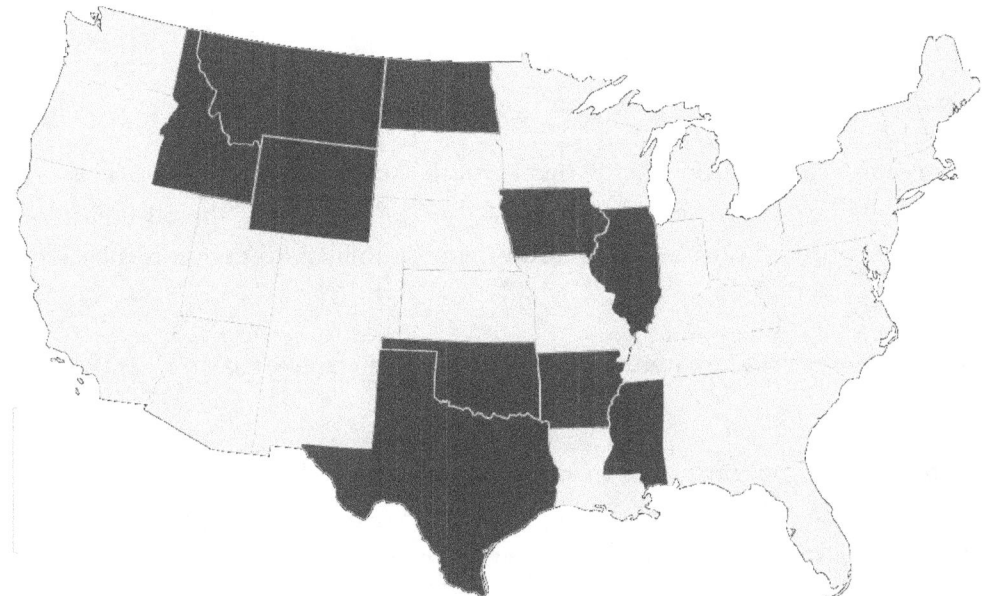

42. North Dakota
43. Oklahoma
44. Iowa
45. Wyoming
46. Idaho
47. Illinois
48. Montana
49. Arkansas
50. Texas
51. Mississippi

Facts About The Best Performing States

1. **Top Performers are both big and small States in population** — "big" population States include New York (3rd biggest) and Ohio (#7) as well as "small" population States such as Hawaii (#40) and the District of Columbia (#49).

2. **Top Performers are both rich and poor States in terms of median family income** — "rich" States include Maryland (2nd richest), Hawaii (8th richest), and D.C. (9th richest) and less affluent States such as Ohio (#40) and South Carolina (#44).

3. **Top Performers are high tax and low tax burden States** — "high tax burden" States include New York (#1), Minnesota (#6), and Maryland (#7) and "low tax burden" States include Arizona (#35), South Carolina (#42), and Missouri and Colorado (tied for #33).

4. **Top Performers are big and low spenders per person served through the Home and Community**- Based Services — "big spender" States are New York (#11) and D.C. (#3) and "low spender" States include Arizona (#50), Maryland (#44), and South Carolina (#45).

5. **Top Performers are politically diverse.** Seven of the top ten are "Blue States," according to their 2012 Presidential Election results, while three "Red States" were in the top ten.

The Proven Parenting And Programs To Help Kids With Intellectual And Developmental Disabilities Become Happy, Productive, Engaged Adults

Life is hard. Change is harder. Everyone struggles with transitions in life. Young adults with developmental disabilities are no different.

And yet, they are. The consequences of bad transitions can be greater and longer term for those with developmental disabilities, even compared to those with other types of disabilities or challenges.

"Youth with intellectual disabilities are more likely than youth with learning disabilities or emotional/behavioral disorders to stay in school until they age out of eligibility for special education services at age 21 and much less likely than almost all other youth with disabilities to earn a regular high school diploma.

Individuals with intellectual disabilities typically require lifelong support and are often at risk of being excluded from participation in society.

Indeed, most recent reports of the post-school outcomes of youth with intellectual disabilities have found that these youth are less likely than youth with other disabilities to attend postsecondary education, work, live independently, or see friends at least weekly in the early years after leaving high school [emphasis added]."

And they are more reliant on others to aid in (or undermine) this process.

Given all this, as part of this year's Case for Inclusion, UCP wanted to dive deeper into the latest research and best practices on transitions. The goals are two-fold:

1. To inform advocates and policymakers of key programming that support better transitions for young adults with developmental disabilities.

2. To empower parents, family members and young adults with developmental disabilities themselves of how to best support the transition from young adult to an adult with a full, inclusive and productive life.

There are many recent and in-depth reports on transitions. This case study will summarize major findings.

How does one define or measure a successful transition? One must have specific, measureable outcomes that approximate a host of softer, less measureable but desired outcomes – happiness, feelings of self-worth and a sense of a meaningful life – that signify a successful transition.

To best measure a successful transition, researchers used a national longitudinal survey of parents, youth, teachers and school officials called the National Longitudinal Transition Study-2 (NLTS2) which ran from 2000 to 2009 (for those ages 13 to 16 at the start of the study) to chart four key outcomes to best measure a successful transition within four years after high school for 490 youth.:

Positive Outcome	Details	Percent Reporting within 2-4 Years after High School
1. Employment	In any job, for any number of hours	41%
2. Postsecondary Education	Enrolled after high school training	35%
3. Enjoyment of Life	Answering "a lot" or "most" of the time to a survey question about how often the individual enjoys life	74%
4. Social Interactions	Answering at least weekly to a survey question about how often the individual gets together with friends outside of organized activities or groups	72%

So if those are the outcomes one wants for youth to have through a successful transition. What does it take to accomplish them? Using regression analysis, researchers identified key characteristics (demographic and family involvement) and best practices (formal school transition program activities) that had the strongest impact on a student having success in all four transition outcome areas. Even more interesting, was the extent of that impact.

Key Family Characteristics for a Successful Transition within Two to Four Years

Positive Outcome	Characteristic	Impact
1. Employment	Parent expects employment	32x more likely to be employed
	High family income	7x more likely to be employed
	Completed high school	6x more likely to be employed
	High functional academics	3x more likely to be employed
2. Postsecondary Education	Parent expects employment	4x more likely to be enrolled
	High functional academics	4x more likely to be enrolled
	Parent expects postsecondary education	3x more likely to be enrolled
	Medium family income	2x more likely to be enrolled
3. Enjoyment of Life	Parent expects employment	6x more likely to enjoy life
4. Social Interactions	Completed high school	12x more likely to be social

From this, it is clear that families have a tremendous impact on the successful transition of their children into a full and rich adulthood. **Most importantly, parents must:**

1. Expect employment for their child

85% of parents said they did

2. Expect postsecondary education for their child

Only 38% of parents said they did

3. Ensure high functional academic skills are realized by their child

Only 45% of students reported high functional skills in four key areas

4. Ensure their child completes high school

81% of students did

And while having a medium to high family income helps with a successful transition to employment and postsecondary education, it is not the most important characteristic and clearly this is not something families can easily change. The other four strategies for parents listed above can be accomplished regardless of income and, often, regardless of location (urban or rural). That's exciting and provides a clear, focused roadmap of how parents can lead their child into a successful transition and, ultimately, a full adult life.

Now, what about the student. What programming should the student receive that will equip him or her to transition successfully into adulthood? This same research asked that question and look at the key programming that aided in that transition.

Most Impactful Programs for a Successful Transition within Two to Four Years

Positive Outcome	Best Practice	Impact
1. Employment	Received work experiences	5x more likely to be employed
	Received youth involvement	5x more likely to be employed
2. Postsecondary Education	Received life skills instruction	41x more likely to be enrolled
	Received life skills instruction	9x more likely to be enrolled
	Received youth involvement	2x more likely to be enrolled
3. Enjoyment of Life	Received interagency involvement	12x more likely to enjoy life
	Received family involvement	6x more likely to enjoy life
4. Social Interactions	Received interagency involvement	2x more likely to be social

Just like with parents, from this program list we can see the profound impact that particular services have on youth successfully transitioning. While this in no way is to suggest that other services are not important or helpful, this list clearly outlines those services most proven to help youth become complete adults. Sadly, some of these program services are not common. That means that a majority of students are not getting what they need to be successful.

In particular, those individuals who had the following programming outcomes enjoyed the best transition outcomes:

1. Received work experiences

- As evidenced by percent of school day in work experiences
- Only 57% reported having work experiences

2. Received youth involvement

- As evidenced by their involvement in transition planning
- Only 58% reported involving youth

3. Had family involvement

- As evidenced by family involvement in transition planning
- 68% of families reported being involved

4. Had life skills instruction

- As evidenced by student receiving life skills or social skills instruction
- 72% reported receiving this

5. Enjoyed interagency involvement

- As evidenced by an adult service agency representative at the transition planning
- Only 43% reported having this involvement

If these are the five program outcomes that position students for a solid transition, then what are the best practices in these programs? Other research answers this with the curriculum and teaching methods that best produce the desired experience or outcome.

Positive Outcome	Best Practice
Functional Life Skills	Backward chaining
	Forward chaining
	Least-to-most prompting
	Most-to-least prompting
	Progressive time delay
	Response prompting
	Simultaneous prompting
Work Experiences	Computer-assisted instruction
	Community-based instruction
	Constant time delay
	Least to most prompting
	Mnemonics
Youth Involvement (through student involvement in the IEP meeting)	Check and Connect
	Computer-assisted instruction
	Published curricula
	Self-advocacy strategy
	Self-directed IEP
	"Whose Future Is It Anyway" program
Family Involvement	Training modules
Life Skills	Response prompting
	Simulations
	Total task chaining
Interagency Involvement	None identified

Transitions are tough. But with the right parent expectations and evidence-based programming for their students, youth with developmental disabilities can have a solid transition to an adult life rich with work, education, experiences and relationships.

How To Use & How The Rankings Were Developed

Using The Case For Inclusion Report

This report puts each State's progress in serving individuals with intellectual and developmental disabilities into a national context. It is intended to help advocates and policymakers understand:

How their State performs overall in serving individuals with intellectual and developmental disabilities?

What services and outcomes need attention and improvement in their State?

Which States are top performers in key areas, so advocates and officials in those top-performing States can act as a resource for those States desiring to improve in key areas?

ADVOCATES should use this information to educate other advocates, providers, families and individuals, policymakers and State administrations on key achievements and areas needing improvement within each State. The facts and figures can support policy reforms and frame debates about resource allocation for the ID/DD population. Advocates can also use the information to prioritize those areas that need the most immediate attention and use the facts to support adequate and ongoing funding to maintain high quality outcomes, eliminate waiting lists and close large institutions.

ELECTED OFFICIALS should use this report as a guiding document on which issues and States need time and attention and, possibly, additional resources or more inclusive State policies to improve outcomes for individuals with intellectual and developmental disabilities.

THOSE WITHIN FEDERAL AND STATE ADMINISTRATIONS should use this report to put their work and accomplishments in context and to chart a course for the next focus area in the quest for continuous improvement and improved quality of life.

The States should replicate this data reporting in more detail at the State and county level to identify areas of excellence and to target critical issues needing attention.

How The Rankings Were Developed

The Case for Inclusion rankings were developed through a broad, data-driven effort. Demographic, cost, utilization, key data elements and outcomes statistics were assembled for all 50 States and the District of Columbia. Ninety-nine individual data elements from numerous governmental non-profit and advocacy organizations were reviewed. Dozens of Medicaid, disability and ID/DD policy experts were consulted as well as members of national advocacy and research organizations. They were asked to consider the attributes of top performing Medicaid programs and offer opinions and recommendations on key data measures and outcomes.

To comprehensively determine the top-performing States, a weighted scoring methodology was developed. Thirty key outcome measures and data elements were selected and individually scored in five major categories on a total 100-point scale. If a person is living in the community, it is a key indicator of inclusion; therefore the "Promoting Independence" category received half of all possible points.

Weighting Of Case For Inclusion Scored — 100 Total Possible Points

Category	Measure		Points Assigned	
Promoting Independence	Community-Based	% of Recipients with ID/DD on HCBS	9	50
		% of ID/DD Expenditures on HCBS	7	
		% of ID/DD Expenditures on non-ICF-MR	8	
	Residential Services in the Community (includes all types)	1–3 Residents %	13	
		1–6 Residents %	11	
		16+ Residents % (smaller %, higher rank)	-4	
		% in Large State Facilities	-3	
	NCI - % Self-Directed		2	
Tracking Health, Safety & Quality of Life	Quality Assurance - NCI Participation		0	14
	NCI - Recent Dental Visit		2.8	
	NCI - Lonely Less than Half the Time		2.8	
	NCI - Not Scared in Own Home		2.8	
	NCI - Inclusion (sum of 4 measures)		2.8	
	NCI - Relationships Other than Staff and Family		2.8	
Keeping Families Together	Family Support per 100k		3	8
	% in a Family Home		3	
	NCI - Child/Family Survey Participation		2	
Promoting Productivity	Has Medicaid Buy-In Program		2	12
	Competitive Employment - %		4	
	Voc Rehab - Rehab Rate (finding a job)		2	
	Voc Rehab - Number of Hours Worked		2	
	Voc Rehab - Retain Job for One Year		2	
Reaching Those in Need	Waiting List - Average % Growth for Residential and HCBS		9	16
	Individuals with ID/DD Served per 100k of Population		2	
	Ratio of Prevalence to Individuals Served		2	
	Uses Federal Functional Definition for Eligibility or Broader		3	
			100	

In general, the top-performing State for each measure was assigned the highest possible score in that category. The worst-performing State was assigned a zero score in that category. All other States were apportioned accordingly based on their outcome between the top- and worst-performing.

As noted, most data is from 2013, but all data is the most recently available from credible national sources. Much of the data is self-reported by the States. These State rankings are a snapshot in time, and policy changes or reforms enacted or beginning in 2014 or later would not have an impact on the data.

When reviewing an individual State's ranking, it is important to consider action taken since 2013, if any, to accurately understand both where that State was and where it is presently. Also, it is important to note that not all individuals with disabilities were considered, only those with intellectual and developmental disabilities. This limited the scope of the effort, allowing focus on subsequent initiatives of meaningful, achievable improvement.

A note of caution: Although more than 56 points separate the top performing State from the poorest performing State, 12 points separate the top 10 States, 16 points separate the top 25 States and only 10 points separate the middle 25 States. Therefore, minor changes in State policy or outcomes could significantly affect how a State ranks on future or past Case for Inclusion reports.

Most Livable U.S. Cities for Wheelchair Users

Data obtained from *The* Christopher & Dana Reeve Foundation (2016)

Introduction:

To get a better understanding of how cities in the U.S. are faring when it comes to accessible living, The Christopher & Dana Reeve Foundation looked at 100 of some of the largest cities in the United States and ranked them based on specific criteria that provides a snapshot of not just accessibility, but livability for people using wheelchairs.

Criteria Examined:

- Climate: A city's climate hospitality for those living with paralysis. Avoidance of cities with extremes in temperature or snowfall.
- Air Quality
- Number of Physicians:
- Number of Rehabilitation Specialist and Rehabilitation Centers
- Number of Accessible Fitness and Recreation Centers
- Paratransit System
- Population of physically disabled people in the city and whether those people have been able to get employment.
- Age of the city (old building are harder to make accessible).
- Spending and eligibility requirements for Medicaid.

<u>**A Cities Mobility:**</u>

Cities are required to make public transportation accessible to everyone, however "…even if a transit system is listed as accessible, it still may be very difficult to use it if you are in a wheelchair or other assistive device," says Yochai Eisenberg, an urban planner and Project Coordinator at the Department of Disability and Human Development at the University of Illinois at Chicago. "People tell us about the lifts on buses not working, or buses passing them by because they are in a wheelchair, or elevators at train stations being out of service for long periods."

Accessibility:

Asking if a building is "accessible" isn't good enough -- learn to ask the right questions, like 'How wide are your doorways?' or 'Is the bathroom on the first floor?'. "There is no organized way to check whether something is truly accessible," says Nary, who has been in situations where her wheelchair couldn't fit into an accessible hotel room bathroom. "We have to be our own police when it comes to ADA compliance."

Independent Living Centers can be a lifeline for people who are moving or even visiting a new city-they can offer first-hand advice when it comes to navigating a city's public transportation system, finding a gym to join or housing referrals. To find a center in your city, go to www.independentliving.org or DO AN Internet search using the words "independent living center" with your city name.

Following is a list of the tops 20 cities in the U.S., ranked order, for being most wheelchair accessible suing the above noted criteria:

1. Seattle, Wash.
2. Albuquerque, N.M.
3. Reno, Nev.
4. Denver, Colo.
5. Portland, Ore.
6. Chicago, Ill.
7. Birmingham, Ala.
8. Winston-Salem, N.C.
9. Orlando, Fla.
10. Lubbock, Texas
11. Miami, Fla.
12. Tampa, Fla.
13. Durham, N.C.
14. Fort Worth, Texas
15. Virginia Beach, Va.
16. Arlington, Texas
17. Baltimore, Md.
18. New Orleans, La.
19. Arlington, Va.
20. Atlanta, Ga.

Veteran's with Disabilities (Best Places)

Veterans with disabilities need to be cognizant of several factors when choosing a place to live. The most important of these factors are 1) access to VA medical facilities; 2) economic considerations; and 3) proximity to a military installation.

Access to VA Medical Facilities

Courtney Miller, in her June 2015 article titled "Top Cities for Veterans in 2015" in Nerdwallet did not consider a city's proximity to VA medical facilities, because "the Senate recently approved legislation to expand veterans' access to treatment outside the VA health care system…." Patricia Kime in her June 5, 2015, article "Senate Pushes for Expansion of VA Choice" in *Military Times* stated that the legislation would "…amend a rule that bars veterans from seeking private health care if they live within 40 miles of a VA facility, even if the clinic in question doesn't provide the services they need." However, the VA Choice program only runs through August 2017, or until the money runs out, and many veterans are voicing concerns regarding the approval process in general and the timeliness of the approval process. Therefore, access to VA medical facilities is of the utmost importance when determining the best places for veterans with disabilities to live.

In his article on Wallethub "2015's Best & Worst States for Military Retirees," John S Kleman, Senior Writer and Editor at Evolution Finance, determined the top five states having the most VA health facilities per 10,000 veterans:

1	New York
2	California
3	Wyoming
4	Texas
5	Florida

Economic Considerations

It is also imperative to consider economic factors such as unemployment rates and housing costs. Disabled veterans may need some type of employment, be it full or part-time, to supplement their military pay, and if they have a family support system, members of their support system will need jobs. Housing costs are another consideration for veterans living primarily on a fixed income.

The following chart ranks cities by percentage of veterans in the population, unemployment, and median income.

Rank	City	Percentage of veterans in the adult population	Veteran unemployment rate in 2013	Median income for veterans	Veterans who live below the poverty line
1	Beavercreek, Ohio	19.0%	3.2%	$68,989	1.4%
2	Madison, Alabama	15.5%	4.2%	$71,425	2.6%
3	Goodyear, Arizona	14.6%	1.5%	$44,372	1.5%
4	Papillion, Nebraska	15.5%	2.0%	$65,219	0.0%
5	Schertz, Texas	21.8%	3.8%	$61,037	2.4%
6	Sierra Vista, Arizona	27.6%	3.8%	$56,675	7.4%
7	Chesapeake, Virginia	15.2%	2.9%	$50,956	3.1%
8	Maricopa, Arizona	14.3%	3.1%	$49,093	4.2%
9	Vacaville, California	13.6%	5.7%	$53,953	3.7%
10	Lake Stevens, Washington	11.6%	4.7%	$54,804	2.9%

*Miller "Top Cities for Veterans in 2015," June 29, 2015, Nerdwallet

The next chart ranks the top five states in regards to most affordable housing.

Affordable Housing

1	Iowa
2	Nebraska
3	North Dakota
4	Kansas
5	Texas

*Kleman, "2015's Best & Worst States for Military Retirees," Wallethub

Proximity to a Military Installation

There are a number of reasons veterans often prefer to live near a military installation, including access to commissary and free services such as legal advice. Military installations also have a morale, welfare, and recreation (MWR) office that give vets access to discounted tickets and equipment rentals for outdoor activities. Mitch Cline in his February 6, 2016, Livability article "10 Best Cities for Veterans" quotes retired Master Sergeant Paul Chester as saying, "… there are lots of friends around military installations who speak the same military lingo that you speak, and you can sit around and tell war stories until the cows come home."

15 Locations to Consider

Beavercreek, Ohio

The close proximity to veterans' services is a key attraction of Beavercreek, which is just 13 miles from Wright-Patterson Air Force Base. The Miami Valley Military Affairs Association sponsors events and offers support for vets, and about 8 miles away, in Xenia, veterans can get employment help from the OhioMeansJobs Greene County Center. Beavercreek, a suburb of Dayton, is about 15 miles from the Dayton VA Medical Center. Also in Dayton, the Military Veterans Resource Center offers support with employment, housing, food and transportation. Honor Flight Dayton provides free trips to see national memorials in Washington, D.C., for veterans of World War II, the Korean and Vietnam wars, as well as for terminally ill veterans.

Goodyear, Arizona

Goodyear, a suburb of Phoenix, is near several places of interest for veterans, including Luke Air Force Base, Sky Harbor Air National Guard Base, Phoenix Vet Center, Phoenix VA Health Care System and West Valley Vet Center. Up By Their Bootstraps, an organization based in Goodyear, provides opportunities and support to members of the military, veterans and families. Veterans in Goodyear have an unemployment rate of 1.5%. The nearby Glendale Community College provides enrollment and referral services for veterans transitioning from military life to an academic environment. The local chapter of the Disabled American Veterans is also in Glendale.

Papillion, Nebraska

Papillion, located outside Omaha, is less than 10 miles from the Offutt Air Force Base. Papillion is home to VFW Post 9675, which serves Sarpy County. In nearby Omaha, veterans can find the Omaha VA Medical Center and the Douglas County Veterans Services Office. The Eastern Nebraska Veterans' Home is located minutes away in Bellevue and provides services for assisted living, intermediate care, skilled care and Alzheimer's disease care.

Schertz, Texas

Schertz, northeast of San Antonio, is a neighbor of Randolph Air Force Base in Universal City. The base is part of Joint Base San Antonio, which also includes the Army's Fort Sam Houston and Lackland Air Force Base. Veterans make up about 22% of Schertz's population. There is a VFW post in Schertz, and the closest VA hospital is Audie L. Murphy Memorial in San Antonio. Guadalupe County Veterans Service offices can help Schertz veterans seeking information about filing for their benefits. Veteran employment specialists are available at the Workforce Solutions Alamo in San Antonio.

Sierra Vista, Arizona

In Sierra Vista, veterans make up about 28% of the total population. When it comes to job opportunities, over 21% of jobs are in public administration and 7% of positions are in transportation, warehousing and utilities, two of the most popular industries among veterans. A prominent fixture in this southeast Arizona city is Fort Huachuca. The fort is home to the Army Intelligence Center and the Army Network Enterprise Technology Command/9th Army Signal Command. There is an Arizona Department of Veterans' Services office in Sierra Vista, and the Sierra Vista Community Based Outpatient Clinic is located in the city as part of the Southern Arizona VA Health Care System, based in Tucson.

Chesapeake, Virginia

Chesapeake and the surrounding areas of southeastern Virginia are a highly concentrated military area. The city is home to the Naval Support Activity Northwest Annex, which provides support services for 11 commands. A Veterans Benefits Service Field Office is in Chesapeake on the campus of Tidewater Community College to serve the large population of veterans in the area. Other nearby military installations include the Coast Guard's Fifth District, just 8 miles away in Portsmouth; the Navy's Norfolk Naval Shipyard; a Naval Medical Center and an office of the Virginia Department of Veterans Services. And in Hampton, less than 30 miles from Chesapeake, veterans will find the Hampton VA Medical Center.

Maricopa, Arizona

Maricopa is the second city on our list located in the Phoenix metro area. Similar to Goodyear, Maricopa is near Luke Air Force Base, Sky Harbor Air National Guard Base, Phoenix Vet Center, Phoenix VA Health Care System and West Valley Vet Center. Maricopa is 35 miles from the former Williams Air Force Base, which shut down in 1993. The space is now used for businesses, colleges and the Phoenix-Mesa Gateway Airport. The county of Maricopa offers services for veterans including programs focusing on health care, homelessness, affordable housing, down-payment assistance, home improvement, court- and law-related programs, continuing education and skills training and employment.

Vacaville, California

The Northern California city of Vacaville is less than 13 miles from Travis Air Force Base. A branch of Disabled American Veterans is in Vacaville. The Solano County Veterans Services Office in nearby Fairfield offers information and referrals, as well as a Veterans Discount ID Card. There are several veterans' halls in the area, including one in Vacaville. These halls are meeting hubs for many veterans groups including the Brotherhood of Vietnam Vets, VFW and American Legion. Vacaville is 45 miles from the Sacramento VA Medical Center in Mather.

Lake Stevens, Washington

Lake Stevens in Snohomish County is close to the Naval Station Everett in Everett and an Armed Forces Reserve Center in Marysville. The VA Puget Sound Health Care System serves veterans in the area. At the Everett Vet Center, run by Veterans Affairs, veterans can find out about Washington State Department of Veterans Affairs services. Eligible Veterans can receive limited emergency assistance from the Veterans' Assistance Fund by applying through Snohomish County. In Lake Stevens, more than one-fifth of all jobs are in manufacturing, one of the most popular industries for veterans.

Cheyenne, Wyoming

Cheyenne is about 90 minutes from Denver, CO and sits at the northern section of the Rocky Mountains. Veterans can find commissary and exchange at F.E. Warren Air Force Base and receive health care at a VA medical center. No state income tax, low property taxes and a low cost of living make this city even more attractive to those on a fixed income.

Tucson, Arizona

While Tucson is home to Davis-Monthan Air Force Base, it is near three other military installations. Just 70 miles away is Fort Huachuca, an Army base. Tucson is 139 miles from Luke Air Force Base; and 273 miles from Camp Navajo, a training site for multiple branches of the military. These bases give veterans a range of options for commissary and access to military services.

Kenner, Louisiana

Kenner is a suburb of New Orleans, and the New Orleans Naval Air Station allows military retirees access to commissary and exchange. The local VA medical center is in New Orleans.

Syracuse, New York

Syracuse is home to a local VA hospital, and the economy is entrenched in education, health care, science and research.

Colorado Springs, Colorado

The city is home to such military installations as Fort Carson, Peterson Air Force Base and Scheiver Air Force Base, and Colorado Springs gives veterans a vast support network and potential job market. There is an outpatient clinic for veterans in Colorado Springs, and a VA medical center about 63 miles away in Denver. The defense industry plays a major role in the economy, employing thousands of vets.

Fayetteville, North Carolina

Home to Fort Bragg, one of the largest military complexes in the world, Fayetteville, North Carolina, has a military history that goes all the way back to the Revolutionary War. It is considered America's First Military Sanctuary Community. Pope Air Force Base is also located near Fayetteville, and Camp Lejeune is about 106 miles away. This gives veterans three options for commissary and access to services. Health care needs are met at the Fayetteville VA Medical Center.

Best Places to Live for People with Disabilities (Overview)

When searching for the best places for people with disabilities to live, many things factor into making a determination. The disabled need to be in close proximity to any treatment they may need, they must be able to travel to and from appointments, and they must be able to access businesses and entertainment venues to have the opportunity to enjoy life in their new home.

Potential Cities

The cities below standout in health care, transportation, and/or accessibility to businesses and entertainment venues.

Orlando, Florida

Orlando's modern, wheelchair accessible construction combined with its transit system and huge healthcare network makes this one of the most disability friendly cities in the United States. The well-known amusement parks in the area are very disability friendly and most, if not all, areas of the parks are wheelchair accessible.

New York City, New York

New York City has much to offer people with disabilities including handicap-friendly sidewalks, a paratransit service along with other forms of wheelchair accessible transit. There are numerous handicap accessible museums, restaurants and business, along with many rehabilitation centers and specialists available in New York City.

Winston-Salem, North Carolina

Winston-Salem has an impressive health care system, with the Novant Health Facilities and Wake Forest Baptist Medical Center located within the city. This area has grown more than 50% in recent years, and the new construction accommodates the disabled.

Chicago, Illinois

Chicago has made almost all of its rail stations handicap accessible and offers discounted fares to those in wheelchairs. The University of Illinois is creating a Healthy Community Mapping System to track the handicap accessibility of fitness centers, sidewalks, and businesses. The city also has a large healthcare system.

Portland, Oregon

Portland has the Oregon Health and Science University Hospital, The Legacy Health System, and many other healthcare facilities to offer the disabled. The city also has different transit options such as bus, light rail, and streetcars, which all accommodate wheelchairs.

Denver, Colorado

Denver has extended its transportation system to include rail and bus both of which are wheelchair accessible. In addition Denver offers the Access-a-ride program which will take wheelchair users anywhere within a mile radius of the transit system. The large downtown area is always busy and most venues are handicap friendly.

Seattle, Washington

Seattle offers handicap accessible buses and light rail lines discounted to wheelchair users. There is also a paratransit van service that will take a user anywhere within the city. Furthermore, Seattle has a rideshare program for the handicapped and maps that show downtown routes that are accessible to those with disabilities. Seattle also has many modern, handicap accessible buildings and facilities and is home to numerous healthcare facilities.

Albuquerque, New Mexico

Albuquerque has a transit system that includes a modern rail and rapid bus service. The transit service gives discounted fares to people with disabilities. In addition Albuquerque is home to the University of New Mexico Hospital, known for its innovative procedures.

Reno, Nevada

Reno has wheelchair accessible buses and bus rapid transit systems that offer discounted fares for people with disabilities. Additionally, Reno provides paratransit services within the city and to some outlying areas. Most of the casinos, shows, and restaurants in Reno are wheelchair accessible, and there are numerous handicapped accessible parks to enjoy.

Birmingham, Alabama

Birmingham has a large variety of healthcare resources with HealthSouth and the University of Alabama at Birmingham. The Birmingham-Jefferson County Transit Authority operates more than 24 paratransit buses within the city.

Baltimore, Maryland

Baltimore offers a myriad of handicap accessible activities including the Fort McHenry National Monument, The National Aquarium, and the Baltimore coast. Baltimore's transit system makes it easy to get around and offers discounts to those in wheelchairs.

Cheyenne, Wyoming

Cheyenne offers a paratransit service in the city to provide safe and reliable transportation. An additionally interesting aspect of Cheyenne is there is no state income tax which is certainly beneficial to people, such as those with disabilities, living on a fixed income.

Tucson, Arizona

Tucson has more than 800 miles of handicap accessible paved paths for those who love to be outdoors and more than 1,500 restaurants that are wheelchair accessible.

Kenner, Louisiana

Kenner has several museums, theaters, and a huge historic district, along with numerous recreational facilities which are handicap accessible.

Lubbock, Texas

Lubbock has a modern transit system which includes hybrid buses equipped to accommodate large wheelchairs.

Other Considerations

Cost of living and job opportunities are two more deciding factors in choosing the best places for people with disabilities to live. Richie Bernardo in his article "2015's Best & Worst Cities for People with Disabilities" on WalletHub identified the best and worst cities for people with disabilities by looking at Economic Environment, Quality of Life, and Health Care. The below charts show the cities with the Lowest Cost of Living and Highest Employment Rate for People with Disabilities as discovered by Richie in his research.

	Lowest Cost of Living Cities
1	Laredo, Texas
2	Memphis, Tennessee
3	Jackson, Mississippi
T4	Augusta, Georgia
T4	Amarillo, Texas

	Highest Employment Rate for People with Disabilities
1	Amarillo, Texas
2	Fremont, California
3	Huntington Beach, California
4	Oceanside, California
5	Tacoma, Washington

Richie stated in his article,

"In the U.S., people with disabilities bring valuable skill sets to the workplace that build upon the strength and diversity of the American labor market. According to the U.S. Bureau of Labor Statistics, nearly five million people with disabilities were employed in 2014. However, the unemployment rate for those with a disability continues to be almost double the rate for persons without one."

In his research Richie compared 150 cities on Economic Environment, Quality of Life, and Health Care then ranked them in order. The following are Richie's top 15 places for people with disabilities to live:

Overall Rank	City
1	Overland Park, Kansas
2	Scottsdale, Arizona
3	Peoria, Arizona
4	Tampa, Florida
5	St. Petersburg, Florida
6	Huntington Beach, California
7	Oklahoma City, Oklahoma
8	Gilbert, Arizona
9	Honolulu, Hawaii
10	Santa Clarita, California
11	Modesto, California
12	Amarillo, Texas
13	San Jose, California
14	Chandler, Arizona
T15	Lincoln, Nebraska
T15	Rancho Cucamonga, California

Conclusion

When searching for a new city to call home, people with disabilities have a large list of considerations. Factors such as the proximity to health care providers, transportation, accessibility of various facilities, cost of living, and employment rates of people with disabilities in the area are all extremely important in directing the individual to a suitable location for his/her new home. The availability of these elements allows people with disabilities to play an important role in the community and make significant contributions to the economy. Which factor, or factors, hold the most weight in helping a person with a disability select a new location is dependent on the individual, the type of disability, and the type of support system he/she has.

Advocacy

Advocacy is an activity by an individual or group which aims to influence decisions within political, economic, and social systems and institutions. Advocacy can include many activities that a person or organization undertakes including media campaigns, public speaking, commissioning and publishing research or conducting exit poll or the filing of an amicus brief. Lobbying (often by lobby groups) is a form of advocacy where a direct approach is made to legislators on an issue which plays a significant role in modern politics.

An advocate is someone who provides advocacy support to people who need it. We were fortunate to find an advocate when we first relocated to California who was not only knowledgeable about the state regulations and services available for special needs children, but who also had the tenacity of a 'pit bull'. Through her assistance, she was able to ensure our daughter received all of the help available to her from the school district and state.

The regulations and services available for special needs children is enormous. However, unless you know about them, how to apply for them, and can legitimately threaten to legally challenge denial of them, they are of no value. The school district and government agencies are of little help. Often they do everything possible to distract, sidetrack, discourage, or deny you these services since it impacts their budget and imposes additional work upon their staff. If you can discover them on your own, these agencies will often try to wear you down through bureaucracy, frustrate you into giving up with lengthy delays, and withhold information from you that would help you and your child. I don't mean to sound cynical, but with firsthand experience in dealing with these agencies and school districts for nearly two decades in multiple jurisdictions I cannot but help to have a negative opinion of them considering what we know now about the laws, regulations, and funding established to help children with special needs, and their typical modus operandi.

We have seen many cases over the years where families without an advocate, or one with an inexperienced advocate, are denied services or are only able to acquire a minimum level of service. The amount of money we pay our advocate has paid for itself tenfold.

My recommendations for hiring an advocate are the following:

1. Find and advocate with experience in addressing school districts and agencies in your geographical area
2. Try to find an advocate with experience in assisting families with similar special needs (an autism advocate for a child with autism, etc.)
3. Try to find an advocate with the personality to call people out on their wrongs, is tenacious, and not afraid to stand up to a group of people in a fierce meeting.
4. Try to find an advocate who will take time to understand your needs.

This Chapter provides an alphabetical list of resources for parents of children with disabilities, and the professionals who work with them. A personalized advocate who will represent you on a local level will be found though your local network and yellow pages. To locate such a person try searching for an advocate or an attorney who specializes in cases similar to yours. Also perform an Internet search by typing in your town and/or county immediately followed by 'Professional Advocacy Consultants'.

Advocacy Resources

Beach Center on Families and Disabilities
www.beachcenter.org

The Beach Center on Families and Disability is a rehabilitation research and training center on public policy affecting families who have children with disabilities. The professionally oriented web site contains research and related information. A separate area is devoted to positive behavioral support. The Beach Center on Families and Disability is a permanent unit of the University of Kansas, a major international center for research and other scholarship, teaching and learning, and service to the citizens of Kansas, the United States of America, and people throughout the world.

Children's Defense Fund
http://www.childrensdefense.org

The Children's Defense Fund is an advocacy organization for children, especially poor and minority children and those with disabilities. Its web site is filled with information, especially relating to issues of concern for people with low incomes.

Family Voices
http://www.familyvoices.org

Family Voices is "a national, grassroots clearinghouse for information and education concerning the health care of children with special health needs." Its web site includes a bimonthly newsletter and weekly news update, as well as information about the organization and its publications.

Families for Early Autism Treatment (FEAT)
http://www.feat.org/

Families for Early Autism Treatment, Inc. (FEAT) is a non-profit organization of parents, family members, and treatment professionals, designed to help families with children of all ages who have an

Autism Spectrum Disorder (ASD), which includes Autistic Disorder, Pervasive Developmental Disorder, Not Otherwise Specified (PDD-NOS), and Aspergers's Disorder (AS). It offers a network of support where families can meet each other to discuss issues surrounding autism and treatment options.

Institute for Child Health Policy
http://health-outcomes-policy.ufl.edu/about/

The Institute focuses on children in managed care with special emphasis on children with special health care needs. Its web site offers a wealth of information about policy/program development, health services research and evaluation programs.

Internet Resources for Special Children (IRSC)
http://www.inclusivechildcare.org/resourcesWeb2/details.cfm/GetRecID/290

An extensive and well organized collection of links. The mission of the Center for Inclusive Child Care is to be a centralized, comprehensive resource network supporting inclusive care for children in community settings.

Kids Together, Inc.
http://www.kidstogether.org/

Nicely arranged by subject, this parent-oriented web site includes general information, short documents, and annotated links relating to children with disabilities.

KidsHealth
http://kidshealth.org/en/parents/about.html

Sponsored by nonprofit Nemours Foundation, this extensive website features separate sections for parents, kids and teens. The parents' section has thousands of easy-to-find, health-related articles; though not specifically geared to parents of children with disabilities, it includes many good articles about specific conditions. The upbeat kids and teens sections likewise include information about specific disabilities and chronic illnesses as well as information that will interest all young people.

Nacersano.org
http://nacersano.marchofdimes.org/

Bienvenidos! This March of Dimes website was developed "to help serve the growing need for education in maternal and infant health for the Spanish-speaking community in the U.S. and around the world." It includes an online health library with information on preparing for pregnancy, the effects of alcohol, tobacco and stress during pregnancy, prenatal and newborn tests, and more.

National Center for Education in Maternal & Child Health (NCEMCH)
http://ncemch.org/

Dedicated to improving the health of children and families through national leadership in state-of-the-art knowledge, program development, and policy analysis and education, this organization's professionally-oriented links include access to its extensive databases and publications.

continued

National Fathers' Network
http://fathersnetwork.org/

"Dedicated to providing support and resources for fathers and families of children with special needs," this site is packed with information by and for fathers of children with disabilities (including articles in Spanish), photos, a special section for providers, and much more.

National Information Center for Children and Youth with Disabilities (NICHCY)
http://www.parentcenterhub.org/nichcy-gone/

NICHCY is the national information and referral center that provides information on disabilities and disability-related issues for families, educators, and other professionals. NICHCY's web site features its excellent fact sheets, resource guides and other publications about specific disabilities and disability-related issues. Many of the publications are available in Spanish.

National Parent Network on Disabilities (NPND)
http://bryanking.net/national-parent-network-on-disabilities-npnd/

Information, legislation, advocacy, and more. This website is especially valuable for its current information and links relating to "hot issues" and legislation affecting children with disabilities.

Our Kids
http://www.our-kids.org/

The home page of a wonderful online support group for parents, caregivers and others who are working with children with physical and/or mental disabilities and delays. The site includes subscription information and archives, members' home pages, links, resources, reading lists, and more.

Parents Helping Parents, Inc.
http://www.php.com/

The web site of this family resource center includes an extensive, easy-to-search database of national organizations involved with children with disabilities.

Pediatric Database (PEDBASE)
http://www.pedbase.org/

This database contains basic medical information about 550 "childhood illnesses," including many rare disorders. The entries may be viewed online, and the entire database can be downloaded.

Points of Pediatric Interest
http://www.hopkinsmedicine.org/

A good guide to medical and related information from John Hopkins University.

Sibling Support Project
https://www.siblingsupport.org/

This web site is packed with resources and ideas for siblings of children with disabilities and their parents and service providers. Includes a national directory of sibling support programs and newsletter.

Special Child Magazine
http://www.specialchild.com/

An online magazine for parents. Sections include success stories, horror stories, family issues, tips, special children, and a handy bulletin board.

T.A. Alliance for Parents (PACER Center)
http://www.taalliance.org/about.html

"The Technical Assistance Alliance for Parent Projects (the Alliance), focuses on providing technical assistance for establishing, developing, and coordinating parent training and information projects under the Individuals with Disabilities Education Act." Its web site includes a national calendar, legislative information, web links, lists of organizations and parent centers, and information about Supplemental Security Income (SSI), and more. Future developments will include electronic study teams for and several databases.

DSNetwork
http://dsnetworkaz.org/about/

DSNetwork is to educate, support and advocate for those in the community impacted by Down syndrome. DSNetwork achieves this goal through an open, supportive and collaborative network that connects individuals and families with needed resources and information.

Employment for Persons with Disabilities and the Best-and Worst-States for Workers with Disabilities

While searching for and finding a job can be an arduous task for anyone, it can be even more daunting for people with disabilities. People with disabilities are faced with more challenges to find work than their counterparts without disabilities, even in a good economy. The chart below highlights several hurdles people with disabilities may encounter while attempting to find meaningful employment:

Possible Obstacles to Overcome

- Problems following a schedule
- Stigma and/or discrimination
- Trouble concentrating
- Difficulty communicating and interacting with others
- Medication side-effects
- Absences from work
- Frequent medical appointments

However, with training and counseling, people with disabilities can handle a variety of jobs. It is often just a matter of showing employers what these prospective employees are capable of. In addition, there are many reasonable accommodations, people with disabilities should not be afraid to request from their potential employers:

Accommodations to Request from Employer

- Flexible work schedules or start times
- Reduced distractions or noise in the work area
- Working from home
- Written or recorded directions
- Flexible break schedule
- Space to rest during breaks

Finding work is vital for people with able disabilities in that it gives them a chance to learn new skills, gain financial security and independence, obtain health benefits, achieve a sense of purpose, encourage social interaction, and create a sense of identity.

Nearly one in five people, or roughly 19% of the population, in the United States has some type of disability. According to the United States Department of Labor website, "The Americans with Disabilities Act (ADA) prohibits discrimination against people with disabilities in employment, transportation, public accommodation, communications, and governmental activities." However, Samantha Cowan, associate culture editor for TakePart found that 70% of working-age people with disabilities are unemployed, compared with 28 percent of working-age people overall. Of course some states are better than others at employing people with disabilities, and people with disabilities looking to relocate should be aware of where the best opportunities are. In September 2015, RespectAbility released their report "The Best-and Worst-States for Workers with Disabilities," which ranked all 50 states by the percentage of people with disabilities who are employed. The chart below indicates the percentage of working-age people with disabilities who are employed in each state.

Rank	State	Percentage employed
1	North Dakota	52.0%
2	Wyoming	50.0%
3	South Dakota	48.0%
4	Alaska	47.0%
5	Minnesota	46.0%
6	Nebraska	45.5%
7	Iowa	44.8%
8	Utah	42.5%
9	Colorado	42.3%
10	New Hampshire	41.8%
11	Kansas	41.7%
12	Wisconsin	40.9%
13	Connecticut	40.0%

14	Maryland	40.0%
15	Montana	39.4%
16	Nevada	39.2%
17	Hawaii	39.1%
18	Texas	38.7%
19	Virginia	36.9%
20	Idaho	36.7%
21	New Jersey	36.6%
22	Delaware	36.4%
23	Washington	36.4%
24	Illinois	36.1%
25	Oklahoma	35.8%
26	New Mexico	35.3%
27	Oregon	35.2%
28	Massachusetts	34.9%
29	Rhode Island	34.3%
30	Pennsylvania	33.9%
31	Indiana	33.8%
32	Arizona	33.6%
33	Ohio	33.5%
34	Vermont	33.3%
35	Missouri	33%
36	California	32.7%
37	New York	32.2%
38	Georgia	31.5%
39	Louisiana	31.3%
40	Maine	31.2%
41	South Carolina	30.7%
42	Florida	30.5%
43	North Carolina	30.3%
44	Michigan	29.9%
45	Tennessee	29.9%
46	Arizona	28.2%
47	Alabama	27.1%
48	Kentucky	26.9%
49	Mississippi	26.3%
50	West Virginia	25.3%

According to RespectAbility, "… people with disabilities are twice as likely to be working in the Dakotas, Alaska and Wyoming than they are in many other states," and "the states with the consistently lowest workforce participation rates are West Virginia, Mississippi, Kentucky, Alabama and Arizona."

The ability to find work is crucial to people with disabilities. Not only does having a job help create a sense of identity and purpose, but people with disabilities often have higher costs of living than those without disabilities. Employment is needed to support these higher costs of living. It is important to note that The Workforce Innovation and Opportunity Act now requires every state to develop plans for career programs for people with disabilities.

Employment Resources for Persons with Disabilities:

Ticket to Work: The Ticket to Work and Work Incentives Improvement Act of 1999 is designed to help people with disabilities seeking employment, primarily by eliminating the disincentives to work for individuals who receive SSI or SSDI, and expanding the availability of health care services to people with disabilities who are working. The free, voluntary program gives users a "ticket" that allows them to get employment services, vocational rehab services or access to other supports, such as assistive technology. The program will be phased in nationally over a three-year period, beginning in 2002.

Ticket to Work Website
https://yourtickettowork.com/web/ttw

This comprehensive, easy-to-use website is from Maximus, the company that administers the Ticket to Work program for the Social Security Administration. The site provides authoritative, extensive information about the program, news, resources, and employment networks.

Barn Builders Network
http://www.amputee-coalition.org/inmotion/may_jun_98/barnnet.html

Barn Builders Network builds an informal peer support network of farmers and ranchers with disabilities across the nation.

The AgrAbility Project
http://www.seals.com

The AgrAbility Project was created to assist people with disabilities employed in agriculture. It links cooperative extension services with nonprofit disability service organizations to provide practical education and assistance that promotes independence in agricultural production and rural living. In just four years, the AgrAbility Project has emerged as one of rural America's most valuable and cost-effective resources.

The AgrAbility Project is helping hundreds of farmers, ranchers, and agricultural workers with disabilities and their families to succeed in agricultural production and rural community life.

DO-IT (Disabilities, Opportunities, Internetworking, and Technology)
http://www.washington.edu/doit/

Based at the University of Washington, DO-IT helps people with disabilities pursue academics and careers, with an emphasis on the use of technology. This site provides information about the program and related resources. The section on college transition and access is particularly useful for students.

Project PURSUIT
http://www.tr.wou.edu/orpti/partnership-for-reading/page9.html

PURSUIT is "a multifaceted approach to encouraging students with disabilities to pursue their academic and professional dreams. PURSUIT focuses on opening doors to classes and careers in science, engineering and mathematics beginning at the high school level. The program offers a wide variety of services for students, parents, professionals, etc.

Disabilities Employment
http://www.disabilityresources.org/EMPLOYMENT.html

Federal Government Employment for Persons with Disabilities
https://www.opm.gov/policy-data-oversight/disability-employment/

The Federal Government is actively recruiting and hiring persons with disabilities. The Federal Government offers a variety of exciting jobs, competitive salaries, excellent benefits, and opportunities for career advancement.

Disabilities Job Exchange
http://www.disabilityjobexchange.com/

Job opportunities and employment resources for people with disabilities.

Ranking of States on Employment of People with Disabilities (PwDs)

Following is information provided by the organization, 'RespectAbility'. RespectAbility is on the front lines in the battle to reduce stigmas, failed government policies, and other obstacles that deny people with disabilities the opportunity to achieve the American Dream. They are highly recommended. More about RespectAbility can be found on their website at: http://respectabilityusa.com

September 4, 2015: Washington, DC. Fully 70 percent of people with disabilities nationwide are out of the workforce. The rates of employment, however, vary widely by state. In some, people with disabilities are twice as likely to be working as those in others.

The states with the consistently lowest workforce participation rates are West Virginia, Mississippi, Kentucky, Alabama and Arizona. When taking into consideration the gap between the employment rate of people with disabilities and those without disabilities, Maine and Vermont are added to the list, with Maine coming in dead last in the country.

Unfortunately, many states have continued to fund failed programs and old ways of thinking but there is good news. **According to U.S. Census Bureau statistics from 2013, the following 10 states are leading the nation in creating more job opportunities for the one-in-five Americans who have a disability:**

- North Dakota: 52 percent of the state's 34,800 working-age people with disabilities are employed.
- Wyoming: 50 percent of Wyoming's 34,000 working-age people with disabilities are employed.
- South Dakota: 48 percent of the state's 47,700 working-age people with disabilities are employed.
- Alaska: 47 percent of Alaska's 47,000 working-age people with disabilities are employed
- Minnesota: 46 percent of Minnesota's 266,400 working-age people with disabilities are employed.
- Nebraska: 45.5 percent of Nebraska's 88,700 working-age people with disabilities are employed.
- Iowa: 44.8 percent of Iowa's 169,300 working-age people with disabilities are employed.
- Utah: 42.5 percent of Utah's 135,100 working-age people with disabilities are employed.
- Colorado: 42.3 percent of Colorado's 260,700 working-age people with disabilities are employed.
- New Hampshire: 41 percent of New Hampshire's 77,800 working-age people with disabilities are employed.

Following is a more in-depth look at the states that are succeeding on the front employment for persons with disabilities:

1) North Dakota

North Dakota has the coveted distinction of being the state with the highest rate of employment for individuals with disabilities, employing 52.8 percent of their citizens with disabilities. North Dakota, which is experiencing and economic boom, is also a part of the Promoting the Readiness of Minors in Supplemental Security Income (PROMISE) Grant, a collaborative effort which promotes career achievement as a means of gaining economic self-sufficiency and a diminished dependence on public benefits among youth who receive Social Security Insurance (SSI). The PROMISE Grant enables states to develop curricula and projects that will improve education for youth with disabilities, thereby equipping these youth with the tools to succeed in the workforce In addition, North Dakota's Division of Vocational Rehabilitation recently launched a website called ND Advantage, which providers employers information about the financial incentives for hiring vocational rehabilitation referrals such as the Work Opportunity Tax Credits. Another benefit that ND Advantage highlights is Disability Access Credit, which provides expenses to companies who employ individuals with disabilities to cover such services as sign language interpreters and assistive technology. Gov. Jack Dalrymple's leadership has led to a more prosperous state and opened the American Dream to many people with disabilities.

2) Wyoming

Wyoming has the second highest percentage of employed people of disabilities (50.7 percent), compared with 79 percent of people without disabilities. The Wyoming Employment First Task Force, which was created last year, fosters collaboration between the public and private sectors to craft solutions for employing people with disabilities. Wyoming also has benefitted from the MentorAbility program, which emulates the strategies used by Project SEARCH. Strong leadership through an earlier Business Leadership Network also brought best practices and enthusiasm to the state. With the new workforce law, Gov. Matt Mead has the chance to ensure that Wyoming sustains it success and creates more jobs.

3) South Dakota

The employment rate for people with disabilities in South Dakota is 48 percent compared to 83 percent of people without disabilities. South Dakota became a model state for disability employment in part because Gov. Dennis Daugaard has a personal interest in the subject as a son of two deaf parents. As a member of the NGA, Gov. Daugaard supported Gov. Markell's Better Bottom Line Initiative and he helped organize hearings on finding employment solutions for people with disabilities. Furthermore, South Dakota created the Employment Works Task Force, which develops hiring solutions for people with disabilities.

In addition, South Dakota's Department of Human Services recently launched its new *Ability for Hire* program, which alters public perceptions and touts the benefits of hiring individuals with disabilities. Ability for Hire's approach to achieving this ambitious goal is through networking, educating, and informing supervisors, businesses, and the general public about what individuals with disabilities have to offer. South Dakota should serve as a model for other states on how implementing strategies that provide employment opportunities for people with disabilities can produce successful results.

4) Alaska

In Alaska roughly half of individuals with disabilities between the ages of 18-64 are employed (47.8 percent) compared to 75.2 percent of people without disabilities. The employment rate for people with disabilities is up nearly 9 percent from 2012.

Recent state efforts have played a significant role in narrowing the employment gap between people with disabilities and those without disabilities. In order to encourage entrepreneurship among low-income individuals with disabilities, Alaska has established an Industry-Driven Support model that provides trainings on a variety of business topics, networking sessions, and one-on-one business support to entrepreneurs. In addition, Alaska has created the State as a Model Employer Task Force, targeting recruitment of individuals with disabilities, and identifying best practices for accommodations and workplace inclusion.

Project SEARCH, which immerses interns into a structured environment, combines education with career exploration and has been one of the most effective programs in transitioning young people with disabilities into the workforce. In Alaska, Project SEARCH has had tremendous success collaborating with the Anchorage school district, Providence Alaska Medical Center, Mat-Su Borough School and the Mat-Su Regional District.

Alaska's success proves that a multifaceted approach improves employment outcomes for people with disabilities. Alaska has put into action a variety of cost effect best practices and proven models. RespectAbility's Disability Employment First Planning contains such practices and has many other ideas to follow. Under Gov. Bill Walker, Alaska appears to be headed in a positive direction, and is looking forward to a bright future of continued progress in ensuring that people with disabilities receiving greater opportunities to thrive in the workforce.

5) Minnesota

In Minnesota, the employment rate of people with disabilities is 46 percent compared to 83 percent of people without disabilities. By 2018, Gov. Mark Dayton has a goal that 7 percent of the state workforce will be people with disabilities. This effort also requires state hiring managers to undergo training for recruiting people with disabilities. While not everyone will want to work in state government, this type of practice is an important step forward to breaking down stigma around hiring. Likewise, the Minnesota

Department of Employment and Economic Development have extensive resources available that emphasize the business case for hiring people with disabilities.

6) Nebraska

45.5 percent of Nebraskans with disabilities are employed, compared to 82.6 percent of Nebraskans without disabilities. Nebraska has invested in a Ticket to Work website, assisting jobseekers with disabilities to network with employers seeking to hire these individuals, and professionals serving both groups. In addition, Nebraska remains an active participant in Project Search, a nationwide initiative to employ individuals with disabilities, boasting programs with 14 different host organizations. Furthermore, Nebraska has distinguished itself by becoming one of the states to pass a state level ABLE Act, which enables individuals with disabilities to save money while maintaining federal benefits and other forms of necessary assistance. The White House recognized David Scott from Embassy Suites Omaha-La Vista as a 2014 White House Champion of Change for his work on a Project SEARCH Program enabling young people with disabilities to transition in careers in the hospitality field. Gov. Pete Ricketts has much reason to be proud of his state and to continue the fight for more jobs for all Nebraskans.

7) Iowa

In Iowa, 44 percent of people with disabilities are employed. After initially returning $2,314,114 to the federal government after failing to spend the money on state Vocational Rehabilitation programs, leaders such as Gov. Terry Branstad and Vocational Rehabilitation Director David Mitchell ensured that the resources were properly utilized. Recently, groups such as the Iowa Vocational Rehabilitation Services (IDVR) and the Iowa Developmental Disabilities Council, in partnership with other organizations, have come together to establish the Iowa Coalition for Integrated Employment. The program transitions people with disabilities into a competitive workforce. The state also is streamlining its paper work to enable Iowans with a variety of barriers to employment and employers to be better served while saving money for taxpayers. Employers including Kwik Trip, Unity Point Hospital, Bankers Trust and Mercy Hospital have set up successful partnerships with Iowa Vocational Rehabilitation Services.

8) Utah

Utah continues to narrow the gap between the 42.5 percent of residents with disabilities who are employed and 76.6 percent of residents without disabilities. Utah employs a series of supports provided to both jobseekers with disabilities and potential employers through the Choose to Work Utah and Work Ability Utah programs, as well as their Employment First Priority Initiative. These programs go beyond job placement services to provide on-the-job training and employment support services, as well as work incentives and benefits planning for people with disabilities transitioning off of government benefit programs like SSI or SSDI. Utah also provides more than 11 financial incentives to employers to hire people with disabilities, including the Welfare to Work Tax Credit and Work Opportunity Tax Credit. At the same time, Utah's Employment First Priority initiative, signed into law by Gov. Gary Herbert in 2011, provides individuals with significant disabilities integrated employment at competitive wages.

9) Colorado

Colorado's employment rate of people with disabilities is up two percentage points from the previous year to 42.3 percent, compared to 77.3 percent of people without disabilities. Gov. Hickenlooper signed an Achieving a Better Life Experience (ABLE) Act into law which allows families to that have cash savings over $2,000 and still be eligible for Medicaid and other government benefits programs, allow beneficiaries to go back to work without quickly losing benefits. Furthermore, Colorado has created Ability Connection Colorado, an exceptional resource in supporting individuals with disabilities in their pursuit of employment.

10) New Hampshire

In New Hampshire, 41.8 percent of people with disabilities are employed compared to the 80.3 percent of people without disabilities. This includes 1,087 job placements by vocational rehabilitation. As a parent of a child with disabilities, Gov. Maggie Hassan has made it a priority to address the employment needs of people with disabilities. As she said upon signing a ban on sub-minimum wage work, including more people with disabilities "into the heart and soul of our democracy, our communities, our economy, has a great ripple effect, not only for individuals and not only for their families, but for our economy, too."

State to Watch – South Carolina

While it may not yet rank in the top 10, one state that deserves closer attention is South Carolina. Not only has there been a 1.3 percent increase in the employment rate of people without disabilities, there has also been a 2.7 percent increase in employment among South Carolinians with disabilities. Just recently, Gov. Nikki Haley talked about the importance of employing people with disabilities.

"Our goal is to get as many people back to work, whether its veterans, whether it's those with disabilities, whether it's those with challenges," Haley said. "We're finding that businesses in South Carolina want to help."

Haley praised Walgreens' distribution center in Anderson for their efforts at integrating employees with disabilities. She went so far as to call Walgreens "a source of pride." However, there's more work to create opportunity for the 340,300 working age people with disabilities living in South Carolina.

BELOW: Ranking 50 States by Employment Rates and Employment Gap Comparisons Table

Column 1 Ranking of States by Employment Rate of People with Disabilities			Column 2 Ranking of States by the Employment Gap Between People With Disabilities and People Without Disabilities				
#	State	% of PWDs Employed	#	State	% of PWDs Employed	% of People Without Disabilities Employed	Employment Gap as a %
1	North Dakota	52.8	1	Alaska	47.8	75.2	27.4
2	Wyoming	50.7	2	Wyoming	50.7	79.4	28.7
3	South Dakota	48.1	3	North Dakota	52.8	83.1	30.3
4	Alaska	47.8	4	Nevada	39.2	73.1	33.9
5	Minnesota	46	5	Utah	42.5	76.6	34.1
6	Nebraska	45.5	6	New Mexico	35.3	70.1	34.8
7	Iowa	44.8	7	South Dakota	48.1	83	34.9
8	Utah	42.5	8	Colorado	42.3	77.3	35
9	Colorado	42.3	9	Texas	38.7	74.7	36
10	New Hampshire	41.8	10	Minnesota	46	82.1	36.1
11	Kansas	41.7	11	Connecticut	40	76.4	36.4
12	Wisconsin	40.9	12	Hawaii	39.1	75.7	36.6
13	Connecticut	40	13	Nebraska	45.5	82.6	37.1
14	Maryland	40	14	Iowa	44.8	82.1	37.3
15	Montana	39.4	15	Kansas	41.7	79	37.3
16	Nevada	39.2	16	Montana	39.4	76.8	37.4
17	Hawaii	39.1	17	Arizona	33.6	71.3	37.7
18	Texas	38.7	18	Maryland	40	78.3	38.3
19	Virginia	36.9	19	Washington	36.4	74.7	38.3
20	Idaho	36.7	20	California	32.7	71.1	38.4
21	New Jersey	36.6	21	Idaho	36.7	75.2	38.5
22	Delaware	36.4	22	New Hampshire	41.8	80.3	38.5
23	Washington	36.4	23	New Jersey	36.6	75.1	38.5
24	Illinois	36.1	24	Delaware	36.4	75.1	38.7
25	Oklahoma	35.8	25	Oregon	35.2	73.9	38.7
26	New Mexico	35.3	26	Illinois	36.1	75	38.9
27	Oregon	35.2	27	Wisconsin	40.9	80.1	38.2
28	Massachusetts	34.9	28	Oklahoma	35.8	75.2	38.4
29	Rhode Island	34.3	29	Georgia	31.5	71.5	40
30	Pennsylvania	33.9	30	Virginia	36.9	76.9	40
31	Indiana	33.8	31	Louisiana	31.3	72.4	41.1
32	Arizona	33.6	32	New York	32.2	73.3	41.1
33	Ohio	33.5	33	Florida	30.5	72.2	41.7
34	Vermont	33.3	34	Pennsylvania	33.9	75.6	41.7

35	Missouri	33	35	South Carolina	30.7	72.7	42
36	California	32.7	36	Rhode Island	34.3	76.3	42
37	New York	32.2	37	Indiana	33.8	76	42.2
38	Georgia	31.5	38	Ohio	33.5	75.9	42.4
39	Louisiana	31.3	39	Massachusetts	34.9	77.9	43
40	Maine	31.2	40	Mississippi	26.3	69.4	43.1
41	South Carolina	30.7	41	North Carolina	30.3	73.5	43.2
42	Florida	30.5	42	Alabama	27.1	70.5	43.4
43	North Carolina	30.3	43	Michigan	29.9	73.4	43.5
44	Michigan	29.9	44	Tennessee	29.9	74.1	44.2
45	Tennessee	29.9	45	Missouri	33	77.1	44.1
46	Arizona	28.2	46	Arkansas	28.2	72.7	44.5
47	Alabama	27.1	47	West Virginia	25.3	70.6	45.3
48	Kentucky	26.9	48	Vermont	33.3	79.6	46.3
49	Mississippi	26.3	49	Kentucky	26.9	73.7	46.8
50	West Virginia	25.3	50	Maine	31.1	78.8	47.6

Independent Living

Independent living means that a person lives in his or her own apartment or house and needs limited or no help from outside agencies. The person may not need any assistance or might need help with only complex issues such as managing money, rather than day-to-day living skills. Independent living services may be home or community based.

Whether an adult with disabilities continues to live at home or moves into the community depends on his or her ability to manage everyday tasks with little or no help. However, more importantly, independent living has to do with self-determination – it is having the right and the opportunity to pursue a course of action and having the freedom to fail.

The National Council on Independent Living (NCIL) is the longest-running national cross-disability, grassroots organization run by and for people with disabilities. Founded in 1982, NCIL represents thousands of organizations and individuals including individuals with disabilities, Centers for Independent Living (CILs), Statewide Independent Living Councils (SILCs), and other organizations that advocate for the human and civil rights of people with disabilities throughout the United States. In summary, NCIL advances independent living and the rights of people with disabilities.

Centers for Independent Living are community-based, cross-disability, non-profit organizations that are designed and operated by people with disabilities. CILs are unique in that they operate according to a strict philosophy of consumer control, wherein people with all types of disabilities directly govern and staff the organization.

Centers for Independent Living Provide:

- Peer Support
- Information and Referral
- Individual and Systems Advocacy
- Independent Living Skills Training

America is home to:

- 403 Centers for Independent Living (CILs)
- 330 branch offices
- 56 Statewide Independent Living Councils (SILCs)

For a directory of Statewide Independent Living Centers for your state go to: http://www.ilru.org/projects/silc-net/silc-directory

Finding safe, affordable and accessible housing can be a significant challenge for disabled Americans. The Americans with Disabilities Act (ADA) mandates that businesses, workplaces, government offices and public services provide accommodations for the disabled, but for many disabled Americans, access to one's own living quarters can be lacking. The U.S. Department of Housing and Urban Development has worked with architects and disability rights advocates to develop accessibility design strategies. The 1968 Fair Housing Act requires that covered multi-family dwellings contain wheelchair- and disabled-accessible pathways and common-use areas, such as parking lots, mailrooms and laundry rooms.

Another major obstacle towards independent living is inadequate or inaccessible transportation, making it difficult for many disabled Americans to get to work, school or perform other tasks that are essential to daily life. Some progress is being made toward accessible transportation in cities such as New York City, Denver, Albuquerque, and Seattle, where they are ensuring their public transportation is handicap accessible, and some cities offer paratransit services.

For many Americans with disabilities, barriers in their communities take away or severely limit their choices. These barriers may be obvious, such as lack of ramped entrances for people who use wheelchairs, lack of interpreters or captioning for people with hearing impairments, lack of Brailed, digital or recorded copies of printed material for people who have visual impairments. Other barriers, however, can be even more limiting to people with disabilities trying to live independently. These are people's misunderstandings and prejudices about disability, and these barriers result in low expectations about things people with disabilities can achieve.

United Cerebral Palsy (UCP) educates, advocates and provides support services through an affiliate network to ensure a life without limits for people with a spectrum of disabilities. Their mission is to advance the independence, productivity and full citizenship of people with disabilities. According to the UCP, their annual report *The Case for Inclusion* ranks all 50 States and the District of Columbia (DC) – not on their spending – but on their outcomes for Americans with ID/DD…. *The Case for Inclusion* is a tool that gives us glimpses at how well each individual State is performing overall." (United Cerebral Palsy's 2015 Report – cfi.ucp.org) UCP's 2015 rankings are listed on the following page:

1	Arizona		27	Florida
2	Maryland		28	New Jersey
3	Missouri		29	Michigan
4	New York		30	West Virginia
5	Hawaii		31	Nevada
6	Colorado		32	Tennessee
7	Minnesota		33	Wisconsin
8	District of Columbia		34	North Carolina
9	South Carolina		35	Delaware
10	Ohio		36	New Mexico
11	Georgia		37	Nebraska
12	Maine		38	South Dakota
13	Alabama		39	Rhode Island
14	Massachusetts		40	Alaska
15	Utah		41	Virginia
16	California		42	North Dakota
17	Connecticut		43	Oklahoma
18	Oregon		44	Iowa
19	Kentucky		45	Wyoming
20	Kansas		46	Idaho
21	Vermont		47	Illinois
22	Pennsylvania		48	Montana
23	Indiana		49	Arkansas
24	Louisiana		50	Texas
25	New Hampshire		51	Mississippi
26	Washington			

Independent Living does not mean people with disabilities want to do everything by themselves or do not need anyone, or they like to live in isolation. Independent Living means that people with disabilities want the same choices and control in their every-day lives that their non-disabled neighbors and friends take for granted. They want to grow up in their families, go to the neighborhood school, use the same bus as their neighbors, work in jobs that are in line with their education and interests, and raise families of their own.

Resources

Disabilities Resources.org
http://www.disabilityresources.org/INDEPENDENT.html

National Institute on Disability, Independent Living, and Rehabilitation Research (NIDILRR)
http://www.acl.gov/Programs/NIDILRR/Index.aspx

Americans with Disabilities Act (ADA) Past, Present, and Future

Definition

Just 22 years ago it was legal to not hire, to fire, or discriminate against Americans with disabilities. The Americans with Disabilities Act (ADA) was signed into law on July 26, 1990, by President George H.W. Bush. It is the nation's first comprehensive civil rights law addressing the needs of people with disabilities, prohibiting discrimination in employment, public services, public accommodations, and telecommunications. The ADA did things_like repeal the last of the ugly discriminatory laws that prohibited people with disabilities from coming out in public, and required employers to provide accommodations for disabled workers on the job. Employers also were not allowed to discriminate against potential employees with disabilities during the interview process and pass them over for a non-disabled applicant. Employers were forbidden to ask if a person is disabled as well during an interview. The ADA empowers the Equal Employment Opportunity Commission (EEOC) to file lawsuits against employers who violate the law. The ADA was intended to guarantee that people with disabilities have the same opportunities as everyone else to participate in the mainstream of American life.

Changes to the ADA

After several Supreme Court decisions narrowly interpreted the ADA's definition of disability which resulted in the denial of the law's protection for many individuals, Congress passed the ADA Amendments Act which was signed into law in 2008. This Act emphasizes that the definition of disability should be construed in favor of broad coverage of individuals to the maximum extent permitted by the terms of the ADA and generally not require extensive analysis. The planned effect was to make it easier for an individual seeking protection under the ADA to establish he has a disability within the meaning of the ADA.

The ADAAA

The ADAAA defines disability as a physical or mental impairment that substantially limits one or more major life activities; a record (or past history) of such an impairment; or being regarded as having a disability.

In 2014 the Department of Justice released a Notice of Proposed Rulemaking to Implement the Americans with Disabilities Act Amendments Act of 2008. The Questions and Answers regarding this Notice of Proposed Rulemaking on the American Disabilities Act website (ada.gov), lists the changes to be incorporated into the revised regulations.

- The definition of disability will be interpreted broadly. The ADAAA makes it clear that the primary object of attention in ADA cases should be whether entities covered under the ADA have complied with their obligations.
- The question of whether an individual's impairment is a disability under the ADA will not demand extensive analysis.

- It will be easier for individuals to establish coverage under the "regarded as" prong of the definition of disability. Under the ADAAA the focus for establishing coverage is on how a person has been treated because of an actual or perceived physical or mental impairment, rather than on what an employer may have believed about the nature or severity of the person's impairment.
- Individuals covered under the "regarded as" prong are entitled to reasonable accommodations.
- The definition of "major life activities" will be expanded by providing a non-exhaustive list of major life activities that includes the operation of major bodily functions.
- There will be specific rules of construction that should be applied when determining whether an impairment substantially limits an individual in a major life activity:
    - The term "substantially limits" shall be construed broadly in favor of expansive coverage, to the maximum extent permitted by the terms of the ADA.
    - An impairment is a disability if it substantially limits the ability of an individual to perform a major life activity as compared to most people in the general population.
    - The primary issue in a case brought under the ADA should be whether the covered entity has complied with its obligations and whether discrimination has occurred, not the extent to which the individual's impairment substantially limits a major life activity
    - In making the individualized assessment required by the ADA, the term "substantially limits" shall be interpreted and applied to require a degree of functional limitation that is lower than the standard for substantially limits applied prior to the ADA Amendment Act
    - The comparison of an individual's performance of a major life activity to the performance of the same major life activity by most people in the general population usually will not require scientific, medical, or statistical evidence
    - Except for ordinary eyeglasses and contact lenses, the ameliorative effects of mitigating measures such as medication or hearing aids, shall not be considered in assessing whether an individual has a disability that substantially limits a major life activity
    - An impairment that is episodic or in remission is a disability if it would substantially limit a major life activity when active
    - An impairment that substantially limits one major life activity need not substantially limit other major life activities in order to be considered a substantially limiting impairment.

(www.ada.gov/nprm_adaaa/adaaa-nprm-qa.htm)

Is the ADA Successful?

In her July 23, 2015, article "The Americans with Disabilities Act: 25 years later," Julian Cardillo interviewed Susan Parish, Ph.D. regarding strengths and weaknesses of the Americans with Disabilities Act. Dr. Parish is the director of the Lurie Institute for Disability Policy and associate dean for research at the Heller School for Social Policy and Management. Dr. Parish stated that the Americans with Disabilities Act "…has had an enormous impact in the sense that it demonstrates our national commitment to the full civil and human rights of people with disabilities and it outlaws discrimination against people with disabilities. However, in terms of changing the daily lives of people with disabilities, it has had mixed results." Dr. Parish went on to note that the ADA is a voluntary compliance law, meaning employers are expected to voluntarily comply, but there are no reporting requirements to ensure they are. Most researchers agree that the ADA has had limited success in increasing the employment of people with disabilities.

However, considerable improvements have been made in accessibility for people with disabilities. Since the inception of the ADA there are significantly more accessible modes of transportation in this country, including fixed route buses, rail transit such as subways, commuter and light rail, and paratransit. People with disabilities are going places on public transportation. The ADA has not made every building in America accessible for people with disabilities but numbers are rising.

Life has improved for people with disabilities since the passage of the ADA. Still, while much progress has been made over 25 years, the nation has not yet fully realized the law's intent. Architecture, transportation, employment, and housing remain areas where drastic improvements can be made to open up opportunities for people with disabilities.

"The ADA was intended as a civil rights bill to establish the foundation that people with disabilities have the right to full participation in all aspects of society, including the right to seek and be hired into jobs that advance their economic self-sufficiency," said Susan Prokop, senior associate advocacy director for Paralyzed Veterans of America. "While the country has fulfilled that ideal in some respects, the workforce participation rate of people with disabilities is not very good; it remains stuck at 30 percent."

Transportation – from air travel to trains, taxis and buses – also remains a challenge. Companies like Amtrak are still working towards ADA compliance, while passenger vessels including cruise ships are waiting for final regulations on accessibility from the United States Access Board. Air travel – while addressed prior to the ADA in the 1986 Air Carrier Access Act (ACAA) – also can prove problematic for individuals with disabilities, said Lee Page, senior associate advocacy director for Paralyzed Veterans of America.

"In some cases, the airlines have met the requirement of the law but not necessarily the spirit of the law," Page said. "The reality is that assistive devices can be damaged, which really puts a cramp on travel for someone with a disability."

Paralyzed Veterans of America along with other advocacy groups also will remain vigilant to ensure states are abiding by the Supreme Court's 1999 Olmstead decision, which ruled that the ADA requires individuals with disabilities be integrated into the community rather than forced into nursing homes and other institutions. Government data shows that by 2010, just 12 states had made acceptable progress in implementing Olmstead.

"That's the next step of the ADA – to make sure that services are delivered in the least restrictive setting," Prokop said.

Meanwhile, the United States also has a role to play in promoting accessibility around the world, which requires in part the ratification by the U.S. Senate of the U.N. Convention on the Rights of Persons with Disabilities (CRPD), a treaty that would promote and protect the rights of people with disabilities in more than 150 countries around the world. While the treaty is modeled after the ADA, the United States is one of only a few countries that have not ratified it.

Still, while much work remains, the ADA has been a positive force not only in improving accessibility but boosting the public's attitudes and perceptions of the contributions and rights of people with disabilities. Looking forward, it is those attitudes and perceptions that ultimately will pave the future of the ADA and accessibility.

"Seeing people with disabilities out in the mainstream of life participating 100 percent makes everyone recognize that disability is part of the human condition and not something to be feared, patronized or specialized," Page said. "Twenty-five years is a long time, but we're still at the beginning because eventually all human aspects will be seamless – to the point where all people are truly equal."

Resources on the Americans with Disabilities Act

www.eeoc.gov/laws/regulations/adaaa_fact_sheet.cfm - Fact Sheet on the EEOC's Final Regulations Implementing the ADAAA

www.ada.gov - Information and Technical Assistance on the Americans with Disabilities Act

http://www.brandeis.edu/now/2015/july/parish-ada-qanda.html - "The Americans with Disabilities Act: 25 years later"

http://www.usccr.gov/pubs/ada/ch2.htm - "Sharing the Dream: Is the ADA Accommodating All?"

Home Modification for People with Disabilities

Accessible housing is essential for people with disabilities as they go about their everyday lives. Obtaining accessible housing could mean building a new, accessible home, or it may require adapting an already-existing house into one that can be enjoyed. Being part of the community and living as independently as possible are among the most important values and goals shared by people with disabilities, their families, and advocates. A home of one's own – either rented or owned – is the cornerstone of independence for people with disabilities.

The Fair Housing Act

Unfortunately, people with disabilities often face discrimination when seeking housing. The Fair Housing Act, enacted in 1968 and amended in 1988, is intended to protect people from discrimination, when they are renting, buying, or securing financing for any housing. Owners of housing facilities are required to make reasonable exceptions in their policies for tenants with disabilities. Landlords must allow tenants with disabilities to make reasonable access-related modifications to their private living space, as well as to common use spaces. However, landlords are not required to pay for these changes. The Act further requires that new multifamily housing with four or more units be designed and built to allow access for persons with disabilities.

However, the reality is that many housing units still do not meet accessibility standards as Glenn Collins discovered in his article in *The New York Times* titled "Accessible Homes? Not Really, Say Disabled Residents." Collins interviewed several apartment building tenants in New York City and found that they struggle with sinks and toilets that are either too high or too low; can be "trapped in corridors too narrow to maneuver wheelchairs in; stymied by unreachable latches, light switches and thermostats;" and are unable to get in their closets because of space restrictions.

New Architecture for Disabilities

Concrete Change (concretechange.org) is an organization that has been promoting the idea of *visitable* housing since before the Americans with Disabilities Act (ADA) was passed. They define Visitability as a movement to change home construction practices so that virtually all new homes offer specific features that make it easier for mobility-impaired people to live in and visit. The spirit of Visitability states, "it's not just unwise, but unacceptable that new homes continue to be built with gross barriers — given how easy it is to build basic access in the great majority of new homes, and given the harsh effects major barriers have on so many people's lives. These easily-avoided barriers cause daily drudgery, unsafe living conditions, social isolation, and forced institutionalization." Three basic changes to the way homes are designed can alleviate numerous hardships for people with disabilities: 1) Zero-step entrances; 2) Wider interior doors; and 3) At least a half bath on the main floor.

The house needs to have at least one zero-step entrance on an accessible route. An accessible route is considered a firm surface at least three feet wide. The entrance may be a ramp, a sloping sidewalk, or a garage floor level with the house. This entrance should be the entrance family and guests usually use.

The entrance must be truly zero-step. Even one small step poses a barrier. In addition, the slope must not be too steep; the ratio of length to height should be at least a foot long for every inch in height (1:12), and less steep than that when possible. The height of the ground at the bottom of a ramp (as opposed to height of the ground at the top of a ramp) is very relevant in determining the proper minimum length of the slope. To determine the length of slope needed, a board can be held out parallel from the porch floor; the board then leveled; and the vertical distance from the board to the ground then measured, at various possible end-points for the slope. The slope must end in a level platform such as a porch or garage floor. The slope should be level from side-to-side, flat from top to bottom, and end smoothly at the bottom, with less than a half-inch drop off. These features are necessary for basic safety.

All interior passage doors need to provide a minimum of 32 inches of clear passage space when the door is open at 90 degrees. A 2'10" door provides this space, and these doors are increasingly available because 32 inches is the width required by the Fair Housing Amendment in new multi-family dwellings. Special attention needs to be paid to the bathroom door because this is the one typically smaller than other doors on house plans. The bathroom door can be hinged to swing out rather than in to provide more room and give a person using a wheelchair or walker enough room to shut the door.

Additional tips for making new homes accessible for people with disabilities include modified furniture, shelves, and cupboards; adding handrails and grab bars throughout the home; easy-to-reach work and storage areas in the kitchen; reaching devices to grab objects on high shelves; lever handles on doors; toilet seat risers; walk-in showers; and bathtub and shower seats.

In Carl Wilkerson's 2012 article "Space and Empathy" found on Psychology Today's website, he discusses the need for house designers to use social empathy when building homes. "A designer has to put herself or himself into the place of the user and see how they will use the design in their everyday lives."

Modifications

The Easter Seals Disability Services developed a brochure titled "Easy Access Housing for Easier Living" that lists tips to make homes accessible. As the brochure states, "These are just a few adaptations that are possible to increase the accessibility and comfort of a home occupied by a person with a disability…." The following chart illustrates adaptations that can be made to alleviate or eliminate existing problems in your home:

Problem	Adaptation
Narrow doors	Remove the door. Replace with lever or handle style. Install special hinges. Swing the door in the opposite direction, or consider widening the doorway.
Round knob fixtures/hardware	Replace with lever or handle style
Switches, outlets and thermostats located too high/low	Use available products for remote control operation of switches and outlets; attach extensions to switches; lower thermostat.
Lack of maneuvering room in the kitchen for wheelchair	Consider removing some base cabinets to provide maneuvering room and knee spaces under countertops.
Wall cabinets that are too high	Lower existing cabinets, add some new cabinets or add a free-standing storage cabinet.
High countertops	Substitute a drop leaf cart with wheels. Leaf can be raised for food preparation and cart can be rolled to stove and refrigerator.
Standard fire alarms	For persons with hearing disabilities, install visual alarm systems that are triggered to go off when the standard alarm does.
Standard doorbells	Again, visual devices can be attached to the doorbell, even the door itself, to alert persons with hearing disabilities to visitors.
Standard height toilets and bathroom fixtures	Most hospital and medical supply companies carry products that can be added on to standard toilets to raise the seat height. Many types of adaptive bathtub and shower aids are also on the market.

Many bath tubs have high sides making it difficult for people with disabilities to get in and out of them. There are several ways this problem can be minimized and/or eliminated. Grab bars can be added to assist entering and exiting the tub. A bath tub with a door for easier access can be installed. Tub transfer seats which allow the person to sit in the tub without lowering can be installed. Roll-in showers can also be installed and utilized.

Bathroom sinks also present problems for people with disabilities. Sinks can be installed to allow wheel chair access. Vanity cabinets can be removed from under sinks to allow more room. The plumbing pipes may be exposed in this instance and will need to be covered.

Modifying homes to be accessible for people with disabilities is needed to maintain people's independence and safety and foster community integration. Home modifications can help prevent injuries and reduce medical costs while allowing people to stay in their own homes.

Defining Adaptable and Accessible Housing

An adaptable house has certain structural features that make it possible to modify it to accommodate people with a wide range of physical abilities. The adaptable house is a lifetime living house. It's similar to insurance for people in that if they, or someone close to them, become disabled or experience a change in their physical abilities, they can modify the house to accommodate their needs. An accessible house or dwelling is equipped with specific features to accommodate people with permanent disabilities or declining physical abilities.

Home Adaptability Checklist

A home is considered adaptable if it has all or most of the following key structural features which allow reasonable entry and circulation without extensive modification.

- ☐ Located on a relatively flat or level site with paved walkways from parking (covered is preferred) and sidewalk areas to level entry.
- ☐ A ground-level entrance or a one or two step entrance clear of any major obstructions, i.e. trees, building corners, etc., that would accept a ramp with a slope no greater than 1" height per 12" in length.
- ☐ No steps or abrupt level changes on main floor.
- ☐ Wider-than-standard doorways (32" or more clear width); 1/2" high maximum thresholds.
- ☐ Wide hallways at least 42"; preferably 48"- 60".
- ☐ At least one large bathroom with a 32" clear door opening and clear 5' x 5' floor space.
- ☐ A kitchen large enough for easy wheelchair mobility (U or L shaped or open plan preferred).

Accessibility Checklist

When you preview a house for accessibility, especially wheelchair accessibility, check each item that is presently available. Individual access needs vary greatly. Wheelchairs are used for different reasons and come in many different sizes so, while one person using a wheelchair may be able to get through a 32 inch doorway, another may need 36 inches. Where a range of measurement is indicated on the accessibility checklist, note the exact width or height in the space provided.

This list will provide the user with a measure of existing accessibility features. Certainly all of these features are not necessary, or even desirable, to meet the needs of an individual with a disability. This checklist is intended to generate enough information about any given home to let people interested in accessibility features know if it warrants consideration. At the end of the checklist, you will find some general tips and resources.

GENERAL

- ☐ One-story building.
- ☐ Multi-level house with main level accessible entrance, bathroom and bedroom.
- ☐ Level entry way or ramp with entry level landing for easy door opening.
- ☐ Wide doorways (32"-36" clear width).
- ☐ Wide hallways (42"- 60").
- ☐ Low-pile carpeting with thin padding or smooth surfaces.
- ☐ Chair-height (48"-54")* doorbell/mailbox.
- ☐ Chair-height electrical controls/outlets (excluding the kitchen, generally controls are 6" lower and outlets are 6" higher than standard).
- ☐ Chair-height push-button telephones/jacks.
- ☐ Accessible, easily operated window controls, i.e. slide to side can be opened with one hand or less than eight pounds of pressure, located 24"- 28" from floor.
- ☐ Direct outside emergency exit from bedroom.
- ☐ Audio and visual smoke detectors.
- ☐ Large windows, overhead lighting or several electrical outlets in each room (Lighting is a big consideration for persons with low vision).

KITCHEN

- ☐ Front control-operated range.
- ☐ Countertop range.
- ☐ Lowered wall oven (30"- 42").
- ☐ Side by side, frost-free, dispenser type refrigerator.
- ☐ Varying countertop and cabinet heights.

continued

- ☐ Counters with pullout cutting boards.
- ☐ Front control-operated, built-in dishwasher.
- ☐ Front loading washer/dryer.

BATHROOM

- ☐ Out swing doors.
- ☐ Non-slip floors.
- ☐ Grab bars.
- ☐ Reinforced walls (i.e. 3/4" plywood backing throughout) for installation of grab bars 5' square clear area (required for most wheelchair users to make a 360 degree turn). Since many wheelchair users can function in smaller areas, measure exact clear floor space if less than 5' Chair-height racks/shelves/cabinets Lever handled faucets.
- ☐ Lowered or tilted mirror.
- ☐ Roll-under vanity top.
- ☐ Hinged, fold-down seat in shower.
- ☐ Roll-in shower with no curb.
- ☐ Hand-held or adjustable shower head.
- ☐ Bathtub with nonskid strips or surface.
- ☐ Toilet seat 17"-19" from floor; or wall mounted toilet.
- ☐ Telephone outlet.

BEDROOM

- ☐ Open floor plan.
- ☐ Built-in cabinets have 6" baseboard recess.
- ☐ Built-in wall bed.
- ☐ Direct access to accessible bathroom.
- ☐ Reinforced ceiling (to accommodate pulleys for lifting mechanisms).

CLOSETS

- ☐ Sliding doors or bi-folding doors.
- ☐ Adjustable shelves and hanging rods.
- ☐ Shallow shelves no more than 18" deep.

GARAGE

- ☐ Attached.
- ☐ Oversized.
- ☐ High ceiling (9'6" needed to accommodate a raised-top van).
- ☐ Automatic door opener.

OTHER CONSIDERATIONS

- ☐ On or near public transportation.
- ☐ Conveniently located to shopping areas.

SOME ADAPTATION TIPS

Many accessibility problems can be avoided or eliminated by making minor structural changes or by utilizing any number of adaptive aids on the market. The following is a brief list of common accessibility problems and some possible adaptations.

Disability Living Conditions and Remodeling Resources

People with disabilities are faced with many decisions, very few of them easy, regarding their homes. It is often difficult to decide whether it is best to try to build a new home, buy a new home that is accessible, or modify the current home. The following list of resources will help in these decisions and also provides resources on financial assistance regarding housing.

http://www.disabilityrights.org/mod3.htm - Home modification - Funding sources

http://www.homemods.org/index.shtml - This web site is university-based and non-profit dedicated to promoting aging in place and independent living for persons of all ages and abilities.

http://www.disabled-world.com/disability/accessibility/homes/ - Accessible home design: Information and Ideas

http://www.wid.org/publications/accessible-housing-database-and-manual - The goal of the Accessible Housing Database package is to provide a tool with which Independent Living Centers can tack accessible rental housing in their community, and from which officials and advocates can draw data in order to assess affordability and availability of accessible housing.

continued

http://www.udservices.org/about/ - UDS is a nonprofit organization that helps the aging, veterans and people with disabilities live safely and more independently in their own homes.

http://www.adaptiveaccess.com/home_changes.php - Adaptive Access was started to create a safer and more comfortable environment for the elderly and those with disabilities and limited mobility.

http://portal.hud.gov/hudportal/HUD?src=/program_offices/fair_housing_equal_opp/progdesc/title8 - Information on The Fair Housing Act

http://www.thearc.org/what-we-do/public-policy/policy-issues/housing - Discusses Housing Issues for People with Disabilities including Affordability, Accessibility, and Housing Discrimination.

http://www.concretechange.org/about-us/ - Concrete Change is an international network whose goal is making all new homes visitable, not just "special" homes.

http://www.homemods.org/resources/links.shtml - This provides a list of links on home modification.

http://www.benefits.va.gov/homeloans/adaptedhousing.asp - Housing Grants for Disabled Veterans

https://www.disability.gov/ - The U.S. federal government website for information on disability programs and services nationwide.

http://www.afb.org/info/low-vision/living-with-low-vision/a-checklist-for-environmental-safety/235 - A Checklist for Environmental Safety

http://www.easterseals.com/shared-components/document-library/easy_access_housing.pdf - This brochure provides an Accessibility Checklist for people with disabilities who are looking to purchase a new home.

Help for the Caregiver

Caregiving duties cannot be skirted and cannot always be delegated. However, it is important to remember that the job does not have to be performed in isolation and it is vital to reach out and connect to others with similar situations.

The Role of a Caregiver

Helping someone you care for to continue living independently at home is valuable work. Caregiving can be a satisfying experience; it demonstrates fulfillment of a commitment to a loved one. True enough, though, caregiving is not a role anyone really chooses. It seems to choose us, emerging from events and circumstances outside our expectations, beyond our control.

Family members provide the vast majority of care for people who are chronically ill or disabled. According to the Caregiver Action Network, family caregivers underpin our healthcare system in a profound way. More than 50 million people provide some level of care for a loved one, which would translate into annual wages of $375 billion – almost twice as much as is actually spent on homecare and nursing home services combined – if it weren't done for "free." As the population ages, and with growing disability population, the number of family caregivers continues to grow.

Caregiving can be frustrating, physically and emotionally draining. It can steal our dreams or break our hearts. It makes us sad for our loved one's loss, and for our own loss. While caring for loved ones can be enormously satisfying, there are days, to be sure, that offer little reward.

The job takes its toll. Caregivers suffer far more depression, stress and anxiety than the general population. Surveys show that up to 70% of caregivers report depression, 51% sleeplessness, and 41% back problems.

Caregivers feel isolated and often report that their lives are not "normal" or that no one else can possibly understand what they are going through. Compounding the problem is the fact that nearly three quarters of family caregivers do not go to the doctor as often as they should, and 55% say they skip doctor appointments; 63% of caregivers report having poor eating habits

There is a financial impact, too. Families helping a person with a disability spend more than twice as much on out-of-pocket medical expenses than families without a disabled person.

Frequently the caregiver must make sacrifices at work to attend to duties at home. But this is your family, your loved one. What are your choices? You can't just walk away. You learn to deal with the frustration while learning how to best get the job done.

The lessons are often learned the hard way – for the most part, caregivers learn by trial and error on how to manage daily routines for food preparation, hygiene, transportation and other activities at home.

Caregiving Support and Assistance

Tips for Making Family Caregiving Easier and More Rewarding:

As a family caregiver for an ailing parent, child, spouse, or other loved one, you're likely to face a host of new responsibilities, many of which are unfamiliar or intimidating. At times, you may feel overwhelmed and alone. But despite its challenges, caregiving can also be rewarding. And there are a lot of things you can do to make the caregiving process easier and more pleasurable for both you and your loved one. These tips can help you get the support you need while caring for someone you love in way that may benefit both of you.

Family Caregiving

Providing care for a family member in need is an act of kindness, love, and loyalty. And as life expectancies increase, medical treatments advance, and increasing numbers of people live with chronic illness and disabilities, more and more of us will participate in the caregiving process.

There are many different types of family caregiver situations. You may be taking care of an aging parent or a handicapped spouse. Or perhaps you're caring for a child with a physical or mental illness. Regardless of your particular circumstances, you're facing a challenging new role.

If you're like most family caregivers, you aren't trained for the responsibilities you now face. And you probably never anticipated you'd be in this situation. You may not even live very close to your loved one. At the same time, you love your family member and want to provide the best care you can. The good news is that you don't have to be a nursing expert, a superhero, or a saint in order to be a good caregiver. With the right help and support, you can be an effective, loving caregiver without having to sacrifice yourself in the process.

- **Learn as much as you can** about your family member's illness or disability and about how to be a caregiver. The more you know, the less anxiety you'll feel about your new role and the more effective you'll be.
- **Seek out other caregivers.** It helps to know you're not alone. It's comforting to give and receive support from others who understand what you're going through.
- **Trust your instincts.** Remember, you know your family member best. Don't ignore what doctors and specialists tell you, but listen to your gut, too.
- **Encourage your loved one's independence.** Caregiving does not mean doing everything for your loved one. Be open to technologies and strategies that allow your family member to be as independent as possible.
- **Know your limits.** Be realistic about how much of your time and yourself you can give. Set clear limits, and communicate those limits to doctors, family members, and other people involved.

Family Caregiving Tip #1: Accept Your Feelings

Caregiving can trigger a host of difficult emotions, including anger, fear, resentment, guilt, helplessness, and grief. It's important to acknowledge and accept what you're feeling, both good and bad. Don't beat yourself up over your doubts and misgivings. These feelings don't mean that you don't love your family member—they simply mean you're human.

What you may feel about being a family caregiver

- **Anxiety and worry** – You may worry about how you will handle the additional responsibilities of caregiving and what will happen to your family member if something happens to you. You may also fear what will happen in the future as your loved one's illness progresses.

- **Anger or resentment** – You may feel angry or resentful toward the person you're caring for, even though you know it's irrational. Or you might be angry at the world in general, or resentful of other friends or family members who don't have your responsibilities.
- **Guilt** – You may feel guilty for not doing more, being a "better" caregiver, having more patience, accepting your situation with more equanimity, or in the case of long distance caregiving, not being available more often.
- **Grief** – There are many losses that can come with caregiving (the healthy future you envisioned with your spouse or child; the goals and dreams you've had to set aside). If the person you're caring for is terminally ill, you're also dealing with that grief.

Even when you understand why you're feeling the way you do, it can still be upsetting. In order to deal with your feelings, it's important to talk about them. Don't keep your emotions bottled up, but find at least one person you trust to confide in.

Places you can turn for caregiver support include:

- Family members or friends who will listen without judgment
- Your church, temple, or other place of worship
- Caregiver support groups at a local hospital or online
- A therapist, social worker, or counselor
- National caregiver organizations
- Organizations specific to your family member's illness or disability

Family Caregiving Tip #2: Don't Try To Do It All

Even if you're the primary family caregiver, you can't do everything on your own, especially if you're caregiving from a distance (more than an hour's drive from your family member). You'll need help from friends, siblings, and other family members, as well as health professionals. If you don't get the support you need, you'll quickly burn out—which will compromise your ability to provide care.

But before you can ask for help, you need to have a clear understanding of your family member's needs. Take some time to list all the caregiving tasks required, being as specific as possible. Then determine which activities you are able to meet (be realistic about your capabilities and time). The remaining tasks on the list are ones you'll need to ask others to help you with.

Asking family and friends for help

It's not always easy to ask for help, even when you desperately need it. Perhaps you're afraid to impose on others or worried that your request will be resented or rejected. But if you simply make your needs known, you may be pleasantly surprised by the willingness of others to pitch in. Many times, friends and family members want to help, but don't know how. Make it easier for them:

- Set aside one-on-one time to talk to the person
- Go over the list of caregiving needs you previously drew up
- Point out areas in which they might be of service (maybe your brother is good at Internet research, or your friend is a financial whiz)
- Ask the person if they'd like to help, and if so, in what way
- Make sure the person understands what would be most helpful to both you and the caregiving recipient

Family Caregiving Tip #3: Attend to your own needs

When done in the right way, caring for a loved one can bring pleasure—to both you, the caregiver, and to the person you're caring for. Being calm and relaxed and taking the time each day to really connect with the person you're caring for can release hormones that boost your mood, reduce stress, and trigger biological changes that improve your physical health. And it has the same effect on your loved one, too.

Even if the person you're caring for can no longer communicate verbally, it's important to take a short time to focus fully on him or her. Avoid all distractions—such as the TV, cell phone, and computer—make eye contact (if that's possible), hold the person's hand or stroke his or her cheek, and talk in a calm, reassuring tone of voice. When you connect in this way, you'll experience a process that lowers stress and supports physical and emotional well-being—for both of you—and you'll experience the "deepest significance and meaning" that Casals talks about.

Of course, if you're distracted, burned out, or otherwise overwhelmed by the daily grind of caregiving, you'll likely find such connection difficult. That's why it's vital that while you're caring for your loved one, you don't forget about your own needs. Caregivers need care, too.

Emotional needs of family caregivers

- **Take time to relax daily** and learn how to regulate yourself and de-stress when you start to feel overwhelmed. As explained above, one way to do that is by really connecting with the person you're caring for. If that isn't possible, employ your senses to effectively relieve stress in the moment and return yourself to a balanced state.
- **Talk with someone** to make sense of your situation and your feelings. There's no better way of relieving stress than spending time face-to-face with someone who cares about you.
- **Keep a journal.** Some people find it helpful to write down their thoughts and feelings to help them see things more clearly.
- **Feed your spirit.** Pray, meditate, or do another activity that makes you feel part of something greater. Try to find meaning in both your life and in your role as a caregiver.
- **Watch out for signs of depression, anxiety, or burnout** and get professional help if needed.

Social and recreational needs of family caregivers

- **Stay social.** Make it a priority to visit regularly with other people. Nurture your close relationships. Don't let yourself become isolated.
- **Do things you enjoy.** Laughter and joy can help keep you going when you face trials, stress, and pain.
- **Maintain balance in your life.** Don't give up activities that are important to you, such as your work or your hobbies.
- **Give yourself a break.** Take regular breaks from caregiving, and give yourself an extended break at least once a week.
- **Find a community.** Join or reestablish your connection to a religious group, social club, or civic organization. The broader your support network, the better.

Physical needs of family caregivers

- **Exercise regularly.** Try to get in at least 30 minutes of exercise, three times per week. Exercise is a great way to relieve stress and boost your energy. So get moving, even if you're tired.
- **Eat right.** Well-nourished bodies are better prepared to cope with stress and get through busy days. Keep your energy up and your mind clear by eating nutritious meals at regular times throughout the day.
- **Avoid alcohol and drugs.** It can be tempting to turn to substances for escape when life feels overwhelming, but they can easily compromise the quality of your caregiving. Instead, try dealing with problems head on and with a clear mind.
- **Get enough sleep.** Aim for an average of eight hours of solid, uninterrupted sleep every night. Otherwise, your energy level, productivity, and ability to handle stress will suffer.
- **Keep up with your own health care.** Go to the doctor and dentist on schedule, and keep up with your own prescriptions or medical therapy. As a caregiver, you need to stay as strong and healthy as possible.

Family Caregiving Tip #4: Take Advantage of Community Services

There are services to help caregivers in most communities. Depending on where you live, the cost may be based on ability to pay or covered by the care receiver's insurance. Services that may be available in your community include adult day care centers, home health aides, home-delivered meals, respite care, transportation services, and skilled nursing.

- **Caregiver services in your community.** Call your local senior center, county information and referral service, family services, or hospital social work unit for contact suggestions. Advocacy groups for the disorder your loved one's suffering from may also be able to recommend local

continued

services. In the U.S., contact your local Area Agency on Aging for help with caring for older family members.

- **Caregiver support for veterans.** If your care recipient is a veteran in the U.S., home health care coverage, financial support, nursing home care, and adult day care benefits may be available. Some Veterans Administration programs are free, while others require co-payments, depending upon the veteran's status, income, and other criteria.
- **Your family member's affiliations.** Fraternal organizations such as the Elks, Eagles, or Moose lodges may offer some assistance if your loved one is a longtime dues-paying member. This help may take the form of phone check-ins, home visits, or transportation.
- **Community transportation services.** Many communities offer free or low-cost transportation services for trips to and from medical appointments, day care, senior centers, and shopping malls.
- **Adult day care.** If your senior loved one is well enough, consider the possibility of adult day care. An adult day care center can provide you with needed breaks during the day or week, and your loved one with some valuable diversions and activities.
- **Personal care services.** Help with activities of daily living, such as dressing, bathing, feeding, or meal preparation may be provided by home care aides, hired companions, certified nurse's aides, or home health aides. Home health aides might also provide limited assistance with things such as taking blood pressure or offering medication reminders.
- **Health care services.** Some health care services can be provided at home by trained professionals such as physical or occupational therapists, social workers, or home health nurses. Check with your insurance or health service to see what kind of coverage is available. Hospice care can also be provided at home.
- **Meal programs.** Your loved one may be eligible to have hot meals delivered at home by a Meals on Wheels program. Religious and other local organizations sometimes offer free lunches and companionship for the sick and elderly. Contact your local senior center or see the Resources section below for useful links.

Family Caregiving Tip #5: Provide Long Distance Care

Many people take on the role of designated caregiver for a family member—often an older relative or sibling—while living more than an hour's travel away. Trying to manage a loved one's care from a distance can add to feelings of guilt and anxiety and present many other obstacles. But there are steps you can take to prepare for caregiving emergencies and ease the burden of responsibility.

- Set up an alarm system for your loved one. Because of the distance between you, you won't be able to respond in time to a life-threatening emergency, so subscribe to an electronic alert system. Your loved one wears the small device and can use it to summon immediate help.
- Manage doctor and medical appointments. Try to schedule all medical appointments together, at a time when you'll be in the area. Make the time to get to know your loved one's doctors and arrange to be kept up-to-date on all medical issues via the phone when you're not in the area. Your relative may need to sign a privacy release to enable their doctors to do this.

- **Use a case manager.** Some hospitals or insurance plans can assign case managers to coordinate your loved one's care, monitor his or her progress, manage billing, and communicate with the family.
- **Investigate local services.** When you're not there, try to find local services that can offer home help services, deliver meals, or provide local transportation for your loved one. A geriatric care manager can offer a variety of services to long-distance caregivers, including providing and monitoring in-home help for your relative.
- **Schedule regular communication with your loved one.** A daily email, text message, or quick phone call can let your relative know that they're not forgotten and give you peace of mind.
- **Arrange telephone check-ins** from a local religious group, senior center, or other public or nonprofit organization. These services offer prescheduled calls to homebound older adults to reduce their isolation and monitor their well-being.

Caregiver Stress and Burnout

Tips for Regaining Your Energy, Optimism, and Hope

The demands of caregiving can be overwhelming, especially if you feel you have little control over the situation or you're in over your head. If the stress of caregiving is left unchecked, it can take a toll on your health, relationships, and state of mind—eventually leading to burnout. When you're burned out, it's tough to do anything, let alone look after someone else. That's why taking care of yourself isn't a luxury—it's a necessity. Read on for tips on how to rein in the stress in your life and regain balance, joy, and hope.

Caregiver stress and burnout: What you need to know

Caring for a loved one can be very rewarding, but it also involves many stressors. Caregiver stress can be particularly damaging, since it is typically a chronic, long-term challenge. You may face years or even decades of caregiving responsibilities. It can be particularly disheartening when there's no hope that your family member will get better.

If you don't get the physical and emotional support your need, the stress of caregiving leaves you vulnerable to a wide range of problems, including depression, anxiety, and burnout. And when you get to that point, both you and the person you're caring for suffer. That's why managing the stress levels in your life is just as important as making sure your family member gets to his doctor's appointment or takes her medication on time.

Signs and symptoms of caregiver stress and burnout

Learning to recognize the signs of caregiver stress and burnout is the first step to dealing with the problem.

Common signs and symptoms of caregiver stress

- Anxiety, depression, irritability
- Feeling tired and run down
- Difficulty sleeping
- Overreacting to minor nuisances
- New or worsening health problems
- Trouble concentrating
- Feeling increasingly resentful
- Drinking, smoking, or eating more
- Neglecting responsibilities
- Cutting back on leisure activities

Common signs and symptoms of caregiver burnout

- You have much less energy than you once had
- It seems like you catch every cold or flu that's going around
- You're constantly exhausted, even after sleeping or taking a break
- You neglect your own needs, either because you're too busy or you don't care anymore
- Your life revolves around caregiving, but it gives you little satisfaction
- You have trouble relaxing, even when help is available
- You're increasingly impatient and irritable with the person you're caring for
- You feel helpless and hopeless

Once you burn out, caregiving is no longer a healthy option for either you or the person you're caring for. So it's important to watch for the warning signs of caregiver burnout and take action right away when you recognize the problem.

Dealing with caregiver stress & burnout tip 1: Find ways to feel empowered

Feeling powerless is the number one contributor to burnout and depression. And it's an easy trap to fall into as a caregiver, especially if you feel stuck in a role you didn't expect or helpless to change things for the better. But no matter the situation, you aren't powerless. This is especially true when it comes to your state of mind. You can't always get the extra time, money, or physical assistance you'd like, but you can always get more happiness and hope.

- **Embrace your caregiving choice.** Acknowledge that, despite any resentments or burdens you feel, you have made a conscious choice to provide care. Focus on the positive reasons behind that choice. Perhaps you provide care to repay your parent for the care they gave you growing up. Or maybe it's because or your values or the example you want to set for your children. These deep, meaningful motivations can help sustain you through difficult times.
- **Focus on the things you can control.** You can't wish your mother's cancer away or force your brother to help out more. Rather than stressing out over things you can't control, focus on the way you choose to react to problems.
- **Celebrate the small victories.** If you start to feel discouraged, remind yourself that all your efforts matter. You don't have to cure your loved one's illness to make a difference. Don't underestimate the importance of making your loved one feel more safe, comfortable, and loved!

Dealing with caregiver stress & burnout tip 2: Practice acceptance

When faced with the unfairness of a loved one's illness or the burden of caregiving, there's often a need to make sense of the situation and ask "Why?" But you can spend a tremendous amount of energy dwelling on things you can't change and for which there are no clear answers. And at the end of the day, you won't feel any better.

Try to avoid the emotional trap of feeling sorry for yourself or searching for someone to blame. Focus instead on accepting the situation and looking for ways it can help you grown as a person. As the saying goes, "What doesn't kill us makes us stronger."

- **Find the silver lining.** Think about the ways caregiving has made you stronger or how it's brought you closer to the person you're taking care of or to other family members. Think about how caregiving allows you to give back and show your love.
- **Share your feelings.** Expressing what you're going through can be very cathartic, even if there's nothing you can do to alter the situation. And don't worry about being a burden to others. Most friends will be flattered that you trust them enough to confide in them, and it will only strengthen your bond.
- **Avoid tunnel vision.** Don't let caregiving take over your whole life. It's easier to accept a difficult situation when there are other areas of your life that are rewarding. Invest in things that give you meaning and purpose—whether it's your family, church, a favorite hobby, or your career.

Getting the appreciation you need

Feeling appreciated can go a long way toward not only accepting a stressful situation, but enjoying life more. Studies show that caregivers who feel appreciated experience greater physical and emotional health. Caregiving actually makes them happier and healthier, despite its demands. But what can you do if the person you're caring for is no longer able to feel or show their appreciation for your time and efforts?

- **Imagine how your loved one would respond if he or she was healthy.** If he or she wasn't preoccupied with illness or pain (or disabled by dementia), how would your loved one feel about the love and care you're giving? Remind yourself that the person would express gratitude if he or she was able.
- **Applaud your own efforts.** If you're not getting external validation, find ways to acknowledge and reward yourself. Remind yourself of the good you're doing. If you need something more concrete, try making a list of all the ways your caregiving is making a positive difference. Refer back to it when you start to feel low.
- **Talk to a supportive family member or friend.** Positive reinforcement doesn't have to come from the person you're caring for. When you're feeling unappreciated, turn to friends and family who will listen to you and acknowledge your efforts.

Dealing with caregiver stress & burnout tip 3: Ask for help

Taking on all of the responsibilities of caregiving without regular breaks or assistance is a surefire recipe for burnout. Don't try to do it all alone. Look into respite care. Or enlist friends and family who live near you to run errands, bring a hot meal, or "baby-sit" the care receiver so you can take a well-deserved break.

Tips for getting the caregiving help you need

- **Speak up.** Don't expect friends and family members to automatically know what you need or how you're feeling. Be up front about what's going on with you and the person you're caring for. If you have concerns or thoughts about how to improve the situation, express them—even if you're unsure how they'll be received. Get a dialogue going.
- **Spread the responsibility.** Try to get as many family members involved as possible. Even someone who lives far away can help. You may also want to divide up caregiving tasks. One person can take care of medical responsibilities, another with finances and bills, and another with groceries and errands, for example.
- **Set up a regular check-in.** Ask a family member, friend, or volunteer from your church or senior center to call you on a set basis (every day, weekly, or how ever often you think you need it). This person can help you spread status updates and coordinate with other family members.
- **Say "yes" when someone offers assistance.** Don't be shy about accepting help. Let them feel good about supporting you. It's smart to have a list ready of small tasks that others could easily take care of, such as picking up groceries or driving your loved one to an appointment.
- **Be willing to relinquish some control.** Delegating is one thing. Trying to control every aspect of care is another. People will be less likely to help if you micromanage, give orders, or insist on doing things your way.

Dealing with caregiver stress & burnout tip 4: Give yourself a break

As a busy caregiver, leisure time may seem like an impossible luxury. But you owe it to yourself—as well as to the person you're caring for—to carve it into your schedule. Give yourself permission to rest and to do things that you enjoy on a daily basis. You will be a better caregiver for it.

There's a difference between being busy and being productive. If you're not regularly taking time-off to de-stress and recharge your batteries, you'll end up getting less done in the long run. After a break, you should feel more energetic and focused, so you'll quickly make up for your relaxation time.

- **Maintain your personal relationships.** Don't let your friendships get lost in the shuffle of caregiving. These relationships will help sustain you and keep you positive. If it's difficult to leave the house, invite friends over to visit with you over coffee, tea, or dinner.
- **Prioritize activities that bring you enjoyment.** Make regular time for things that bring you happiness, whether it's reading, working in the garden, tinkering in your workshop, knitting, playing with the dogs, or watching the game.
- **Find ways to pamper yourself.** Small luxuries can go a long way in relieving stress and boosting your spirits. Light candles and take a long bath. Ask your hubby for a back rub. Get a manicure. Buy fresh flowers for the house. Or whatever makes you feel special.
- **Make yourself laugh.** Laughter is an excellent antidote to stress—and a little goes a long way. Read a funny book, watch a comedy, or call a friend who makes you laugh. And whenever you can, try to find the humor in everyday situations.
- **Get out of the house.** Seek out friends, family, and respite care providers to step in with caregiving so you can have some time away from the home.

Dealing with caregiver stress & burnout tip 5: Take care of your health

Think of your body like a car. With the right fuel and proper maintenance, it will run reliably and well. Neglect its upkeep and it will start to give you trouble. Don't add to the stress of your caregiving situation with avoidable health woes.

- **Keep on top of your doctor visits.** It's easy to forget about your own health when you're busy with a loved one's care. Don't skip check-ups or medical appointments. You need to be healthy in order to take good care of your family member.
- **Exercise.** When you're stressed and tired, the last thing you feel like doing is exercising. But you'll feel better afterwards. Exercise is a powerful stress reliever and mood enhancer. Aim for a minimum of 30 minutes on most days. When you exercise regularly, you'll also find it boosts your energy level and helps you fight fatigue.
- **Meditate.** A daily relaxation or meditation practice can help you relieve stress and boost feelings of joy and well-being. Try yoga, deep breathing, progressive muscle relaxation, or mindfulness meditation. Even a few minutes in the middle of an overwhelming day can help you feel more centered.

continued

- **Eat well.** Nourish your body with fresh fruit, vegetables, whole grains, beans, lean protein, and healthy fats such as nuts and olive oil. Unlike sugar and caffeine—which provide a quick pick-me-up and an even quicker crash—these foods will fuel you with steady energy.
- **Don't skimp on sleep.** Cutting back on time in bed is counterproductive—at least if your goal is to get more done. Most people need more sleep than they think they do (8 hours is the norm). When you get less, your mood, energy, productivity, and ability to handle stress will suffer.

Dealing with caregiver stress & burnout tip 6: Join a support group

A caregiver support group is a great way to share your troubles and find people who are going through the same experiences that you are living each day. If you can't leave the house, many Internet groups are also available.

In most support groups, you'll talk about your problems and listen to others talk; you'll not only get help, but you'll also be able to help others. Most important, you'll find out that you're not alone. You'll feel better knowing that other people are in the same situation, and their knowledge can be invaluable, especially if they're caring for someone with the same illness as you are.

Local vs. Online Support Groups for Caregivers	
Local support groups:	Online support groups:
<ul><li>People live near each other and meet in a given place each week or month.</li><li>You get face-to-face contact and a chance to make new friends who live near you.</li><li>The meetings get you out of the house, get you moving provide a social outlet, and reduce feelings of isolation.</li><li>Meetings are at a set time. You will need to attend them regularly to get the full benefit of the group.</li><li>Since the people in the support group are from your area, they'll be more familiar with local resources and issues.</li></ul>	<ul><li>People are from all over the world and have similar interests or problems.</li><li>You meet online, through email lists, websites, message boards, or social media.</li><li>You can get support without leaving your house, which is good for people with limited mobility or transportation problems.</li><li>You can access the group whenever it's convenient for you or when you need help most.</li><li>If your problem is very unusual—a rare disease, for example—there may not be enough people for a local group, but there will always be enough people online.</li></ul>

To find a community support group, check the yellow pages, ask your doctor or hospital, or call local organizations that deal with the health problem you would like to address in a support group. To find an Internet support group, visit the website of an organization dedicated to the problem.

Caregiving Tips Summarized

There are 44 million family caregivers in the U.S., making up 20 percent of the whole U.S. adult population. Family caregivers make significant sacrifices to provide essential societal and financial contributions toward the health of their loved ones.

Caregivers also face difficult emotions and significant financial burdens. They make noble sacrifices, but these decisions often have a negative impact on their mental and physical wellbeing. With unpaid family caregivers on the rise, the need for emotional and physical support has become more prevalent. Here are 16 tips for caregivers to stay happy and healthy.

1. Research and make a list. Learn as much as you can about your loved one's illness or disability and about how to be a caregiver. The more you know, the less nervous you'll feel about the tasks you need to perform. You will become a more effective caregiver once you are confident in your actions. Take some time to list all the tasks you will need to carry out. Then decide which tasks you are able to meet. When you create this list, try to be as realistic as possible, taking into consideration your time and energy. The remaining tasks on the list are ones you'll need to find others to help with (either another family member or a home care agency).

2. Find people like you. It is comforting to know you're not alone. Join a support group to find others like you. This will help you with the emotional support you need. Often care providers like Wesley Homes offer support groups that are open to the greater community.

3. Know your limits and vocalize them. Try to be as realistic about how much of your time and energy you can give. Set defined limits, and communicate those limits to doctors, family members and your loved one.

4. Accept your feelings. Caregiving can trigger difficult emotions, including anger, fear, resentment, guilt, helplessness and grief. It's important to acknowledge and accept what you're feeling, both good and bad. Be easy on yourself, and try not to feel guilt or anger about your doubts or misgivings. Remember, your feelings don't mean that you don't love your family member; these are all human traits.

5. Encourage independence for yourself and your loved one. Caregiving does not mean doing everything for your loved one. Be open to the help of family members, friends or home care agencies to create an atmosphere of independence for your loved one. Look into available technologies like a Health Monitoring System, Medication Dispenser System, Medication Reminder System or Personal Emergency Response Systems.

6. Stay social. Make it a priority to see your friends, and don't let yourself become isolated.

7. Stay happy. Laughter and joy can help keep you going when you face trials, stress and pain.

continued

8. Keep your balance. Don't give up activities that are important to you, such as your work or your hobbies.

9. Take breaks. Take regular breaks from caregiving, and give yourself an extended break at least once a week.

10. Find a community. Join or reestablish your connection to a religious group, social club or civic organization. The broader your support network, the better.

11. Exercise regularly. Try to get in at least 30 minutes of exercise, three times per week. Exercise is a great way to relieve stress and boost your energy. So get moving, even if you're tired.

12. Eat right. Well-nourished bodies are better prepared to cope with stress and get through busy days. Keep your energy up and your mind clear by eating nutritious meals at regular times throughout the day.

13. Avoid alcohol and drugs. Excessive drinking or drug use can compromise the quality of your caregiving. Instead, try dealing with problems head on and with a clear mind.

14. Get enough sleep. Try to get eight hours of solid, uninterrupted sleep every night. Sleep is essential to elevate your energy level, improve productivity and maintain your ability to handle stress.

15. Stay healthy. Go to the doctor and dentist on schedule, and keep up with your own prescriptions. You need to stay as strong and healthy as possible.

16. Ask for help. Even if you're the primary family caregiver, you can't do everything on your own, especially if you're caregiving from a distance (classified as more than an hour's drive from your family member). You'll need help from friends and other family members, as well as health professionals, including home care aides. If you don't get the support you need, you'll burn out quickly. This will significantly compromise your ability to provide care.

If you feel overwhelmed and are physically or mentally unable to give as much of the time or support that is necessary for your loved one, consider receiving extra help from a home care agency. Home care agencies offer a wide variety of services that often include:

- Transportation
- Exercise
- Medication reminders
- Respite / relief care
- Light housekeeping and laundry
- Grocery shopping and errands
- Meal planning and preparation
- Pet care
- Live-in care
- Companionship
- Hygiene assistance

Caregiver Resources

Alzheimers.gov
This site is the government's resource for Alzheimer's and related dementias.

Alzheimer's & Dementia Caregiver Center
This site provides information about day-to-day help and services in your community; getting support; or preparing for the future.

ARCH National Respite Network
The ARCH National Respite Network and Resource Center provides resources to help families locate respite and crisis care services.

Consumer Information

Respite Locator

Family Caregiver Alliance
The site contains a wide array of publications and services based on caregiver needs, including a Family Care Navigator.

National Alliance for Caregiving
The site contains publications and resources for caregivers, including the Family Care Resource Connection, where you can find reviews and ratings on over 1,000 books, videos, Web sites, and other materials on caregiving.

Caregiver Action Network
The site offers a virtual library of information and educational materials for family caregivers.

eXtension
This website was created by the United States Department of Agriculture (USDA), Cooperative Extension System. Here, caregivers and advocates can access a wide range of information and materials designed to help them learn about and provide supportive services to family and relative caregivers. Topics include disaster preparedness, military families, grandparents raising grandchildren, housing, and nutrition.

HHS Office of Women's Health (OWH)
The OWH website provides an extensive list of links of interest to caregivers.

Top 15 Cheapest States for Long-Term Care Costs

Genworth's 11th annual study provides data on the states with the lowest costs across a range of LTC services.

If you or a client are a caregiver for someone who really needs long-term care, you know how draining the experience can be, no matter how willing you may be to fill the gap between need and coverage.

According to Genworth's annual study on the cost of LTC, not only are caregivers in for long hours—a third of caregivers say that they provide 30 hours or more per week—and higher expenses, but work can be seriously affected, too. The study says 65% have been subject to lateness or absenteeism, have lost jobs or had to go into another line of work altogether as they struggle to add caregiving to an already full professional life.

The study uses data that span more than 14,800 LTC providers from 440 regions across the country, covering all 50 states and Washington, D.C.

And since more than 70% of people over 65, according to the National Medicare Handbook, will need some kind of LTC at some point—not necessarily admittance to a nursing home, but perhaps residence at an assisted living facility, access to adult day care or the help of a licensed home health care aide—the question of coverage for LTC is something that needs to be addressed before, not when, people need help.

Of course, cost is always a factor in choosing any kind of insurance. Those worried that rates will skyrocket once they've bought a policy, even in the cheapest states, might want to take comfort from Jesse Slome, director of the American Association for Long Term Care Insurance (AALTCI). While policies did experience massive rate increases in the recent past, Slome said that that's not as likely to happen for new policies in the future.

Following are the 15 cheapest states in which to receive some form of LTC. Categories included are adult day care, licensed home care, assisted living and nursing home private rooms.

15. Nebraska

Average Annual Cost: $43,532
Adult day care: $12,927
Licensed home care: $48,048
Assisted living: $39,570
Nursing home (private room): $73,584

14. Iowa

Average Annual Cost: $43,151
Adult day care: $14,300
Licensed home care: $49,764
Assisted living: $41,016
Nursing home (private room): $67,525

13. Utah

Average Annual Cost: $42,468
Adult day care: $12,090
Licensed home care: $48,048
Assisted living: $36,732
Nursing home (private room): $73,000

12. North Carolina

Average Annual Cost: $42,390
Adult day care: $13,260
Licensed home care: $38,896
Assisted living: $35,280
Nursing home (private room): $82,125

11. Kansas

Average Annual Cost: $42,005
Adult day care: $18,200
Licensed home care: $41,184
Assisted living: $44,760
Nursing home (private room): $63,875

10. Tennessee

Average Annual Cost: $41,888
Adult day care: $14,300
Licensed home care: $39,582
Assisted living: $41,580
Nursing home (private room): $72,088

9. Mississippi

Average Annual Cost: $41,077
Adult day care: $16,250
Licensed home care: $36,608
Assisted living: $34,800
Nursing home (private room): $76,650

8. South Carolina

Average Annual Cost: $40,131
Adult day care: $13,000
Licensed home care: $40,040
Assisted living: $34,485
Nursing home (private room): $73,000

7. Texas

Average Annual Cost: $39,531
Adult day care: $8,970
Licensed home care: $41,184
Assisted living: $42,270
Nursing home (private room): $65,700

6. Georgia

Average Annual Cost: $38,702
Adult day care: $15,600
Licensed home care: $39,308
Assisted living: $30,000
Nursing home (private room): $69,898

5. Arkansas

Average Annual Cost: $38,558
Adult day care: $18,720
Licensed home care: $38,896
Assisted living: $34,200
Nursing home (private room): $62,415

4. Missouri

Average Annual Cost: $38,208
Adult day care: $19,500
Licensed home care: $43,472
Assisted living: $30,000
Nursing home (private room): $59,860

3. Oklahoma

Average Annual Cost: $37,813
Adult day care: $15,600
Licensed home care: $41,184
Assisted living: $36,978
Nursing home (private room): $57,488

2. Alabama

Average Annual Cost: $37,344
Adult day care: $6,500
Licensed home care: $36,608
Assisted living: $34,728
Nursing home (private room): $71,540

1. Louisiana

Average Annual Cost: $35,743
Adult day care: $14,300
Licensed home care: $32,032
Assisted living: $37,875
Nursing home (private room): $58,765

Part IV

Best Places to Live for Autism, Intellectual Developmental Disabilities, and Mental/Cognitive Disabilities

Chapter Definitions

Federal Medical Assistance Percentages (FMAP):

Federal Medical Assistance Percentages (FMAP) are the percentage rates used to determine the matching funds rate allocated annually to certain medical and social service programs in the United States of America.

Intermediate Care Facilities for individuals with Intellectual disability (ICF/ID):

Intermediate Care Facilities for individuals with Intellectual disability (ICF/ID) is an optional Medicaid benefit that enables states to provide comprehensive and individualized health care and rehabilitation services to individuals to promote their functional status and independence. Although it is an optional benefit, all states offer it, if only as an alternative to home and community-based services waivers for individuals at the ICF/ID level of care.

Eligibility for ICF/ID Benefit:

ICF/ID is available only for individuals in need of, and receiving, active treatment (AT) services. AT refers to aggressive, consistent implementation of a program of specialized and generic training, treatment and health services. AT does not include services to maintain generally independent clients who are able to function with little supervision and who do not require a continuous program of habilitation services. States may not limit access to ICF/ID service, or make it subject to waiting lists, as they may for HCBS. Therefore in some cases ICF/ID services may be more immediately available than other long term care options. Many individuals who require this level of service have already established disability status and Medicaid eligibility.

Services Included in the ICF/ID Benefit:

ICFs/ID provides active treatment (AT), a continuous, aggressive, and consistent implementation of a program of specialized and generic training, treatment, and health or related services, directed toward helping the enrollee function with as much self-determination and independence as possible. ICF/ID is the most comprehensive benefit in Medicaid.

Federal rules provide for a wide scope of required services and facility requirements for administering services. All services including health care services and nutrition are part of the AT, which is based on an evaluation and individualized program plan (IPP) by an interdisciplinary team. Facility requirements include staffing, governing body and management, client protections, client behavior and physical environment, which are specified in the survey and certification process.

ICF/ID Day Programs:

Many ICF/ID residents work in the community, with supports, or participate in vocational or other activities outside of the residence, and engage in community interests of their choice. These activities are collectively often referred to as day programs. The ICF/ID is responsible for all activities, including day programs, because the concept of AT is that all aspects of support and service to the individual are coordinated towards specific individualized goals in the IPP.

Where ICF/ID Services are Provided:

Medicaid coverage of ICF/ID services is available only in a residential facility licensed and certified by the state survey agency as an ICF/ID. Medicaid ICF/ID services are available only when other payment options are unavailable and the individual is eligible for Medicaid. There are few resources similar to an ICF/ID under any payment source.

Long-Term Services and Supports (LTSS):

Long-term services and supports (LTSS) are defined as the services and supports used by individuals of all ages with functional limitations and chronic illnesses who need assistance to perform routine daily activities such as bathing, dressing, preparing meals, and administering medications.

Social Services Block Grants (SSBG):

Social Services Block Grants (SSBG) enables each state or territory to meet the needs of its residents through locally relevant social services. SSBGs support programs that allow communities to achieve or maintain economic self-sufficiency to prevent, reduce or eliminate dependency on social services.

SSBGs fund a variety of initiatives for children and adults including:

- Daycare
- Protective services
- Special services to persons with disabilities
- Adoption
- Case management
- Health related services
- Transportation
- Foster care
- Substance abuse
- Housing
- Home-delivered meals
- Independent/transitional living
- Employment services

Each state determines which services to provide and who is eligible to receive these services.

Title XX:

Title XX of the Social Security Act, **also referred to as the Social Services Block Grant (SSBG)**, is a capped entitlement program. Thus, States are entitled to their share, according to a formula, of a nationwide funding ceiling or ``cap,'' which is specified in statute. Block grant funds are given to States to help them achieve a wide range of social policy goals, which include preventing child abuse, increasing the availability of child care, and providing community-based care for the elderly and disabled. Funds are allocated to the States on the basis of population. The allotments for Puerto Rico, Guam, the Virgin Islands and the Northern Marianas from the national total are based on their allocation for fiscal year 1981 adjusted to reflect the new total funding level. The Omnibus Budget Reconciliation Act (OBRA) of

1987 (Public Law 100-203) extended eligibility for title XX funds to American Samoa. The Federal funds are available to States without a State matching requirement.

Supplemental Security Income (SSI):

Supplemental Security Income (SSI) is a Federal income supplement program funded by general tax revenues (not Social Security taxes). It is designed to help aged, blind, and disabled people, who have little or no income; and it provides cash to meet basic needs for food, clothing, and shelter.

What is intellectual disability?

Intellectual disability is a disability characterized by significant limitations both in intellectual functioning (reasoning, learning, problem solving) and in adaptive behavior, which covers a range of everyday social and practical skills. This disability originates before the age of 18.

Is intellectual disability the same as mental retardation? Why do some programs and regulations still say mental retardation?

The term intellectual disability covers the same population of individuals who were diagnosed previously with mental retardation in number, kind, level, type, duration of disability, and the need of people with this disability for individualized services and supports. Furthermore, every individual who is or was eligible for a diagnosis of mental retardation is eligible for a diagnosis of intellectual disability.

While intellectual disability is the preferred term, it takes time for language that is used in legislation, regulation, and even for the names of organizations, to change.

Is intellectual disability the same as developmental disabilities?

"Developmental Disabilities" is an umbrella term that includes intellectual disability but also includes other disabilities that are apparent during childhood.

Developmental disabilities are severe chronic disabilities that can be cognitive or physical or both. The disabilities appear before the age of 22 and are likely to be lifelong. Some developmental disabilities are largely physical issues, such as cerebral palsy or epilepsy. Some individuals may have a condition that includes a physical and intellectual disability, for example Down syndrome or fetal alcohol syndrome.

Intellectual disability encompasses the "cognitive" part of this definition, that is, a disability that is broadly related to thought processes. Because intellectual and other developmental disabilities often co-occur, intellectual disability professionals often work with people who have both types of disabilities.

Is intellectual disability determined by just an IQ test?

No. The evaluation and classification intellectual disability is a complex issue. There are three major criteria for intellectual disability: significant limitations in intellectual functioning, significant limitations in adaptive behavior, and onset before the age of 18.

The IQ test is a major tool in measuring *intellectual functioning*, which is the mental capacity for learning, reasoning, problem solving, and so on. A test score below or around 70—or as high as 75—indicates a limitation in intellectual functioning.

Other tests determine limitations in *adaptive behavior*, which covers three types of skills:

- **Conceptual skills**—language and literacy; money, time, and number concepts; and self-direction
- **Social skills**—interpersonal skills, social responsibility, self-esteem, gullibility, naïveté (i.e., wariness), social problem solving, and the ability to follow rules, obey laws, and avoid being victimized
- **Practical skills**—activities of daily living (personal care), occupational skills, healthcare, travel/transportation, schedules/routines, safety, use of money, use of the telephone

What causes intellectual disability?

There are a number of causes. Our understanding of the causes of intellectual disability focuses on the types of risk factors (biomedical, social, behavioral, and educational) and the timing of exposure (prenatal, perinatal, and postnatal) to those factors.

What is the most modern thinking about how to help people with intellectual disability?

The overarching reason for evaluating and classifying individuals with intellectual disability is to tailor supports for each individual, in the form of a set of strategies and services provided over a sustained period.

Our goal is to enhance people's functioning within their own environment in order to lead a more successful and satisfying life. Some of this enhancement is thought of in terms of self-worth, subjective well being, pride, engagement in political action, and other principles of self-identity.

"Cognitive Disabilities" versus "Intellectual Disability"

The term "cognitive disabilities" includes a broad range of cognitive conditions that can impact quality of life and independent living. Cognitive disabilities include intellectual disability, autism spectrum disorders, severe, persistent mental illness, brain injury, stroke, and Alzheimer's disease and other dementias. Technology and information access is essential for all people to live an inclusive life in our society today. People with intellectual disability and other cognitive disabilities together pose a formidable block of potential users of technology: An estimated 28.5 million Americans, more than 9% of the U.S. population, had a cognitive disability in 2012. People with cognitive disabilities worldwide are believed to exceed 630 million individuals, according to recent World Health Organization estimates (2011).

NOTE: For simplicity purposes the term 'intellectual disabilities' will be used in this book. Although this term does not accurately represent the message being addressed in this book (cognitive disabilities would be more accurate), intellectual disabilities is a term more widely recognized and accepted by the public.

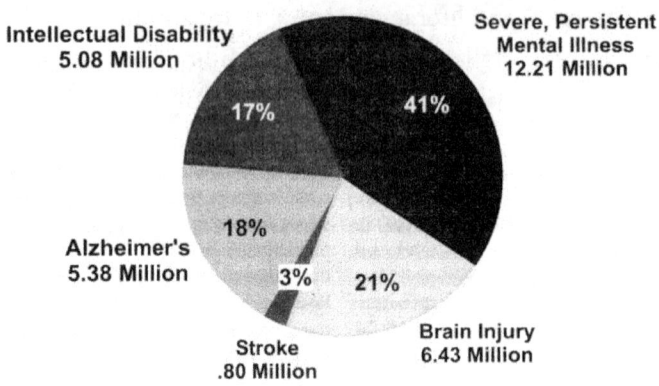

Services and Funding Data for States and State Comparisons

As of 2016, the time of this writing, the most recent 'compiled' data available for the following issues, is presented below. How3ever, before making a relocation decision it is prudent to verify that there have not been any major changes. For instance, Louisiana received some fairly good ratings on several categories, but due to a significant state budget shortfall recently services and funding across the board were cut in the first few months of 2016. Never the less, the data presented in this section will provide a fairly accurate picture of the state and how states compare with one another in regards to funding and services.

BELOW: Overview of fiscal year 2013 Intellectual Developmental Disabilities (IDD) spending in the United States. Summary: 38 states increased spending. 13 states decreased funding. Data obtained from the University of Colorado.

State	% Change	State	% Change	State	% Change
Missouri	12%	North Dakota	4%	Illinois	1%
Kentucky	10%	Oklahoma	3%	Kansas	1%
Mississippi	9%	South Carolina	3%	Oregon	0%
Alaska	9%	Michigan	3%	Delaware	0%
Georgia	8%	Washington	3%	Arizona	-0.5%
West Virginia	8%	Iowa	3%	Maine	-1%
Nebraska	7%	Nevada	3%	Indiana	-1%
Virginia	7%	Tezxas	2%	Louisiana	-1%
Massachusetts	6%	Maryland	2%	North Carolina	-1%
Pennsylvania	6%	Montana	2%	Minnesota	-2%
Wisonsin	6%	New Jersey	2%	Connecticut	-3%
Vermont	5%	New York	2%	Colorado	-3%
District of Columbia	5%	South Dakota	2%	Hawaii	-3%
New Hampshire	4%	Rhode Island	2%	Florida	-4%
Utah	4%	New Mexico	1%	Idaho	-4%
Tennessee	4%	Ohio	1%	Wyoming	-5%
California	4%	Alabama	1%	Arkansas	-7%
				UNITED STATES	**2.4%**

BELOW: Growth of federal, state, and local spending for IDD services in the United States from 1977 to 2013. Data obtained from the University of Colorado.

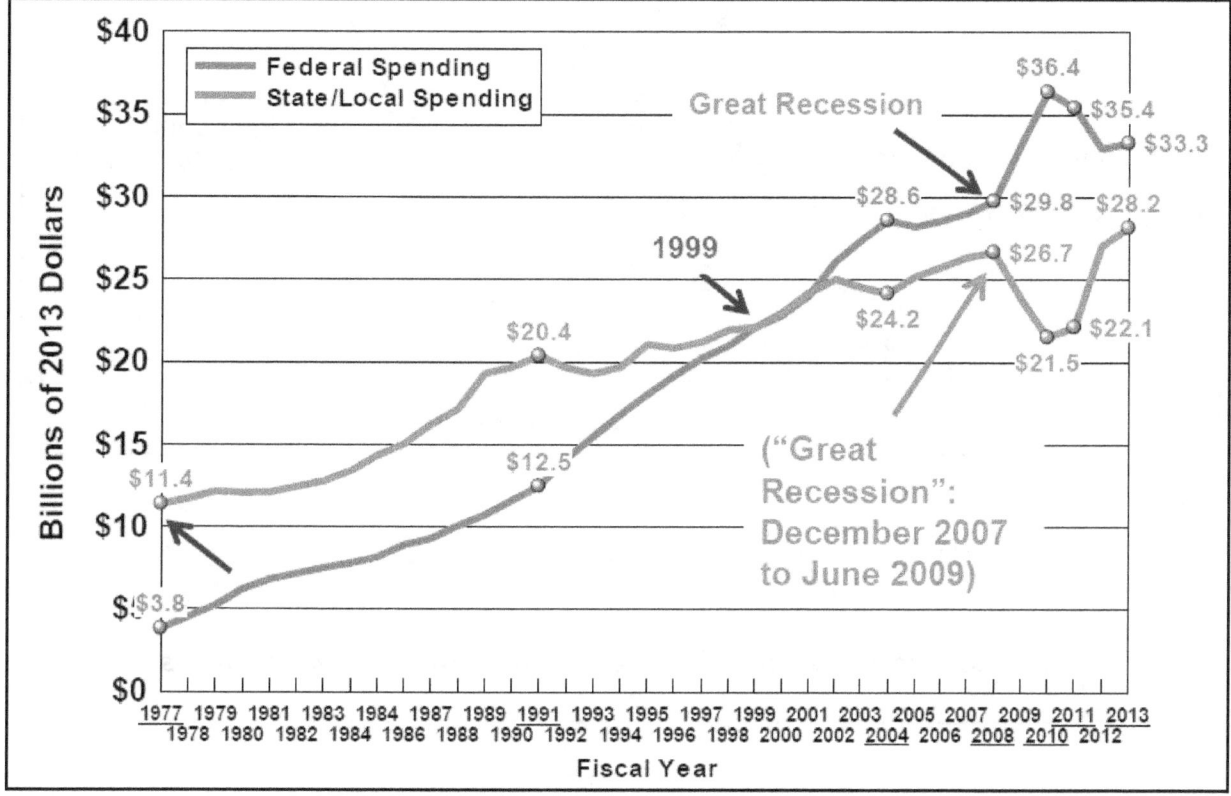

BELOW: Spending for IDD services per category in the United States during fiscal year 2013. Data obtained from the University of Colorado.

Spending for IDD services per category in the United States

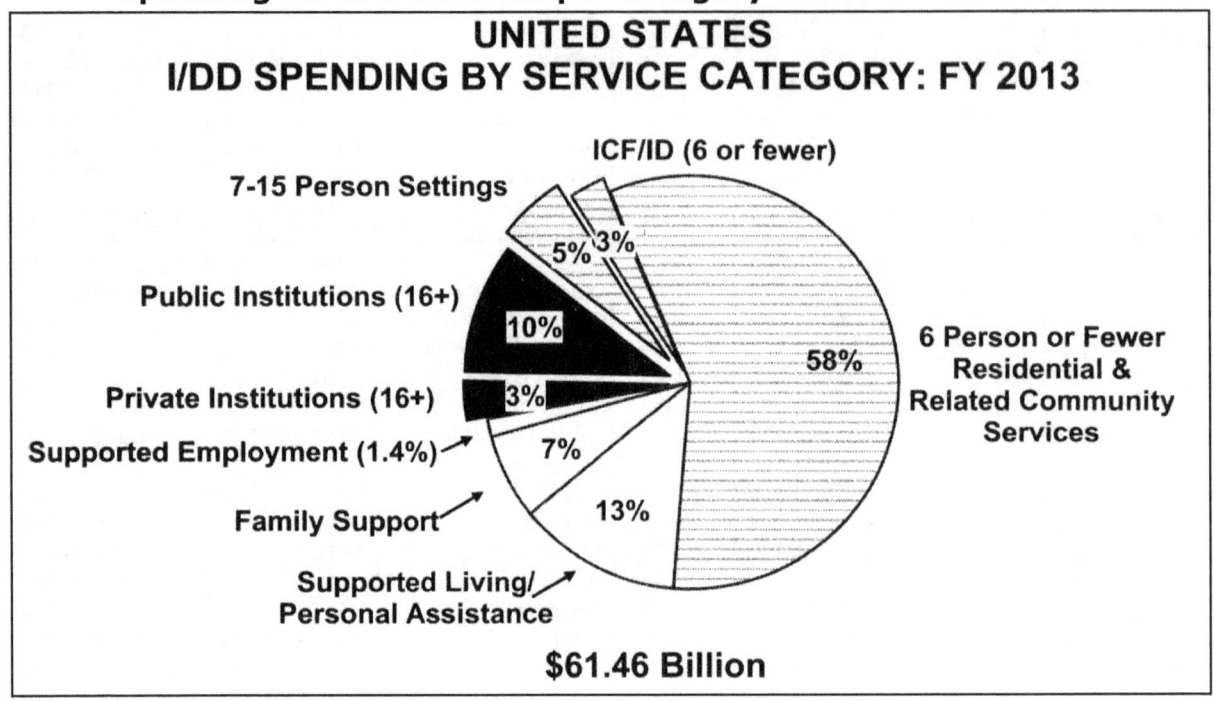

BELOW: Total IDD services and support spending in the United States during fiscal year 2011 ($56 Billion). Data obtained from the University of Colorado.

Total IDD services and support spending in the United States

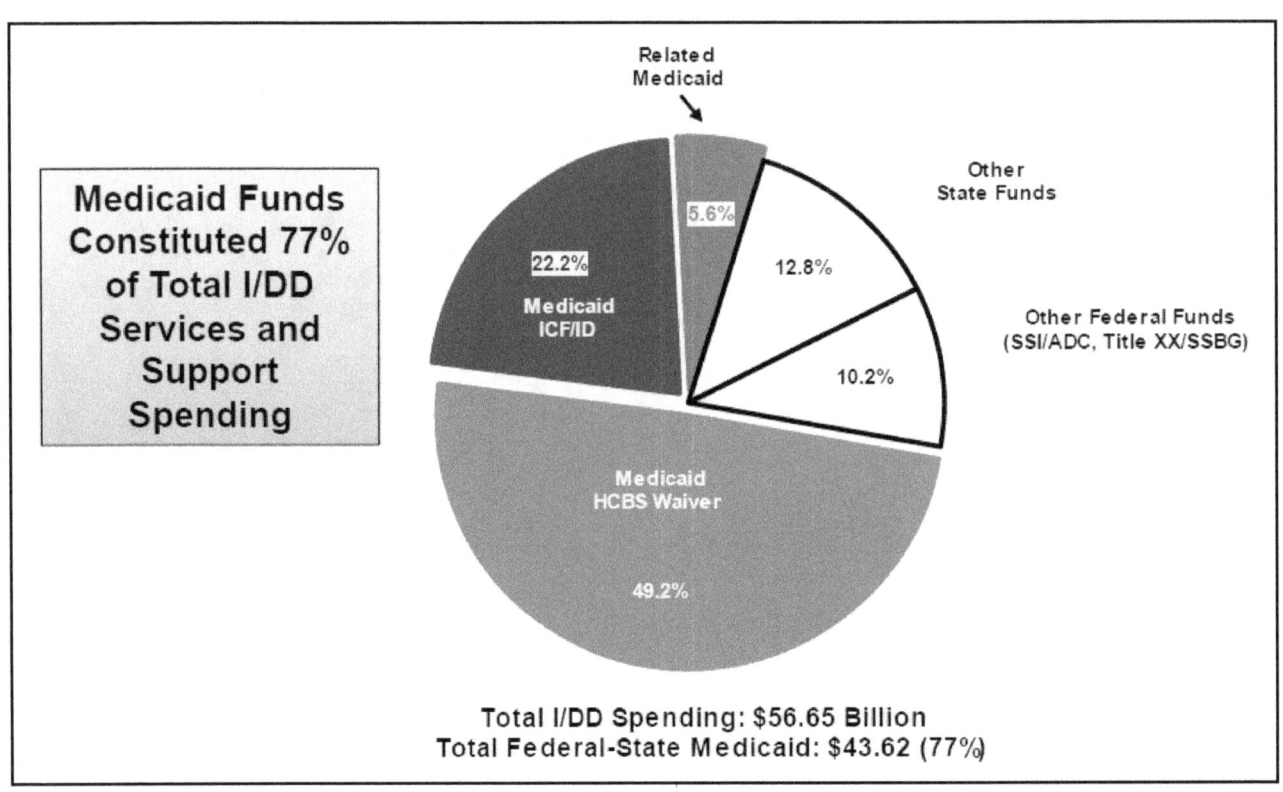

Distribution of services available through the HCBS Waivers

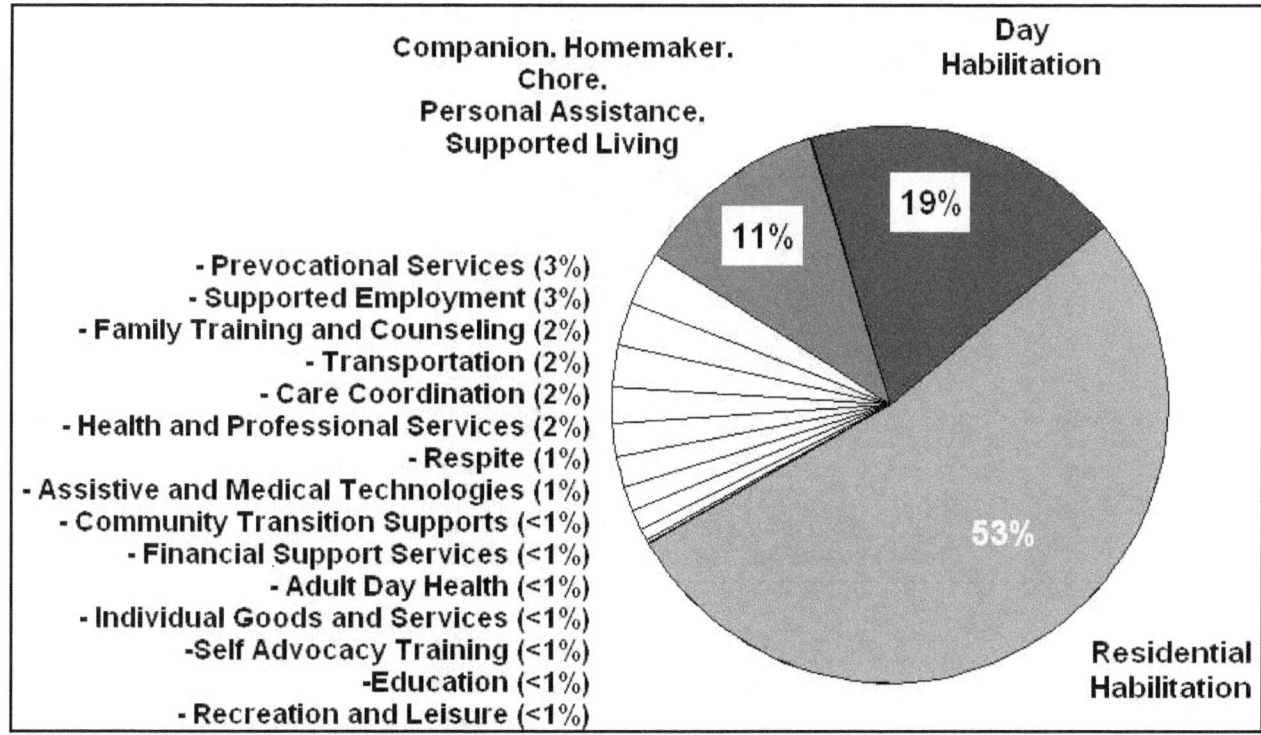

BELOW: Public IDD spending by revenue source in the United States for fiscal year 2013. Data obtained from the University of Colorado.

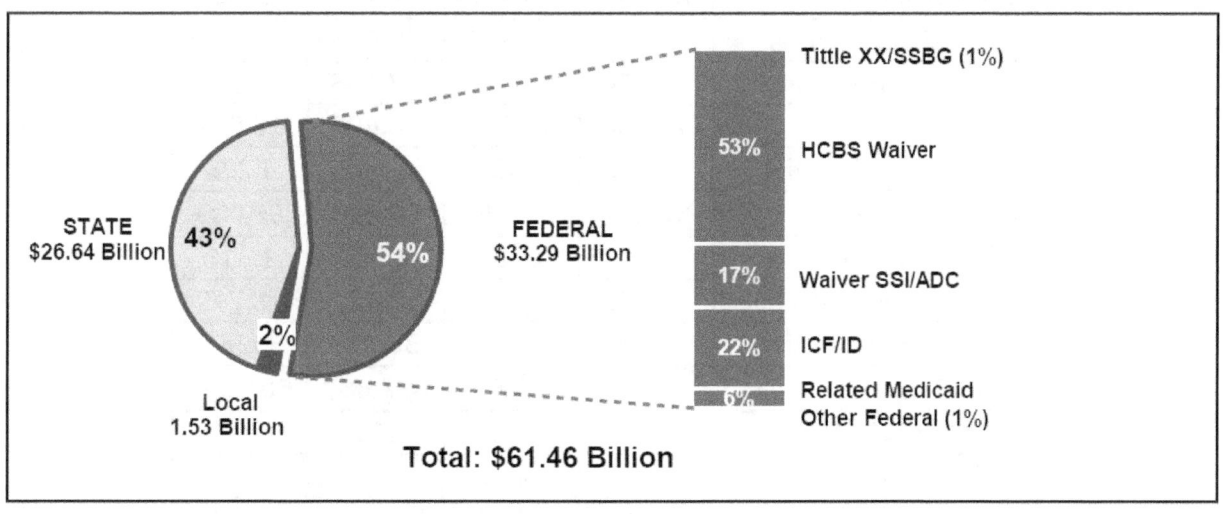

Federal-State Medicaid as a Percentage of total IDD Spending
TOTAL I/DD SPENDING IN FY 2013

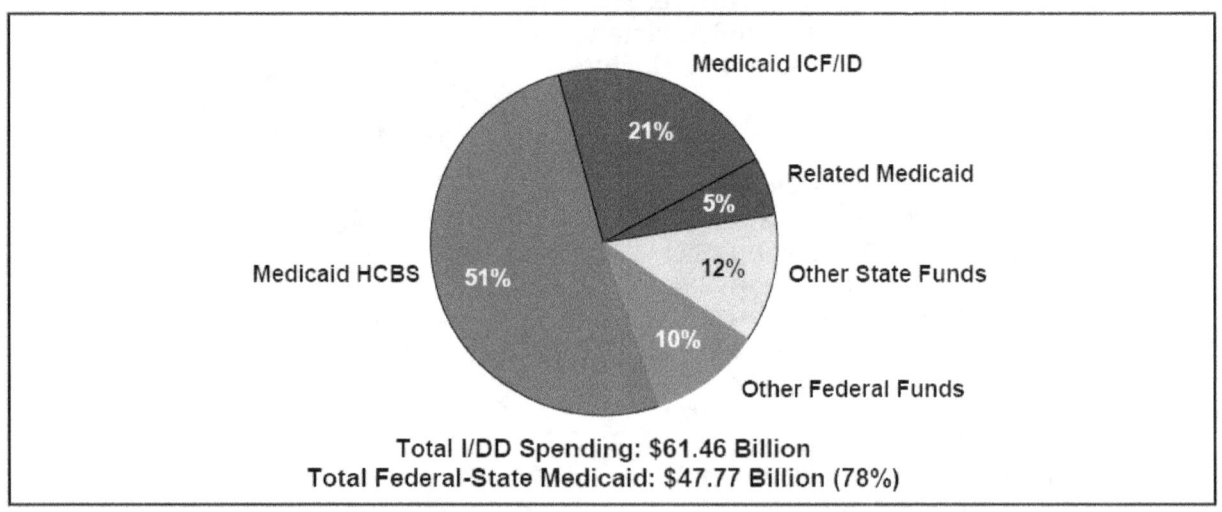

Total I/DD Spending: $61.46 Billion
Total Federal-State Medicaid: $47.77 Billion (78%)

IDD Living Arrangement Types (Estimated Numbers)

	2010	2011	2012	2013
TOTAL	**599,715**	**613,744**	**628,402**	**634,509**
16+ PERSONS	**86,569**	**83,691**	**79,135**	**73,609**
Nursing Facilities	31,420	31,345	29,033	26,678
State Institutions	31,854	29,576	27,166	24,675
Private ICF/ID	18,266	17,770	18,404	18,027
Other Residential	5,028	5,001	4,532	4,229
7-15 PERSONS	**56,342**	**56,240**	**56,600**	**56,003**
Public ICF/ID	1,397	1,383	1,343	1,318
Private ICF/ID	19,180	19,351	18,927	18,777
Other Residential	35,765	35,506	36,330	35,907
≤6 PERSONS	**456,805**	**473,814**	**492,667**	**504,897**
Public ICF/ID	252	220	231	257
Private ICF/ID	20,213	20,303	20,413	20,326
Supported Living	260,331	272,224	282,961	293,956
Other Residential	176,008	181,067	189,062	190,358

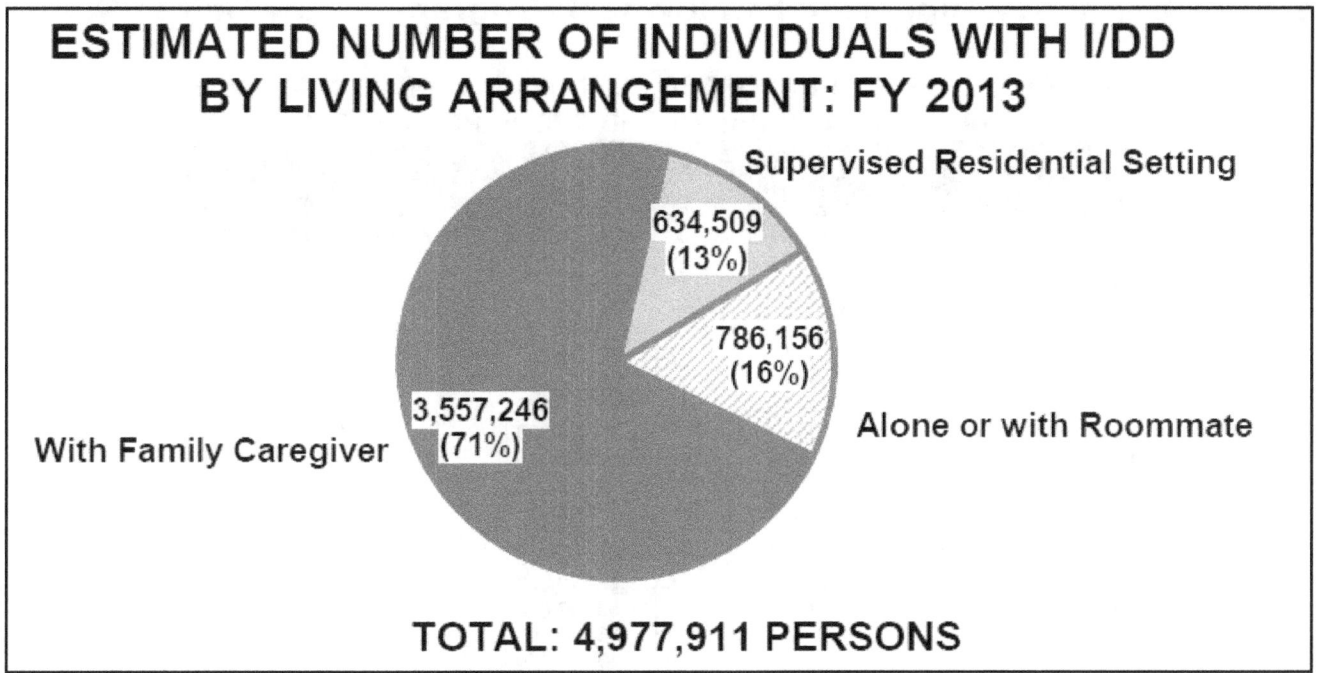

Estimated Number of Individuals with IDD by Age Group Living with Family Caregivers

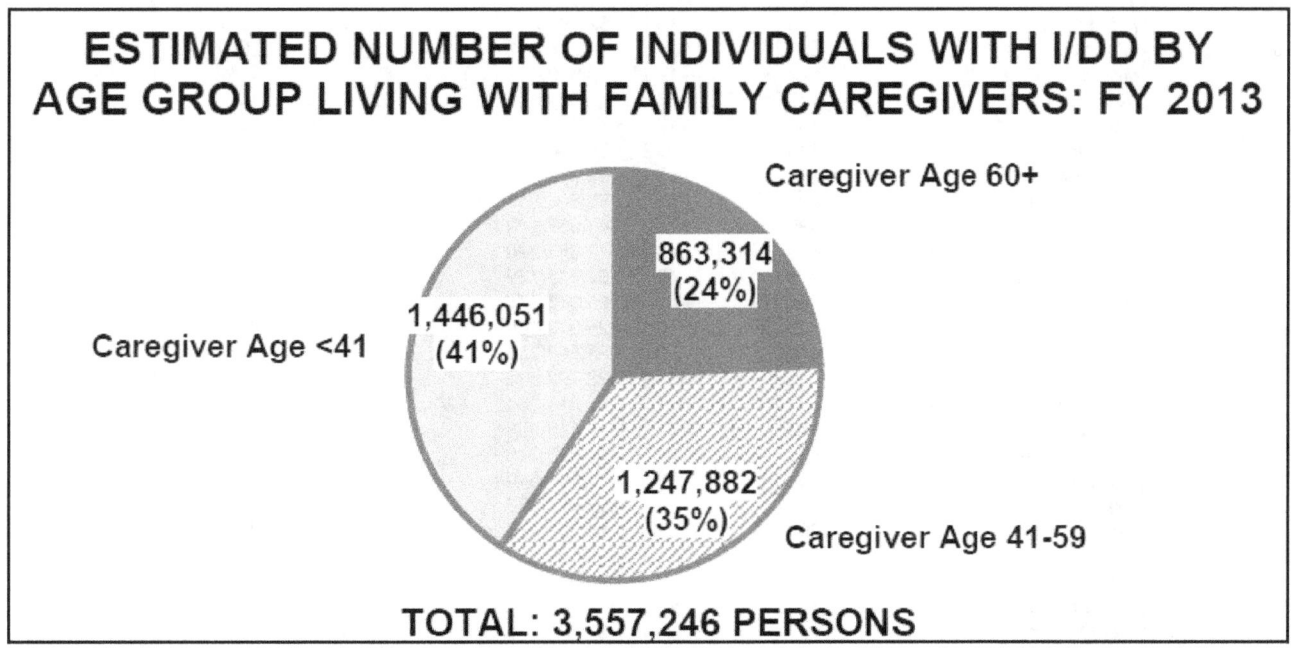

State IDD Agency Supported Employment Programs in the United States

STATE I/DD AGENCY SUPPORTED EMPLOYMENT PROGRAMS IN THE STATES: PARTICIPANTS AND SPENDING IN FY 2013

State	Participants[1]	Utilization Rate[2]	Spending	Spending Per Capita[3]	Supported Employment %[4]
Alabama	222	5	$2,557,191	$0.53	5%
Alaska	540	74	$7,833,820	$10.69	22%
Arizona	2,080	32	$17,244,175	$2.62	19%
Arkansas	97	3	$651,263	$0.22	8%
California	9,927	26	$87,713,652	$2.30	12%
Colorado	2,038	39	$10,227,289	$1.96	33%
Connecticut	4,422	123	$56,773,603	$15.80	47%
Delaware	432	47	$5,400,000	$5.86	22%
District of Columbia	261	41	$1,316,743	$2.05	36%
Florida	2,019	10	$6,246,357	$0.32	15%
Georgia	2,407	24	$10,202,717	$1.02	23%
Hawaii	17	1	$207,650	$0.15	12%
Idaho	845	53	$3,475,125	$2.17	12%
Illinois	1,059	8	$8,720,090	$0.68	6%
Indiana	2,894	44	$9,347,643	$1.43	17%
Iowa	2,486	81	$8,419,945	$2.73	25%
Kansas	246	9	$3,955,120	$1.37	13%
Kentucky	942	21	$3,497,041	$0.80	8%
Louisiana	1,683	36	$12,185,013	$2.64	48%
Maine	994	75	$3,915,616	$2.95	23%
Maryland	4,765	81	$80,419,975	$13.61	40%
Massachusetts	2,312	35	$34,969,180	$5.24	14%
Michigan	4,015	41	$26,818,518	$2.71	31%
Minnesota	2,906	54	$19,971,991	$3.70	20%
Mississippi	476	16	$2,509,818	$0.84	23%
Missouri	688	11	$6,816,562	$1.13	26%
Montana	172	17	$990,469	$0.98	17%
Nebraska	1,430	77	$10,309,682	$5.54	45%
Nevada	458	17	$3,614,543	$1.30	21%
New Hampshire	346	26	$5,100,300	$3.86	45%
New Jersey	1,157	13	$9,266,786	$1.04	18%
New Mexico	1,106	53	$9,804,561	$4.70	32%
New York	8,896	45	$45,657,142	$2.33	12%
North Carolina	1,608	16	$12,368,270	$1.26	19%
North Dakota	299	42	$2,781,762	$3.90	16%
Ohio	7,039	61	$95,373,875	$8.25	23%
Oklahoma	2,525	66	$25,212,400	$6.58	67%
Oregon	1,149	29	$51,868,233	$13.25	15%
Pennsylvania	3,842	30	$28,703,586	$2.25	17%
Rhode Island	533	51	$2,914,534	$2.77	14%
South Carolina	1,479	31	$8,218,206	$1.73	25%
South Dakota	578	69	$7,527,249	$8.97	24%
Tennessee	1,202	19	$11,163,540	$1.72	25%
Texas	2,214	8	$2,677,823	$0.10	7%
Utah	608	21	$4,561,824	$1.59	22%
Vermont	1,088	174	$10,989,831	$17.55	44%
Virginia	1,357	17	$25,639,959	$3.12	31%
Washington	6,418	93	$49,794,507	$7.18	84%
West Virginia	462	25	$2,503,735	$1.35	25%
Wisconsin	1,624	28	$8,622,601	$1.50	10%
Wyoming	241	42	$1,211,921	$2.09	15%
United States	**98,604**	**31**	**$868,273,437**	**$2.76**	**19%**

[1] Table does not include 16,031 follow-along work support workers assisted by I/DD agencies in 19 states: AZ, CT, DC, GA, HI, IA, KS, LA, MI, MO, MT, NE, NH, NJ, NY, NC, OH, SC, and WA.

[2] Supported employment participants per 100,000 citizens of the general population of the state.

[3] Spending per citizen of the general population.

[4] Percentage in supported employment includes persons in follow-along work support (referenced in Note 1).

Above Illustration Source: Univ. of Colorado

Estimated Number of IDD Caregiving Families and Families Supported by IDD

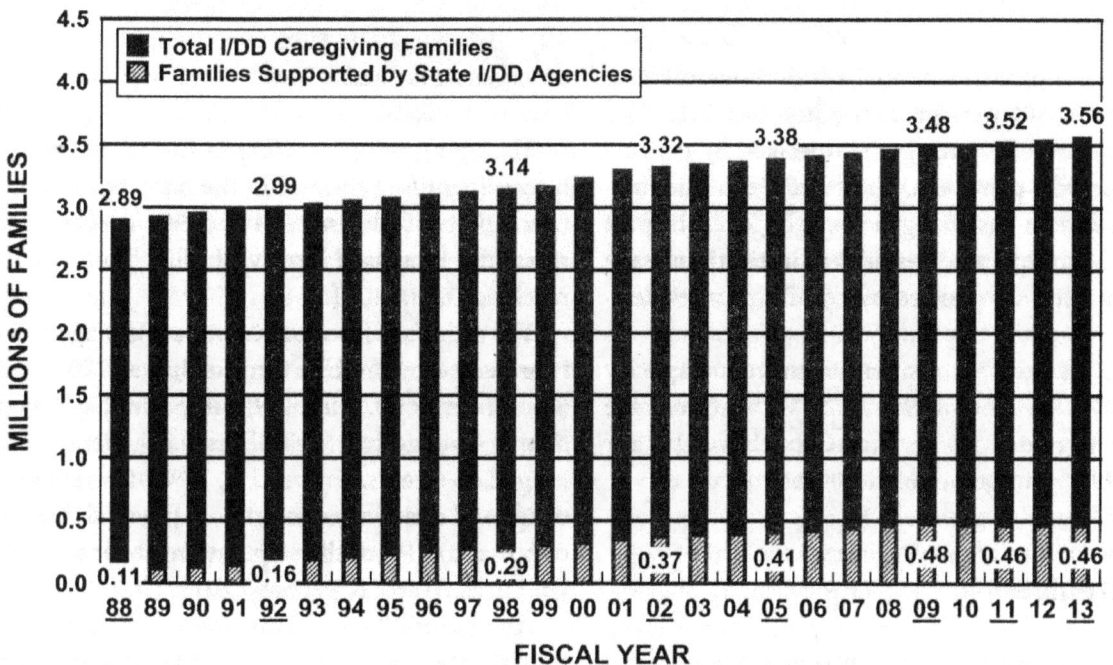

Above Illustration Source: Univ. of Colorado

Estimated Number of Individuals with IDD by Age Group Living with Family Caregivers

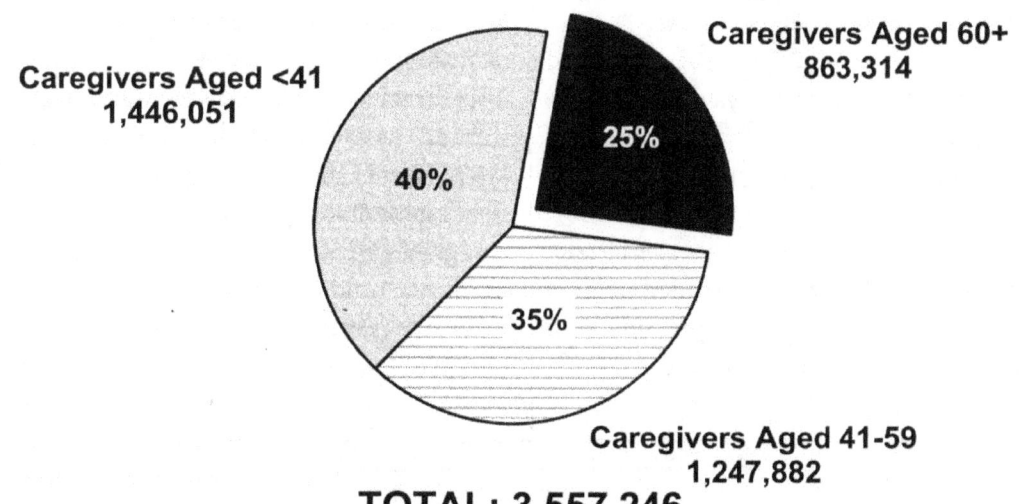

Above Illustration Source: Univ. of Colorado

Estimated Number of Persons with IDD Living with a Caregiver who is 60-years of Age and Older

State	Persons with I/DD
Alabama	15,455
Alaska	1,298
Arizona	21,210
Arkansas	8,730
California	96,375
Colorado	12,118
Connecticut	10,645
Delaware	2,911
DC	1,450
Florida	77,467
Georgia	22,627
Hawaii	4,256
Idaho	4,031
Illinois	32,732
Indiana	17,460
Iowa	9,137
Kansas	8,150
Kentucky	12,479
Louisiana	12,603
Maine	4,230
Maryland	15,794
Massachusetts	19,092
Michigan	24,123
Minnesota	12,401
Mississippi	8,355
Missouri	17,633
Montana	3,198
Nebraska	5,311
Nevada	7,843
New Hampshire	3,631
New Jersey	26,301
New Mexico	6,361
New York	50,487
North Carolina	25,635
North Dakota	2,116
Ohio	30,310
Oklahoma	11,613
Oregon	9,470
Pennsylvania	41,085
Rhode Island	3,071
South Carolina	14,481
South Dakota	2,306
Tennessee	18,991
Texas	58,158
Utah	5,825
Vermont	1,794
Virginia	23,019
Washington	17,536
West Virginia	5,860
Wisconsin	14,721
Wyoming	1,429
United States	**863,314**

Above Table Source: Univ. of Colorado

Estimated number of IDD caregiving families compared to families supported by state IDD agency Federal, State, and Local funds.

(Fiscal year 2013)

State	Total IDD Caregiving Families	Families Supported by I/DD Agencies	% of Families Supported	Rank[1]
Alabama	58,602	987	2%	48
Alaska	8,349	1,377	16%	17
Arizona	81,495	19,002	23%	11
Arkansas	32,708	414	1%	49
California	445,877	104,099	23%	10
Colorado	60,240	2,183	4%	43
Connecticut	39,585	3,069	8%	33
Delaware	10,993	2,610	24%	8
Dist. of Columbia	6,833	753	11%	24
Florida	234,210	15,617	7%	37
Georgia	118,188	3,273	3%	46
Hawaii	15,891	1,740	11%	25
Idaho	18,040	0	0%	51
Illinois	142,194	4,945	3%	44
Indiana	74,095	6,661	9%	31
Iowa	32,953	739	2%	47
Kansas	32,798	2,811	9%	32
Kentucky	51,201	2,771	5%	39
Louisiana	53,458	12,558	23%	9
Maine	14,437	480	3%	45
Maryland	69,653	7,516	11%	26
Massachusetts	74,991	11,759	16%	19
Michigan	101,261	16,699	16%	18
Minnesota	53,920	13,711	25%	5
Mississippi	35,057	4,859	14%	20
Missouri	68,387	4,621	7%	36
Montana	11,378	2,856	25%	6
Nebraska	20,796	2,569	12%	23
Nevada	34,167	2,426	7%	34
New Hampshire	15,005	3,142	21%	13
New Jersey	103,375	4,564	4%	42
New Mexico	23,879	5,725	24%	7
New York	198,592	54,309	27%	2
North Carolina	110,692	10,021	9%	30
North Dakota	7,445	779	10%	27
Ohio	119,026	21,882	18%	15
Oklahoma	45,279	4,496	10%	28
Oregon	38,885	2,030	5%	40
Pennsylvania	142,608	25,429	18%	16
Rhode Island	11,736	1,575	13%	21
South Carolina	56,541	11,764	21%	14
South Dakota	8,529	1,922	23%	12
Tennessee	76,416	4,761	6%	38
Texas	296,704	20,156	7%	35
Utah	34,542	1,723	5%	41
Vermont	6,652	1,774	27%	3
Virginia	98,928	325	0.3%	50
Washington	76,927	7,436	10%	29
West Virginia	19,656	2,544	13%	22
Wisconsin	58,660	23,192	40%	1
Wyoming	5,413	1,389	26%	4
UNITED STATES	**3,557,246**	**464,043**	**13%**	

[1] States ranked, highest to lowest, on percent of family caregivers receiving I/DD state agency support.

Above Table Source: Univ. of Colorado

BELOW: Low wages discourage people from entering the caregiver profession. Most caregivers earn slightly more than the defined poverty level (see below illustration).

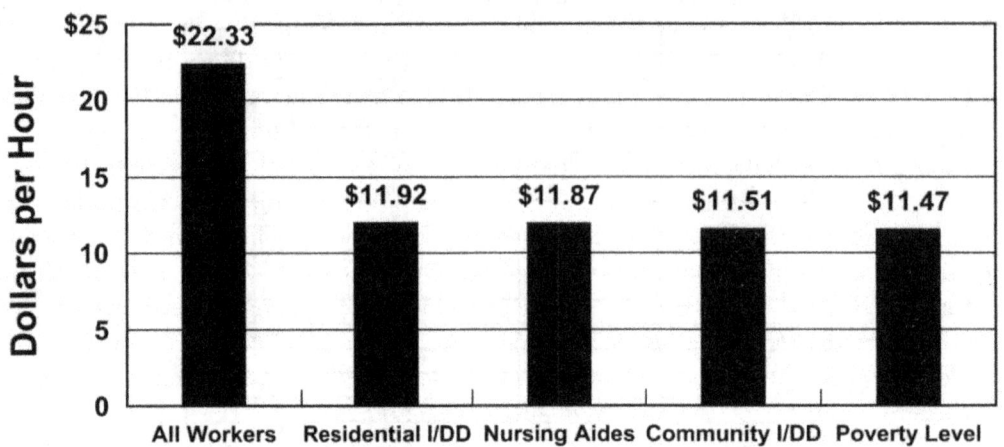

Above Illustration Source: U.S. Bureau of Labor Statistics, April 2014

Part IV - Best Places to Live for Autism, Intellectual Developmental, and Mental/Cognitive Disabilities

BELOW: Family financial support in each of the states for participants with IDD. (Fiscal year 2013)

Family Financial Support in each of the States for Participants with IDD

State	Total Family Support[1] Families	Total Family Support[1] Spending	Spending Per Family	Rank[2]	Families Supported Per 100K	Rank[3]	Cash Subsidy Families	Cash Subsidy Spending	Other Family Support Families	Other Family Support Spending
Alabama	987	$502,775	$509	49	20	48	0	$0	987	$502,775
Alaska	1,377	$10,429,966	$7,574	22	188	17	0	$0	1,377	$10,429,966
Arizona	19,002	$363,769,803	$19,144	8	288	2	1	$4,647	19,001	$363,765,156
Arkansas	414	$523,859	$1,265	46	14	49	0	$0	414	$523,859
California	104,099	$729,359,025	$7,006	23	273	8	0	$0	104,099	$729,359,025
Colorado	2,183	$2,348,496	$1,076	47	42	43	0	$0	2,183	$2,348,496
Connecticut	3,069	$54,980,964	$17,915	10	85	34	1,738	$2,955,493	1,331	$52,025,471
Delaware[4]	2,610	$2,037,800	$781	48	283	3	95	$575,100	2,610	$1,462,700
District of Columbia	753	$15,610,362	$20,731	7	117	27	0	$0	753	$15,610,362
Florida	15,617	$327,858,454	$20,994	5	80	35	39	$117,735	15,578	$327,740,720
Georgia	3,273	$17,908,146	$5,471	30	33	46	0	$0	3,273	$17,908,146
Hawaii	1,740	$24,457,501	$14,056	14	125	25	0	$0	1,740	$24,457,501
Idaho	0	$0			0		0	$0	0	$0
Illinois	4,945	$33,757,975	$6,827	24	38	44	139	$924,048	4,806	$32,833,927
Indiana	6,661	$44,076,198	$6,617	26	102	31	0	$0	6,661	$44,076,198
Iowa	739	$28,027,869	$37,927	1	24	47	217	$659,515	522	$27,368,354
Kansas	2,811	$50,180,281	$17,851	11	97	32	0	$0	2,811	$50,180,281
Kentucky	2,771	$11,592,149	$4,183	35	63	39	0	$0	2,771	$11,592,149
Louisiana	12,558	$374,835,470	$29,848	2	272	9	1,647	$4,475,278	10,911	$370,360,192
Maine	480	$8,447,527	$17,599	12	36	45	480	$600,000	0	$7,847,527
Maryland	7,516	$62,678,938	$8,339	20	127	24	0	$0	7,516	$62,678,938
Massachusetts	11,759	$37,855,140	$3,219	40	176	18	0	$0	11,759	$37,855,140
Michigan	16,699	$61,707,193	$3,695	37	169	19	6,914	$18,272,323	9,785	$43,434,870
Minnesota	13,711	$284,989,320	$20,785	6	254	10	3,164	$13,071,304	10,547	$271,918,016
Mississippi	4,859	$30,769,279	$6,332	28	163	20	0	$0	4,859	$30,769,279
Missouri	4,621	$43,138,430	$9,335	18	77	37	0	$0	4,621	$43,138,430
Montana	2,856	$12,892,812	$4,514	33	283	5	0	$0	2,856	$12,892,812
Nebraska	2,569	$20,619,859	$8,026	21	138	22	0	$0	2,569	$20,619,859
Nevada	2,426	$5,866,890	$2,418	43	88	33	595	$2,671,856	1,831	$3,195,034
New Hampshire	3,142	$6,392,547	$2,035	44	238	13	0	$0	3,142	$6,392,547
New Jersey	4,564	$39,868,869	$8,736	19	51	42	0	$0	4,564	$39,868,869
New Mexico	5,725	$16,710,745	$2,919	42	275	7	0	$0	5,725	$16,710,745
New York	54,309	$545,479,789	$10,044	17	277	6	0	$0	54,309	$545,479,789
North Carolina	10,021	$39,325,866	$3,924	36	102	30	0	$0	10,021	$39,325,866
North Dakota	779	$17,004,084	$21,828	3	109	28	6	$86,529	773	$16,917,554
Ohio	21,882	$98,410,606	$4,497	34	189	16	0	$0	21,882	$98,410,606
Oklahoma	4,496	$75,002,046	$16,682	13	117	26	2,113	$5,792,470	2,383	$69,209,576
Oregon	2,030	$970,552	$478	50	52	41	0	$0	2,030	$970,552
Pennsylvania	25,429	$81,087,979	$3,189	41	199	15	0	$0	25,429	$81,087,979
Rhode Island	1,575	$33,084,019	$21,006	4	150	21	43	$144,743	1,532	$32,939,276
South Carolina	11,764	$59,768,916	$5,081	32	248	11	2,350	$1,211,100	9,414	$58,557,816
South Dakota	1,922	$6,324,861	$3,291	39	229	14	0	$0	1,922	$6,324,861
Tennessee	4,761	$7,133,400	$1,498	45	74	38	0	$0	4,761	$7,133,400
Texas	20,156	$238,841,452	$11,850	16	77	36	0	$0	20,156	$238,841,452
Utah	1,723	$11,240,253	$6,524	27	60	40	1	$58	1,722	$11,240,195
Vermont	1,774	$21,184,286	$11,942	15	283	4	0	$0	1,774	$21,184,286
Virginia	325	$1,845,355	$5,678	29	4	50	325	$1,845,355	0	$0
Washington[4]	7,436	$50,276,399	$6,761	25	107	29	2,122	$5,078,384	6,170	$45,198,015
West Virginia	2,544	$48,347,261	$19,004	9	137	23	0	$0	2,544	$48,347,261
Wisconsin	23,192	$77,504,036	$3,342	38	404	1	0	$0	23,192	$77,504,036
Wyoming	1,389	$7,329,504	$5,277	31	240	12	0	$0	1,389	$7,329,504
United States	464,043	$4,144,355,306	$8,931		147		21,989	$58,485,938	443,005	$4,085,869,367

[1] Total family support consisted of cash subsidy and "other family support" that included respite care, family counseling, architectural adaptation of the home, in-home training, sibling support, education and behavior management services, and the purchase of specialized equipment.

[2] States' ranking, highest to lowest, on total family support spending per family supported.

[3] States' ranking, highest to lowest, on total families supported per 100,000 citizens of the general population.

[4] In Delaware each of the families receiving cash subsidies also received other family support; and in Washington, the majority of cash subsidy families also received other (i.e., non-subsidy) family support.

Above Table Source: Univ. of Colorado

NOTE: Louisiana reduced funding substantially in 2016.

IDD Funding Budget of Each State

This section provides a summary view of each state. The last page of this section shows the United States average. Below are noted items that should be carefully considered when examining a state for relocation purposes.

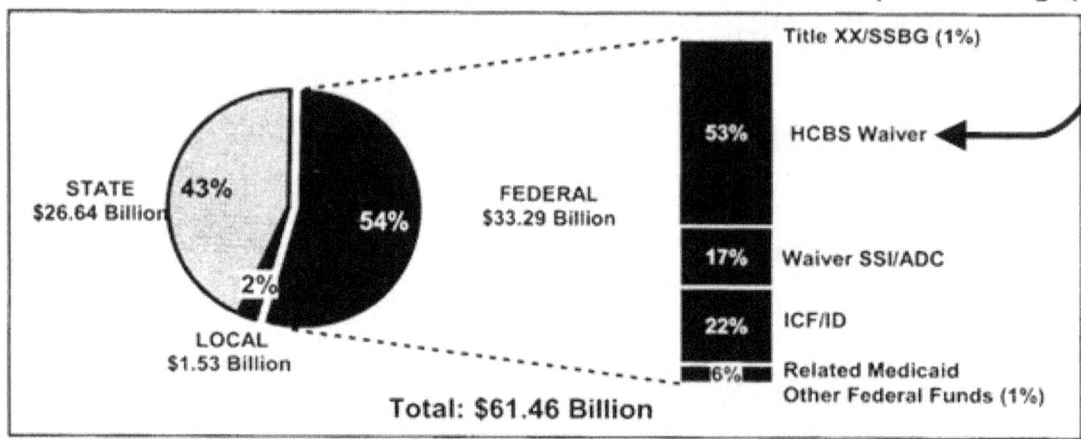

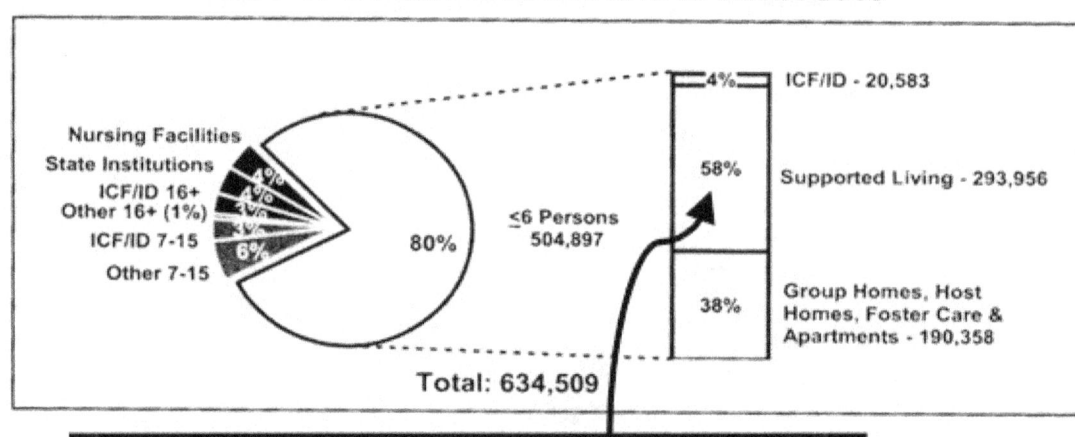

ALABAMA
PUBLIC I/DD SPENDING BY REVENUE SOURCE: FY 2013

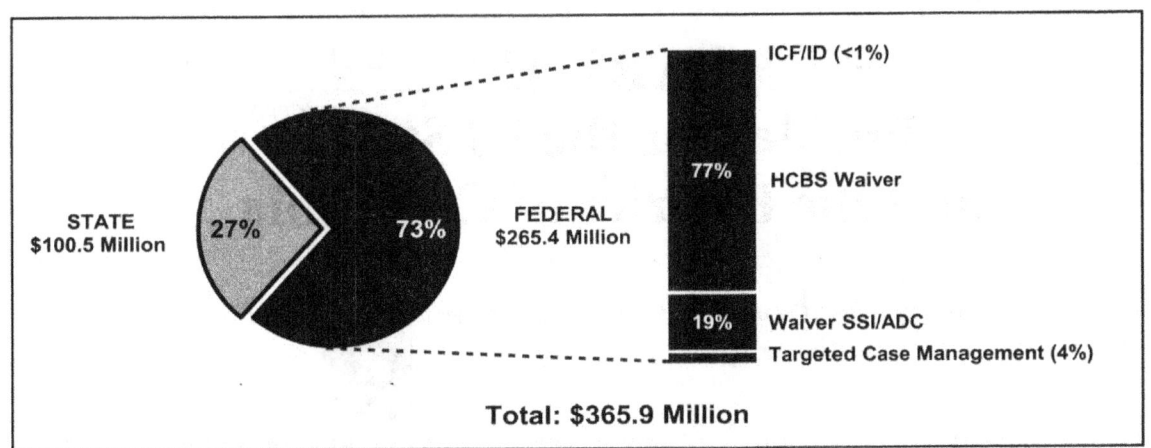

ALABAMA
PERSONS BY SETTING IN FISCAL YEAR 2013

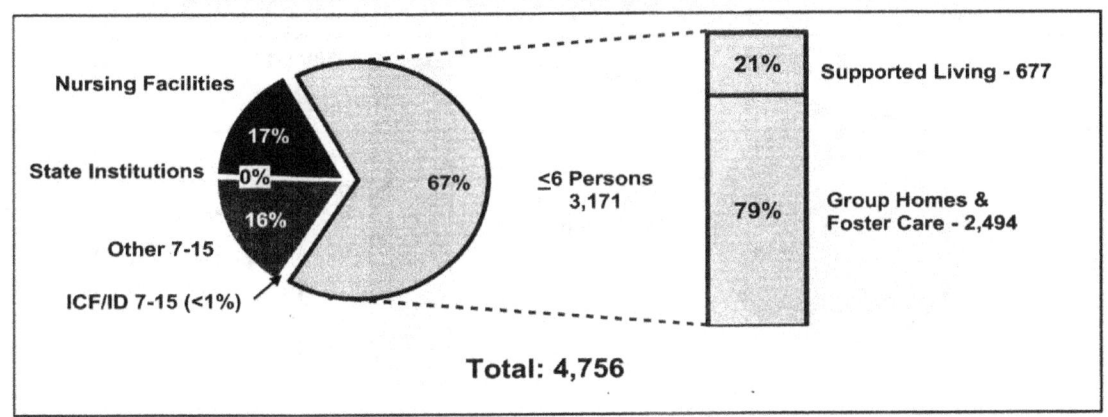

ALASKA
PUBLIC I/DD SPENDING BY REVENUE SOURCE: FY 2013

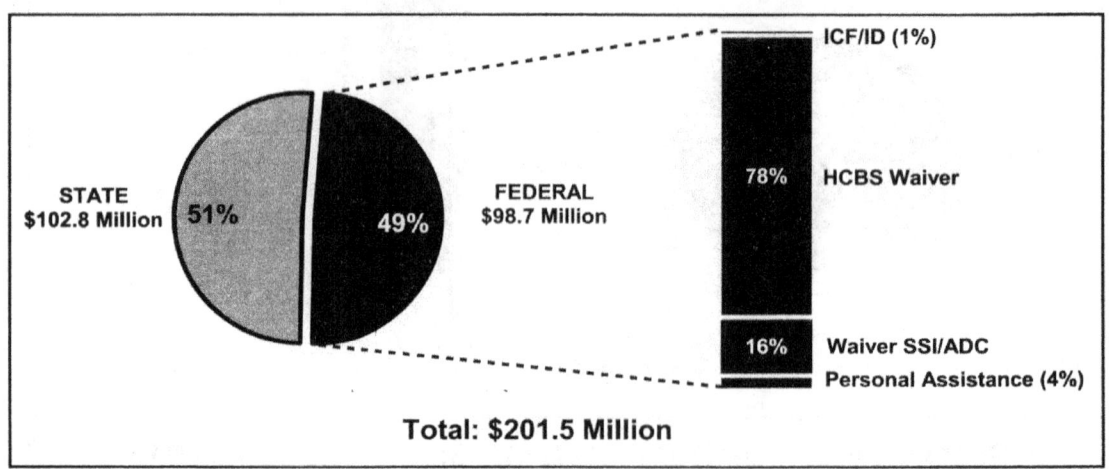

ALASKA
PERSONS BY SETTING IN FISCAL YEAR 2013

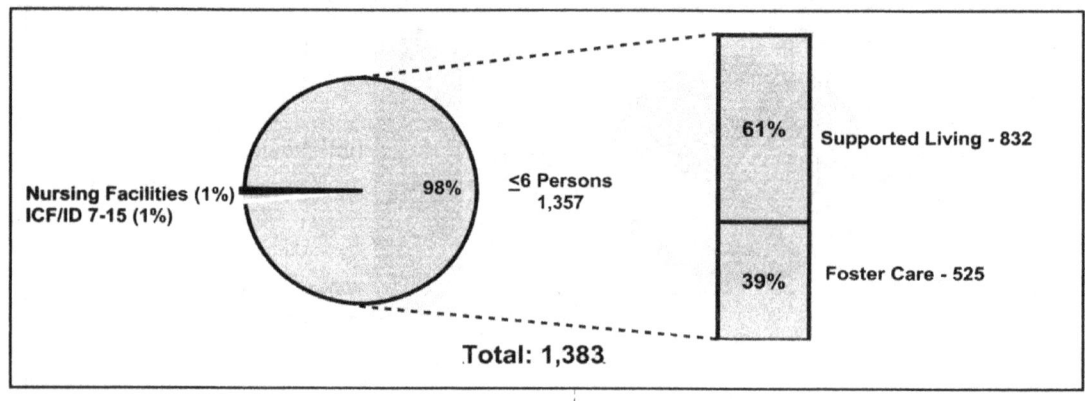

ARIZONA
PUBLIC I/DD SPENDING BY REVENUE SOURCE: FY 2013

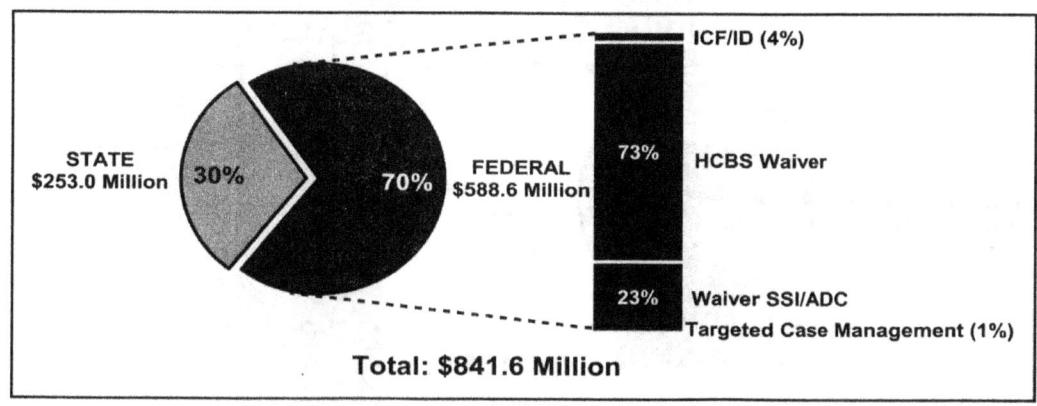

Total: $841.6 Million

ARIZONA
PERSONS SERVED BY SETTING IN 2013

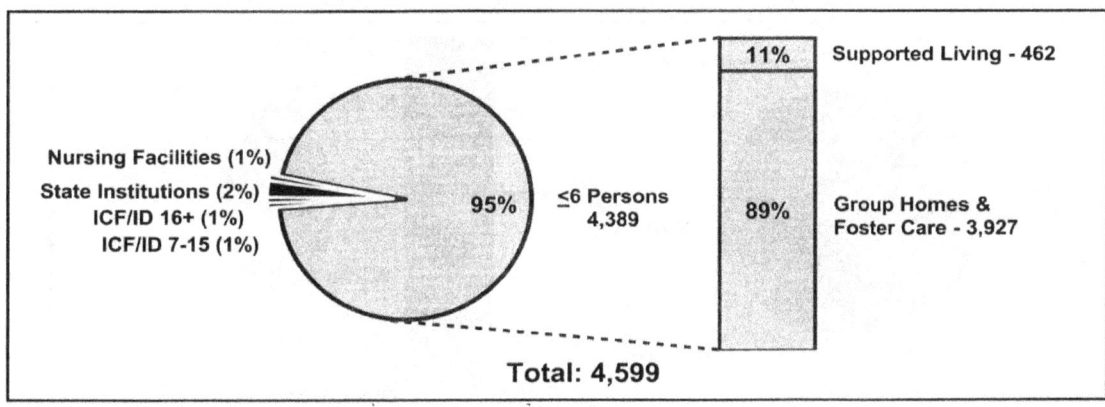

Total: 4,599

ARKANSAS

PUBLIC I/DD SPENDING BY REVENUE SOURCE: FY 2013

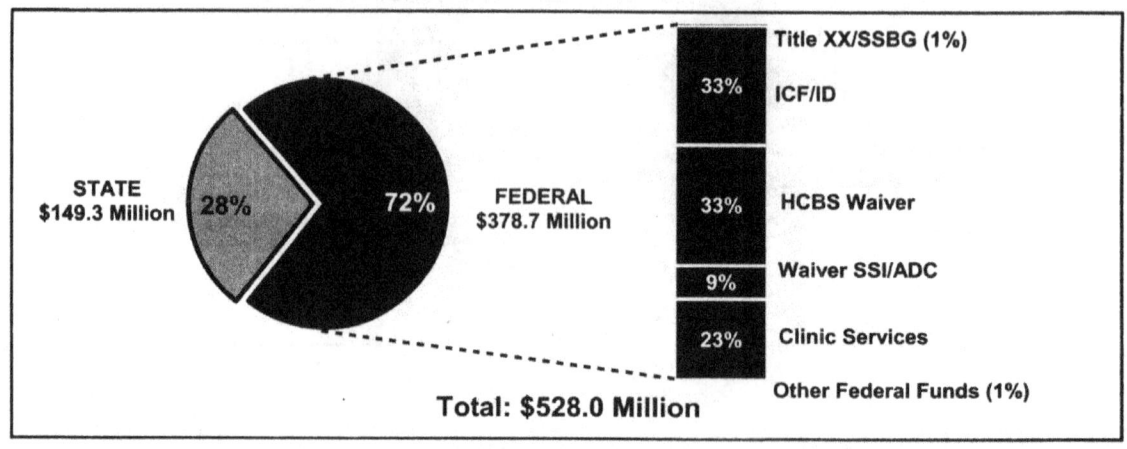

ARKANSAS

PERSONS BY SETTING IN FISCAL YEAR 2013

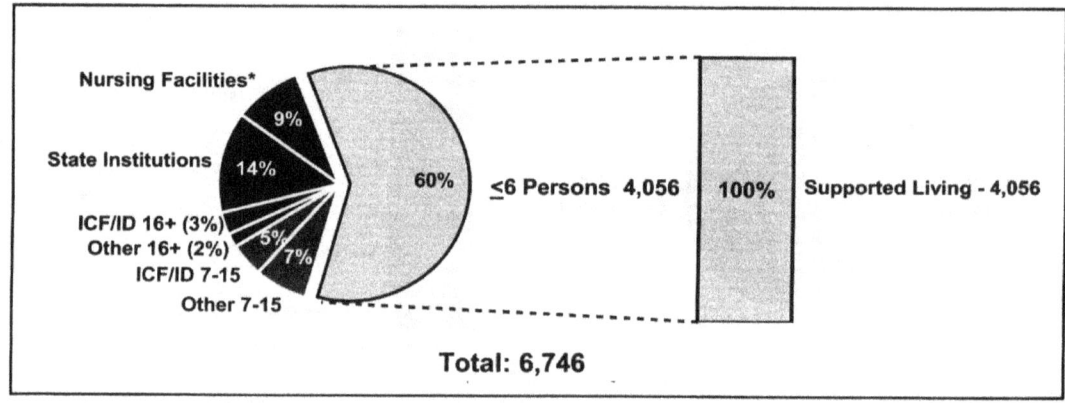

CALIFORNIA
PUBLIC I/DD SPENDING BY REVENUE SOURCE: FY 2013

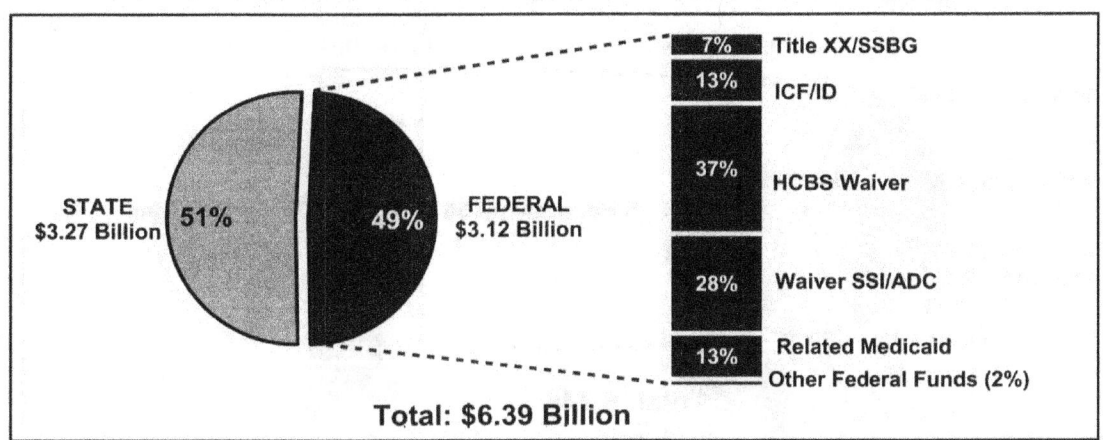

CALIFORNIA
PERSONS SERVED BY SETTING IN FISCAL YEAR 2013

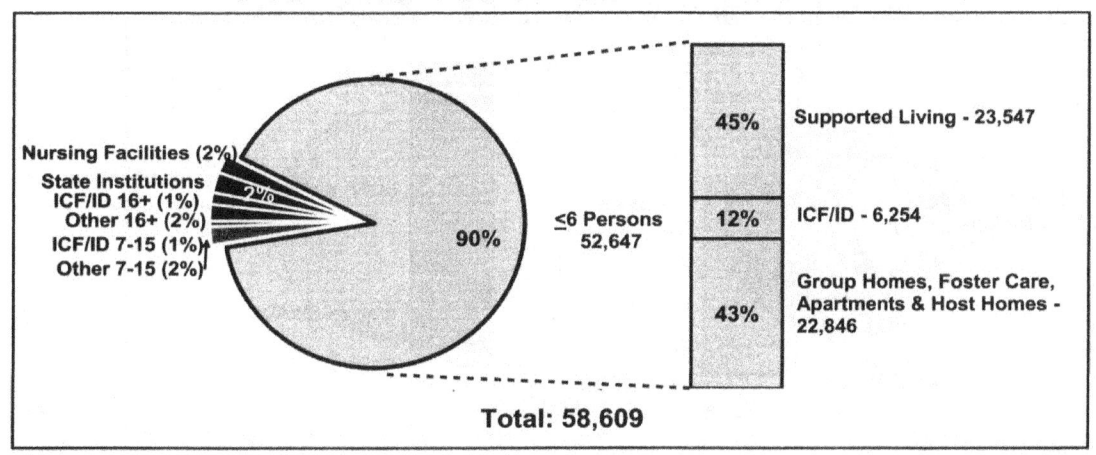

COLORADO
PUBLIC I/DD SPENDING BY REVENUE SOURCE: FY 2013

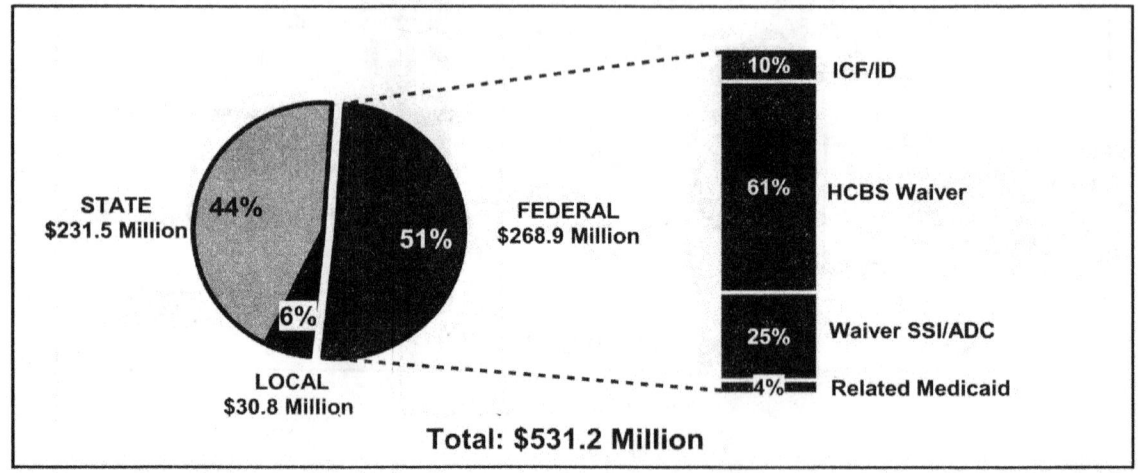

COLORADO
PERSONS BY SETTING IN FISCAL YEAR 2013

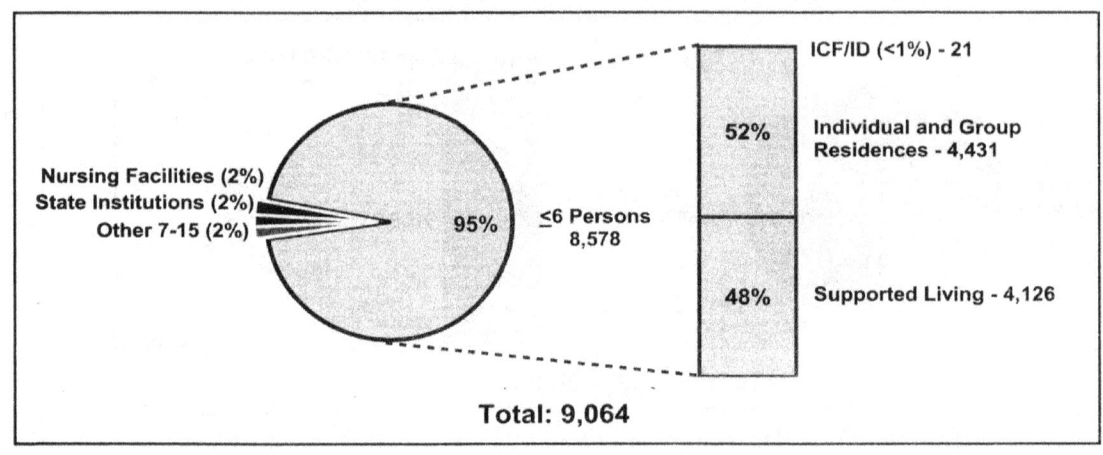

CONNECTICUT
PUBLIC I/DD SPENDING BY REVENUE SOURCE: FY 2013

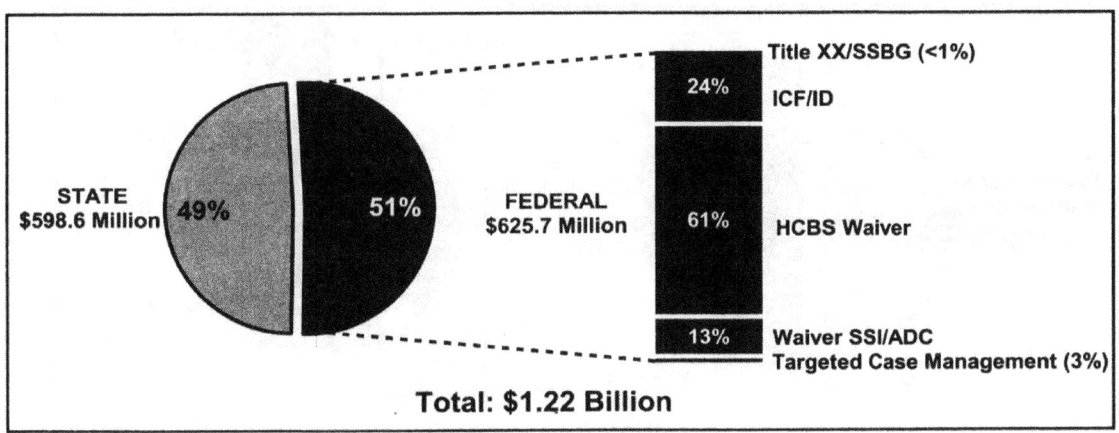

CONNECTICUT
PERSONS BY SETTING IN FISCAL YEAR 2013

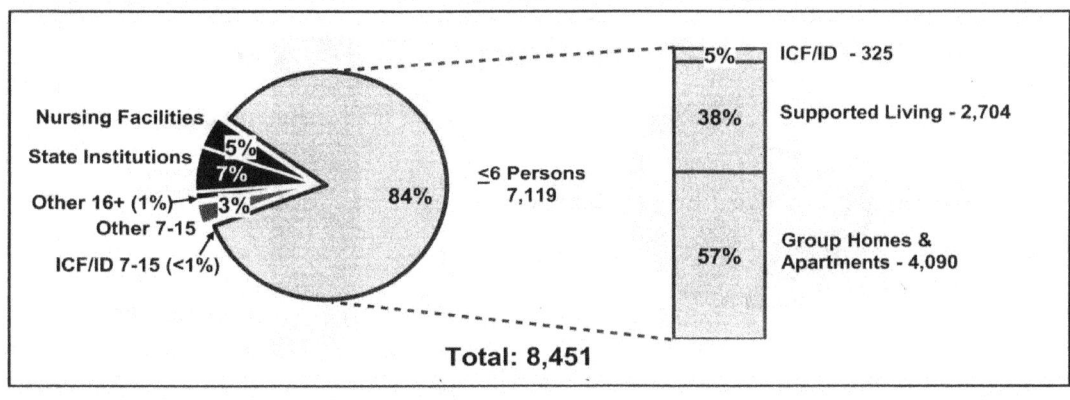

DELAWARE
PUBLIC I/DD SPENDING BY REVENUE SOURCE: FY 2013

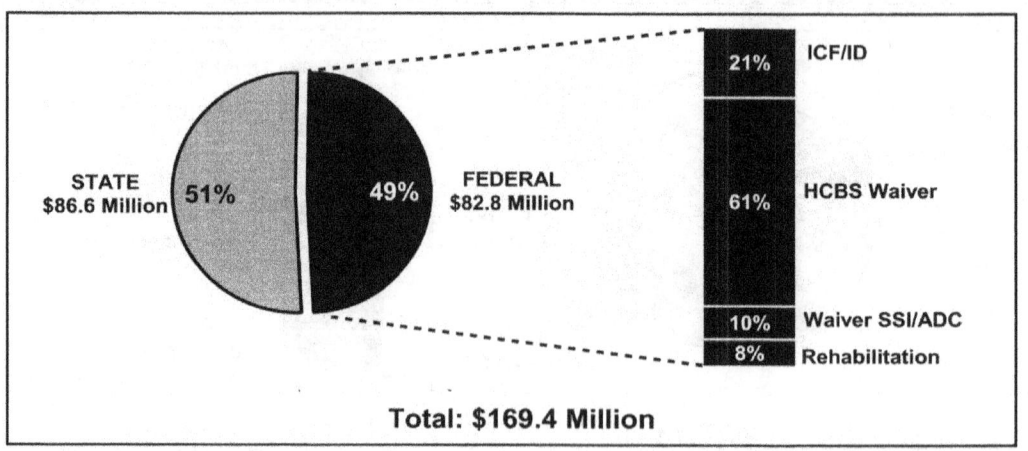

DELAWARE
PERSONS BY SETTING IN FISCAL YEAR 2013

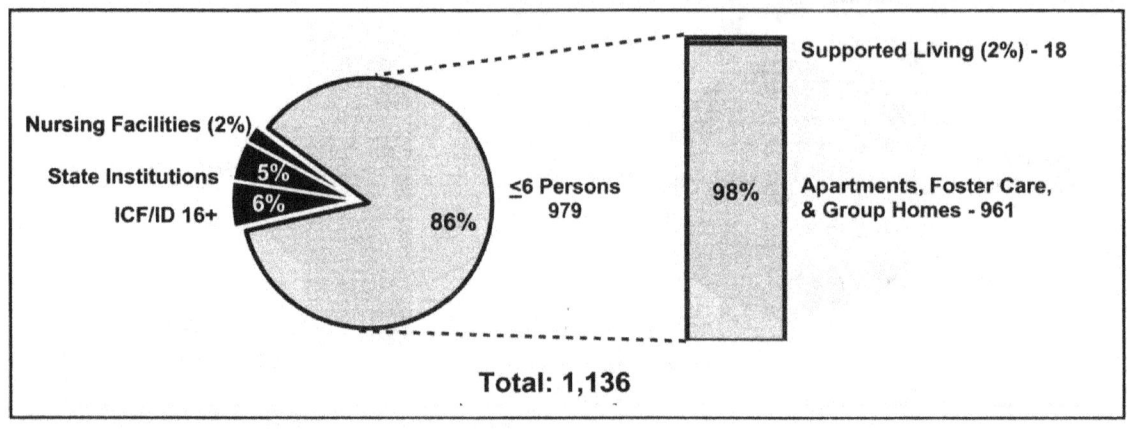

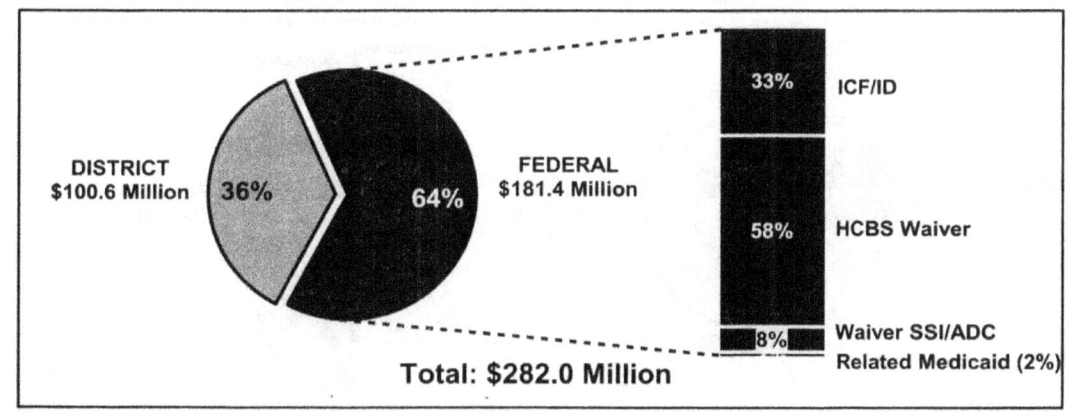

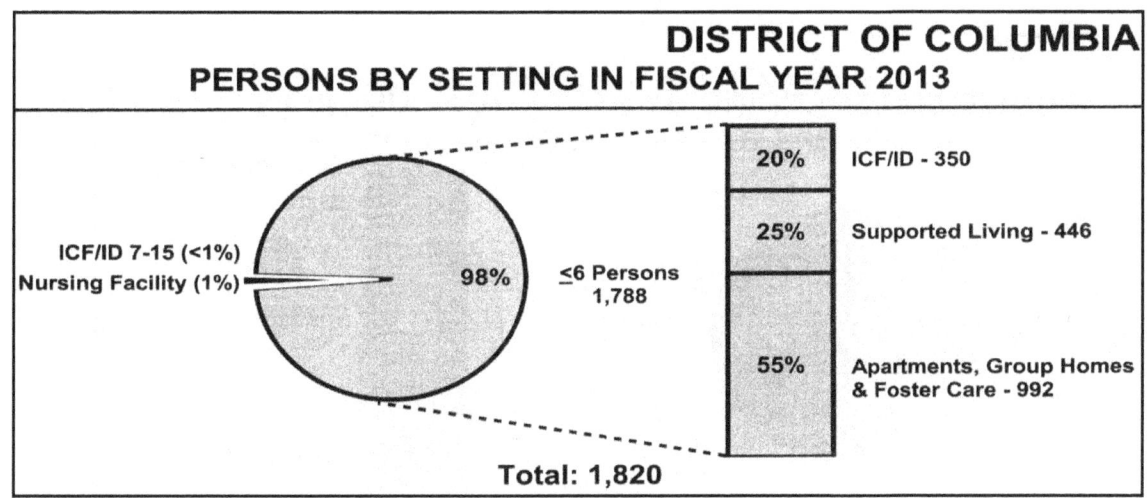

FLORIDA
PUBLIC I/DD SPENDING BY REVENUE SOURCE: FY 2013

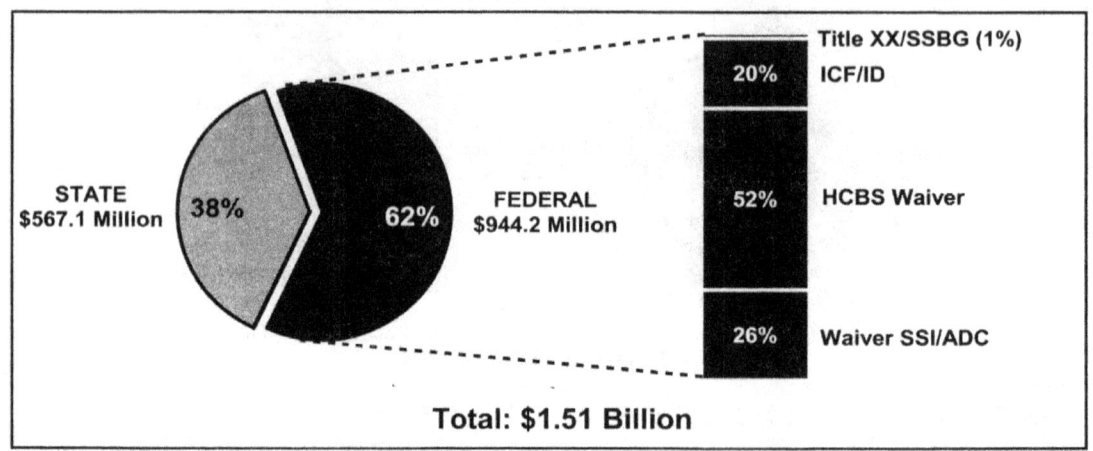

FLORIDA
PERSONS BY SETTING IN FISCAL YEAR 2013

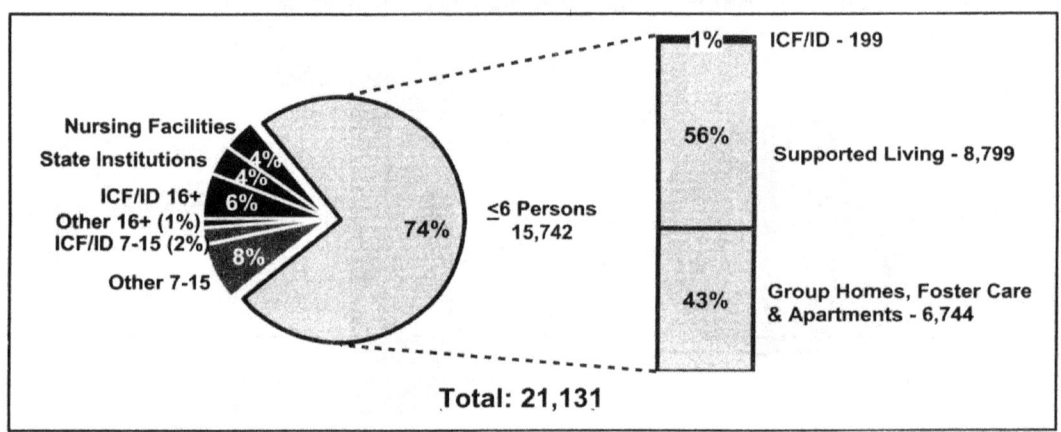

HAWAII
PUBLIC I/DD SPENDING BY REVENUE SOURCE: FY 2013

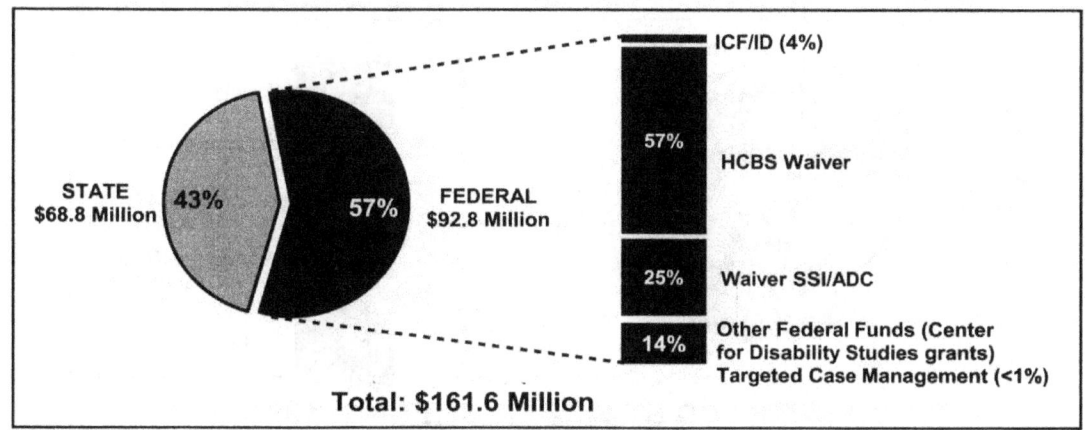

HAWAII
PERSONS BY SETTING IN FISCAL YEAR 2013

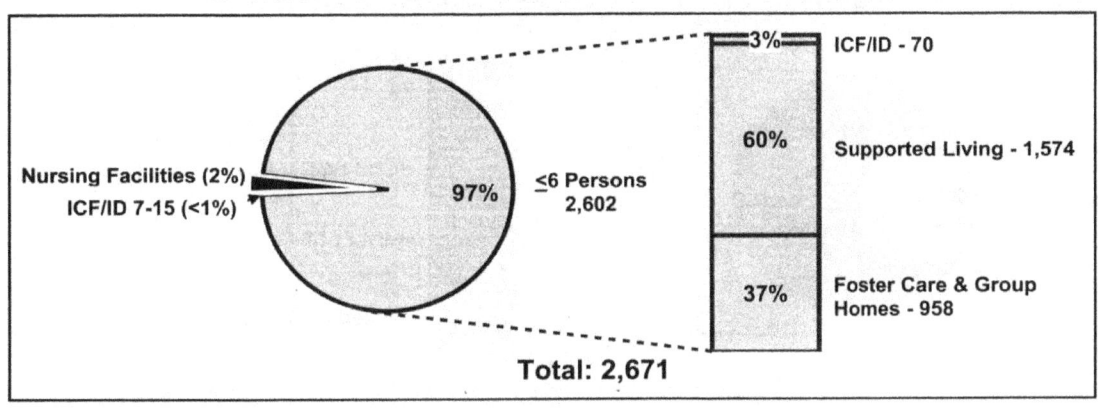

IDAHO
PUBLIC I/DD SPENDING BY REVENUE SOURCE: FY 2013

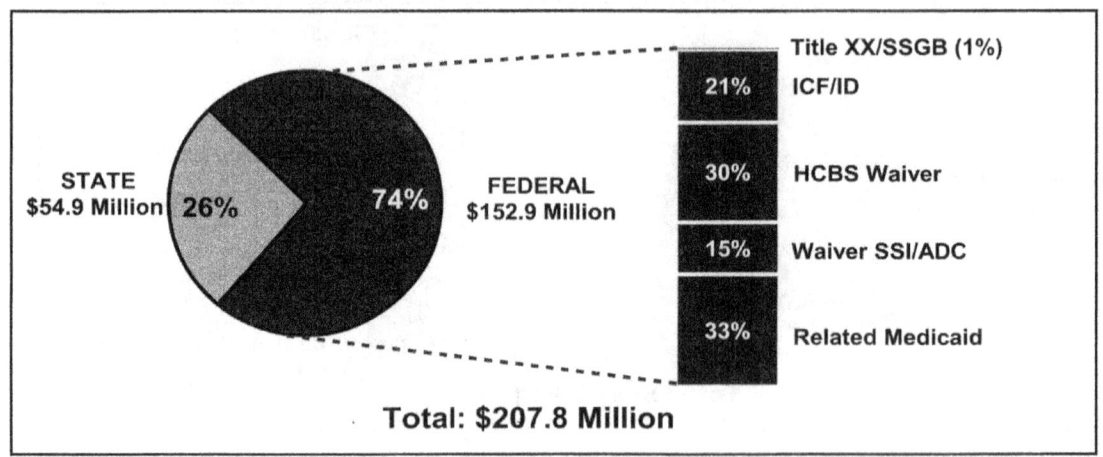

IDAHO
PERSONS BY SETTING IN FISCAL YEAR 2013

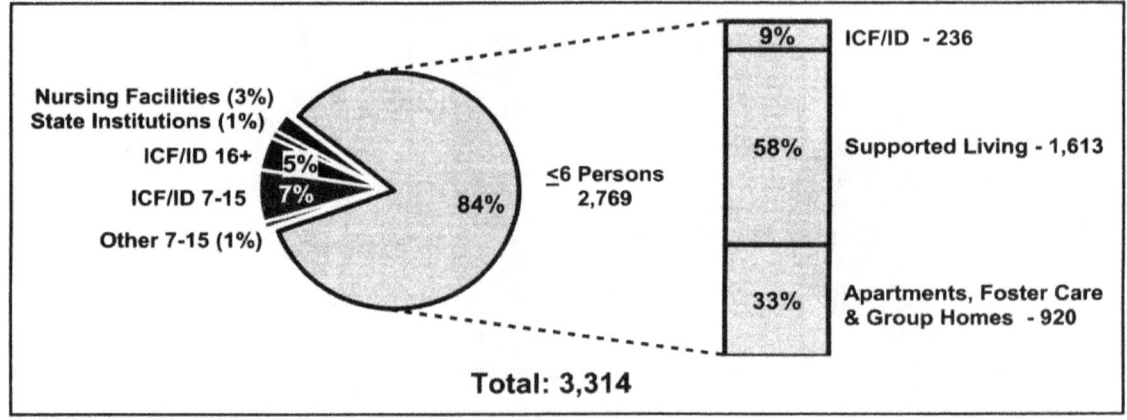

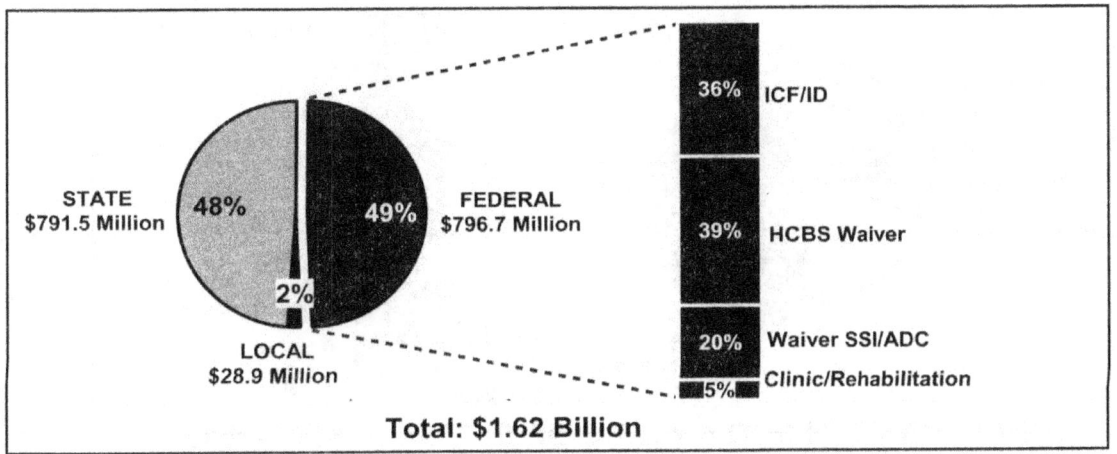

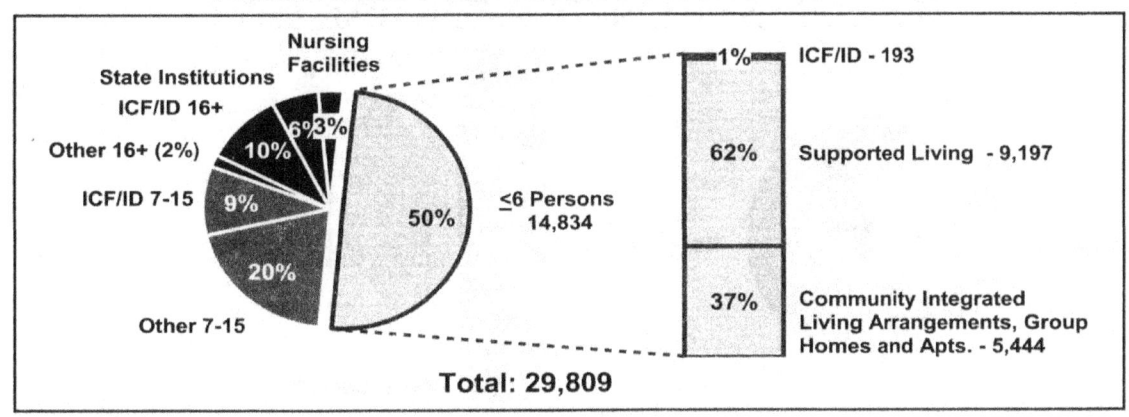

INDIANA
PUBLIC I/DD SPENDING BY REVENUE SOURCE: FY 2013

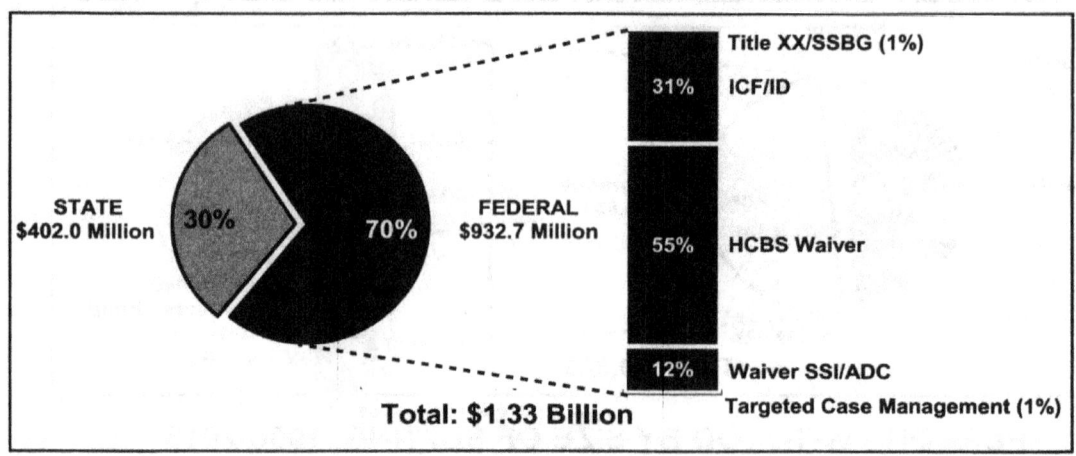

INDIANA
PERSONS BY SETTING IN FISCAL YEAR 2013

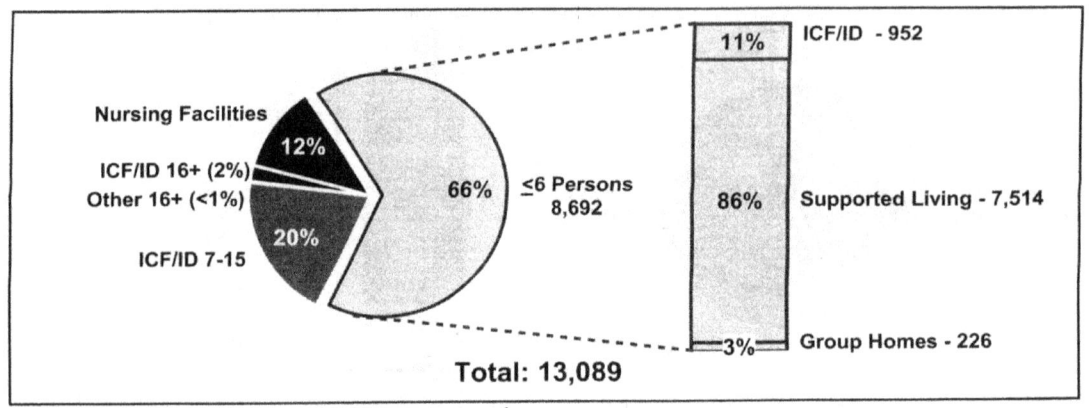

IOWA
PUBLIC I/DD SPENDING BY REVENUE SOURCE: FY 2013

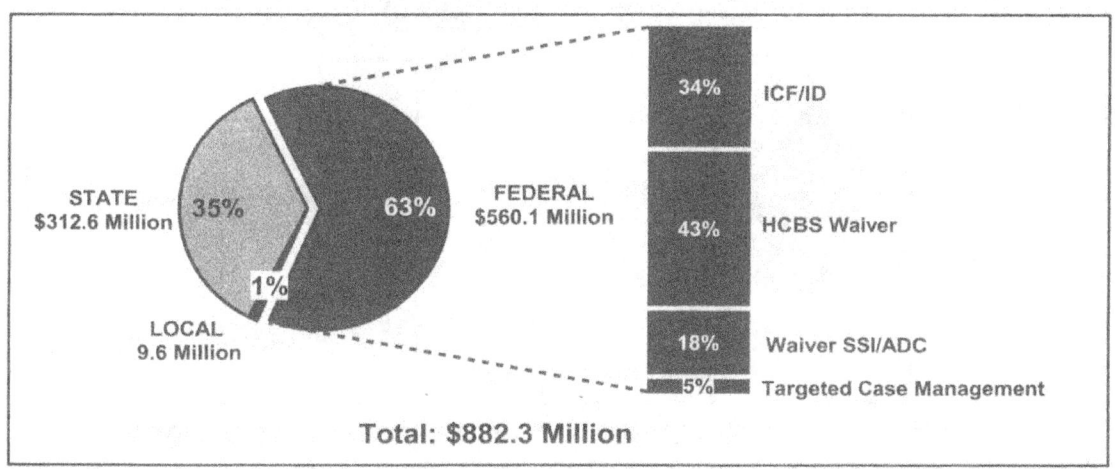

IOWA
PERSONS BY SETTING IN FISCAL YEAR 2013

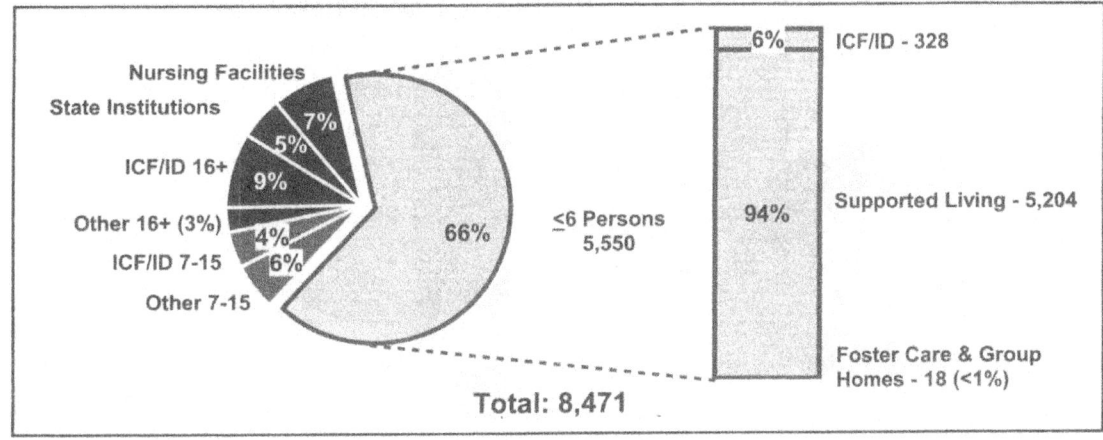

KANSAS
PUBLIC I/DD SPENDING BY REVENUE SOURCE: FY 2013

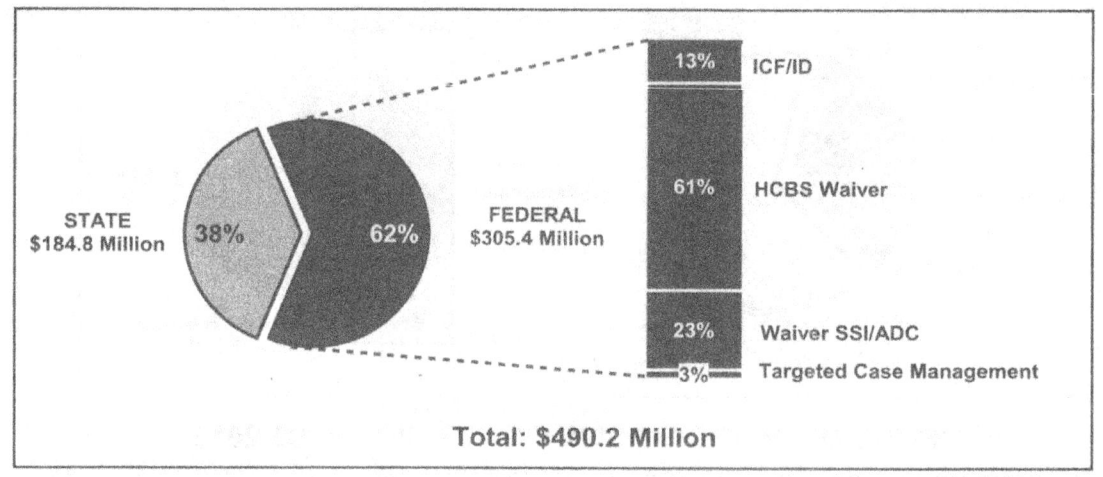

KANSAS
PERSONS BY SETTING IN FISCAL YEAR 2013

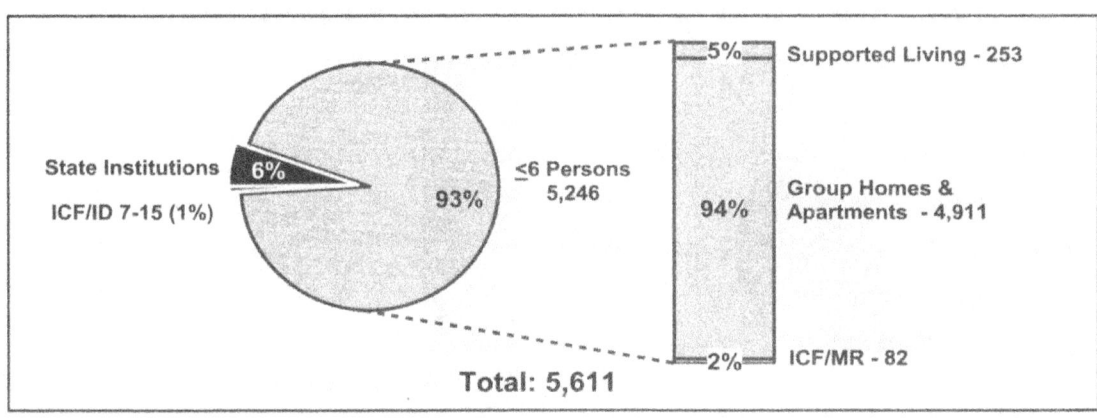

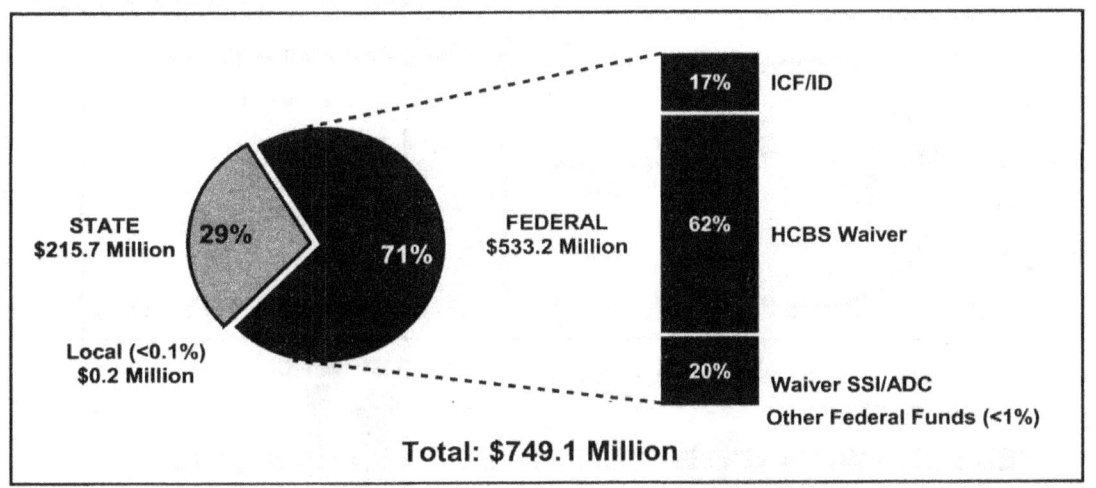

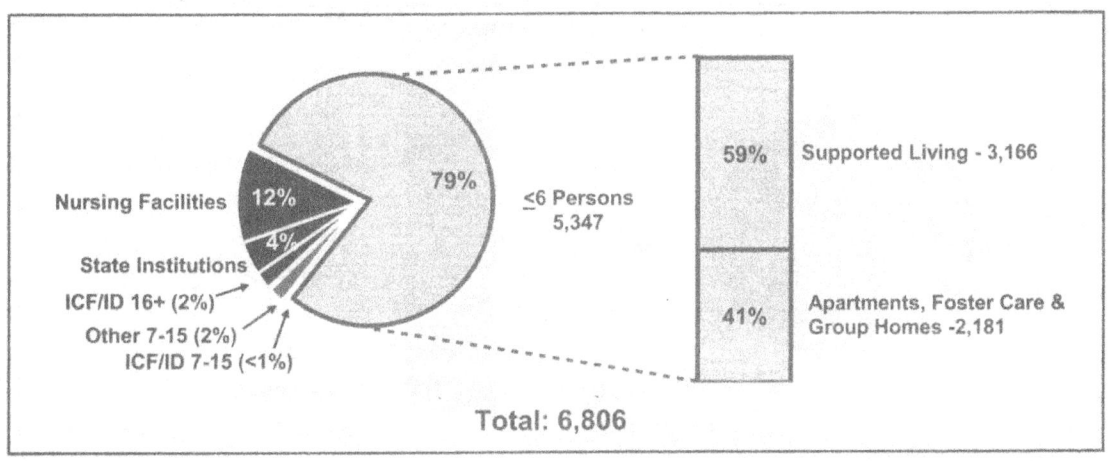

LOUISIANA

The national Mental Health Association's 2015 report lists Louisiana as one of the states with the highest prevalence of mental illness and lowest rates of access to care. To make matters worse, in 2016 Louisiana had to address a $940 million budget deficit, further reducing funding for all departments and mental health services in the state. Louisiana mental health care had to shave another $131 million of state funds out of their budget in 2016. Because these state funds attract federal matching dollars, the total impact of both plans is $346.5 million funding reduction for mental health related services.

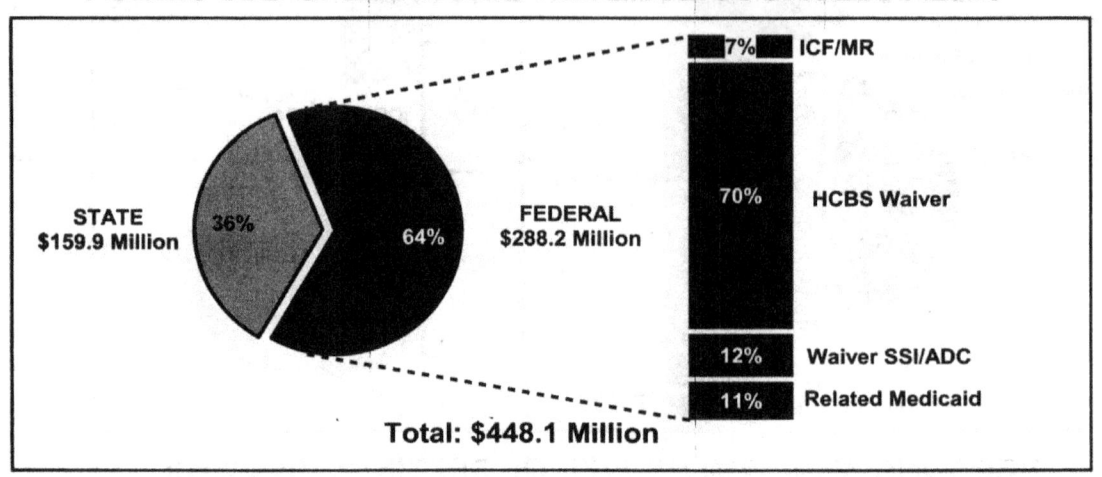

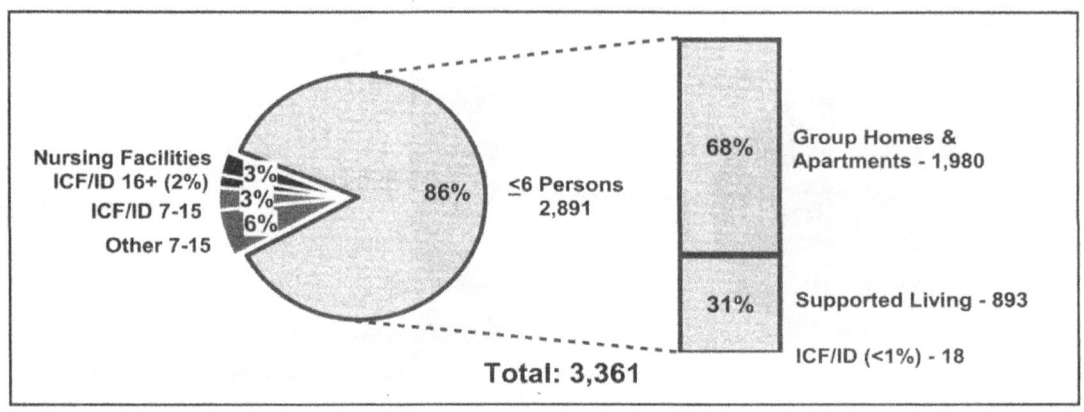

MARYLAND
PUBLIC I/DD SPENDING BY REVENUE SOURCE: FY 2013

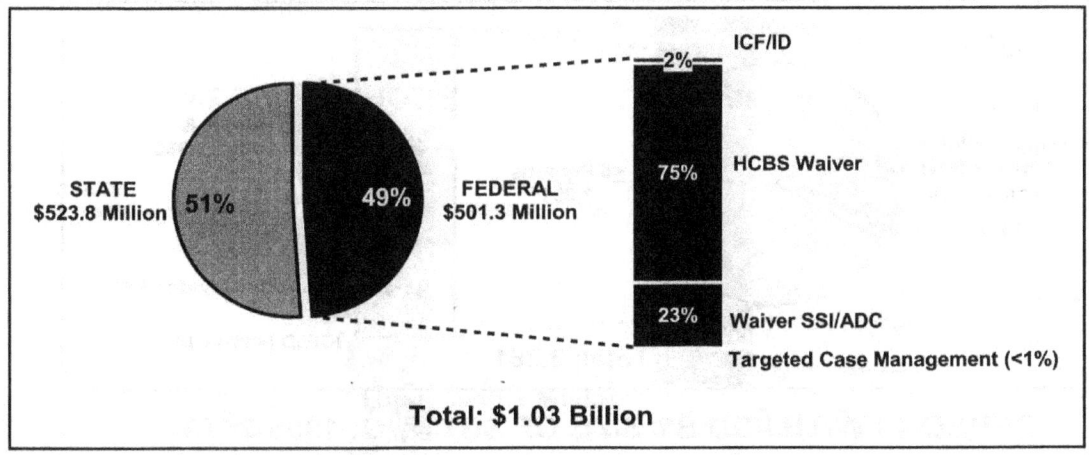

MARYLAND
PERSONS BY SETTING IN FISCAL YEAR 2013

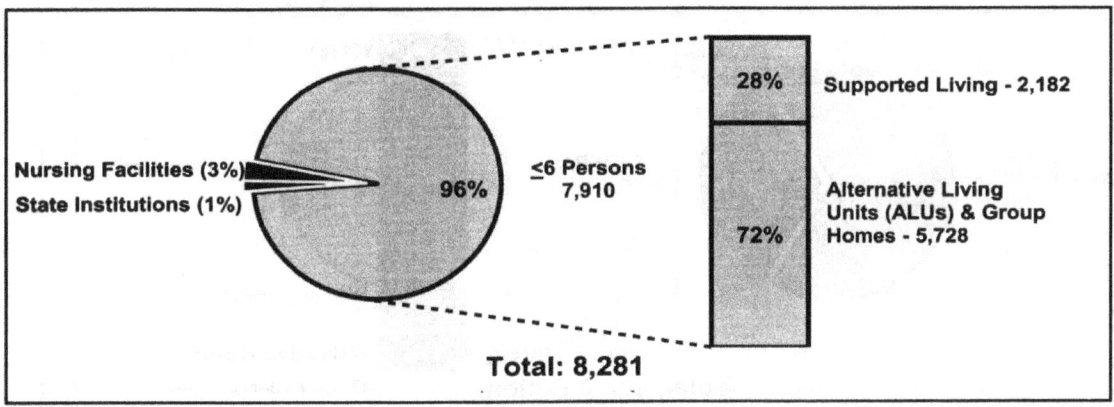

MASSACHUSETTS
PUBLIC I/DD SPENDING BY REVENUE SOURCE: FY 2013

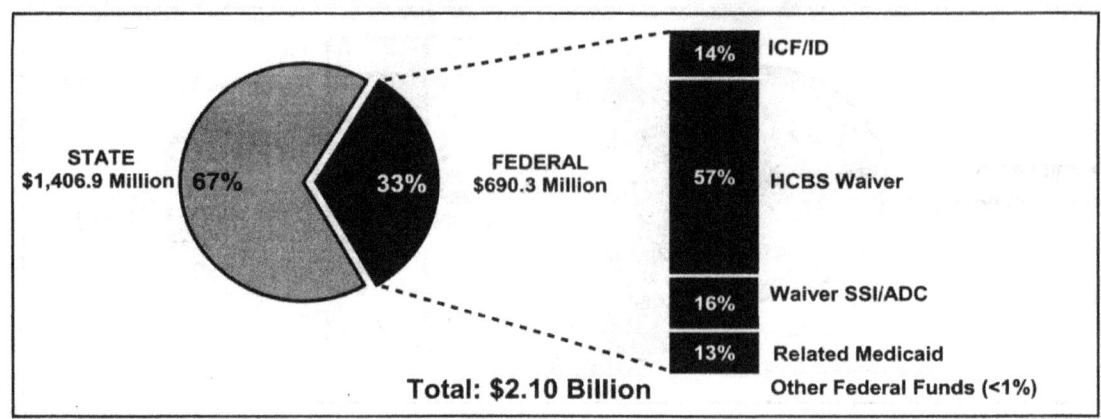

MASSACHUSETTS
PERSONS BY SETTING IN FISCAL YEAR 2013

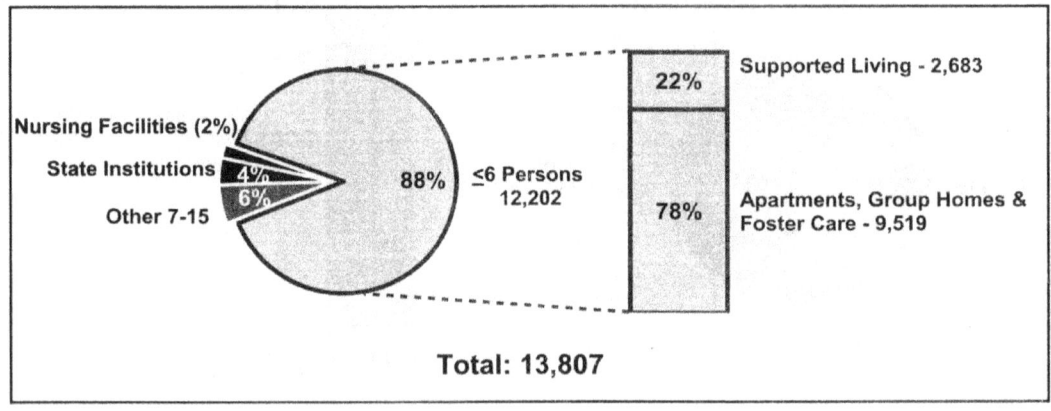

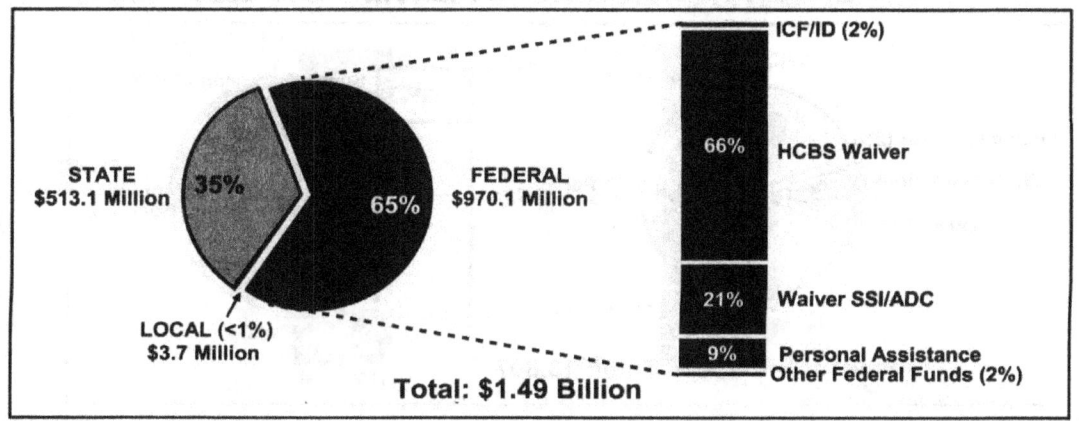

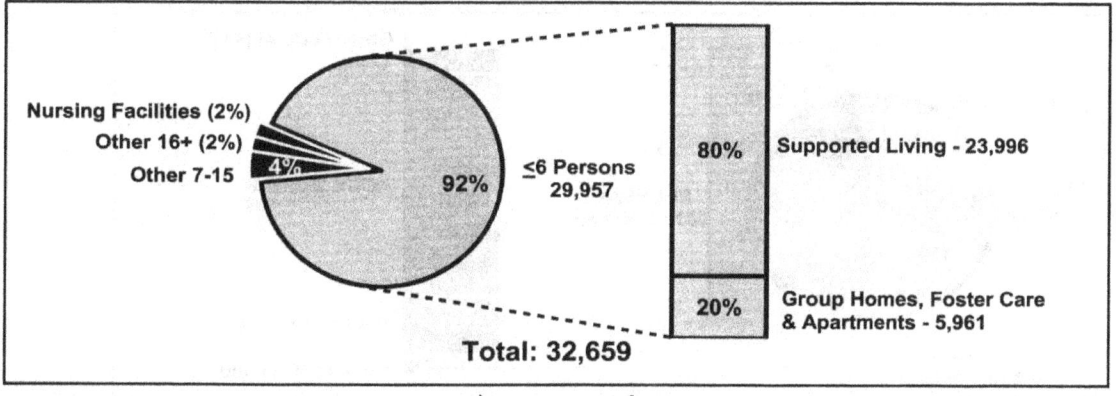

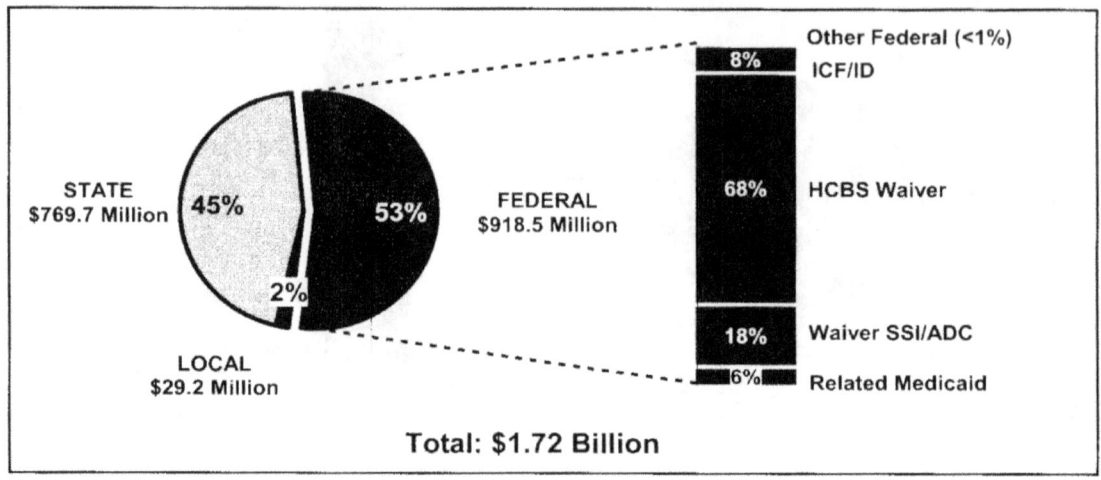

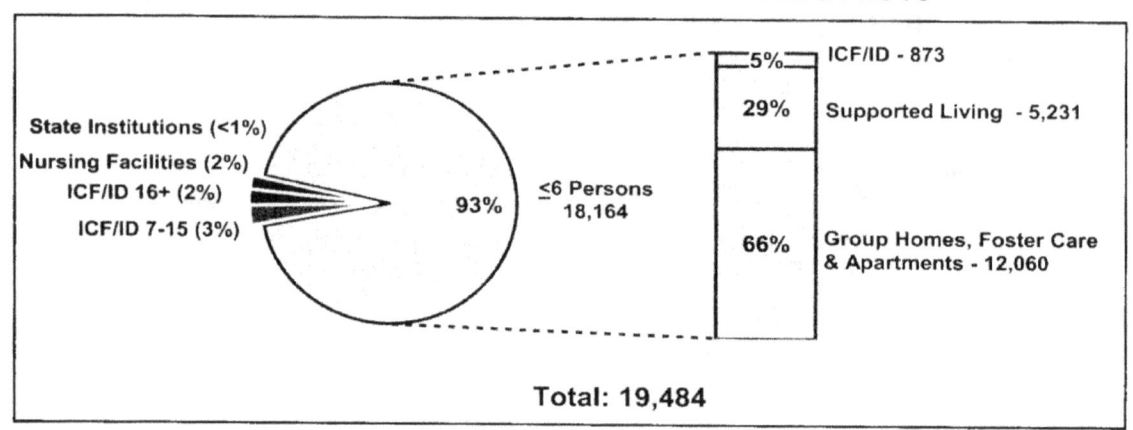

MISSISSIPPI
PERSONS BY SETTING IN FISCAL YEAR 2013

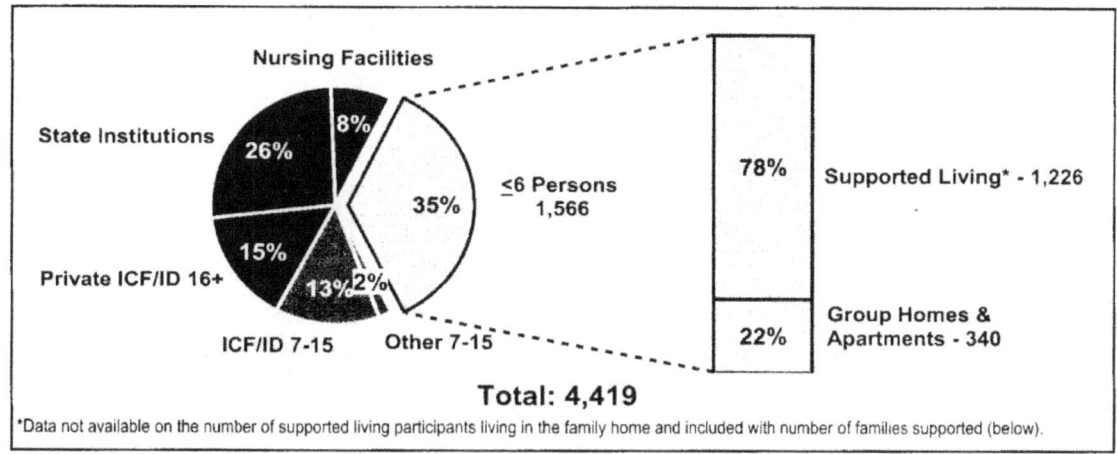

Total: 4,419

*Data not available on the number of supported living participants living in the family home and included with number of families supported (below).

MISSISSIPPI
PUBLIC I/DD SPENDING BY REVENUE SOURCE: FY 2013

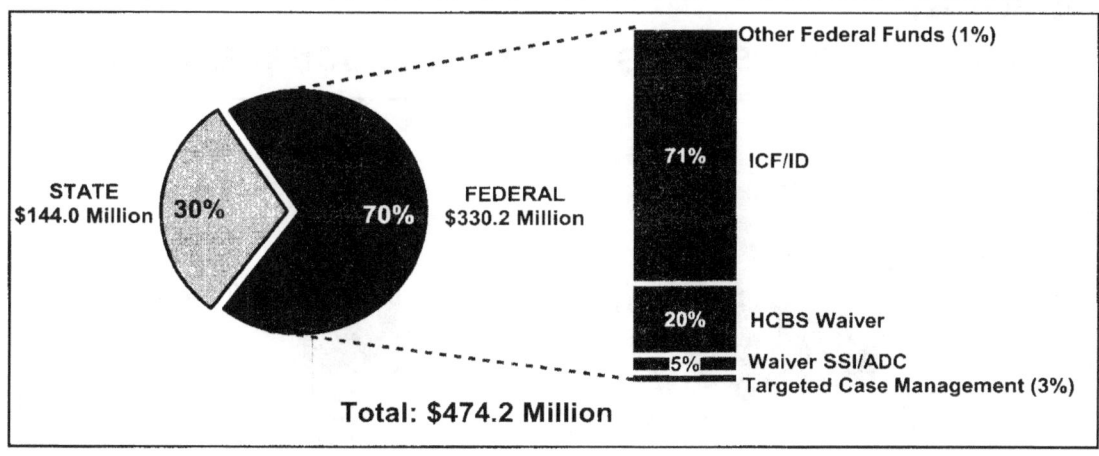

Total: $474.2 Million

MISSOURI
PERSONS BY SETTING IN FISCAL YEAR 2013

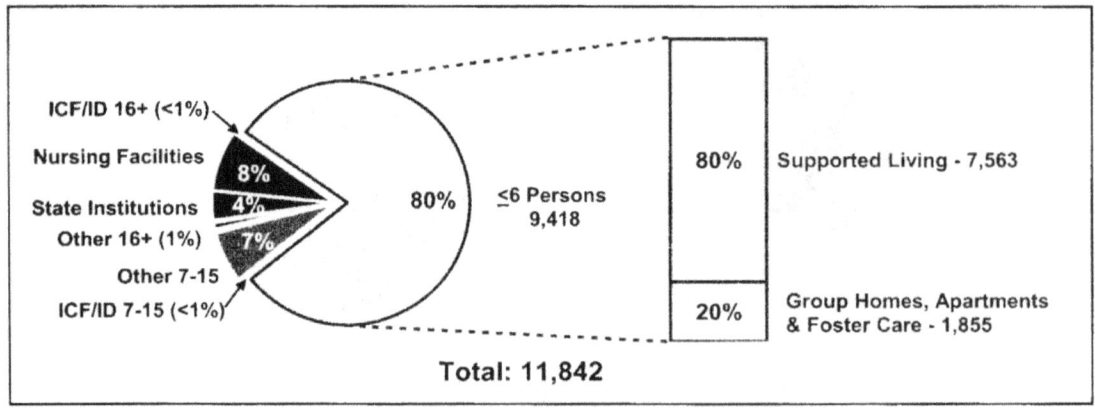

MISSOURI
PUBLIC I/DD SPENDING BY REVENUE SOURCE: FY 2013

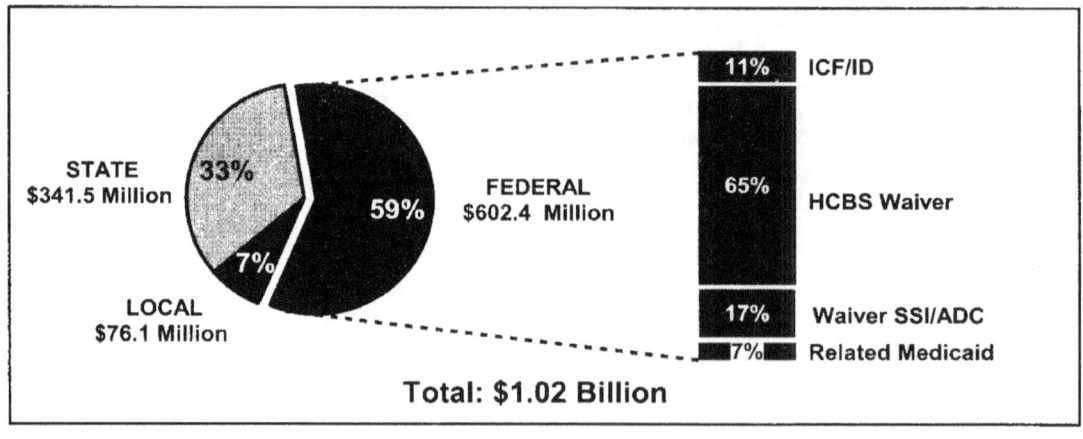

MONTANA
PERSONS BY SETTING IN FISCAL YEAR 2013

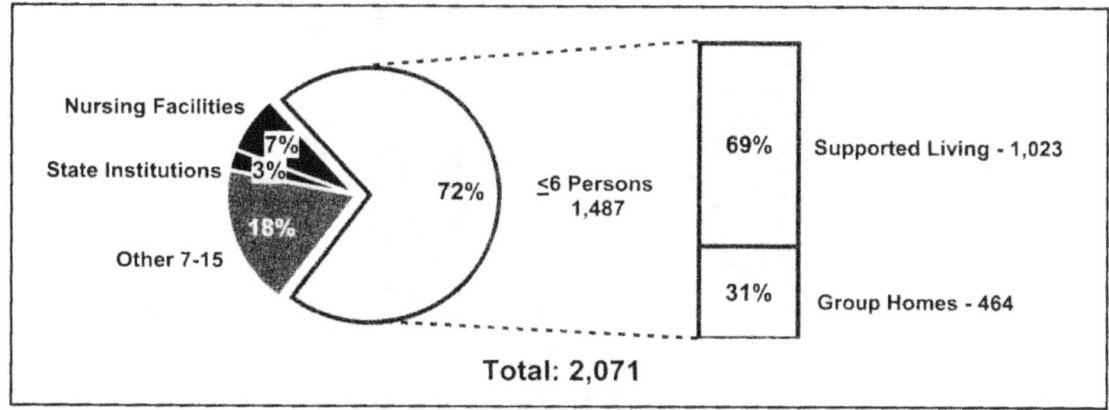

Total: 2,071

MONTANA
PUBLIC I/DD SPENDING BY REVENUE SOURCE: FY 2013

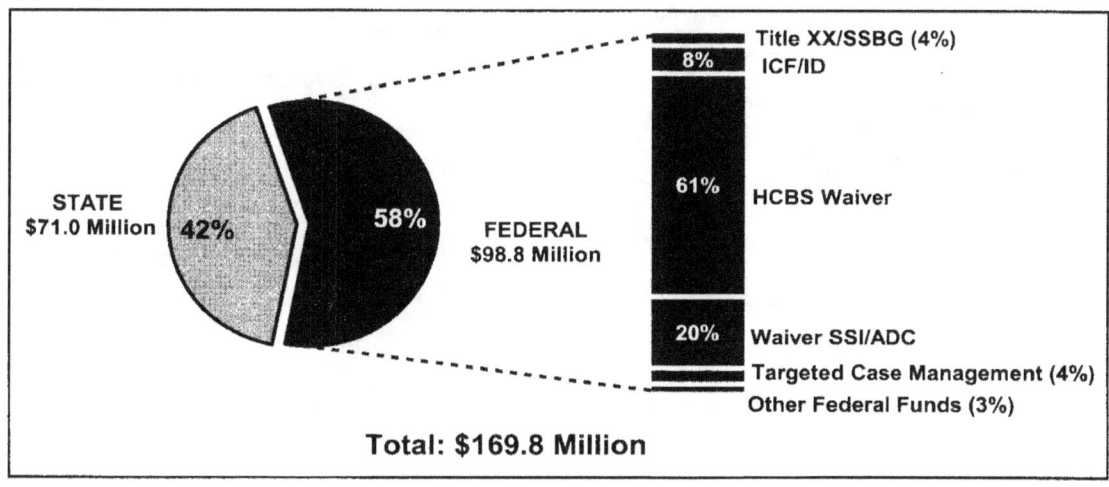

Total: $169.8 Million

NEBRASKA
PUBLIC I/DD SPENDING BY REVENUE SOURCE: FY 2013

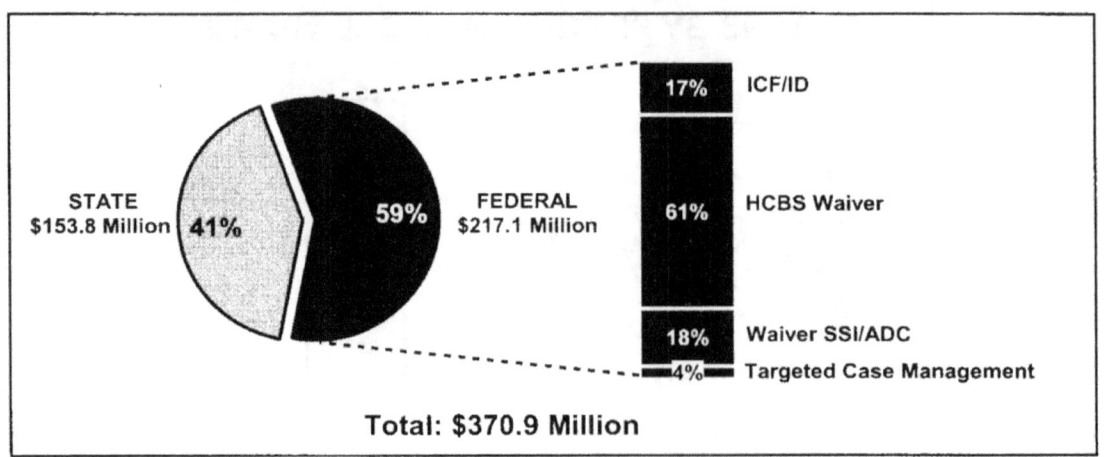

NEBRASKA
PERSONS BY SETTING IN FISCAL YEAR 2013

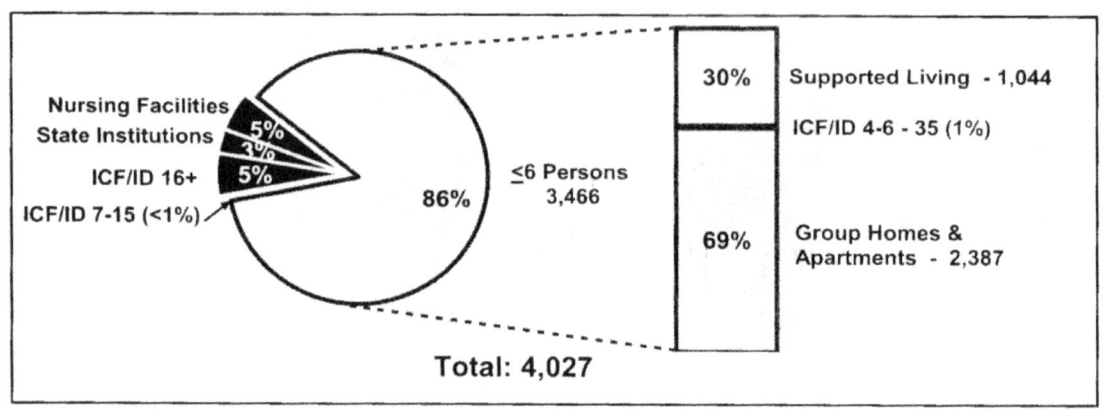

NEVADA
PUBLIC I/DD SPENDING BY REVENUE SOURCE: FY 2013

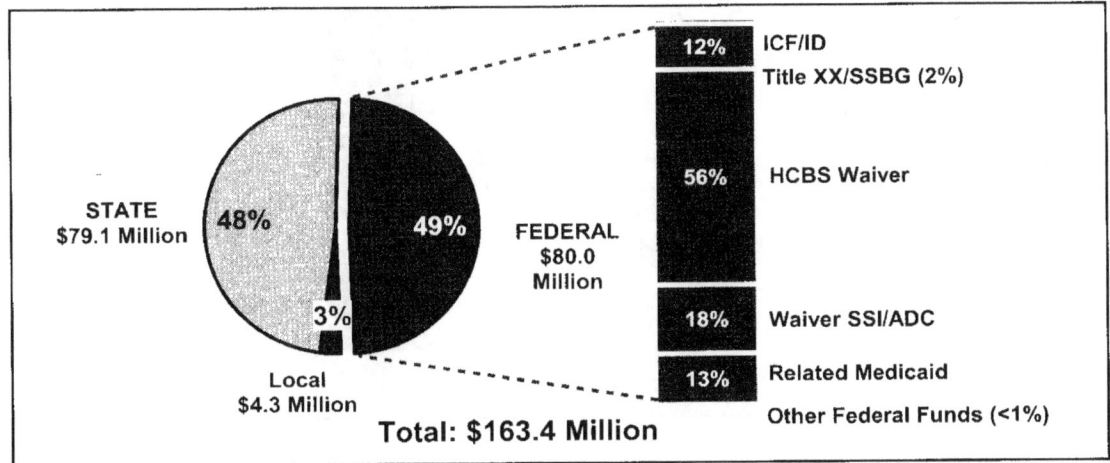

NEVADA
PERSONS BY SETTING IN FISCAL YEAR 2013

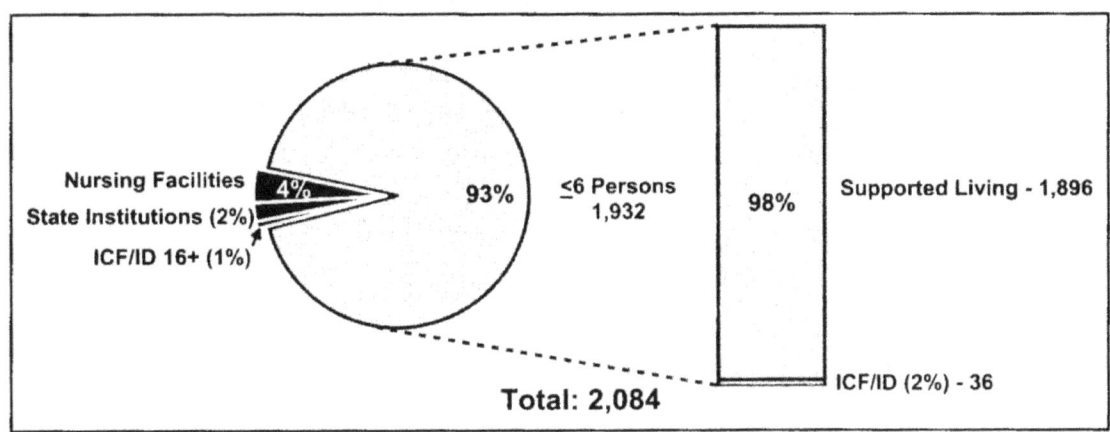

NEW JERSEY
PUBLIC I/DD SPENDING BY REVENUE SOURCE: FY 2013

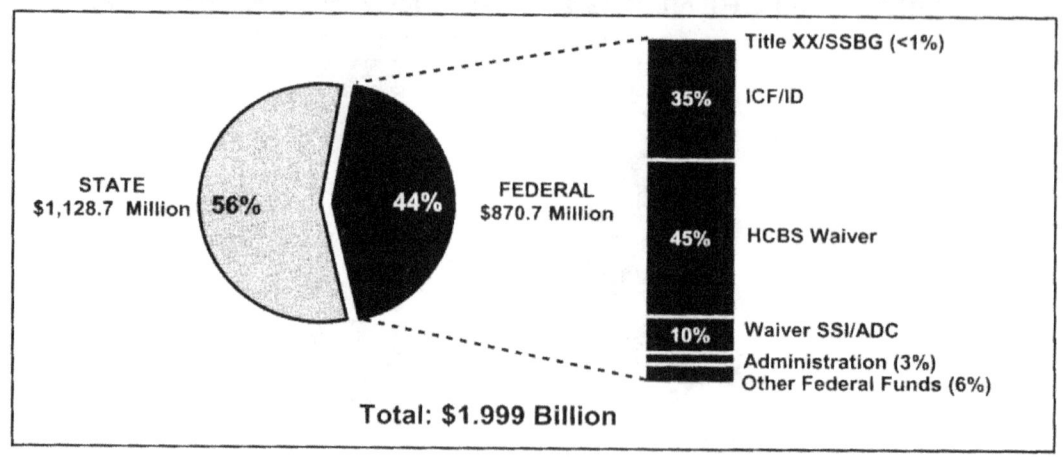

NEW JERSEY
PERSONS BY SETTING IN FISCAL YEAR 2013

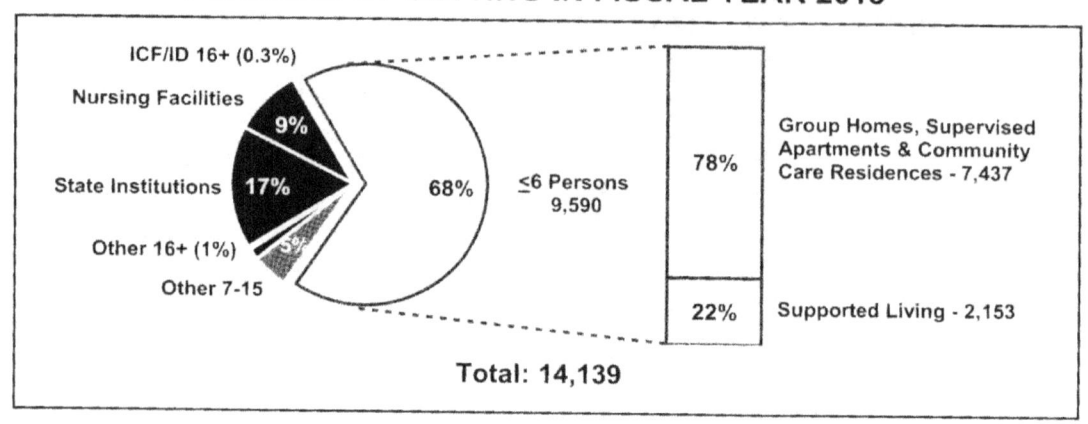

NEW HAMPSHIRE
PUBLIC I/DD SPENDING BY REVENUE SOURCE: FY 2013

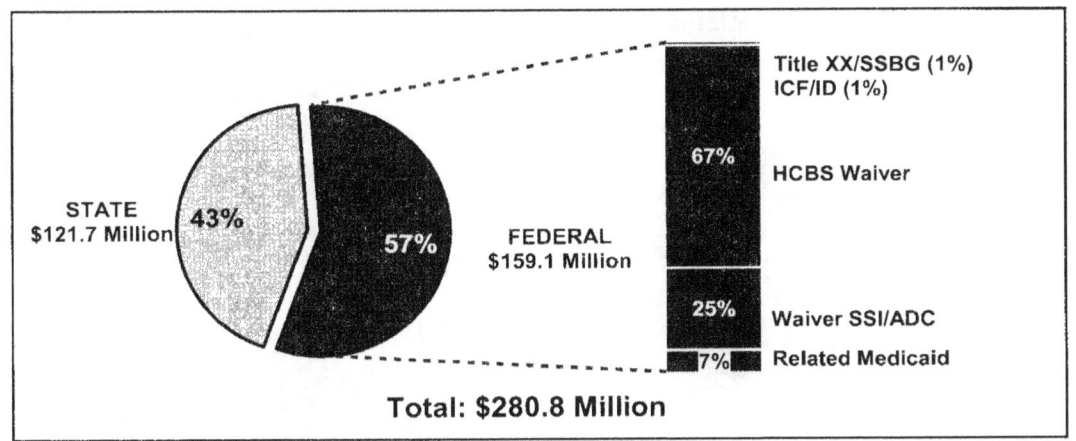

NEW HAMPSHIRE
PERSONS BY SETTING IN FISCAL YEAR 2013

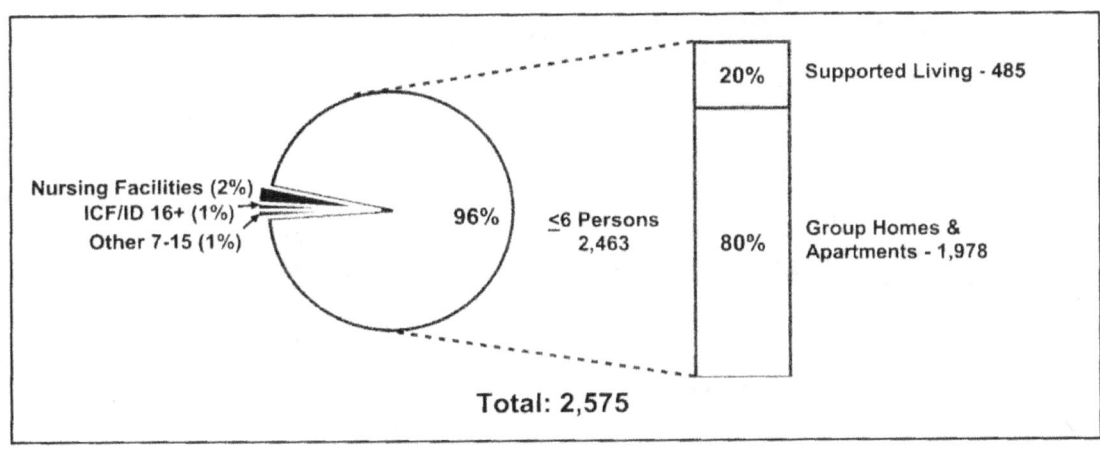

NEW MEXICO
PUBLIC I/DD SPENDING BY REVENUE SOURCE: FY 2013

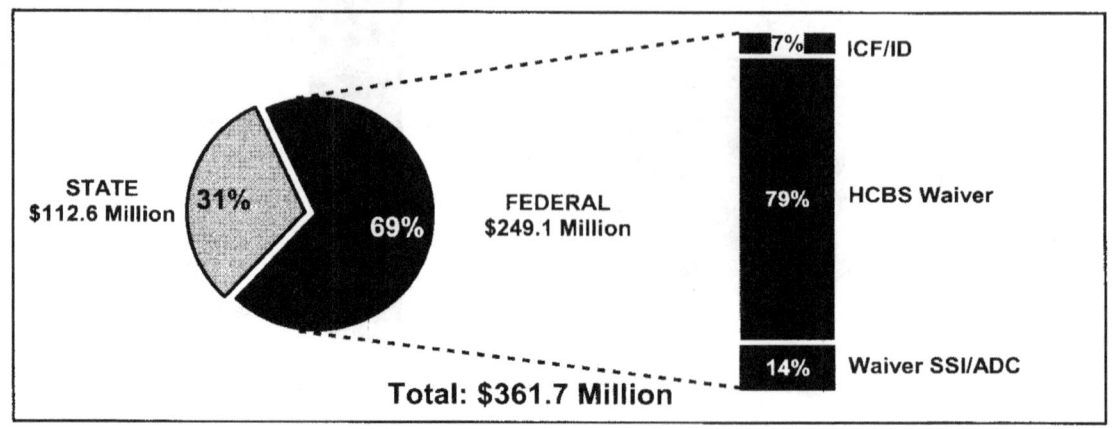

NEW MEXICO
PERSONS BY SETTING IN FISCAL YEAR 2013

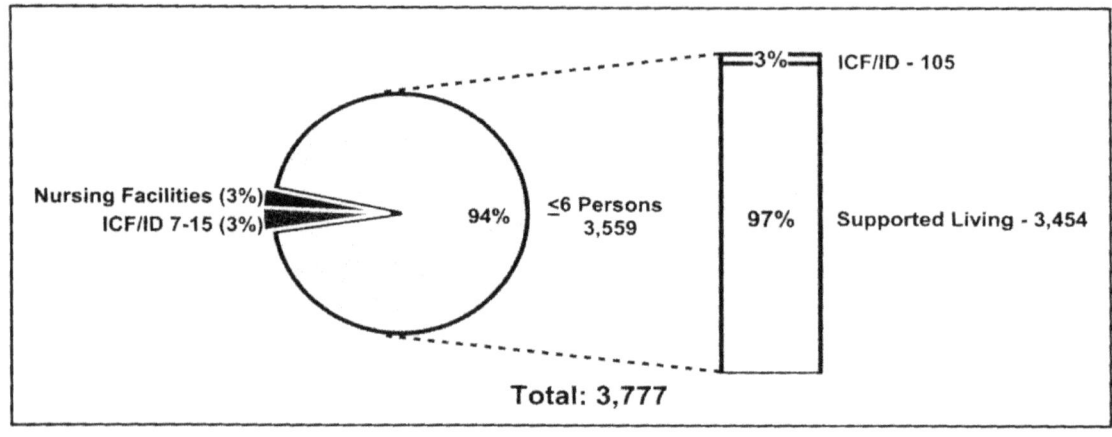

NEW YORK
PUBLIC I/DD SPENDING BY REVENUE SOURCE: FY 2013

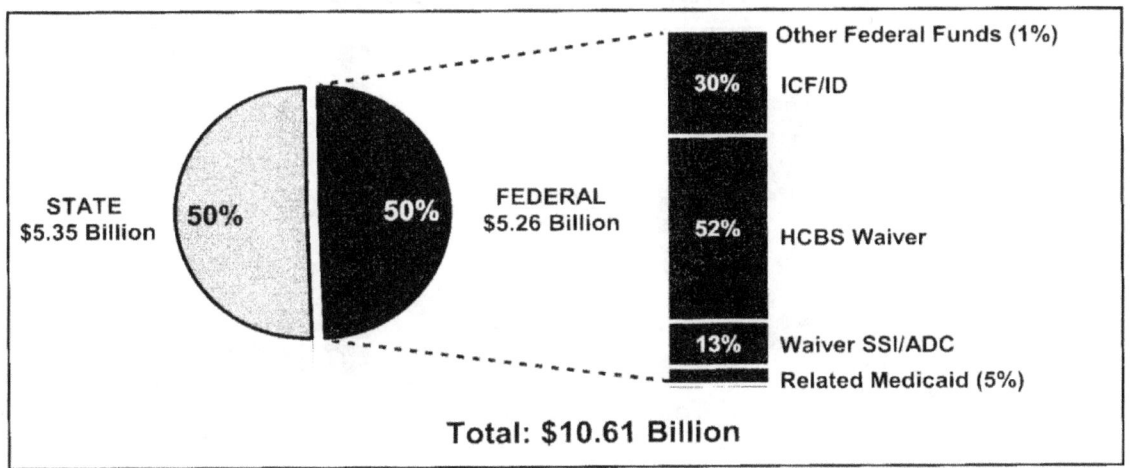

NEW YORK
PERSONS BY SETTING IN FISCAL YEAR 2013

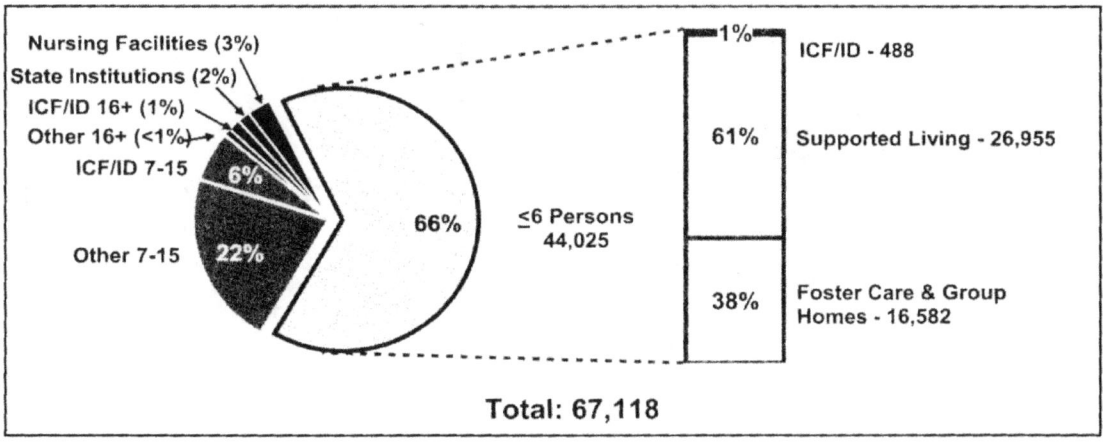

NORTH CAROLINA
PUBLIC I/DD SPENDING BY REVENUE SOURCE: FY 2013

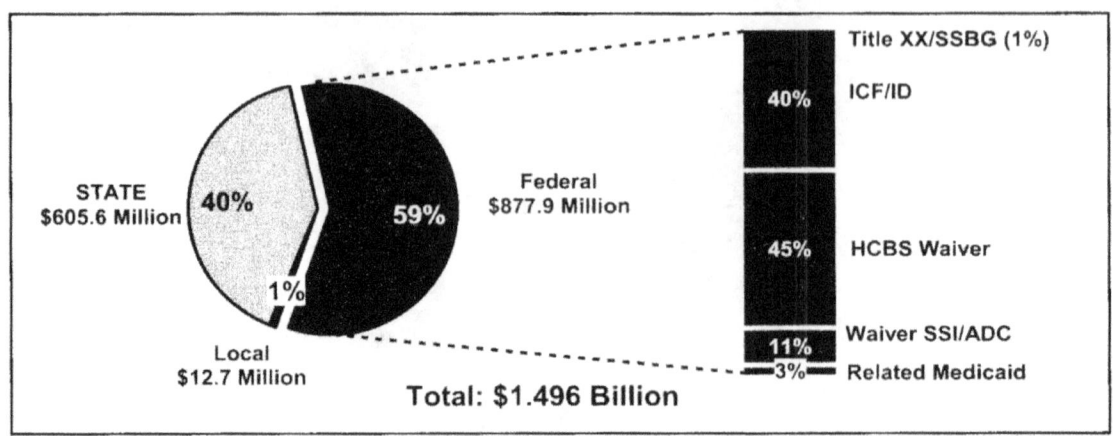

NORTH CAROLINA
PERSONS BY SETTING IN FISCAL YEAR 2013

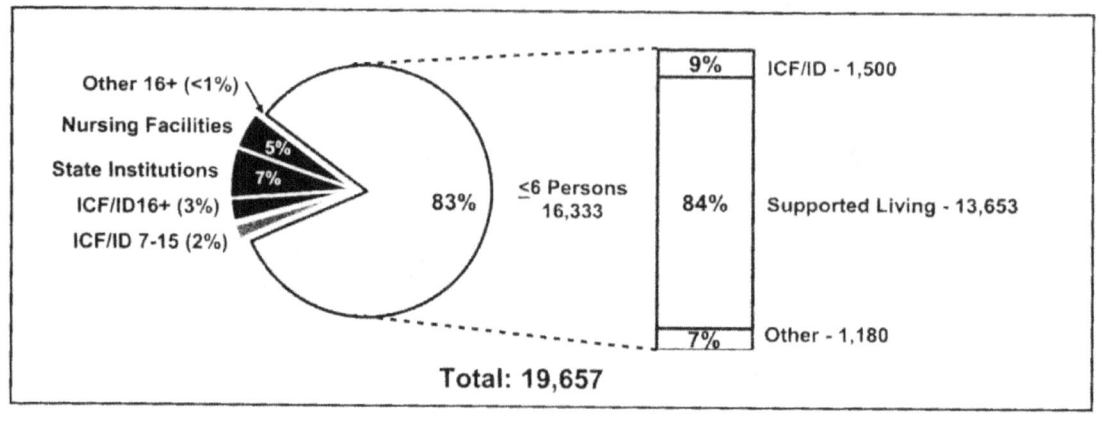

NORTH DAKOTA
PUBLIC I/DD SPENDING BY REVENUE SOURCE: FY 2013

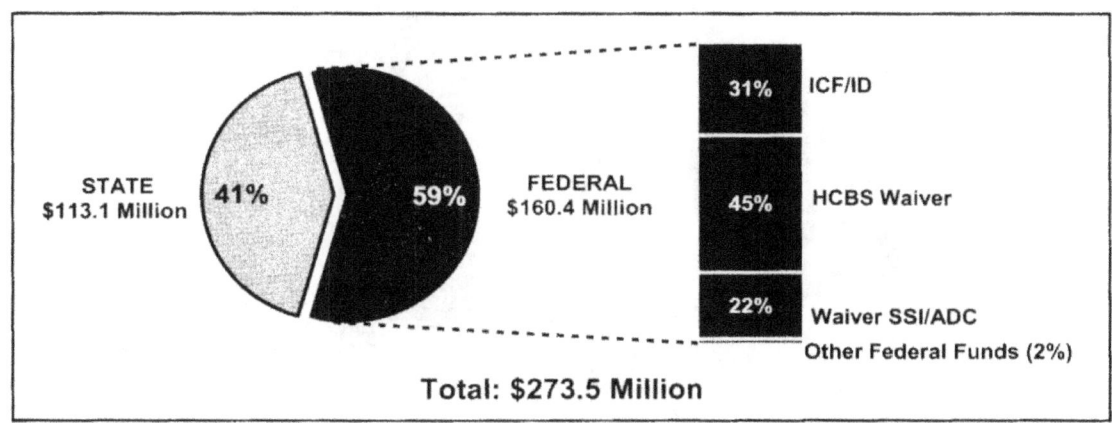

NORTH DAKOTA
PERSONS BY SETTING IN FISCAL YEAR 2013

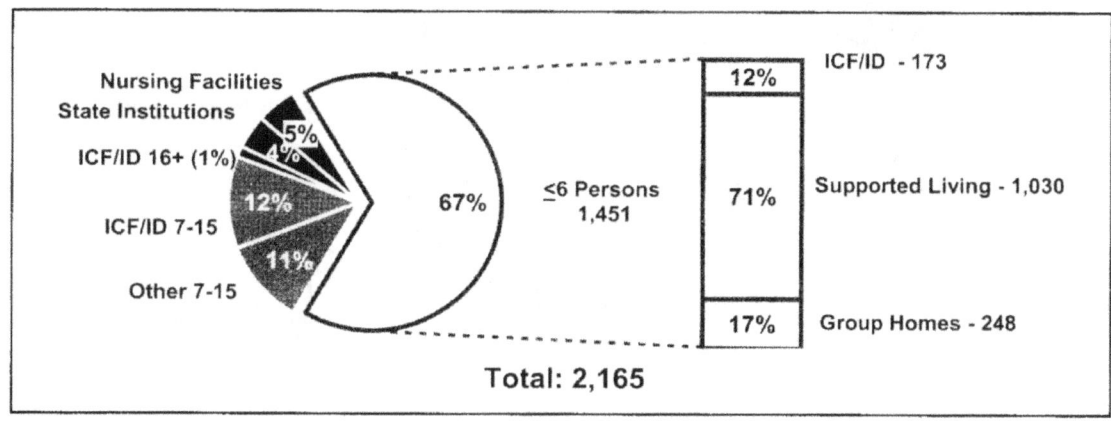

OHIO
PUBLIC I/DD SPENDING BY REVENUE SOURCE: FY 2013

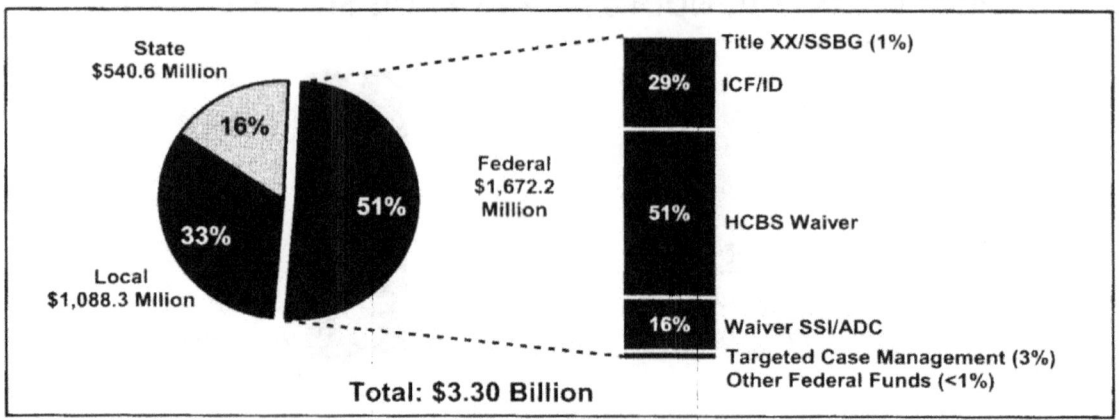

OHIO
PERSONS BY SETTING IN FISCAL YEAR 2013

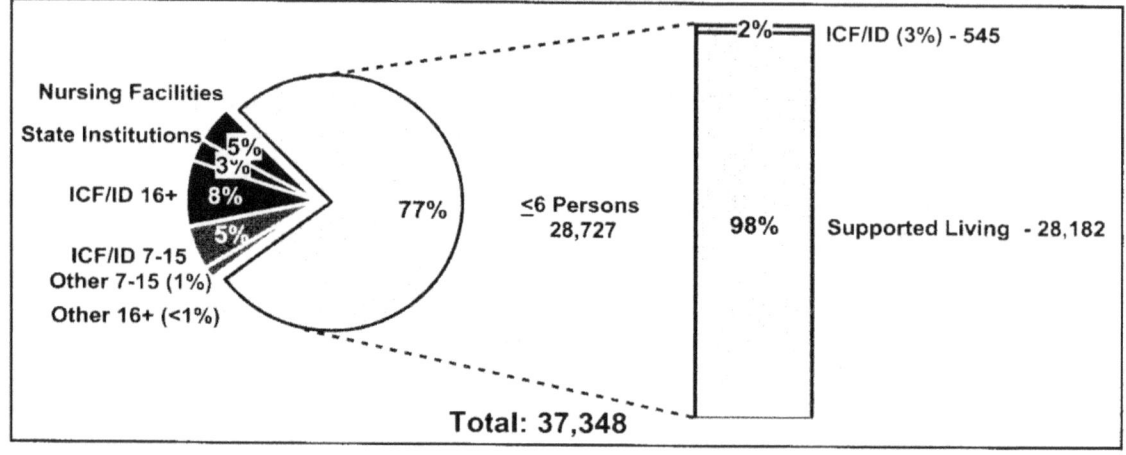

OKLAHOMA
PUBLIC I/DD SPENDING BY REVENUE SOURCE: FY 2013

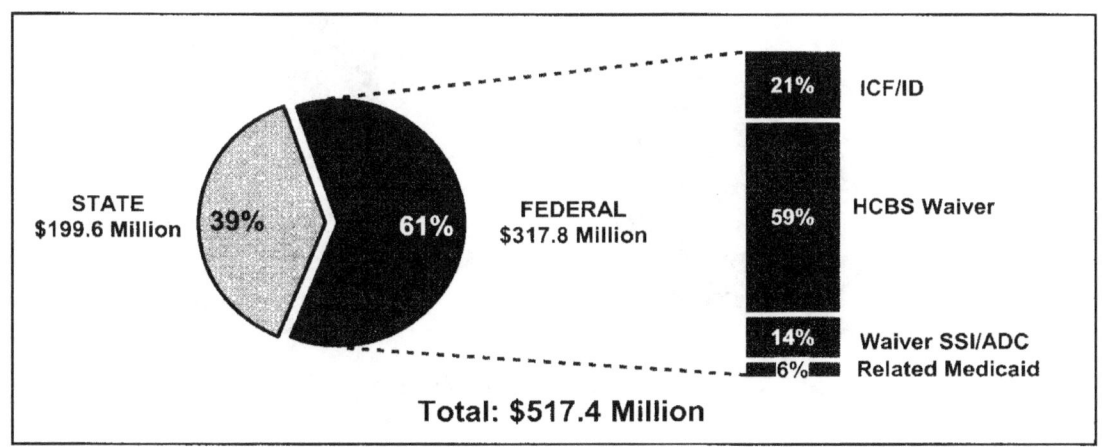

OKLAHOMA
PERSONS BY SETTING IN FISCAL YEAR 2013

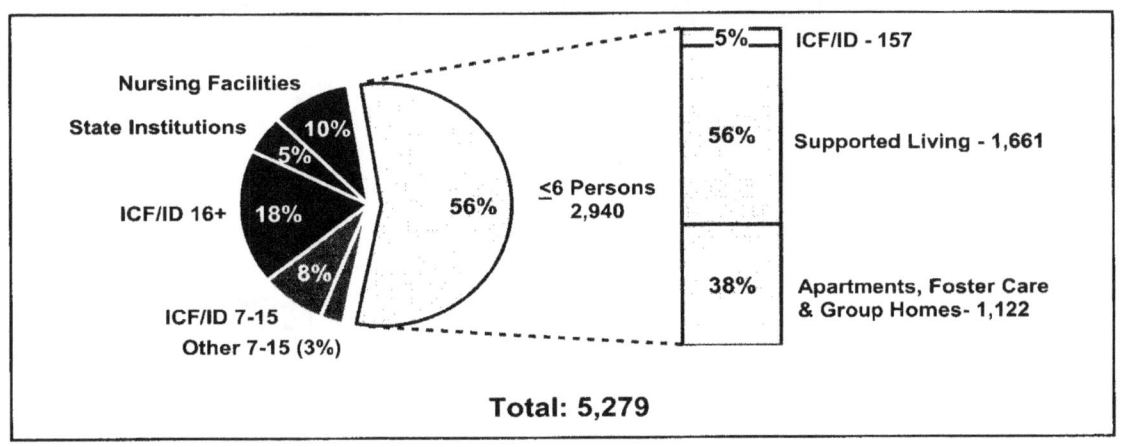

OREGON
PUBLIC I/DD SPENDING BY REVENUE SOURCE: FY 2013

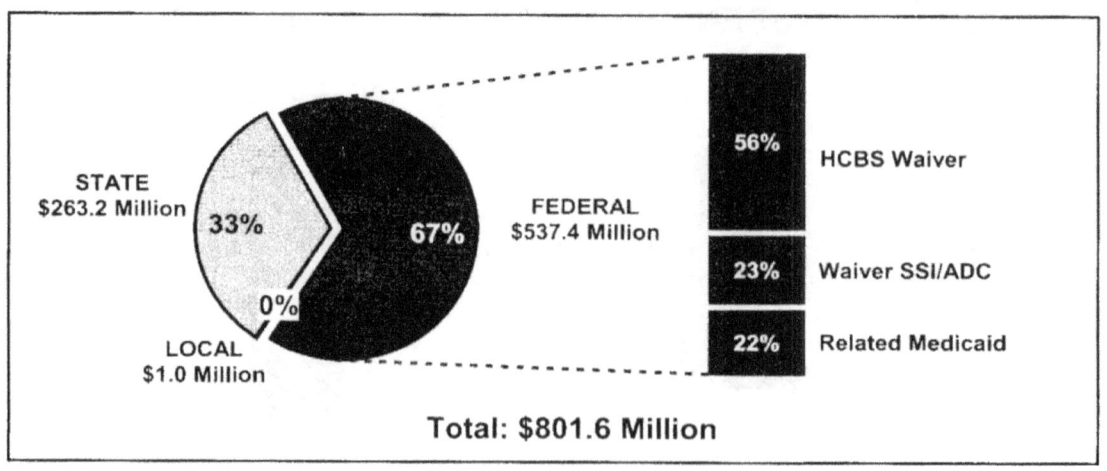

OREGON
PERSONS BY SETTING IN FISCAL YEAR 2013

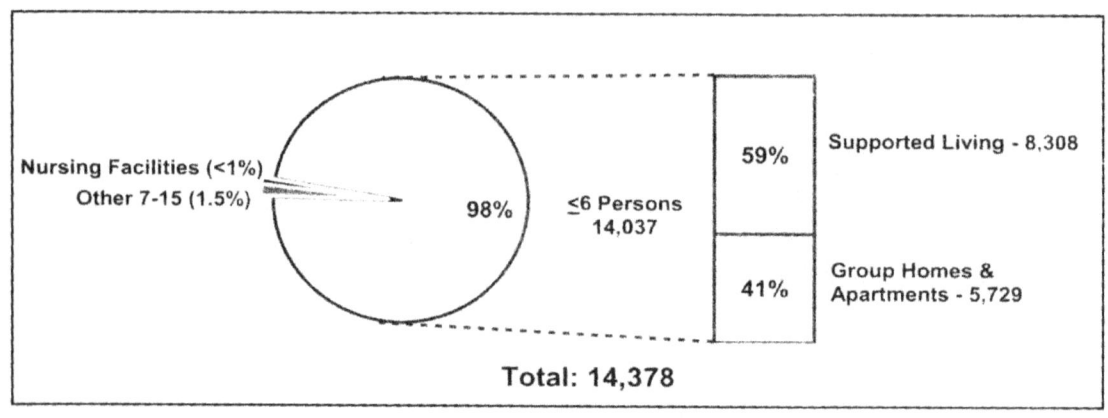

PENNSYLVANIA
PUBLIC I/DD SPENDING BY REVENUE SOURCE: FY 2013

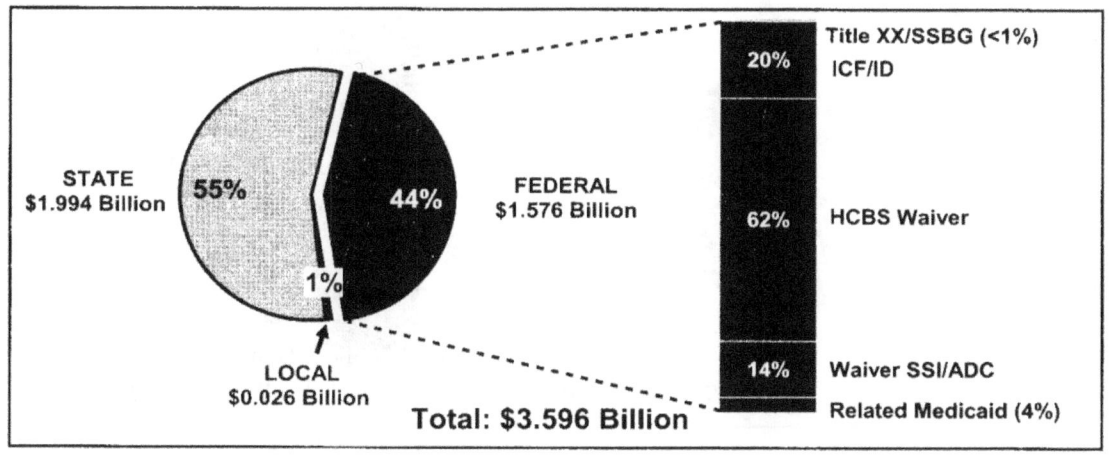

PENNSYLVANIA
PERSONS BY SETTING IN FISCAL YEAR 2013

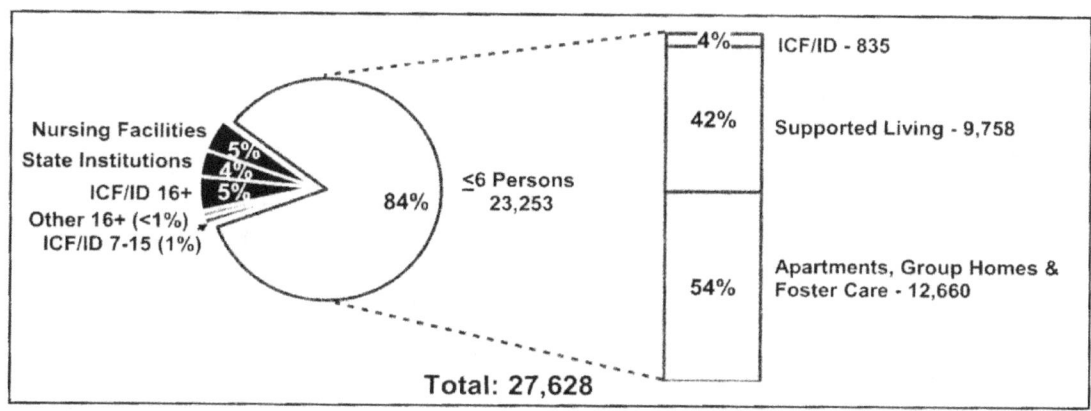

RHODE ISLAND
PUBLIC I/DD SPENDING BY REVENUE SOURCE: FY 2013

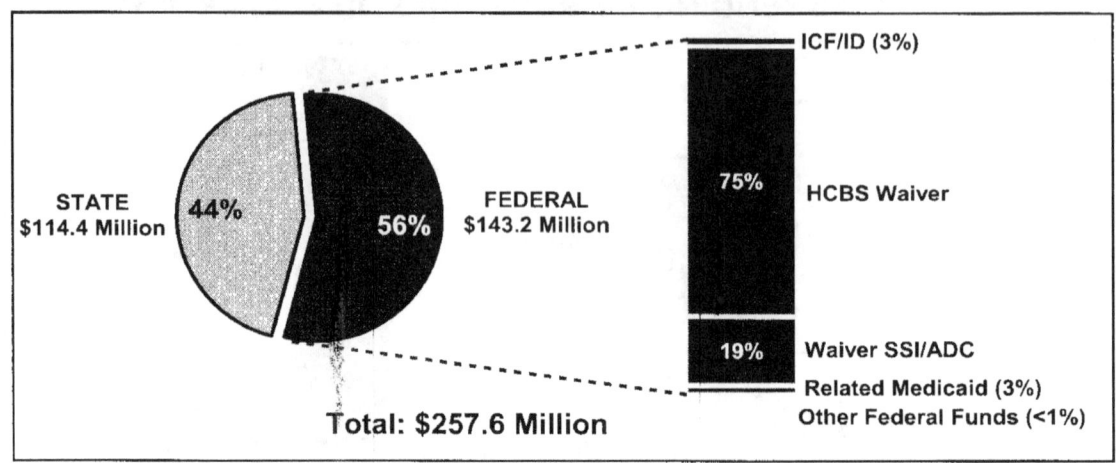

RHODE ISLAND
PERSONS BY SETTING IN FISCAL YEAR 2013

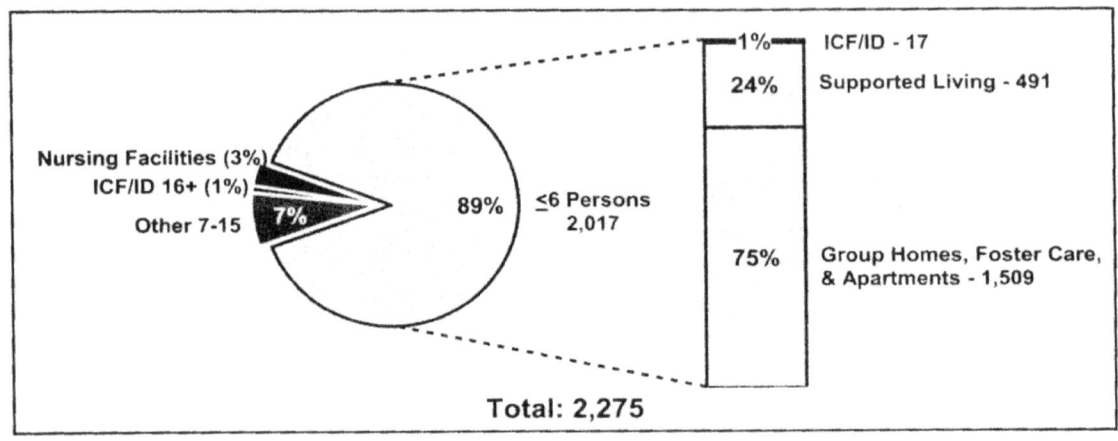

SOUTH CAROLINA
PUBLIC I/DD SPENDING BY REVENUE SOURCE: FY 2013

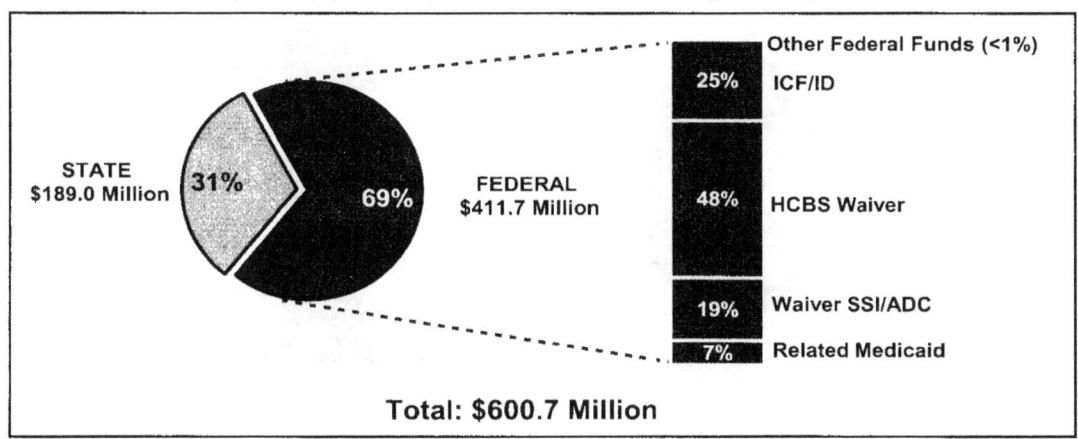

SOUTH CAROLINA
PERSONS BY SETTING IN FISCAL YEAR 2013

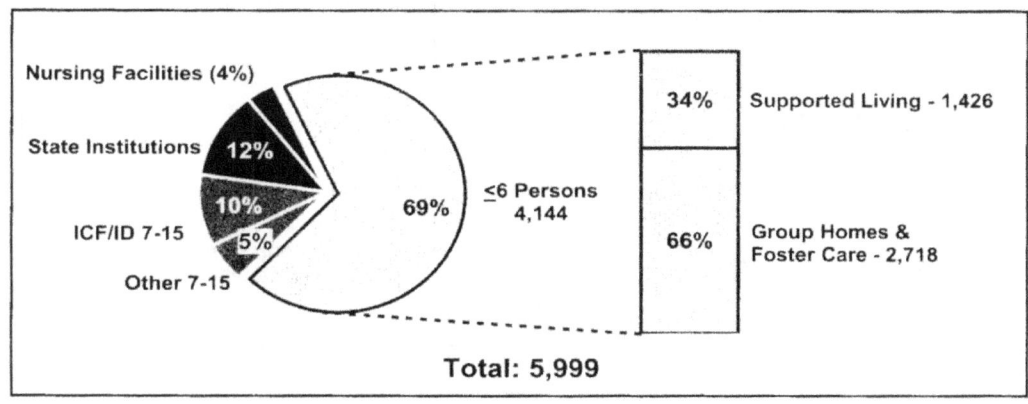

TENNESSEE
PUBLIC I/DD SPENDING BY REVENUE SOURCE: FY 2013

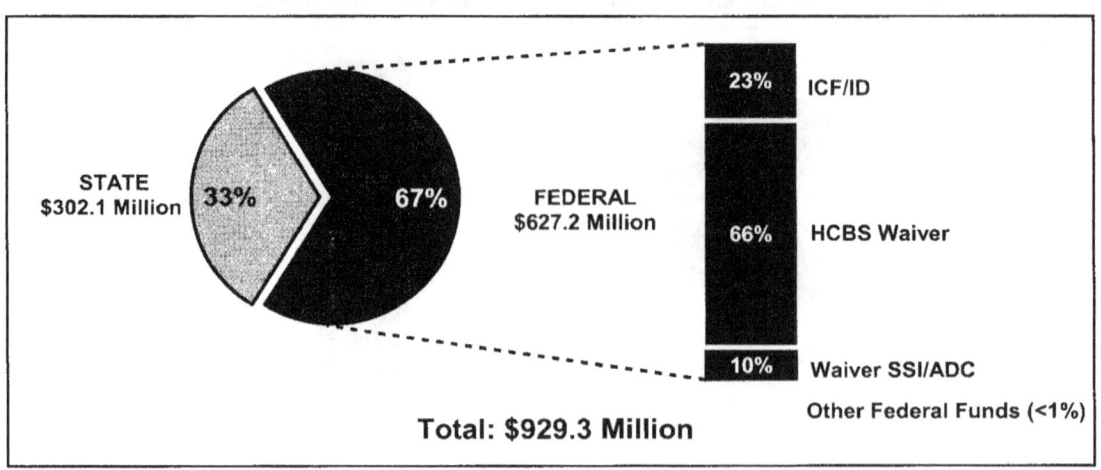

TENNESSEE
PERSONS BY SETTING IN FISCAL YEAR 2013

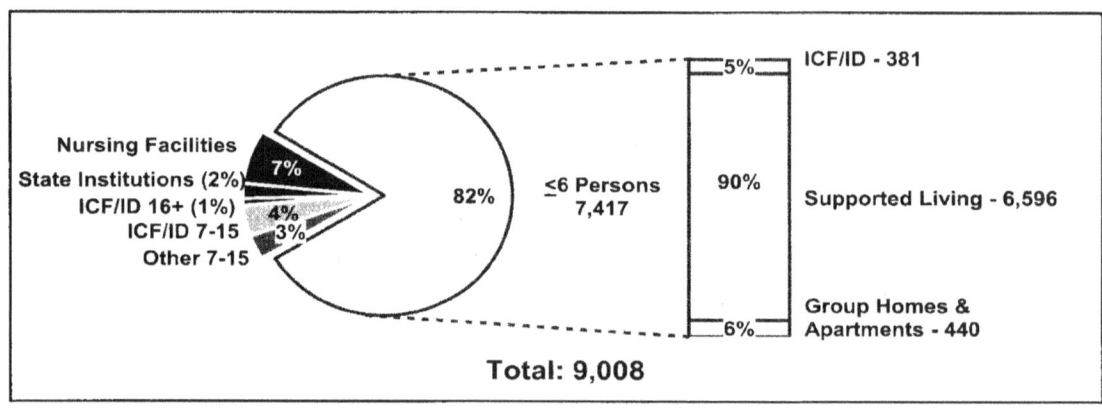

TEXAS
PUBLIC I/DD SPENDING BY REVENUE SOURCE: FY 2013

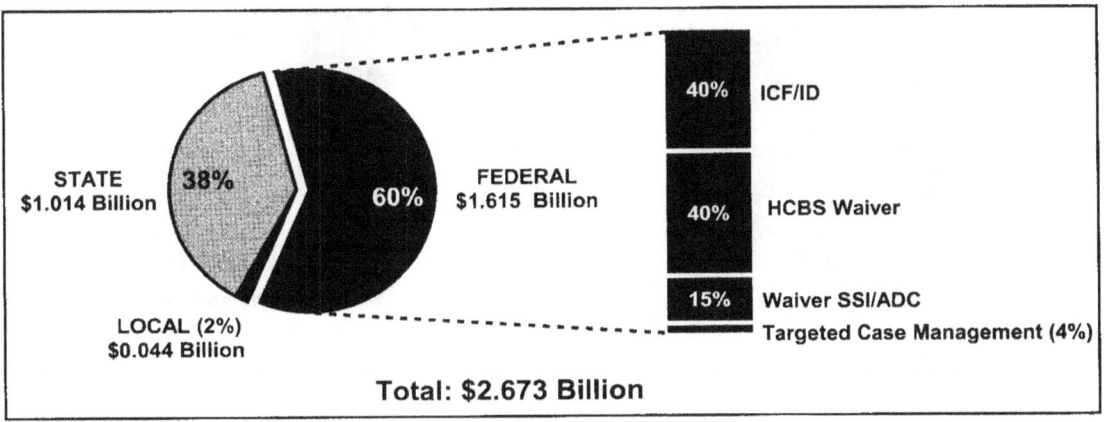

TEXAS
PERSONS BY SETTING IN FISCAL YEAR 2013*

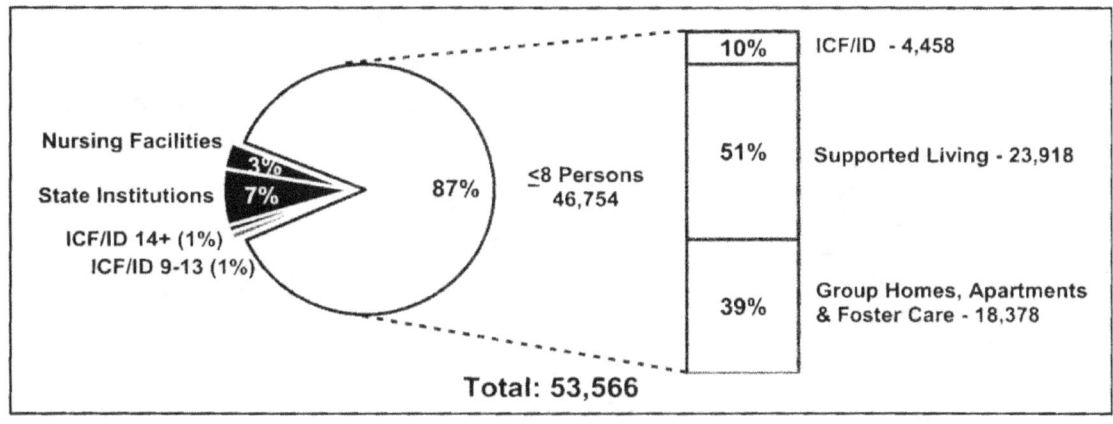

*Texas reported out-of-home placements in the following categories: 8 or fewer, 9-13 and 14+ persons.

UTAH

PUBLIC I/DD SPENDING BY REVENUE SOURCE: FY 2013

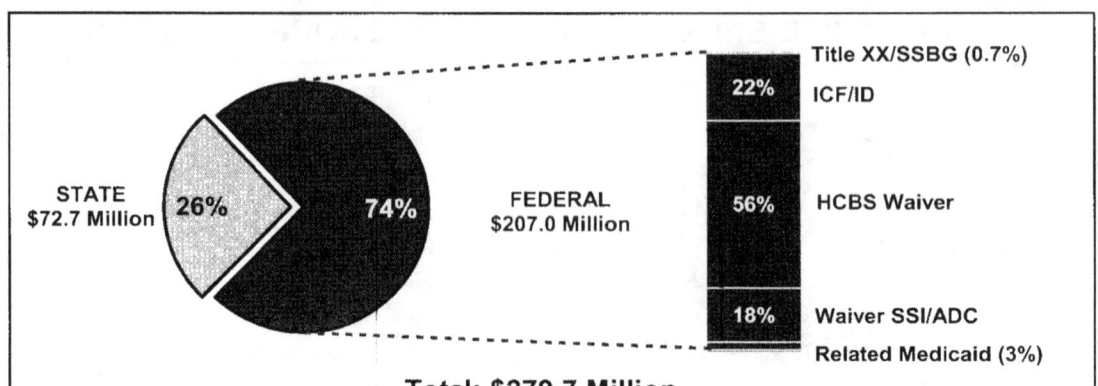

UTAH

PERSONS BY SETTING IN FISCAL YEAR 2013

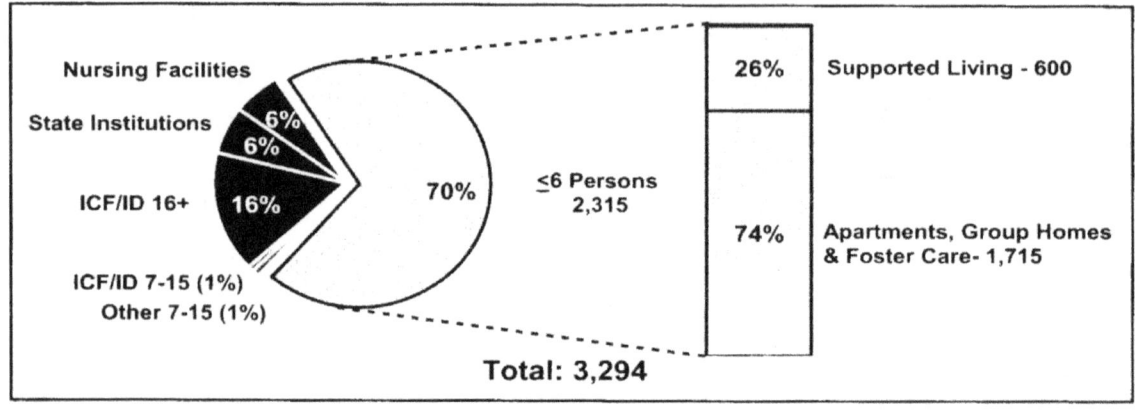

VERMONT
PUBLIC I/DD SPENDING BY REVENUE SOURCE: FY 2013

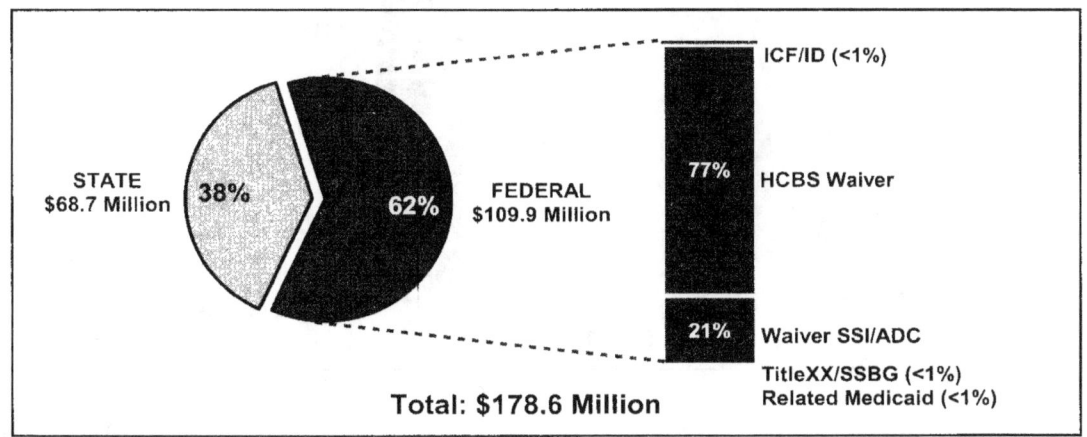

VERMONT
PERSONS BY SETTING IN FISCAL YEAR 2013

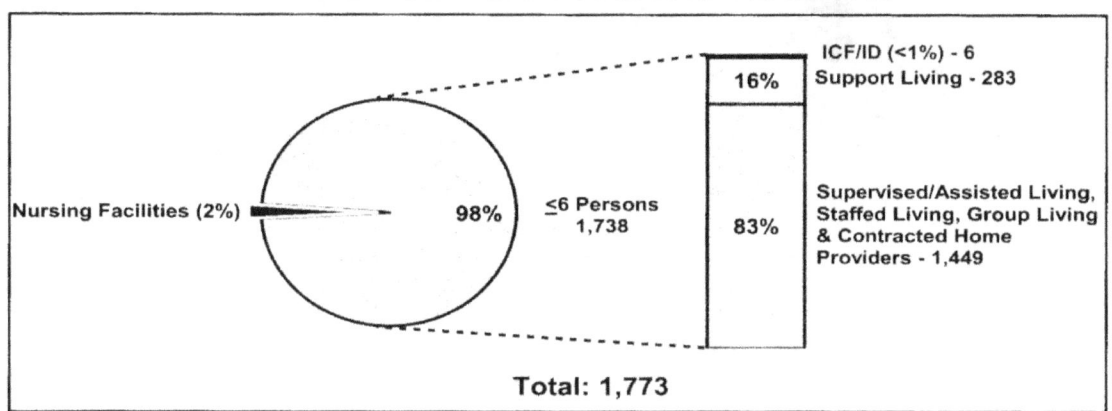

VIRGINIA

PUBLIC I/DD SPENDING BY REVENUE SOURCE: FY 2013

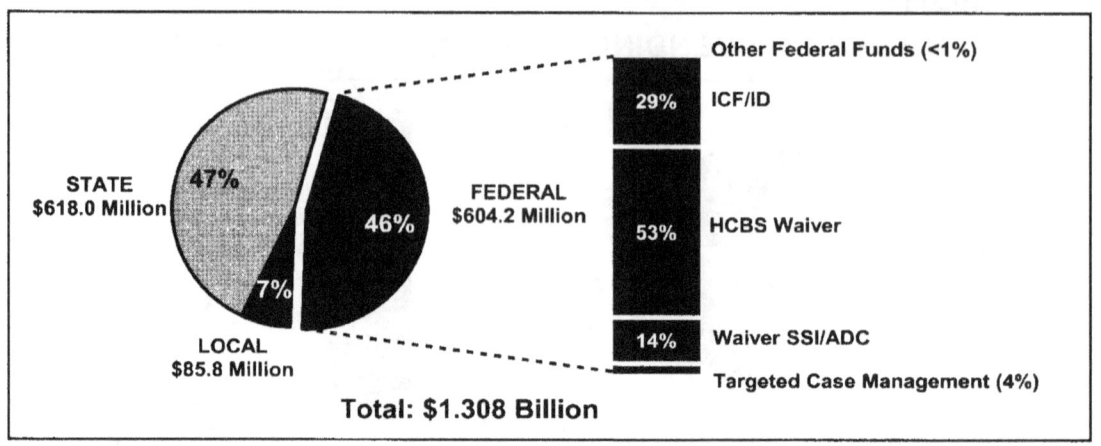

VIRGINIA

PERSONS BY SETTING IN FISCAL YEAR 2013

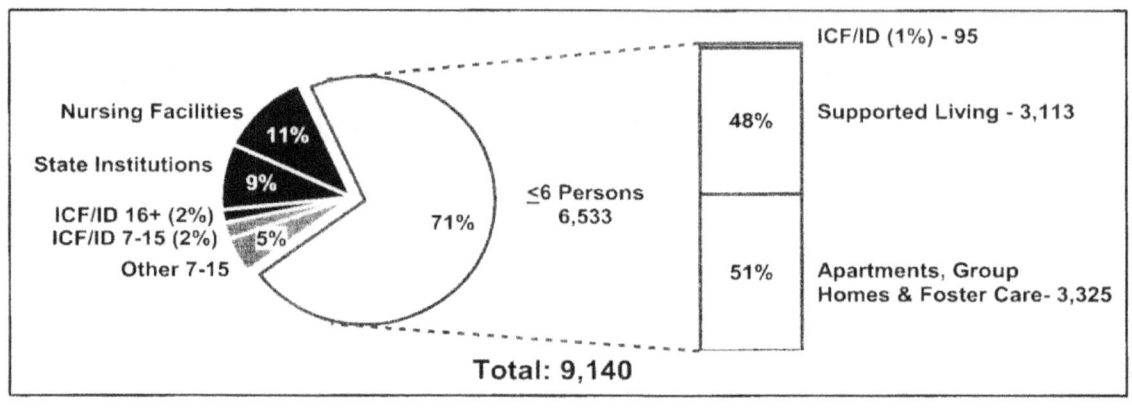

WASHINGTON
PUBLIC I/DD SPENDING BY REVENUE SOURCE: FY 2013

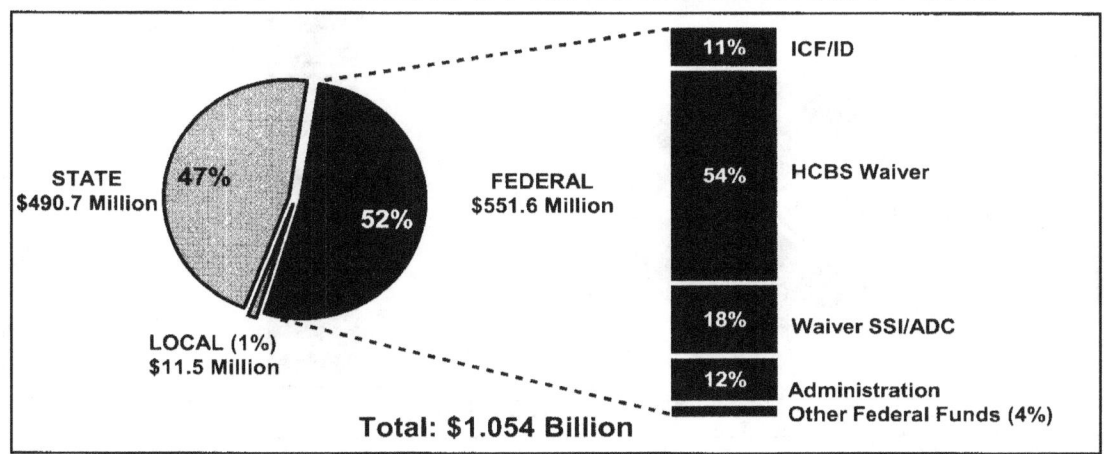

WASHINGTON
PERSONS BY SETTING IN FISCAL YEAR 2013

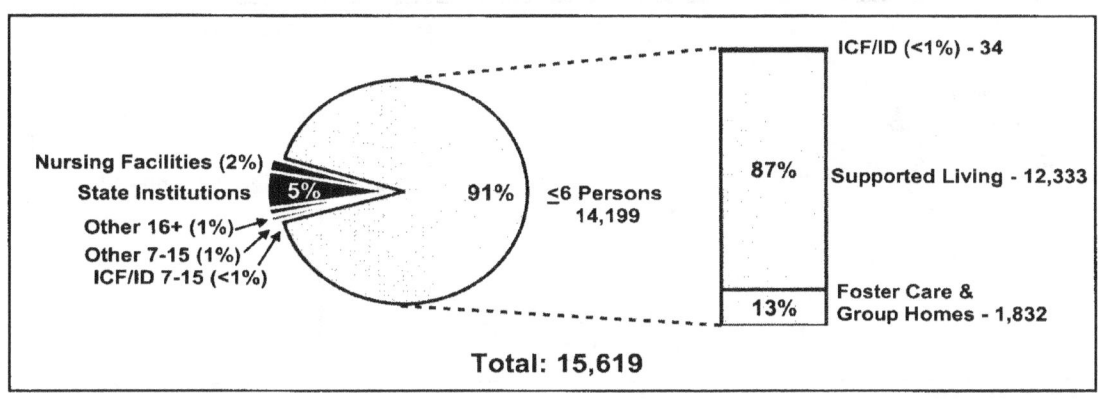

WEST VIRGINIA
PUBLIC I/DD SPENDING BY REVENUE SOURCE: FY 2013

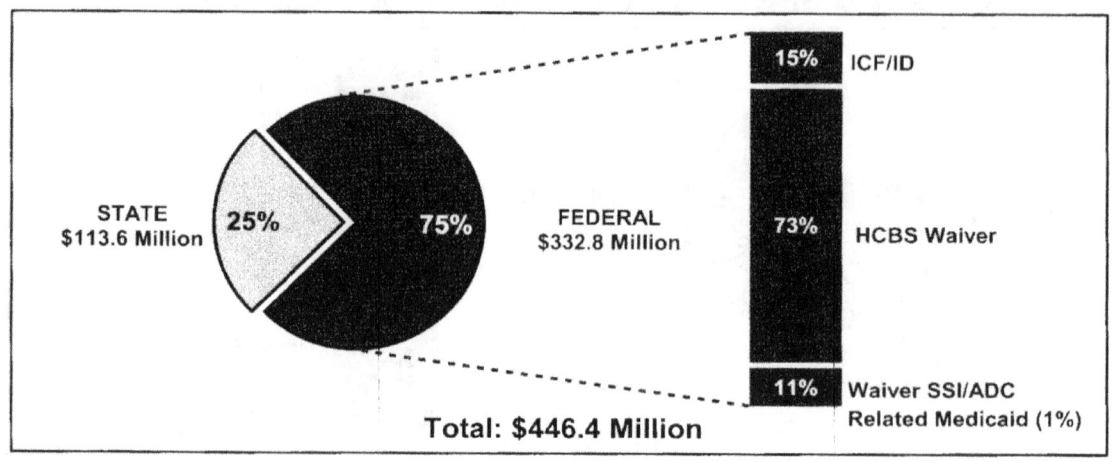

WEST VIRGINIA
PERSONS BY SETTING IN FISCAL YEAR 2013

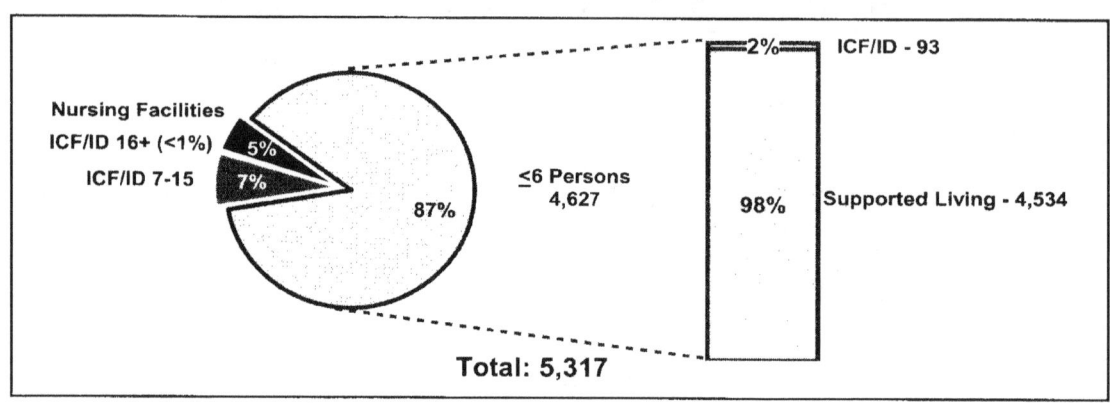

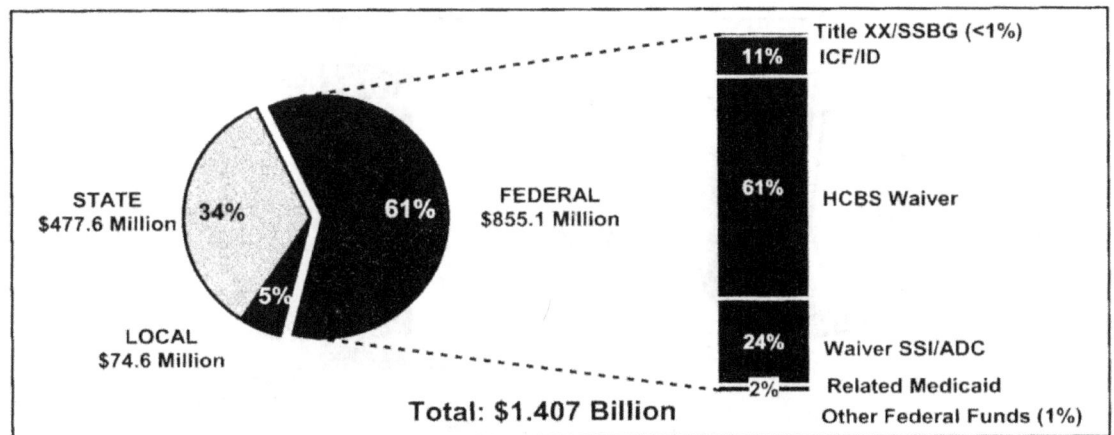
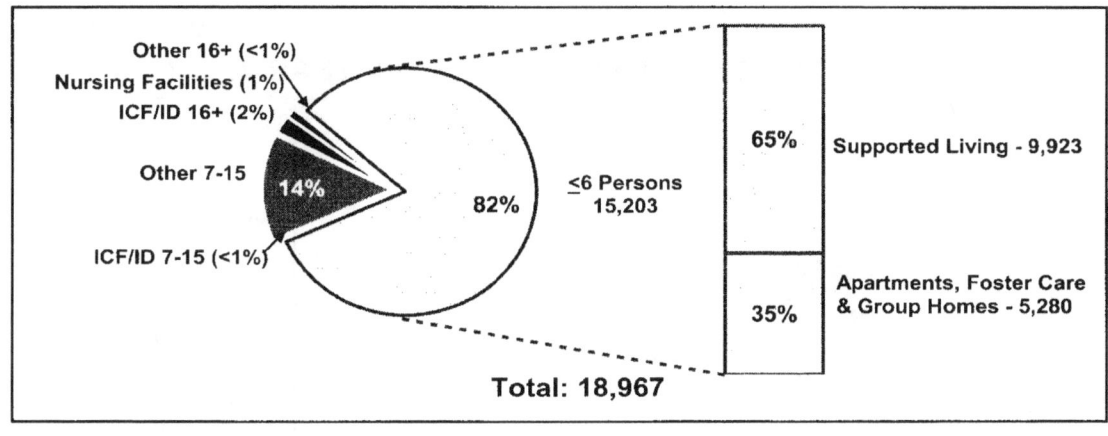

WYOMING
PUBLIC I/DD SPENDING BY REVENUE SOURCE: FY 2013

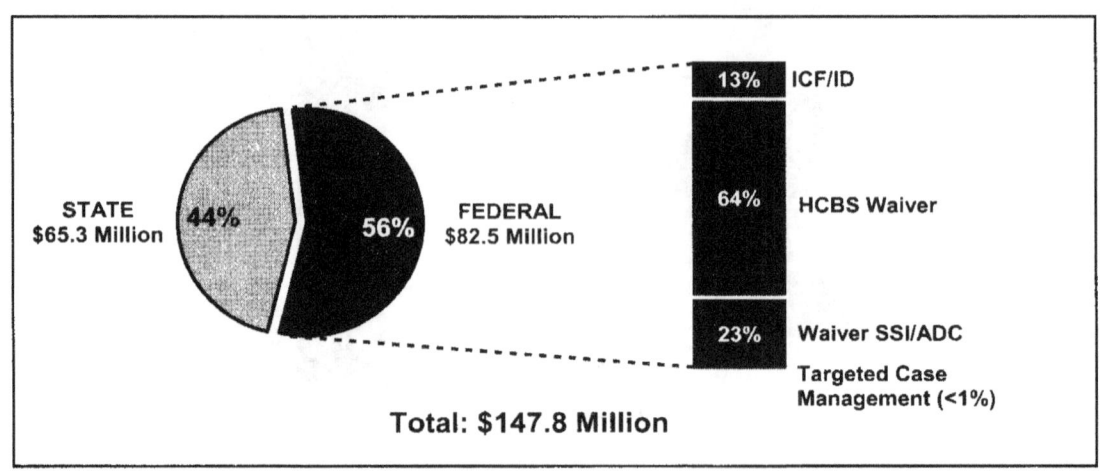

WYOMING
PERSONS BY SETTING IN FISCAL YEAR 2013

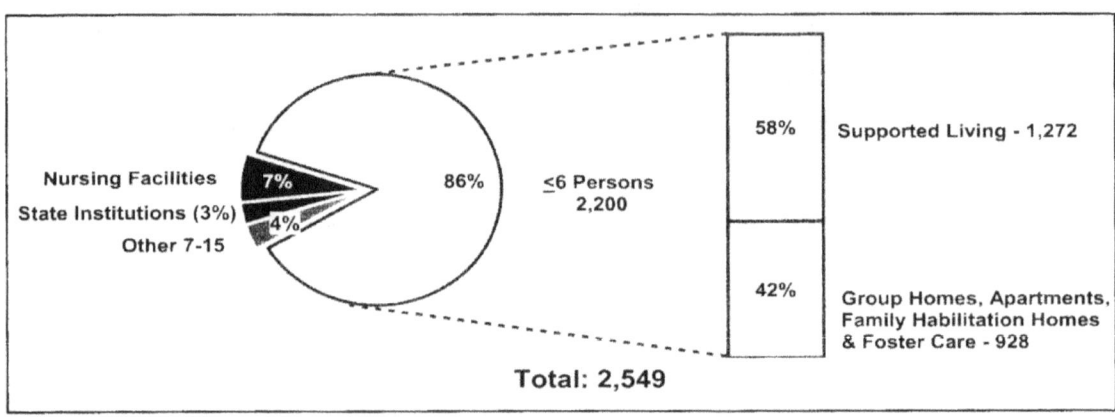

IDD Funding Budget in United States

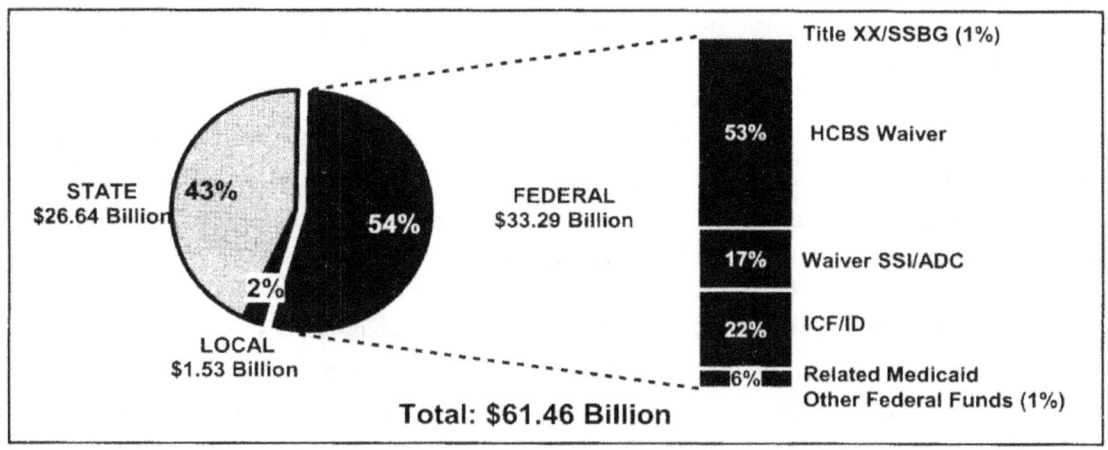

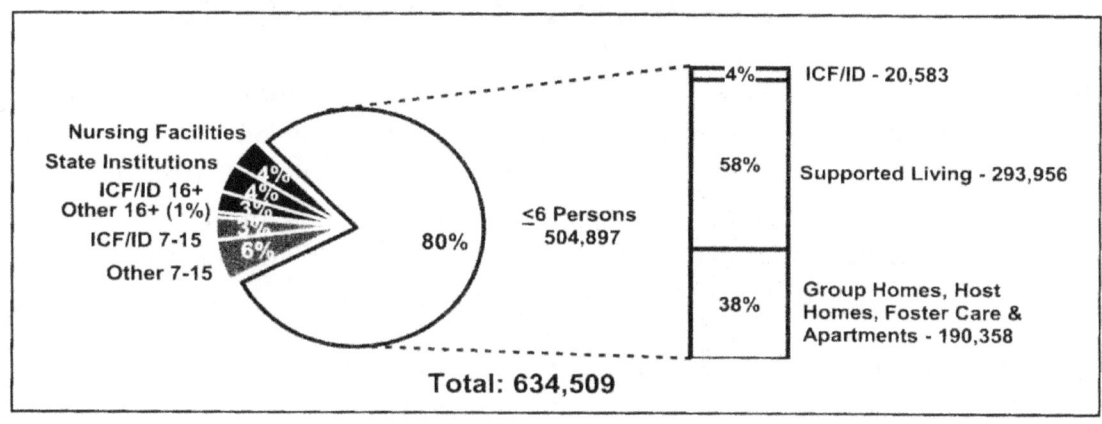

What is Applied Behavior Analysis (ABA)?

Behavior analysis focuses on the principles that explain how learning takes place. Positive reinforcement is one such principle. When a behavior is followed by some sort of reward, the behavior is more likely to be repeated. Through decades of research, the field of behavior analysis has developed many techniques for increasing useful behaviors and reducing those that may cause harm or interfere with learning.

Applied behavior analysis (ABA) is the use of these techniques and principles to bring about meaningful and positive change in behavior.

Behavior analysts began working with young children with autism and related disorders in the 1960s. Early techniques often involved adults directing most of the instruction. Some allowed the child to take the lead. Since that time, a wide variety of ABA techniques have been developed for building useful skills in learners with autism – from toddlers through adulthood.

These techniques can be used in structured situations such as a classroom lesson as well as in "everyday" situations such as family dinnertime or the neighborhood playground. Some ABA therapy sessions involve one-on-one interaction between the behavior analyst and the participant. Group instruction can likewise prove useful.

How Does ABA Benefit Those with Autism?

Today, ABA is widely recognized as a safe and effective treatment for autism. It has been endorsed by a number of state and federal agencies, including the U.S. Surgeon General and the New York State Department of Health. Over the last decade, the nation has seen a particularly dramatic increase in the use of ABA to help persons with autism live happy and productive lives. In particular, ABA principles and techniques can foster basic skills such as looking, listening and imitating, as well as complex skills such as reading, conversing and understanding another person's perspective.

More information about behavior analysis and ABA is available at the websites of the *Association of Professional Behavior Analysts*, the *Association for Behavior Analysis International* and the *Behavior Analyst Certification Board*.

What Does Research Tell Us About ABA and Autism?

A number of completed studies have demonstrated that ABA techniques can produce improvements in communication, social relationships, play, self care, school and employment. These studies involved age groups ranging from preschoolers to adults. Results for all age groups showed that ABA increased participation in family and community activities.

A number of peer-reviewed studies have examined the potential benefits of combining multiple ABA techniques into comprehensive, individualized and intensive early intervention programs for children with autism. "Comprehensive" refers to interventions that address a full range of life skills, from communication and sociability to self-care and readiness for school. "Early intervention" refers to programs designed to begin before age 4. "Intensive" refers to programs that total 25 to 40 hours per week for 1 to 3 years.

The studies can be accessed via the following link:

https://www.ncbi.nlm.nih.gov/pubmed?term=autism%20%22applied%20behavior%20analysis%22%20OR%20%22early%20start%20denver%20model%22

These programs allow children to learn and practice skills in both structured and unstructured situations. The "intensity" of these programs may be particularly important to replicate the thousands of interactions that typical toddlers experience each day while interacting with their parents and peers.

Such studies have demonstrated that many children with autism experience significant improvements in learning, reasoning, communication and adaptability when they participate in high-quality ABA programs. Some preschoolers who participate in early intensive ABA for two or more years acquire sufficient skills to participate in regular classrooms with little or no additional support. Other children learn many important skills, but still need additional educational support to succeed in a classroom.

Across studies, a small percentage of children show relatively little improvement. More research is needed to determine why some children with autism respond more favorably to early intensive ABA than others do. Currently, it remains difficult to predict the extent to which a particular child will benefit.

In some studies, researchers compared intensive ABA with less intensive ABA and/or other early intervention or special education programs for children with autism. Generally, they found that children who receive intensive ABA treatment make larger improvements in more skill areas than do children who participate in other interventions. In addition, the parents of the children who receive intensive ABA report greater reductions in daily stress than do parents whose children receive other treatments.

ABA and Adults with Autism

A number of recent studies confirm that ABA techniques are effective for building important life skills in teens and adults with autism. Many comprehensive autism support programs for adults employ and combine ABA techniques to help individuals transition successfully into independent living and employment. However, the benefits of intensive ABA programs remain far less studied in teens and adults than they have been with young children. This is a research area of particular interest to Autism Speaks and its supporters.

These studies can be accessed via the following link:

https://www.ncbi.nlm.nih.gov/pubmed/20160648

What Does ABA Intervention Involve?

Effective ABA intervention for autism is not a "one size fits all" approach and should never be viewed as a "canned" set of programs or drills. On the contrary, a skilled therapist customizes the intervention to each learner's skills, needs, interests, preferences and family situation. For these reasons, an ABA program for one learner will look different than a program for another learner. That said, quality ABA programs for learners with autism have the following in common:

Planning and Ongoing Assessment

- A qualified and trained behavior analyst designs and directly oversees the intervention.
- The analyst's development of treatment goals stems from a detailed assessment of each learner's skills and preferences and may also include family goals.
- Treatment goals and instruction are developmentally appropriate and target a broad range of skill areas such as communication, sociability, self-care, play and leisure, motor development and academic skills.
- Goals emphasize skills that will enable learners to become independent and successful in both the short and long terms.
- The instruction plan breaks down desired skills into manageable steps to be taught from the simplest (e.g. imitating single sounds) to the more complex (e.g. carrying on a conversation).
- The intervention involves ongoing objective measurement of the learner's progress.
- The behavior analyst frequently reviews information on the learner's progress and uses this to adjust procedures and goals as needed.
- The analyst meets regularly with family members and program staff to plan ahead, review progress and make adjustments as needed.

ABA Techniques and Philosophy

- The instructor uses a variety of behavior analytic procedures, some of which are directed by the instructor and others initiated by the learner.
- Parents and/or other family members and caregivers receive training so they can support learning and skill practice throughout the day.
- The learner's day is structured to provide many opportunities – both planned and naturally occurring - to acquire and practice skills in both structured and unstructured situations.
- The learner receives an abundance of positive reinforcement for demonstrating useful skills and socially appropriate behaviors. The emphasis is on positive social interactions and enjoyable learning.
- The learner receives no reinforcement for behaviors that pose harm or prevent learning.

What Kind of Progress Can Be Expected with ABA?

Competently delivered ABA intervention can help learners with autism make meaningful changes in many areas. However, changes do not typically occur quickly. Rather, most learners require intensive and ongoing instruction that builds on their step-by-step progress. Moreover, the rate of progress – like the goals of intervention – varies considerably from person to person depending on age, level of functioning, family goals and other factors.

Some learners do acquire skills quickly. But typically, this rapid progress happens in just one or two particular skill areas such as reading, while much more instruction and practice is needed to master another skill area such as interacting with peers.

Who Is Qualified to Provide ABA Intervention?

Just as a medical treatment program should be directed by a qualified medical professional, ABA programs for learners with autism should be designed and supervised by qualified professionals, which include either licensed clinical psychologists with training in applied behavior analysis or behavior analysts, who are board certified with supervised experience providing ABA treatment for autism or who can clearly document that they have equivalent training and experience.

Because of the huge demand for ABA intervention for autism, many individuals and programs now claim to provide ABA. Some are private practitioners or agencies that offer services in a family's home. Others operate private schools. And still others provide consultation services to public schools. Unfortunately, some who claim to offer ABA lack the field's established minimum requirements in education and practical experience. Family members, teachers and others involved in developing an individual's therapy and support program should keep the following in mind when choosing an ABA program or practitioner:

Always check credentials of those who claim to be qualified in behavior analysis. For example, for licensed clinical psychologists, you should inquire about the level of training in behavioral interventions for autism, including training in applied behavior analysis. For behavior analysts, you should determine whether the person has been credentialed with the *Behavior Analyst Certification Board* or the *Association of Professional Behavior Analysts*. These professionals often supervise other people, including paraprofessionals, who will be working directly with your child. Thus, it is important that you feel confident that the licensed clinical psychologist or behavior analyst is providing regular supervision to anyone working directly with your child. Parents, guardians and other care givers should monitor the program by observing sessions and participating in training sessions and consultations.

The Best & Worst States to live in to get ABA

IMORTANT NOTE: *This article compares states by their autism insurance coverage laws. It does not take into account school district and other autism services.*

The following article (study) was produced by the Mental Health & Autism Health Insurance Project in 2015. The Mental Health & Autism Health Insurance Project is a nonprofit organization that helps families and providers secure insurance coverage for interventions related to autism and mental health disorders. On a sliding scale fee, the act on behalf of families, filing appeals and grievances with health plans and state regulators in order to secure coverage of all needed treatments entitled by law.

Certain states have passed strong laws requiring insurers to cover autism treatments, while other states have not. A smaller number of states have gone a step further and required that intensive autism treatments be a required benefit in Affordable Care Act plans sold on the state exchange. And finally, while the federal government has told states that their Medicaid programs must offer ABA therapy for children under 21, so far only a handful of states have put this directive into action. Read on to see how your state fares.

As of 2015 forty two states mandated some degree of insurance coverage of autism treatments, however five states in the nation had no such laws or plans to introduce laws which allow people with autism to access medically necessary treatments. As of 2015 the worst states to live in if you have a child with autism are: Alabama, Idaho, North Dakota, Oklahoma and Wyoming.

Ohio, Tennessee and North Carolina were on the list but they have since either introduced autism health insurance legislation or are in the process of doing so. If you live in a state without a benefit, the only way to receive ABA is to work for an employer that voluntarily offers the benefit, or to obtain it through the school district, which frequently involves a protracted legal fight.

Important Side Note: There is a significant difference in the amount of ABA services, funding, and assistance provided by school districts. A city with many districts will typically have some or one district that is very favorable to autism students and ABA programs and others that would rate very poorly. Therefore, it is extremely important to research and pick the school district in which to live very carefully.

Utah, Hawaii, Mississippi, and Georgia passed favorable ABA legislation in 2016. However, all have opted out of offering the benefit through their exchanges.

16 STATES OFFERING ABA FOR MEDICAID FAMILIES

Very low-income families on Medicaid, despite their low socioeconomic status, may fare better in some states than their higher wage earning peers. In July 2014, the Centers for Medicaid and Medicare released guidance that ABA therapy must be offered to children under 21 across the nation, as part of the federal statute Early Periodic Screening Diagnosis and Treatment. This is a huge boon to low-income families impacted by autism as well as children who may qualify for Medicaid based on the degree of their disability. CMS has stressed that care must not be denied or delayed, and has suggested that all states must be in compliance by 2019.

As of 2015, California, Connecticut, Florida, Louisiana, Massachusetts, New Mexico, Oregon, Pennsylvania, Rhode Island, South Carolina, Vermont, Virginia and Washington are offering or in final stages of establishing EPSDT services for autism treatments through their Medicaid programs. Washington D.C. offers some ABA through Medicaid with age limits, as does Michigan to age 6. Some of this coverage has been the result of litigation. Some states offer behavior intervention through Medicaid waivers, which waive traditional income requirements, rather than due to the recent Federal directive. Connecticut's implementations is questionable, as autism advocates argue that the state's strict requirements—such as requiring a licensed caregiver to be present at all times during treatment-create too high a barrier to access. Tennessee's Tenncare offers ABA, but require BCBA's (board certified behavior analysts) only, not line therapist, which makes it nearly impossible to implement. South Carolina has begun offering the benefit but there are problems with implementation. West Virginia is technically offering the benefit but obstacles exist to getting providers on board. Some states have only been able to offer it in limited geographic locales, implementation for Medicaid through EPSDT in other states is a moving target. A number of states including Texas, New York, Utah, Montana and Georgia are in implementation discussions with their state Medicaid departments. Still other states are handling claims on a case by case basis or providing some coverage through Managed Care Organizations. Improved and more formalized coverage will likely occur in the coming year but will require sustained and consistent efforts. Autism Speaks has taken an active role in advocating for full and prompt compliance with EPSDT coverage requirements. Kids on Medicaid are entitled to medically necessary treatments under the law regardless of what state they happen to live in.

STATES OFFERING ABA ON AFFORDABLE CARE ACT PLANS

As of 2015 a total of 29 states have passed autism insurance mandates requiring private insurers to offer ABA therapy in state regulated plans. These states are Alaska, Arizona, Arkansas, California, Colorado, Connecticut, Delaware, Illinois, Indiana, Kentucky, Louisiana, Maine, Maryland, Massachusetts, Michigan, Missouri, Montana, Nevada, New Hampshire, New Jersey, New Mexico, New York, Ohio, Oregon, Texas, Vermont, West Virginia, Washington Wisconsin, and Minnesota.

SIDE NOTE: At the time of this publication, the Trump administration is preparing to greatly improve funding, health care, and service options for children and adults with special needs.

Among the states, some laws mandate treatment without limitation, while others set age caps, limits on hours per week, and annual financial limits. Maine, for example, only requires insurers to provide the behavioral therapy Applied Behavior Analysis (ABA) until a child is 10-years-old, -- this represents improvement over their initial law, which mandated services until age 6. Nebraska has capped the hours of ABA at 25 per week. The status of these limits is somewhat in flux, however, as the ACA prohibits financial limitations on essential health benefits and other limits are increasingly being challenged and in many cases withdrawn in light of state and federal mental health parity requirements. Also, several state legislatures have recently or are in the process of expanding their mandates to treat children up to an older age, to provide more hours, or cover the individual market. (Kansas, Maine, South Carolina, Virginia). Many states only mandate ABA for employers with more than 50 employees. The specifics of the mandates differ in each state.

BEST ABA STATES FOR AUTISM

Of the 29 states listed above, California, Massachusetts, Oregon, and Washington hold the distinction of the best ABA states to live in if you have a child with autism. Each of these states:

1. Mandates ABA with no age cap, visit or financial limits.
2. Offer the ABA benefit on their ACA plans
3. Has an ABA benefit for Medicaid through EPSDT.

NOTES:
- EPSDT - Early and Periodic Screening, Diagnostic and Treatment (**EPSDT**) is the child health component of Medicaid. Federal statutes and regulations state that children under age 21 who are enrolled in Medicaid are entitled to **EPSDT** benefits and that States must cover a broad array of preventive and treatment services.
- Unfortunately, there are often bureaucratic and administrative obstacles to accessing benefits; however these states have the best laws in place with regards to insurance.

| Best Worst ABA States in Year 2015 ||
BEST STATES	WORST STATES
California	Alabama
Massachussetts	Idaho
Oregon	North Dakota
	Oklahoma
Washington	Wyoming
	Tennessee

SO-SO ABA STATES

The remaining states have passed autism health insurance mandates requiring private insurers to offer ABA therapy. The states are Kansas, Minnesota, Iowa, Pennsylvania, Florida, South Carolina, Mississippi, Georgia, Hawaii and Virginia. In some of these states (Florida, Pennsylvania, South Carolina), the mandate only applies to state-regulated plans with 50 or more employees.

The latest numbers (2015) from the Centers for Disease Control and Prevention report that 1 in 45 children (ages 3 through 17) have an autism spectrum disorder (ASD). This number is up from 1 in 88 children in 2012. Applied Behavior Analysis is still the strongest, evidence-based treatment proven to make a difference in children with autism. Without these therapies, states will pay more and pay later, by missing the early intervention window to maximize potential. States that have passed autism health insurance mandates and chosen to offer ABA in their health exchanges and through Medicaid are to be commended.

States with ABA Benefits in Exchange

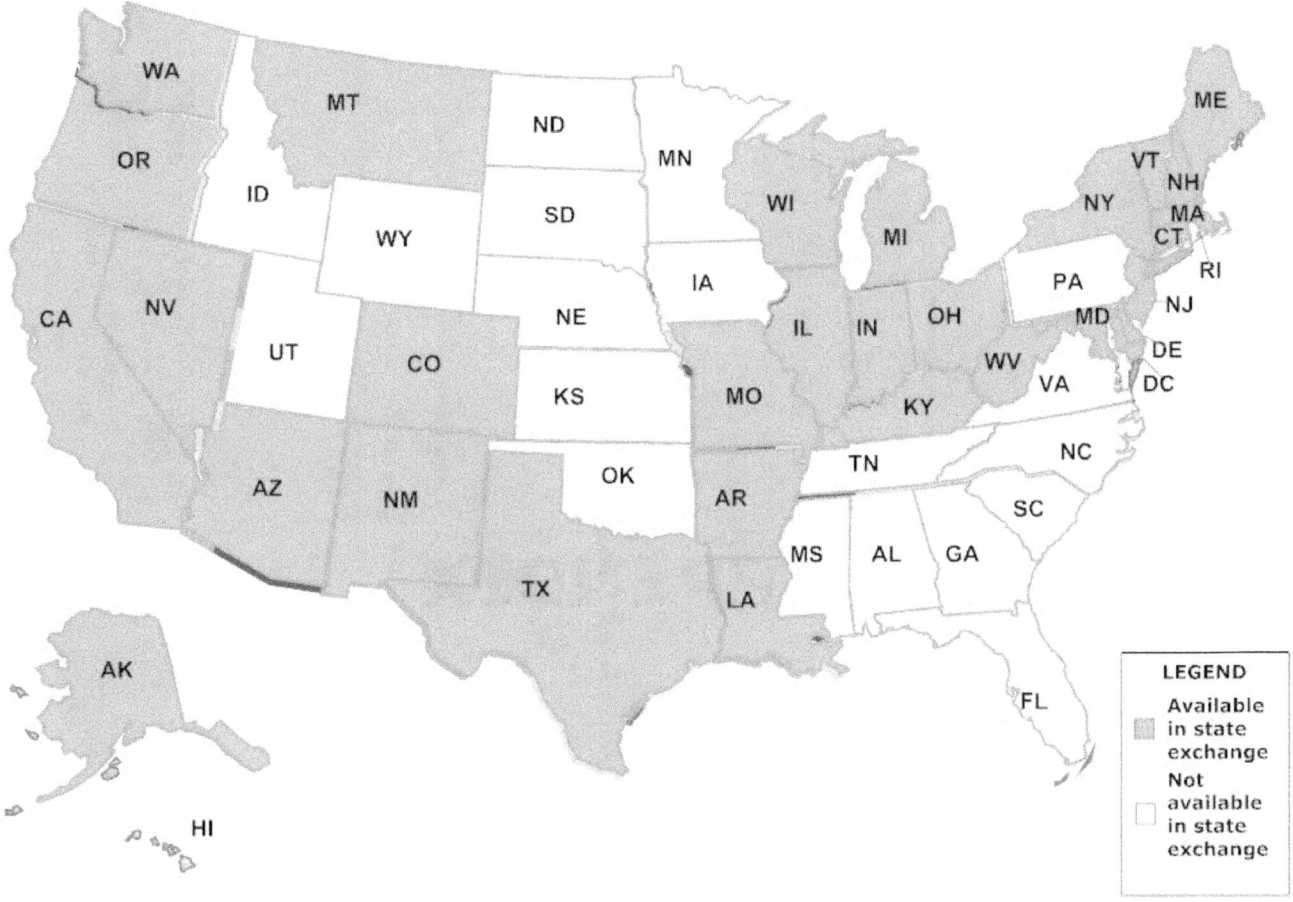

http://www.autismhealthinsurance.org/the-best-worst-states-to-live-in-if-you-have-a-child-with-autism

APPENDIX

APPENDIX 1

Aquaponics

Please be sure to read the author's other books on the subject of 'Aquaponics'. The book offering the most comprehensive overview and specific "how-to" instructions available on the market is **"Aquaponic Design Plans & Everything You Need to Know from Backyard to Profitable Business"** by David H. Dudley.

Aquaponics is the marriage of aquaculture (raising fish) and hydroponics (the soil-less growing of plants) that grows fish and plants together in one integrated system. The fish waste provides a food source for the growing plants and the plants provide a natural filter for the water the fish live in.

The result is environmentally-friendly grown organic food. Aquaponics provides yields much greater, with higher nutrient density, and uses 95% less water than traditional agriculture.

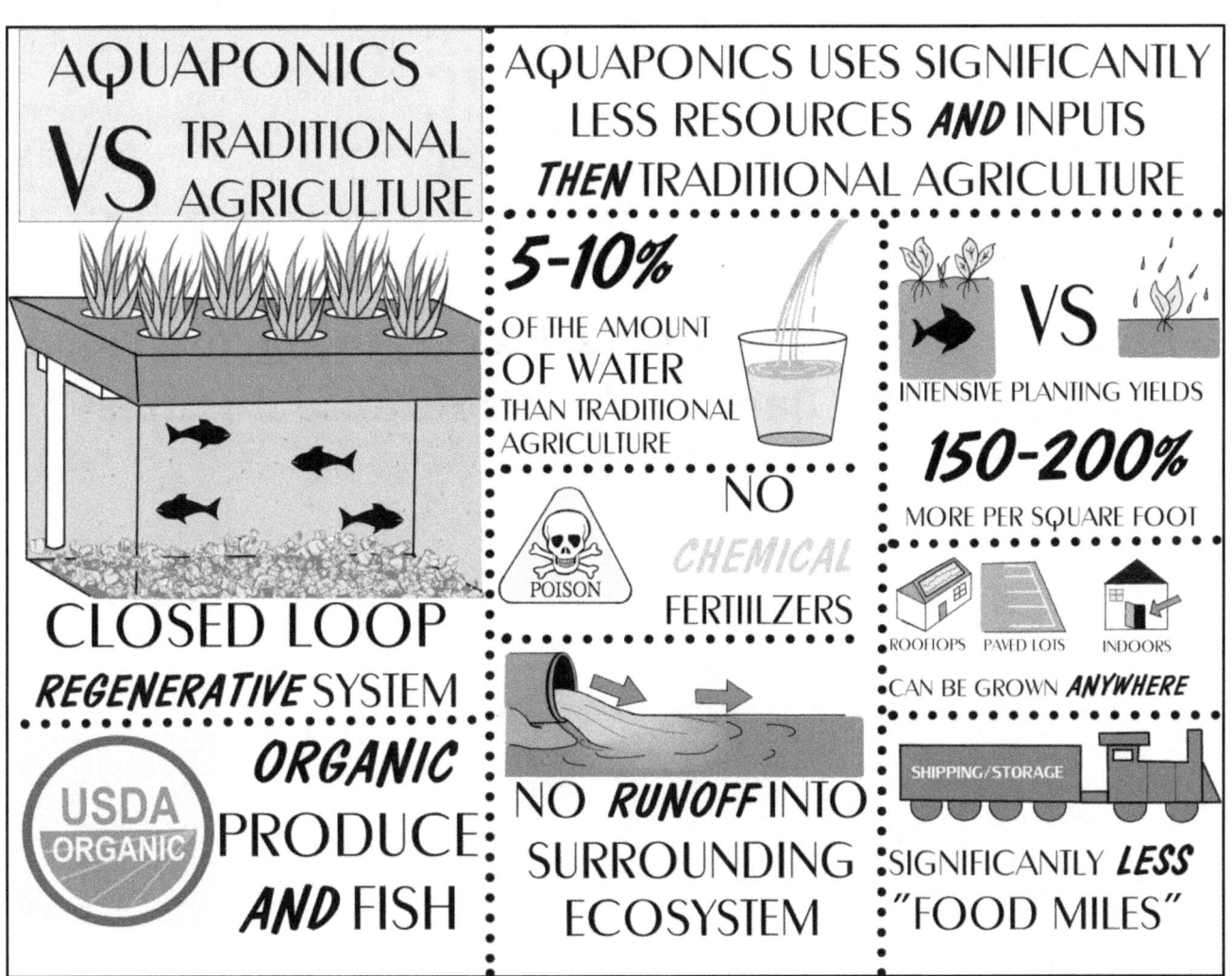

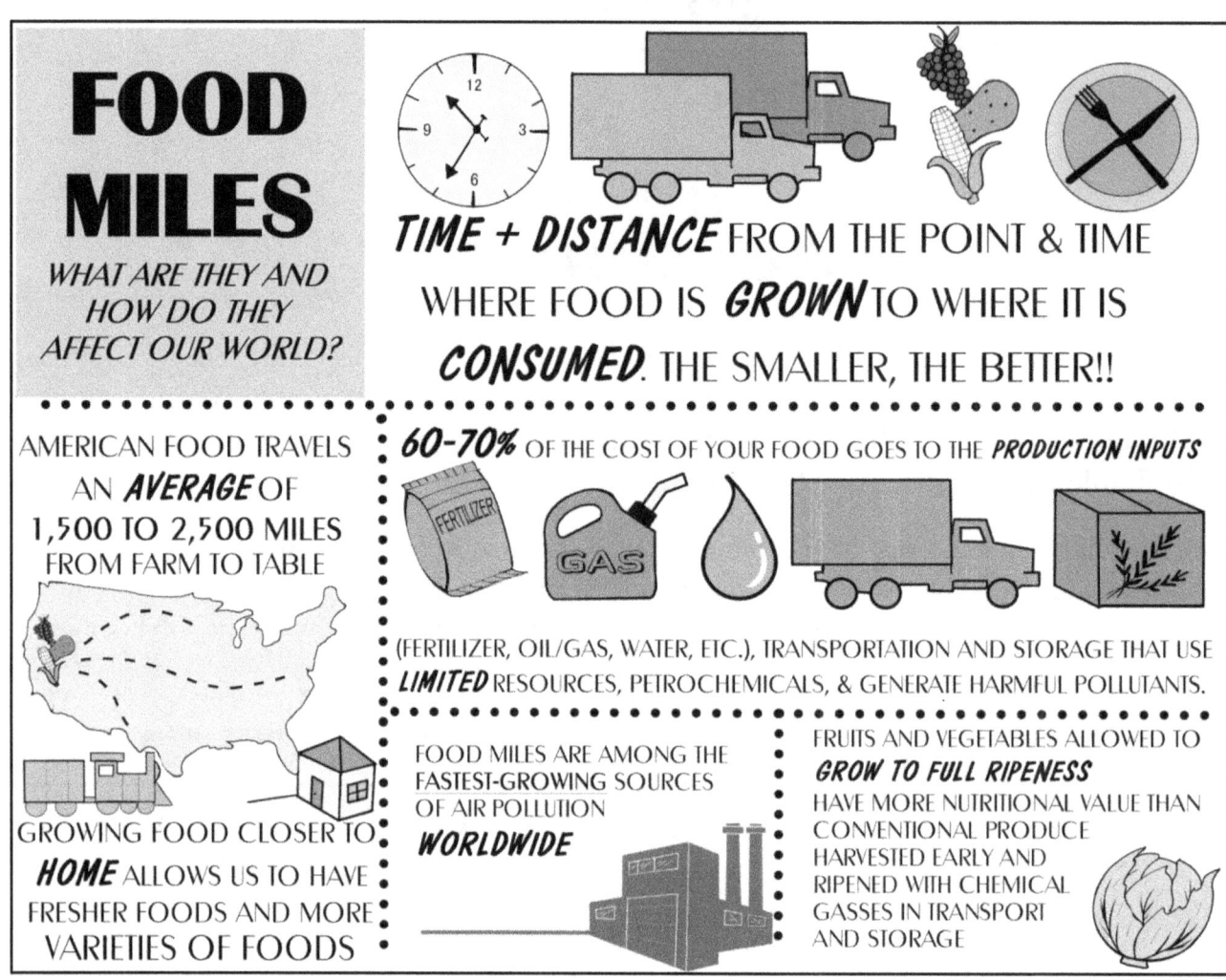

"Aquaponic Design Plans & Everything You Need to Know from Backyard to Profitable Business"

by David H. Dudley

Aquaponics
How to Do Everything
From Backyard to Profitable Business

- Fresh Organic Vegetables and Plentiful Healthy Fish
- Feed Your Family Healthy Low Cost Food, Barter and/or Sell Surplus
- Beginning Basics to Operating a Profitable Commercial Business
- Everything You Need to Know

Expensive university courses and lengthy on-site training workshops that cost thousands of dollars do not provide as much valuable, comprehensive material, as presented in this a user-friendly 'how-to' book.

This 550+ page book (how-to-guide) consists of three very important sections:

- Everything You Need to Know About Aquaponics
- How to Set-Up & Operate an Aquaponic System of Any Size
- How to Successfully Operate a Profitable Commercial Aquaponics Business

Within these sections you will be provided everything you need to know, in an understandable, easy to follow approach; so that you can enjoy environmentally-friendly sustainable farming, consistently feed your family plentiful healthy organic lost cost food, and earn as much extra income as desired (the sky really is the limit). Best of all, this book will show you how to accomplish these objectives in the most efficient way possible. Aquaponics truly is a worthwhile and rewarding endeavor

APPENDIX 2

Aquaponic Design Plans

Aquaponic Design Plans
Everything You Need to Know
from
Backyard to Profitable Business
2nd EDITION

David H. Dudley, PE

Aquaponic Design Plans, Instructions & All You Need to Know

- Fresh Organic Produce and Plentiful Healthy Fish
- Feed Your Family Healthy Food + Barter and/or Sell Surplus
- Everything from Beginner Basics to Operating a Profitable Aquaponic Business

Expensive university courses and lengthy on-site training workshops which cost thousands of dollars do not provide as much valuable, comprehensive material as presented in this comprehensive user-friendly 'how-to' book.

This 534-page book provides detailed directions to create and maintain different types of aquaponic systems of all sizes so you can consistently feed your family environmentally friendly sustainable healthy organic food and earn extra income. This valuable how-to resource consists of three important sections:

- Design Plans, Instructions & Everything You Need to Know About Aquaponics
- How to Set up & Operate different types of Aquaponic Systems of any Size
- How to Turn Aquaponics Into a Profitable Venture

APPENDIX 3

Aquaponics for Profit

Aquaponics for Profit

- What are the best methods for making money with aquaponics?
- Which edible aquaponic fish species will generate the most revenue per pound?
- Which aquaponic vegetables provide the highest profit margin?
- Which fish and vegetables are in highest demand by consumers?
- Do you know about all of the non-vegetable plants that can provide you with greater revenue than vegetable plants?
- What costs are involved in setting-up and operating an aquaponic system?
- What is the cost-benefit analysis of an aquaponic system?
- Where and how can I sell my aquaponic harvest?
- What regulations and legalities are involved in setting-up and operating an aquaponic business?
- Did you know that there are other aquatic species that can be grown in aquaponics which can generate more revenue than the commonly grown edible aquaponic fish species?
- What is the best way to barter my aquaponic harvest?
- How can I get my products officially labeled as 'organic'?
- What is the best approach to having a successful aquaponics business that will produce the largest profit margin?
- How can I earn extra money with my small backyard aquaponic system?
- Which type of aquaponic system – Media-Bed/Flood-and-Drain, Nutrient Film Technique (NFT), Raft System / Deep Water Culture (DWC) – is the most profitable?
- What are the pros and cons to each of these types of aquaponic systems?
- In addition to selling your harvest, are you aware of all the other ways in which you can earn revenue from your aquaponic system?
- How much time would I need to invest to have an aquaponic system that will feed my family and provide us with some extra income?

This user-friendly easy read book will answer the above a questions. This valuable resources is also packed with the necessary information that will not only show you how to make extra money with your aquaponic system, but to grow it into a successful commercial business; if that is your desire. **Also included are two real-world aquaponic business plans.** This book is an excellent investment that will reward you greatly with the knowledge needed to earn extra money through aquaponics or optimize revenue from a commercial aquaponic operation.

APPENDIX 4

Aquaponics Plans and Instructions

AQUAPONICS
PLANS AND INSTRUCTIONS
MEDIA-BED (FLOOD-AND-DRAIN) SYSTEMS

David H. Dudley, P.E.

AQUAPONICS PLANS AND INSTRUCTIONS
MEDIA-BED (FLOOD-AND-DRAIN) SYSTEMS

- Aquaponic Plans and Instuctions
- Fresh Organic Produce and Plentiful Healthy Fish
- An Abundance of Fish and Vegetables throughout the Year at a Very Low Cost
- User-Friendly Plans and Instructions from Beginner to Scaling-Up to Any Size
- Aquaponics is Fun and a Conversation Topic Others Find Very Interesting.
- An Excellent Investment with Tremendous Personal and Financial Rewards.

This 400+ page user-friendly book shows you how to easily produce an abundance of Fresh Organic Produce and Plentiful Healthy Fish through a Media-Bed (Flood-and-Drain) Aquaponic System; so you can:

Feed Your Family Healthy Organic Food, Barter and/or Sell Surplus, Substantially Lower Your Food Cost.

This VALUABLE resource has everything from Beginner Basics to showing you how to scale-up as you desire to grow your system. Easy to follow step-by-step Instructions and SO much more.

Expensive university courses and lengthy on-site training workshops which cost thousands of dollars do not provide as much valuable, comprehensive material as presented in this comprehensive user-friendly 'how-to' book.

Included are Media-Bed Design Plans, Instructions & Everything You Need to Know about Aquaponics.

Along with the instructions are over 350 photos and illustrations which show you how to set-up and operate a productive and successful media-bed aquaponic system of any size; and how to scale-up in size to produce even more organic vegetables and fish as you desire grow.

This book empowers you with the knowledge needed to consistently feed your family environmentally friendly sustainable healthy organic food and greatly lower your food bill. Fun, Financially Rewarding, Enjoyable, Healthy, and an Interesting Conversation Topic at social functions.

David H. Dudley is a professional aquaponics consultant who has helped many individuals and companies develop aquaponics systems. His accomplished career in aquaponics, hydroponics, and aquaculture includes serving as the Construction Manager of the Oklahoma Aquarium, Engineering Manager of the nation's largest caviar producing company, overseeing life support systems of four large aquaculture facilities, designing a $5M aquaculture operation for white sturgeon, and Project Manager of a large fishing clinic facility for the U.S. Department of Wildlife. David holds advanced degrees in civil engineering and nutrition/dietetics, owns a commercial nursery, and has several decades of experience in vegetable gardening. David understands every facet of aquaponics and clearly communicates aquaponics in a way that truly helps others.

www.FarmYourSpace.com

APPENDIX 5

Reliable Alternative News Sources

A total of 90 percent of all news media outlets in the USA are owned by a total of only six companies. The owners and/or head of all these companies are members of the Bilderberg Group, and attend the annual Bilderberg Club meeting every year. Bilderberg is a highly secretive, elitist, international think tank and policy forming group. This globalist establishment of government leaders and media company heads work together to execute a covert globalist liberal agenda. Also, advertisers support media companies with billions of dollars in ads. These business transactions come with strings attached. In addition, the Obama administration dished out tremendous amount of funding, grants, and special favors to mainstream media companies. These forces influence mainstream media to the point where the truth gets buried under a scripted narrative resulting in propaganda or fake news.

As a result of the above, it is next to impossible to obtain unbiased truth from the mainstream media. Mainstream news is corrupt with corporate, government, Bilderberg influences. Therefore, to get accurate reporting of the news one must depend upon the other 10 percent of media sources which are independent and provide more reliable information and news which can be trusted. Several of these valuable media outlets are listed below.

- www.DrudgeReport.com
- www.InfoWars.com
- www.Brietbart.com
- www.DailyCaller.com
- www.NatrualNews.com
- www.fluoridealert.org
- www.fluoridealert.org/articles/50-reasons (50 reasons why fluoride in H2O is bad)
- www.organicconsumers.org
- www.NaturalSociety.com
- www.GeoEngineeringWatch.org

The following 'YouTube' channels also provide accurate reporting:
- Paul Joseph Watson, www.youtube.com/user/PrisonPlanetLive
- Stefan Molyneux, www.youtube.com/user/stefbot
- Mike Dice, www.youtube.com/user/MarkDice

APPENDIX 6

Recommended Resources

Now that I am entering into my senior years of life I am able to look back and recognize certain things which really made a positive impact on me. Beyond education, life experiences, and people who played an instrumental role in my life, I have been blessed beyond measure by certain documentaries and books. These resources have either greatly inspired me or better educated me to a point of positive change. I wanted to dedicate this portion of this book to pay it forward in the hope that you may be able to benefit from them as well. Following you will find resources that have truly improved my quality of life. I very much recommend the below resources and hope that you will find value in them, too.

Documentaries

I absolutely love documentaries. I learn so much from them. Following are my favorite documentaries that I highly recommend. Most of these recommended documentaries received a review rating of at least 4.5 stars out of 5 stars.

Food / Nutrition / Health Documentaries (Highly Recommended)

- Cowspiracy
- Eating - 3rd Edition (by Mike Anderson)
- Fat, Sick & Nearly Dead
- Fat, Sick & Nearly Dead 2
- Fed Up
- Food Chains
- Food Choices
- Food Matters
- Food, Inc.
- Forks Over Knives
- Fresh
- GMO OMG
- Hungry for Change
- Killer at Large
- King Corn
- Plant Pure Nation
- Processed People
- Scientists Under Attack - Genetic Engineering in the Magnetic Field of Money
- Sugar Coated
- Supersize Me
- The Beautiful Truth (nutrition for cancer patients)
- The Future of Food
- The Gerson Miracle
- The Kids Menu
- The Weight of a Nation
- Vegucated

Social, Environmental, or Nature Documentaries (Highly Recommended)

- (Dis)Honesty: The Truth About Lies
- A Crude Awakening
- Bag It
- Blue Gold: World Water Wars
- Cowspiracy
- Earthlings (by Shaun Monson)
- End of the Line (by filmmaker Rupert Murray)
- Flow: For Love of Water
- Gasland
- God of Wonders
- Happy
- In the Womb (National Geographic)
- Inside Job
- Inside Planet Earth
- Life
- Living on One Dollar
- Minimalism: A Documentary About the Important Things
- Nature's Most Amazing Events
- No Place on Earth
- Planet Earth
- Plastic Paradise: The Great Pacific Garbage Patch
- Poverty, Inc.
- SlingShot
- Tapped
- The College Conspiracy (a documentary on YouTube)
- The Great Rift: Africa's Greatest Story
- The Human Experiment
- The Lee Strobel Film Collection
- The World According to Monsanto
- Vanishing of the bees
- Waste Land directed by Lucy Walker (Arthouse Studio)
- Winter on Fire: Ukraine's Fight for Freedom

Historical Documentaries (Highly Recommended)

- Above and Beyond
- Auschwitz: The Nazis and the 'Final Solution'
- Brothers in War
- Desperate Crossing: Mayflower
- Diaries of the Great War
- Escape from a Nazi Death Camp
- Reader's Digest WWII in the Pacific
- The Civil War
- The First World War (the complete series)
- The Long Way Home
- The Longest Day by 20th Century Fox
- The War
- The World at War
- Treblinka
- World War II - War in the Pacific

Inspirational Films (Highly Recommended)

Below is a list of my favorite inspirational movies.

- Courageous
- Facing the Giants
- Fire Proof
- Flywheel

Classics (Highly Recommended)

Following is my list favorite classical films. These films received excellent reviews.

- An American in Paris
- Fiddler on the Roof
- It's a Wonderful Life
- Oklahoma!
- Seven Brides for Seven Brothers
- Singin' in the Rain
- The General (this silent movie filmed in 1926 is the funniest movie I have ever seen)
- The Great Locomotive
- The Music Man
- The Sound of Music
- White Christmas

Books & Audio Books (Highly Recommended)

The below books are the best books I have ever read in my life. Coincidently, most all received a customer review rating of 5 stars out of 5 stars.

- 1776 by David McCullough
- 50/50: Secrets I Learned Running 50 Marathons in 50 Days
- 7 Habits of Highly Successful People
- A Thousand-Mile Walk to the Gulf by John Muir
- As A Man Thinketh by James Allen
- Awaken the Giant Within
- Band of Brothers by Stephen E. Ambrose
- Born to Run: A Hidden Tribe, Superathletes, and the Greatest Race the World Has Never Seen
- Brian Tracy (all books by Brian Tracy are excellent)
- Bringing Up Boys by James Dobson
- Bringing Up Girls by James Dobson
- Caffeine Blues
- China Study
- Coming Back Stronger: Unleashing the Hidden Power of Adversity
- Desiring God by John Piper
- Disciplines of a Godly Man by R. Kent Hughes
- Don't Waste Your Life by John Piper
- Driven: How To Succeed In Business And In Life by Robert Herjavec
- Eat and Run: My Unlikely Journey to Ultramarathon Greatness
- Eat to Live: The Amazing Nutrient-Rich Program for Fast and Sustained Weight Loss by Joel Fuhrman
- Evangelism and the Sovereignty of God, J.I. Packer
- Extreme Pursuit by John E. Davis
- From Pride to Humility by Stuart Scott
- God's Wisdom in Proverbs by Phillips
- Good to Great: Why Some Companies Make the Leap and Others Don't
- Grace to You by John MacArthur
- Handwriting of the Famous and Infamous by Sheila Lowe
- Happy is the man by Robert V. Ozment
- Happy, Happy, Happy
- Have a New Kid by Friday by Leman
- Healthy Eating, Healthy World: Unleashing the Power of Plant-Based Nutrition, by J. Morris Hicks

continued

- How successful people think by John Maxwell
- How to Win Friends & Influence People, Dale Carnegie
- Lincoln the Unknown, Dale Carnegie
- Love Dare
- Love for a Lifetime: Building a Marriage That Will Go the Distance
- Making Men by Chuck Holton
- Men Are from Mars, Women Are from Venus
- No Happy Cows by John Robbins
- Nothing to Envy
- One Minute Manager
- Parenting Collection by James Dobson
- Pursuit of Holiness by Jerry Bridges
- Quiet Strength by Tony Dungy
- Raising a Modern-Day Knight by Robert Lewis (book for Dad's with sons)
- Remember Names by Dale Carnegie
- Respectable Sins by Jerry Bridges (*best book I have ever read in my life*)
- Rich Dad, Poor Dad
- Running Man: A Memoir
- Seeking Allah, finding Jesus
- Shaken: Discovering Your True Identity in the Midst of Life's Storms
- Shepherding a Child's Heart by Tedd Tripp
- Strong Willed Child by James Dobson
- The 10 natural laws of successful time and life management
- The 5 Love Languages: The Secret to Love that Lasts
- The Attributes of God, Arthur W. Pink
- The Autobiography of Benjamin Franklin
- The Backyard Homestead
- The Endurance: Shackleton's Legendary Antarctic Expedition
- The Exemplary Husband by Stuart Scott
- The Gluten Connection: How Gluten Sensitivity May Be Sabotaging Your Health - And What You Can Do to Take Control Now
- The Greatest Miracle in the World by O.G. Mandino
- The Greatest Salesmen in the World
- The Guide to Confident Living, by Norman Vincent Peale
- The Human Body Book (Book & DVD)
- The Marriage You've Always Wanted by Gary Chapman
- The Path Between the Seas: The Creation of the Panama Canal, 1870-1914
- The Personal MBA by Josh Kaufman
- The Power of Positive Thinking by Norman Vincent Peale
- The Power of Positive Thinking, Norman Vincent Peale
- The Psychology of Winning by Dr. Dennis Waitley
- The Quest for Character, John MacArthur
- The Success Principles: How to get from where you are to where you want to be, by Jack Canfield with Janet Switzer.
- The Truth War: Fighting for Certainty in an Age of Deception by John F. MacArthur
- Think and Grow Rich
- Through My Eyes By Tim Tebow
- Ultramarathon Man: Confessions of an All-Night Runner
- Undaunted Courage: Meriwether Lewis, Thomas Jefferson, and the Opening of the American West
- Way of the Master by Ray Comfort
- Whitewash: The Disturbing Truth About Cow's Milk and Your Health

Best of the Best (Highly Recommended)

Although I highly recommend all of the above resources, selecting the best of the best out of each category, following is my 'must see/read' list:

Environmental — the documentaries 'Cowspiracy' and 'Plastic Paradise'.
Nutrition/Health/Weight Loss — 'Food Choices' (documentary) and 'China Study' (book or audiobook).
Social — the documentaries 'Tapped', 'Poverty, Inc.' and "Flow: for the Love of Water'.
Business/Entrepreneurship/Success — all books by Brain Tracy, and the book 'As A Man Thinketh' by James Allen
Spiritual — the books 'Respectable Sins' and 'Pursuit of Holiness' by Jerry Bridges
Nature — the documentaries 'Planet Earth' and 'The Blue Planet'.
Inspirational — the films noted above in the Inspirational category.
Relationships — 'Fire Proof' (film), 'The 5 Love Languages: the Secret to Love that Last (book), Men are from Mars, Women are from Venus' (book), and 'Love for a Lifetime' book by Dobson).
Child Rearing — 'Parenting Collection' (book by Dobson).

Comment and Feedback

As mentioned previously, I am an avid fan of documentaries and non-fiction books. The above resources have greatly helped me grow as a person through the decades and I hope my sharing these recommendations will help you grow as well. Unfortunately, I have not been able to find any good resources as of yet on three topics that I think are very important. Those topics are: (1) the dangers of nuclear power plants and nuclear waste, (2) the dangers and probability of an EMP event, and (3) the Student Loan problem in America. Hopefully, in the next edition of this book or through my website, I will be able to share valuable resources with you on those topics.

I welcome your comments, recommendations, and feedback on these and other resources. Thank you.

www.FarmYourSpace.org

APPENDIX 7

Encouragement & Keys to Success

Do not be afraid of failure. *"Failure is simply the opportunity to begin again, this time more intelligently." -- Henry Ford*

Don't let discouragement stop you from pressing on. *"Let no feeling of discouragement prey upon you, and in the end you are sure to succeed." – Abraham Lincoln*

Be brave enough to follow your intuition. *"Have the courage to follow your heart and intuition. They somehow already know what you truly want to become. Everything else is secondary." – Steve Jobs*

Setting goals, whether they are to be achieved in 5 or 50 years, is the first step to success. The next big step is to take actions in life that increase the likelihood of your **goal** being achieved. Setting **goals** gives you long-term vision and short-term motivation . It focuses your acquisition of knowledge, and helps you to organize your time and your resources so that you can make the very most of your life.

New Year's resolutions don't work. Get this:

- 25 percent of people abandon their New Year's resolutions after one week.
- 60 percent of people abandon them within six months. (The average person makes the same New Year's resolution ten separate times without success.)
- Only 5 percent of those who lose weight on a diet keep it off; 95% regain it. A significant percentage gain back more than they originally lost.
- Even after a heart attack, only 14 percent of patients makes any lasting changes around eating or exercise.

While New Year's resolutions don't work, writing down goals does work. The research is conclusive. The Dominican University in California did a study on goal-setting with 267 participants. They found that you are 42 percent more likely to achieve your goals just by writing them down.

Harvard's graduate students were asked if they have set clear, written goals for their futures, as well as if they have made specific plans to transform their fantasies into realities.

The result of the study was only 3 percent of the students had written goals and plans to accomplish them, 13 percent had goals in their minds but haven't written them anywhere and 84 percent had no goals at all.

After 10 years, the same group of students were interviewed again and the conclusion of the study was totally astonishing. The 13 percent of the class who had goals, but did not write them down, earned twice the amount of the 84 percent who had no goals. The 3 percent who had written goals were earning, on average, 10 times as much as the other 97 percent of the class combined.

People who don't write down their goals tend to fail easier than the ones who have plans. The Harvard study proves that statement, even if the only criteria was the monetary reward of each graduate in the study. When you don't have a plan, you don't know how you will reach your destination. Sure, you know what your destination is and you have a general idea about how you can reach it, but it's not something that will lead you there for sure.

The secret to accomplishing what matters most to you is committing your goals to writing. This is important for the five reasons.

1. **Putting your goals in writing forces you to clarify what you want.** Writing down your goals forces you to select something specific and decide what you want.
2. **Writing down your goals will motivate you to take action.** Writing down your goals and reviewing them regularly provokes you to take action.
3. **Writing down your goals will provide a filter for other opportunities.** Writing down your goals keeps you on course and keeps you from getting distracted by everything else always popping up in life.
4. **Putting your goals in writing will help you overcome resistance.** Every meaningful intention, dream, or goal encounters resistance. From the moment you set a goal, you will begin to feel it. But if you focus on the resistance, it will only get stronger. The way to overcome it is to focus on the goal.
5. **Writing down your goals will enable you to see—and celebrate—your progress.** Life is hard. It is particularly difficult when you aren't seeing progress. However, written goals are like mile-markers on a highway. They enable you to see how far you have come and how far you need to go. They also provide an opportunity for celebration when you attain them.

S.M.A.R.T. Goals

S.M.A.R.T. goals are designed to provide structure and guidance throughout a project, and better identify what you want to accomplish. That's why setting **SMART goals** - **S**pecific, **M**easurable, **A**chievable, **R**ealistic and **T**imely - is a critical to bringing your goals to reality.

S - specific, significant, stretching
M - measurable, meaningful, motivational
A - agreed upon, attainable, achievable, acceptable, action-oriented
R - realistic, relevant, reasonable, rewarding, results-oriented
T - time-based, time-bound, timely, tangible, trackable

SPECIFIC – Your goal should be clear and specific, otherwise you won't be able to focus your efforts or feel truly motivated to achieve it. When drafting your goal, try to answer the five "W" questions:

- **What** do I want to accomplish?
- **Why** is this goal important?
- **Who** is involved?
- **Where** is it located?
- **Which** resources or limits are involved?

MEASURABLE – It is important to have measurable goals, so that you can track your progress and stay motivated. Assessing progress helps you to stay focused, meet your deadlines, and feel the excitement of getting closer to achieving your goal.

A measurable goal should address questions such as:

- How much?
- How many?
- How will I know when it is accomplished?

ACHIEVABLE – Your goal also needs to be realistic and attainable to be successful. In other words, it should stretch your abilities but still remain possible. When you set an achievable goal, you may be able to identify previously overlooked opportunities or resources that can bring you closer to it.

An achievable goal will usually answer questions such as:

- How can I accomplish this goal?
- How realistic is the goal, based on other constraints, such as financial factors?

RELEVANT – This step is about ensuring that your goal matters to you, and that it also aligns with other relevant goals. We all need support and assistance in achieving our goals, but it's important to retain control over them. So, make sure that your plans drive everyone forward, but that you're still responsible for achieving your own goal.

A relevant goal can answer "yes" to these questions:

- Does this seem worthwhile?
- Is this the right time?
- Does this match our other efforts/needs?
- Am I the right person to reach this goal?
- Is it applicable in the current socio-economic environment?

TIME-BOUND – Every goal needs a target date, so that you have a deadline to focus on and something to work toward. This part of the SMART goal criteria helps to prevent everyday tasks from taking priority over your longer-term goals.

A time-bound goal will usually answer these questions:

- When?
- What can I do six months from now?
- What can I do six weeks from now?
- What can I do today?

SMART is an effective tool that provides the clarity, focus and motivation you need to achieve your goals. It can also improve your ability to reach them by encouraging you to define your objectives and set a completion date. SMART goals are also easy to use by anyone, anywhere, without the need for specialist tools or training. When you use SMART, you create clear, attainable and meaningful goals, and develop the motivation, action plan, and support needed to achieve them.

Success Advice from Brian Tracy

The following is great advice from Brian Tracy. Brian Tracy is Chairman and CEO of Brian Tracy International, a company specializing in the training and development of individuals and organizations. He is also the author of over 70 books that have been translated into dozens of languages. Prior to founding his company, Brian Tracy International, Brian was the Chief Operating Officer of a $265 million dollar development company. He has had successful careers in sales and marketing, investments, real estate development and syndication, importation, distribution and management consulting. He has conducted high level consulting assignments with several billion-dollar plus corporations in strategic planning and organizational development. He has traveled and worked in over 107 countries on six continents, and speaks four languages. http://www.briantracy.com/

Realize that you have to pay the price. *"The price of success must be paid in full, in advance."*

Nothing you really want in life is free. You have to put in hard work to get it. And usually over a long time period. You have to make hard choices and sacrifices.

Now, doing so can produce a lot of happiness along the way and when you reach your destination. But when you take the step from comfortable dreams about success and happiness to actually start doing things then there is always a price to pay. So be prepared for that.

Keep going. *"Every great success is an accumulation of thousands of ordinary efforts that no one else sees or appreciates."*

How do you put in all that time and effort if no will reward you right now? Well, you find things you love doing, things you do for yourself – rather than to get someone else's attention and appreciation – and when things feel rough you just do what you know is the right thing to do anyway. You keep going with persistence but also simple the joy of doing what you love as two supporting friends.

Take responsibility for your life. *"The happiest people in the world are those who feel absolutely terrific about themselves, and this is the natural outgrowth of accepting total responsibility for every part of their life."*

"The more you like yourself, the better you perform in everything that you do."

"Disciplining yourself to do what you know is right and important, although difficult, is the high road to pride, self-esteem and personal satisfaction."

When you take full responsibility for your own life you will start doing many of these things naturally like making decisions, putting in hard work and really trying to keep your focus in the right place.

When you decide to take responsibility for your life and doing what you know deep down is right – for example, going to gym instead of lying on the couch eating potato chips – you like yourself more and more as your self-respect increases.

When your self-respect goes up you feel more worthy of any success and you are less likely to self sabotage in subtle and not so subtle ways. This is crucial as it impact every area of your life. You tend to behave in alignment with your own self image.

Taking responsibility for your own life and doing the right thing are not the only things you can do to increase your self-respect and success. Another powerful tip is to like/love other people. Why? Because how you view, judge and think about people is usually how you view, judge and think about yourself.

Look at the world through the eyes of a successful person.

"You cannot control what happens to you, but you can control your attitude toward what happens to you, and in that, you will be mastering change rather than allowing it to master you."

Success comes from being uncomfortable so aim to put yourself in a state of discomfort.

"Move out of your comfort zone. You can only grow if you are willing to feel awkward and uncomfortable when you try something new."

Become one with your thoughts, emotions, and feelings.

"Just as your car runs more smoothly and requires less energy to go faster and farther when the wheels are in perfect alignment, you perform better when your thoughts, feelings, emotions, goals, and values are in balance."

Use the law of attraction to your advantage. Like attracts like. Focus on what you want.

"The key to success is to focus our conscious mind on things we desire not things we fear."

Your actions are the result of habits. If you have successful habits, you will succeed. If you don't, you will fail. Therefore, form good habits and kill your bad ones.

"Successful people are simply those with successful habits."

Be relentless. **Life will throw some horrible things your way, but don't lose faith. Don't let life break you.** *"Your decision to be, have and do something out of ordinary entails facing difficulties that are out of the ordinary as well. Sometimes your greatest asset is simply your ability to stay with it longer than anyone else."*

Set the bar high. **"We will always tend to fulfill our own expectation of ourselves."**

Autism Community Advice

1. **Laugh.** "Life is so hard. Parenting is hard. Parenting kids with disabilities is hard. Finding things to laugh about makes it not just better, but kind of awesome. Laugh about yourself. Laugh with your kids. Find yourself a goofy pet and laugh at it. When something is so terrible that you say, 'It'll be funny later,' take the time and laugh now. Just like I learned from a motivational board on Pinterest (the best advice always comes from Pinterest): Laughter is the difference between an ordeal and an adventure. Life is an adventure. Treat it as one." -- *Jean Winegardner, blogger at Stimeyland and mom of an autistic child*

2. **Don't lose yourself.** "Everybody always tells you to let people know that your child is not only his or her diagnosis -- that there is so much more to them than their autism, or their extra chromosome, or their cerebral palsy. What they often fail to mention is that you need to make sure that you don't pigeon-hole yourself into that same corner. For the first few years of my son's life, I truly began to lose myself while buried under all of the appointments and evaluations and therapies. It took me a long time to figure out that my entire identity had somehow been overtaken and that I needed to stop and take some time to remember who I was beforehand. Don't forget to continue to find time for the hobbies, friends, and little luxuries you have always enjoyed -- be it a massage or a cup of coffee solo." -- *Jamie Krug, blogger behind Jamie Krug, Author and mom of a little boy with autism*

3. **Ask questions!** "You are your child's best advocate. If a doctor or specialist tells you something that doesn't feel right, ask more questions. Even if it may take more time, visit a different specialist or call different therapists and ask extra questions. Additional research can help you make decisions especially if they are different from a doctor's recommendation." -- *Jen Lee Reeves, blogger at Born Just Right and mom of a little girl with a limb difference*

4. **Find your safe space.** "For every new, uncomfortable, and out of the comfort zone experience we attempt as a family, I need at least a dozen hours in my safe space. With my people. With people who understand that [my son] is just ... [my son]." -- *Jessi Bennion, blogger at Life With Jack and mom of a little boy who was a micropremie at birth*

5. **Find THEIR safe space.** "In hopes of avoiding a meltdown, and because self-harm is not an issue, I leave my kids alone and give them time to self-soothe and gain control over their situation when they are experiencing overload. Because I am autistic and experience these things as well, I know that when someone steps in with the intention of calming or 'helping' me, they are (unknowingly) controlling the situation and doing what they feel is best without taking into consideration what I want or need. For my kids and me, this is seen as an intrusion and causes more aggravation and stress and tends to prompt or intensify the meltdown rather than avoid it. Respect your child's needs, find out what he or she prefers: A Safe Place? Headphones with music? A walk outside, maybe? It's important for parents to find out what their child wants instead of what they feel they would want if the situation were reversed." -- *Renee Salas, blogger behind S.R. Salas Autism Blog and autistic mom to autistic kids*

6. **Think before you speak.** "Watch how you talk about your child's disability in front of them, or how you let others talk about it. They internalize more than you may realize." -- *Maya, blogger behind MarfMom and mom of two little boys, one who has autism and the other Marfan syndrome; Maya also has Marfan*

7. **Get used to waiting.** "Be prepared for waiting rooms and doctor's offices with a bag of familiar toys and books or have games that you play each time you wait so the time goes by quickly and your child is less focused on trauma and instead focused on fun. We have played 'I Spy' hundreds of times!" -- *Diane Lang, blogger behind Momo Fali and mom of an autistic child*

8. **Set a good example.** "When people stare at you child, especially disapprovingly, don't bother telling them off. Instead, be an example to them by showing them how you communicate with your child. This takes practice (and patience), but it is the thing that works best for me." -- *Laura Shumaker, blogger at LauraShumaker.com and mom to a 28-year-old son with autism*

9. **Laugh.** What? We said that already? It's that important, folks. "Humor is a very powerful and healthy coping technique that helps release endorphins, the body's natural painkillers. It's also supposed to tighten abdominal muscles though we have no evidence to support this in our own lives. Despite laughing all the time, we still have belly weight left over from our babies (who are now ages 15 and 17 respectively)." -- *Gina Gallagher and Patty Terrasi, sisters behind Shut Up About Your Perfect Kid and moms to kids with special needs*

10. **"I am different, not less."** — Temple Grandin, (an autistic adult)

The Importance of Prayer

"Any concern too small to be turned into a prayer is too small to be made into a burden." - Corrie Ten Boom

"Prayer is not so much an act as it is an attitude -- an attitude of dependency, dependency upon God." - Arthur Pink

Daily prayer gives us an opportunity to share all aspects of one's life with God. God calls us to bring our concerns to Him for disposition and potential blessing. He also calls us to share our joys and triumphs with Him. In fact, Jeremiah 33:3 states, "Call to me and I will answer you and tell you great and unsearchable things you do not know." God wants us to call on Him so that He can answer our prayers. He also wants to share with us incredible blessings that we might otherwise have missed had we not reached out to Him through prayer. And finally, James 4:8 tells us to "draw near to God, and he will draw near to you." God wants us to be close to Him at all times.

Daily prayer gives us the chance to express gratitude for the things in life that He provides. It is no secret that we must give thanks to the Lord for all the things that He provides and all of the things He does on our behalf. His goodness and lovingkindness to us should be recognized on a daily basis. In 1 Chronicles 16:34, we are commanded to "give thanks to the LORD, for he is good; his love endures forever."

Daily prayer provides the platform for confessing our sin and asking for help repenting of that sin. Let's face it, we all sin daily whether we know it or not. Unconfessed sin that hinders our personal relationship with Christ. Daily prayer is asking God for the strength to repent of our sins. Only God can help us turn from our sins, and, for this to be so, He needs to hear our plea to repent.

Daily prayer is an act of worship and obedience. Perhaps no other verse better summarizes why we should pray on a daily basis than 1 Thessalonians 5:16-18: "Be joyful always; pray continually; give thanks in all circumstances, for this is God's will for you in Christ Jesus." It's God's will for His children to rejoice in Him, to pray to Him and give thanks to Him. To pray without ceasing simply means that we should make prayer a regular habit and never stop doing so. Prayer also is an act of worship because by praying to Him we are showing Him how much we adore Him. Daily prayer is also an act of obedience that brings joy to the Lord to see His children following His commands.

Daily prayer is a way to acknowledge who is really in control of our lives. God is above all things and before all things. He is the alpha and the omega, the beginning and the end. He is immortal, and He is present everywhere so that everyone can know Him (Revelation 21:6). God is in control of all things and rules over all things. He has power and authority over nature, earthly kings, history, angels, and demons. Even Satan himself has to ask God's permission before he can act (Psalm 103:19) God controls every aspect of our lives. Each day we should acknowledge His proper place in our lives humbly and with a reverence reserved for such a great and awesome King.

Finally, prayer is something that we all should want to do on a daily basis. Yet for many people it is a challenge to humble one's self in daily prayer. prayer should always be considered as THE best way to speak to God. Imagine not speaking to a loved one or a close friend. How long would the relationship last? Daily prayer with God is daily fellowship with our heavenly Father. It is truly amazing that God would want to have fellowship with us at all. In fact, the psalmist asks, "What is man that you are mindful of him, the son of man that you care for him?" (Psalm 8:4). Daily prayer is a good way to understand this incredible truth and the marvelous privilege God has given us; a privilege that benefits us, strengthens us, gives us peace, and helps us in every way.

Request for Input and Feedback

I invite you to share your comments and provide input about this book, as it will help me improve it for future editions and the companion website, which is currently under construction.

Thank you for your interest in this book. My hope and desire is that it will make a positive contribution to your life, as well as your loved ones. In addition to your feedback, I would love to hear your story and would welcome the opportunity to pray for you. Please feel free to contact me via the web-link provided below.

Respectfully yours,

David Dudley

www.BestPlacesToLiveWithAutism.com

www.ingramcontent.com/pod-product-compliance
Lightning Source LLC
Chambersburg PA
CBHW080408300426
44113CB00015B/2434